The Guise of Exceptionalism

CRITICAL CARIBBEAN STUDIES

Series Editors: Yolanda Martínez-San Miguel, Carter Mathes, and Kathleen López

Focused particularly in the twentieth and twenty-first centuries, although attentive to the context of earlier eras, this series encourages interdisciplinary approaches and methods and is open to scholarship in a variety of areas, including anthropology, cultural studies, diaspora and transnational studies, environmental studies, gender and sexuality studies, history, and sociology. The series pays particular attention to the four main research clusters of Critical Caribbean Studies at Rutgers University, where the coeditors serve as members of the executive board: Caribbean Critical Studies Theory and the Disciplines; Archipelagic Studies and Creolization; Caribbean Aesthetics, Poetics, and Politics; and Caribbean Colonialities.

For a list of all the titles in the series, please see the last page of the book.

The Guise of Exceptionalism

*Unmasking the National Narratives
of Haiti and the United States*

Robert Fatton Jr.

RUTGERS UNIVERSITY PRESS

NEW BRUNSWICK, CAMDEN, AND NEWARK,
NEW JERSEY, AND LONDON

Library of Congress Cataloging-in-Publication Data

Names: Fatton, Robert, author.
Title: The guise of exceptionalism : unmasking the national narratives of Haiti
    and the United States / Robert Fatton Jr.
Description: New Brunswick, New Jersey : Rutgers University Press, [2021] |
    Series: Critical Caribbean studies | Includes bibliographical references and index.
Identifiers: LCCN 2020032419 | ISBN 9781978821323 (hardcover) |
    ISBN 9781978821316 (paperback) | ISBN 9781978821330 (epub) |
    ISBN 9781978821347 (mobi) | ISBN 9781978821354 (pdf)
Subjects: LCSH: Exceptionalism—Haiti—History. | Exceptionalism—United States—
    History. | National characteristics, Haitian—History. | National characteristics,
    American—History. | Haiti—Relations—United States. | United States—
    Relations—Haiti.
Classification: LCC F1916 .F38 2021 | DDC 972.94—dc23
LC record available at https://lccn.loc.gov/2020032419

A British Cataloging-in-Publication record for this book is available from the British
Library.

⊜ The paper used in this publication meets the requirements of the American National
Standard for Information Sciences—Permanence of Paper for Printed Library Materials,
ANSI Z39.48-1992.

www.rutgersuniversitypress.org

Manufactured in the United States of America

For the "new one," Frey

Not everything that is faced can be changed, but nothing can be changed until it is faced.

—James Baldwin

Contents

Preface and Acknowledgments

Being from one country but living in and taking on the citizenship of another is an advantage insofar as it generates deep ties of affection for both places. At the same time, however, it creates a sense of detachment and rootlessness. As a native Haitian and a naturalized American, I live this fractured reality. Opting for a new citizenship alters one's identity but does not erase original bonds. Instead, it creates a liberating but ambiguous detachment. As an intellectual, I find that this detachment gives me latitude to criticize ruthlessly the claims of exceptionalism invoked not only in my two "homes" but also elsewhere.

This is a book that will probably displease many. It is at odds with nationalist renderings of both Haitian and American history. In fact, after giving a recent lecture on Haiti's ongoing crises, a few Haitian students told me, "I do not like your take." "Why?" I asked. "You are right on everything," they responded, "but you should not expound in this way in front of the *blans*."[1] Similarly, Americans often object or feel uneasy when anyone denies both their country's God-given "indispensability" and their society's easy commingling with the "city on the hill." This is especially the case when such antagonistic pronouncements are voiced abroad, beyond the safe boundaries of the United States.

President Donald Trump has recently expressed this view in extreme terms. He condemned as "anti-American" any comments that were critical of the United States, suggesting that criticizing America or its policies calls into question not only one's patriotism but even one's citizenship and right to remain on U.S. soil. Singling out four liberal congresswomen of color, Reps. Alexandria Ocasio-Cortez (New York), Ayanna Pressley (Massachusetts), Ilhan Omar (Minnesota), and Rashida Tlaib (Michigan), the president announced in an incendiary tweet:

So interesting to see "Progressive" Democrat Congresswomen, who originally came from countries whose governments are a complete and total catastrophe,

the worst, most corrupt and inept anywhere in the world (if they even have
a functioning government at all), now loudly ... and viciously telling the
people of the United States, the greatest and most powerful Nation on earth,
how our government is to be run. Why don't they go back and help fix the
totally broken and crime infested places from which they came. Then come
back and show us how ... it is done. These places need your help badly, you
can't leave fast enough.[2]

That all four congresswomen are American citizens, and that three of the
four were born in the United States is not the important issue. What matters is
Trump's misguided notion that to be a true citizen requires an unreflective and
uncritical idolatry of country. That the four are minorities in Congress—they
are women, they are people of color, and three of the four have immigrant
backgrounds—made them all the more vulnerable to Trump's xenophobic and
racist "othering" rhetoric. This xenophobic syndrome is not peculiar to Trump,
however, nor is it particularly American. It may be expressed in different ways
and various degrees, but it exists in virtually every nation-state. Moreover, in
most countries, there is an unspoken norm that to the extent that criticism is
voiced, it should remain in the "family"; otherwise it morphs into an indecent
denunciation that almost rivals treason. It is as if the "insider" were terrified by
publicly displaying the country's dirty laundry, and the "other" were incapable
of thinking through the reality of what she observes. Like a magical eraser,
silence will, it is assumed, remove the very visible issues and predicaments
raised by criticisms. It seems to me that this is an infantile but all too common
nationalist reaction that has to be rejected.

It is in this unabashedly antagonistic vein that I analyze Haitian and American exceptionalisms as mystifying narratives that "invent" their national histories by both purging them of their injurious stains and embellishing them with
mythical innocence. This book is written in the spirit of what Karl Marx called
"ruthless criticism of all that exists." He defined this spirit in an 1803 letter to
Arnold Ruge as "ruthless both in the sense of not being afraid of the results it
arrives at and in the sense of being just as little afraid of conflict with the powers that be."[3] My goal is to expose exceptionalism's omissions for what they
are—a nationalist mask hiding depravities and crimes.

Exceptionalism is the conviction that a particular nation is both unique and
superior to other nations. By glorifying a country's uniqueness, exceptionalism
transforms the entire polity into a sacred "city on the hill" and its citizens into
agents of a superior civilization. In its more extreme version, the city is not
merely on a hill but is in fact sacred, chosen by God for an exclusive people to
carry his mission on earth. Exceptionalism is thus an unforgiving narrative
legitimizing expansion and conquest in the name of a divine mandate. In his
inaugural address in 2009, Barack Obama, the first African American presi-

dent and the son of a Kenyan, delivered a stirring rendition of American exceptionalism: "We remain the most prosperous, powerful nation on Earth . . . and
we are ready to lead once more. . . . We will not apologize for our way of life, nor
will we waver in its defense. . . . Let it be said by our children's children that
when we were tested we refused to let this journey end. . . . And with eyes fixed
on the horizon and God's grace upon us, we carried forth that great gift of freedom and delivered it safely to future generations."[4]

Obama's invocation of God in defense of America's freedom and "way of
life" is not new; it is a fundamental element of American exceptionalism. In
fact, this invocation precedes the very foundation of the republic; it is as old as
the first European settlers who set foot on its shores. It has always legitimized
the project of those in power, whether it be their massive and brutal appropriation of the so-called unoccupied lands of the indigenous populations,[5] their
defense of slavery and white supremacy, or their exclusion of those who had yet
to be among the "chosen" or were altogether the "other." Belief in the nation's
exceptionalism is thus closely bound to founding national myths. While it
cements unique bonds of fellowship among citizens, it excludes those who are
deemed unfit to belong to the "God-chosen" community. The reasons for exclusion vary. They can be tied to ethnicity, race, class, religion, or gender;[6] they can
also change over time. As this book will show, exceptionalism is not a frozen
and fixed narrative. As a social invention, it can be continuously modified, and
while greater inclusion can be written in most versions, the core exclusionary
principles remain.

This reinventing is in turn dependent on the hegemonic capacity of the ruling class—on whether it has the infrastructural power to gradually coopt and
include into its national project those that it had hitherto excluded without
altering the fundamentals of the system. Not surprisingly, the material wealth
and cultural dominance of the American ruling class has facilitated its coopta-
tion of those who had remained politically and economically marginalized, or
"otherized" from the community of the "chosen." The inclusionary reach of
American exceptionalism developed slowly. Over a very long period, the foundational principles of America's revolutionary constitutional claims of freedom,
democracy, and equality coexisted with, first, the annihilation of indigenous
people and slavery, and later, a limited franchise and segregation. That most
Americans rarely evoke the true chasm between reality and national narrative
is an indication of the continuing hold that exceptionalism has on their collective imagination. Similarly, Haitian exceptionalism has rooted itself in revolutionary claims of individual equality and racial justice, but in fact it has always
been ridden by extreme patterns of class and color exclusions.

All nation-states have their myths of origin and celebrate their presumed
uniqueness, but not all exceptionalisms are the same. Haiti's extolling of itself
as the only nation to have a successful slave revolution and as the world's first

black independent country not only has had a significant influence on its own citizens, but it has also inspired colonized and subjugated peoples more broadly, especially those of African descent. Yet like its American counterpart, Haitian exceptionalism is a fabricated narrative. It glosses over the despotic tendencies of the Haitian founders who ruled with an iron fist and lorded it over the vast majority of the emancipated population. The ideals of democracy, equality, and liberty unleashed in the struggle against slavery and foreign control had little to do with the daily routine of Haitians; class, gender, geographical location, and, indeed, color remained powerful markers of inequality and marginalization. The revolution ushered in liberation from enslavement, a radical rupture with Western racism, and the first—albeit constrained—black national sovereignty, but it also left a persisting legacy of inequalities, authoritarianism, and messianic rule.[7]

Exceptionalism is always a very truncated and embellished national narrative that ultimately serves the interests of ruling classes. Certain versions of it can legitimate imperialism, especially when in the hands of great powers. In such cases, expansionist forces justify their annexations, conquests, and wars against "backward" and "rogue" societies in terms of their alleged civilizational and moral superiority. Theodore Roosevelt, who served as the twenty-sixth president of the United States from 1901 to 1909, aptly summarized the imperial vocation of American exceptionalism:

> Of course our whole national history has been one of expansion. While we had a frontier the chief feature of frontier life was the endless war between the settlers and the red men. . . . [The] ultimate cause was simply that we were in contact with a country held by savages or half-savages. . . . In the long run civilized man finds he can keep the peace only by subduing his barbarian neighbor; for the barbarian will yield only to force. . . . [That] the barbarians recede or are conquered, with the attendant fact that peace follows their retrogression or conquest, is due solely to the power of the mighty civilized races which have not lost the fighting instinct, and which by their expansion are gradually bringing peace into the red wastes where the barbarian peoples of the world hold sway.[8]

Roosevelt's blunt racist claims and unadulterated imperial vision are no longer publicly espoused by current policy makers. Their spirit, however, still informs America's understanding of its mission whether it be expressed in President Trump's condescending description of African and Caribbean nations as "shitholes,"[9] or Hillary Clinton's unilateral declaration that America "is an exceptional nation" that is also "indispensable" because the rest of the world looks to the United States for "leadership,"[10] or again, President Trump taking a page from Hillary Clinton's repertoire[11] and threatening Iran with "obliteration"[12] because it may either desire the same kind of weapons that the United States has in its arsenal or attack Israel. Clearly such self-important assertions are only taken seriously when uttered by the leaders of a "hyper-hegemonic" global power; admonishments and hyperbolic threats of this sort would be met with utter ridicule if they were made by any other ruler. Just imagine how farcical it would be if a Haitian president were to try to menace the United States with military intervention or economic sanctions because of its treatment of African Americans. And yet such threats are the embodiment of U.S. foreign policy; they are the ordinary, acceptable, and "rational" ramifications of American exceptionalism.

The effectiveness of exceptionalism thus correlates with a nation's infrastructural power. As the dominant military and economic world power, the United States has justified its global and imperial reach in the name of its own exceptionalism, a feat that is clearly not in the cards for an outer peripheral country like Haiti whose ruling class is utterly dependent on foreign financial and security forces for its very survival.[13] Sitting in the outer periphery of the world economy, Haiti's exceptionalism has little resonance beyond its borders and sounds increasingly hollow in Haiti itself. However, by nourishing the collective imaginary with the story of a world historical emancipation that crystallized against all odds, Haitian exceptionalism still generates some hope that change is possible. After all, if enslaved people could revolt and overthrow a white supremacist colonial order, there is no reason to believe that Haitians could not now again take matters into their own hands and extricate their country from its disastrous predicament. The possibility of fundamental change that the memory of 1804 opens up is nonetheless unlikely to suffice.

Because Haitian exceptionalism has, among other things, hidden the original roots of discord—the internecine divisions of color, the exclusionary patterns of governance, and the system of class rule that characterized the island nation at its inception—Haiti's mythic view of itself cannot offer a programmatic solution to the country's modern quandary. Like its American counterpart, Haitian exceptionalism must be demystified. It is only by confronting reality that it can be changed.

When I completed a draft of this book, I forwarded it to my dear friend and kindred spirit, Alex Dupuy, for his critique. I am most grateful to him for his careful reading of the text and for offering invaluable suggestions to improve it. He not only forced me to clarify important aspects of my analysis, but he also spared me from engaging in some reckless theoretical arguments. There is hardly an issue raised in this book that we have not discussed at some length. While conceptualizing this project over the last four years and presenting parts of it at various conferences and symposia, I have benefitted from feedback from a number of scholars and friends. I am particularly thankful to Bob Maguire, Laurent Dubois, Marlene Daut, Jean-Eddy Saint Paul, François Pierre Louis, Chip Carey, Carolle Charles, and Asselin Charles. I would be remiss if I did not thank Nicky Demitry, an exemplary graduate student at UVA, for doing the tedious work of formatting the manuscript's bibliography and footnotes.

I am very grateful to the many people at Rutgers University Press for carefully overseeing this project in its final stages. In particular, I want to thank Editorial Director Kimberly Guinta, and Jasper Chang of the editorial department. I also wish to express my appreciation to The Critical Caribbean Studies Series Editors: Yolanda Martínez-San Miguel, Carter Mathes, and Kathleen López. Production editor Mary C. Ribesky and copyeditor Don Burgard, both at Westchester Publishing Services, did a superb job of shepherding the production of the book and improving my prose.

This book would have been impossible without Cin, my colleague, companion, and wife, even if she feels guilty "for not having contributed more" to its making. For over thirty years she has consistently blessed me with her support, love, and patience and has enlightened me with her acute intelligence. I extend to her my greatest and most heartfelt thank you for "everything."

It is clear that these *compagnons de route* I am citing are not responsible for whatever faults this book may have. The sins of omission and commission committed during its writing are irredeemably my own.

Finally, I want to dedicate this book to the "new one," my beloved first grandchild, Frey Jacmel Fatton-Larsen. In a strange way he embodies the transnational cosmopolitan citizen who transcends notions of exceptionalism. Born in New York of a Haitian American mother and a Danish émigré father, he has multiple roots. A descendant of slaves, *affranchis*, and privileged Haitians, he is also rooted in "the Empire" as well as a social democratic Scandinavia. Born in the rich world, he will undoubtedly benefit from what Branko Milanovic has termed the "citizenship premium," receiving a "location premium or a location rent."[14] He should know so, and he should know too that it is chance that has given him this premium. More critically, he should learn that this privilege is in many ways the product of ugly historical processes that our exceptionalisms have hidden so well. This book is an attempt to unmask the dreadful faces of these exceptionalisms, in the hopes of stripping away the hold they have over us. Perhaps Frey's generation will come to see that in a better world there is little room for claims of uniqueness or "chosenness" and that what truly matters is respecting the equality, dignity, and humanity of each individual.

Charlottesville, Virginia
June 2020

The Guise of Exceptionalism

CHAPTER 1

Introduction

Exceptionalism is the belief that a nation is inherently unique and extraordinarily different from other nations. The concept is deeply embedded in national narratives that affirm the special history and, in some instances, the inherent and God-given superiority of a people and their institutions. The claim to exceptionalism is common to all nations; to this extent, exceptionalism is utterly unexceptional. All societies formulate their own allegories and create their own legends to demarcate themselves from others. This active fabrication, however, betrays the banality of exceptionalism. And yet the claim of exceptionalism requires that the invented historical narrative be perceived as truly real.[1] If all nations are exceptional, however, not all of them are exceptional to the same degree or are viewed by others as exceptional at all. As Michel-Rolph Trouillot explains, "If all historical products are unique, not all of them are distinguishable in the same way. It is quite probable that a particular configuration of circumstances will lead to a historical product of which the uniqueness is dazzling: an individual, a group of individuals, an institution, or a phenomenon that strikes us more than otherwise similar entities. In short, some historical products are more remarkable than others, at least to certain groups of observers."[2]

The capacity to transform the exceptionalism of one's own historical products into something distinctive is largely dependent on the extent to which one can effectively deploy one's power. Similarly, it is such power that contributes to the denigration, dismissal, and denial of the exceptionalism of others. So, for instance, defining certain cultures as different, weird, or so strange that they are beyond comprehension is not merely the lazy and unconscious reflection of one's own exceptionalism but is contingent upon having the power to impose one's view. Simply put, condescending ignorance is a sign of power, a sign that there is neither the need nor the time to understand the "other." As Trouillot puts it, "When we are being told over and over again that Haiti is unique, bizarre, unnatural, odd, queer, freakish, or grotesque, we are also being told, in varying degrees that it is unnatural, erratic, and therefore unexplainable. We are being told that Haiti is so special that modes of investigation applicable to other societies are not relevant here."[3]

Exceptionalism is not some mysterious, impenetrable, and inexplicable phenomenon. In fact, exceptionalism is quite understandable even if its substance varies across time and country, and reflects power relations, class struggles, ethnic conflicts, and geopolitical realities. It is, however, contradictory. It legitimizes at once imperial expansion as well as retrenchment, patterns of conquest as well as resistance. It frames national victories and defeats and exalts both cultural distinctiveness and universalism.[4]

In this book, I contend that the contradiction between universalism and exceptionalism that Perry Anderson sees at the heart of American nationalism is in fact the very stuff of exceptionalism itself. Political leaders, particularly the "founding fathers," articulate the original creed of exceptionalism, which becomes a civil religion with the help of "organic intellectuals" who sustain, redefine, and propagate it through educational institutions and the media.[5] Exceptionalism erases the imperfections and limitations of foundational struggles and experiences; it idealizes them in imagined versions of a history that is partial at best. Rulers deploy it to explain and justify the present, while subordinate groups seek to appropriate and transform it to advance their own interests and social projects. Exceptionalism is full of ambiguities and contradictions; Janus-like, it serves different constituencies, but it confines them to the narrow parameters of its discursive framework. It is not a frozen product, however; when successful, it absorbs new historical processes and events and fits them within its transcript.

Exceptionalism is thus a changing narrative that expresses the commonsense of a community with which people explain their day-to-day experiences and their relations with the outside world. It is an interpretation of history that need not be accurate but that nonetheless is very real to the community of believers while perhaps mystifying to anyone not belonging to it. Like ideologies, exceptionalisms—to appropriate Barbara Fields and Karen Fields's words—"do not need to be plausible, let alone persuasive, to outsiders. They do their job when they help insiders make sense of the things they do and see—ritually, repetitively— on a daily basis."[6] Founding national myths on which exceptionalism is rooted are particularly prone to embellishment and inventions, and they can in fact be pure historical fiction. The point, however, is that they seek to unify people into a community of believers by giving them a sense of purpose and of belonging to a unique and glorious history.

Thus, as I will seek to demonstrate in the forthcoming chapters, certain events like Haiti's Bois-Caïman ceremony are transformed into foundational myths. Such myths rest on real historical episodes, but episodes poetically magnified and embellished by postrevolutionary generations of organic intellectuals. Foundational myths, however, nurture the national consciousness, giving it meaning and a sense of transcendence. They create the logic of exceptionalism that informs each nation's perceptions of itself as well as its role in the international community. Not all exceptionalisms are the same, nor do they all have the capacity to shape particular types of behavior at particular historical moments. Exceptionalism both structures and is structured by material force; it shapes cultural predispositions and frames strategic possibilities, but its capacity to effect these possibilities into the real world is ultimately dependent on economic and military power.

In this book, I will examine how exceptionalism as a belief system shaped relations between the United States and Haiti from the inception of both republics. I will first study the period of the late 1700s to 1934 during which race and racism were dominant realities in both nations. This period covers not only the formative and conflictual moments in the early history of both exceptionalisms, but also the first and longest American occupation of Haiti (1915–1934), which ultimately served to undermine core elements of those very exceptionalisms. I will then examine the long dictatorship of François Duvalier and that of his son, Jean-Claude, both of whom manipulated their negritude and deep anticommunism to gain international and domestic support while masking their massive dependence on the American empire during the Cold War. Haitian exceptionalism became a form of *marronage* to avoid total subjection to the hegemonic exceptionalism of the United States. Finally, I will analyze the more recent past in the aftermath of the civil rights movement and the Cold War when on the one hand American exceptionalism revisited its conception of race and achieved for a short decade a virtual universalism, and on the other hand Haiti entered an unending transition to democracy punctuated by two other, albeit shorter, American occupations that emptied Haitian exceptionalism of any meaningful content.

Comparing the United States to Haiti may seem odd, and yet the history of the two countries is decisively entwined. They share the violent bonds of slavery and their contradictory legacy. On the one hand, slavery generated pervasive and persisting forms of racism and exclusion; on the other hand, it fueled the development of modern capitalism. The latter was inherently inegalitarian, producing on a world scale both massive wealth and poverty. Haiti was quarantined to the periphery of the global economy and ultimately confined to outer peripheral underdevelopment,[7] while the United States established itself at the very core of this economy to initiate its imperial ascendancy. In both cases, African people had to endure the torture and the lasting racial and social injuries of slavery. As Edward Baptist puts it, "The suffering enslaved people experienced in their bodies and minds and how they survived, coped with, and tried to avoid and alleviate that suffering was an essential component of worldwide economic growth and transformation."[8]

The United States and Haiti thus have common bonds, and as Elizabeth Maddock Dillon and Michael J. Drexler have emphasized, "It should no longer be possible to write a history of the early republic of the United States without mentioning Haiti, or St. Domingue."[9] Similarly, Haiti's history is not a strange history of isolation from the world and its political, cultural, and economic currents. In fact, it is irrevocably linked to that of imperial powers, and the United States in particular. Thus, comparing the two nations is a logical exercise that will show that in spite of their vast differences in power, culture, wealth, and size, they share a common revolutionary narrative rooted in their successful struggle for independence. They became the first two colonies to achieve nationhood, and not surprisingly, their founders believed they had invented new, unique, democratic, and egalitarian models of popular governance.[10] Despite this belief in the uniqueness of their respective societies, the first rulers of the United States and Haiti failed to establish anything resembling a genuine democracy.[11] The former, regrouping a large class of slave owners, defeated the British Empire to create a *Herrenvolk* state of white propertied men;[12] the latter, made up of former slaves, abolished slavery and routed Napoleon's army to build an authoritarian black republic.[13] For Haiti, however, the moment of its revolutionary triumph became its curse. By emancipating a black people in an age of white supremacy, it was condemned to endure the contempt and constant attacks of a vengeful West incapable of accepting defeat and fearful of other slave revolts.[14] Remaining a pariah, "rogue" nation for over a century exacerbated the crisis of Haiti's domestic political economy and reinforced its authoritarian forms of governance.[15]

In both societies, only fragments of the population enjoyed democratic rights. At the time of their creation, American and Haitian regimes had exclusionary foundations rooted in class, property, religion, race, and gender. This is not to diminish the historical significance of both revolutions in expanding individual and social rights, but rather to point out that they represented truncated and incomplete emancipatory projects. Thus, the material and political basis of the American and Haitian republics imposed profound limitations to universal popular participation. The economic realities of slavery and the plantation system had profound consequences for both the preservation of, and the fight against, white supremacy, which in turn decisively shaped relations between Haiti and the United States. In addition, these relations were inevitably marked by the inherent racism of the United States' manifest destiny and imperial impulses. American leaders viewed Haiti as an unfathomable and dangerous society that had to be quarantined like a deadly virus and rescued from the backwardness of its African roots by the modernizing forces of American capitalism.[16] For Haitians, the United States has always been a paradox and a contradiction. In their eyes, it has always represented a constant and formidable menace to their national sovereignty and dignity. But from the mid-twentieth century on, it also embodied a needed source of foreign assistance and a migratory haven for those fleeing the island's repressive regimes, poverty, and underdevelopment.

I will thus also analyze the contemporary transformation of both nations' claims to exceptionalism since World War II. I will argue that American exceptionalism offered a tale of morality that justified and consolidated a global imperial drive nurtured by the development of its increasingly dominant role in the world capitalist system.[17] It is true that it has also exhibited a streak of isolationism, a desire to withdraw from the quarrels of the world into what has historically been defined as "Fortress America." In reality, however, isolationism has never been the driving force of U.S. foreign policy; from its inception America has been expansionist.[18] While Thomas Jefferson may have wanted to insulate the republic's virtues from the spoiling affairs of international politics, he was always bent on opening up America's *Lebensraum* to create what he called the "empire for liberty."[19] This empire of liberty was not, however, for everyone; it had to be a white *Herrenvolk* without the "blot or mixture" of people of African descent.[20] In a 1801 letter to James Madison, Jefferson suggested that "these people" should be moved to new geographical destinations, of which he thought "the island of St Domingo" was the "most promising" because there "the blacks are established into a sovereignty de facto, & have organised themselves under regular laws & government."[21]

In practice, however, the pursuit without "blot or mixture" of the white *Herrenvolk* meant also, as Anders Stephanson explains, "to declare any potential enemy *an objective obstruction* to the course of natural freedom, in effect to call for elimination and liquidation. A great deal of that would indeed follow."[22] And yet American exceptionalism has transmogrified elimination and liquidation into legitimate acts of self-defense, fulfilling the destiny of God's chosen nation. It has managed to describe America's vast territorial expansion and its subsequent global hegemony as a noble tale of moral obligations. American exceptionalism has always covered up U.S. expansionism with what Sidney Lens has called the "rhetoric of defense:"

> Each act of aggrandizement in the American chronicle has been valiantly camouflaged in the rhetoric of defense.... The myth of morality, however, wears thin against the aggregate of history. True, the spirit of expansion often lay dormant for extended periods... [but] with the growth of power and opportunity imperial ambition enlarged its vistas.... American policy has been motivated ... by America's own desire for land, commerce, markets, spheres of influence, investments, as well as strategic impregnability to protect such prerogatives. The primary focus has not been moral, but imperial.[23]

By contrast, as I have contended elsewhere, Haiti has become an outer periphery of the world capitalist system.[24] Thus, its exceptionalism, which never achieved to impose its hegemony on society, has now become a rather weak, if not an altogether purely symbolic invocation of black resistance against Western encroachments. Currently it masks the reality of its utter economic and security dependence on the United States, lesser foreign powers, and international financial institutions. Lacking basic political and material means, Haitian rulers have been unable to establish their hegemony in spite of their continued appeals to exceptionalism. These appeals are now falling on the deaf ears of the majority of the population, which is no longer prepared to accept vain claims about black independence and resistance. Haitian exceptionalism has become nothing more than a symbolic invocation of the revolutionary past hiding the country's dependence on foreign actors.

I will thus argue that the hegemony of exceptionalism is dependent on the material power of the ruling class. The more expansive is that power, the more likely is the ruling class capable of integrating hitherto marginalized and excluded groups into the moral community of the nation. Not surprisingly, the overwhelming infrastructural power of America's ruling class has allowed it to co-opt gradually and in varying degrees former slaves, exploited workers, and waves of global immigrants; these dispossessed have all come to adhere to some form of American exceptionalism. American exceptionalism continues therefore to show its vitality and capacity to seduce; by contrast, its Haitian counterpart has become an imaginary relic, a last and increasingly weak cultural line of defense against the realities of national decomposition and mass exodus to more prosperous lands.

CHAPTER 2

American Exceptionalism

In his celebrated book *Democracy in America*, published in 1835, Alexis de Tocqueville provided the classic thesis of American exceptionalism. His thesis not only captured the founders' conception of their creation, but it also framed the dominant interpretations of American liberal democracy. He argued that America was a unique regime because it enshrined the absolute sovereignty of the people in a distinctively democratic and egalitarian political order. Unlike Europe, America was basically free of an aristocratic past and thus could avoid the typical hierarchies that characterized the other societies of his day.[1] Commenting on his travels throughout the United States, Tocqueville stressed that "nothing struck me more forcibly than the general equality of condition among the people."[2] He continued:

> The social condition of the Americans is eminently democratic. . . . Great equality existed among the immigrants who settled on the shores of New England. Even the germs of aristocracy were never planted in that part of the Union. . . . In America, the aristocratic element has always been feeble from its birth. . . . It is . . . so completely disabled that we can scarcely assign to it any degree of influence on the course of affairs.
>
> The democratic principle, on the contrary, has gained so much strength . . . as to have become not only predominant, but all-powerful. . . . The Anglo-Americans are the first nation who . . . have been happy enough to escape the dominion of absolute power. They have been allowed by their circumstances, their origin, their intelligence, and especially by their morals to establish and maintain the sovereignty of the people.[3]

In an ode to American democracy, Tocqueville concluded, "The people reign in the American political world as the Deity does in the universe. They are the cause and the aim of all things; everything comes from them, and everything is

absorbed in them."[4] This view was articulated not only by the American founders and their successors, but also by most of their compatriots and particularly
the republic's organic intellectuals.[5]

While Tocqueville recognized that systematic exclusions based on race, gender, and class existed in America's system of governance, he was convinced that
they did not undermine the democratic nature of America. He shared with the
American founders the belief that democracy was not only compatible with
white supremacy, but that it was in fact premised on the exclusivist *Herrenvolk*
community of white propertied men. In Tocqueville's eyes, black slaves had a
taste for servility; their desire for freedom, if it ever existed, had been annihi-
lated by slavery itself: "Violence made him a slave, and the habit of servitude
gives him the thoughts and desires of a slave, he admires his tyrants more than
he hates them, and finds his joy and his pride in the servile imitation of those
who oppress him. His understanding is degraded to the level of his soul. . . . In
short, he is sunk to such a depth of wretchedness that while servitude brutal-
izes, liberty destroys him."[6]

The black body was thus utterly debased, existing only as "an intermediate
being between brute and man;"[7] it was incompatible with democracy except if
it was enslaved. As congressman and future Virginia governor Henry A. Wise
put it in 1842, "Break down slavery, and you would with the same blow destroy
the great democratic principle of equality among men."[8] Far from being an
anomaly or an irrational remnant of a hierarchical past in an otherwise egalitarian liberal order, as conventional analysts of American politics would have
it, slavery and American "democracy" were mutually constitutive. In the blunt
words of David Waldstreicher, the U.S. founders produced "a proslavery constitution, in intention and effect."[9] Thus, the American Constitution declared that
"all men are created equal," but as Ibram X. Kendi contends, "it embraced Black
inferiority—and in the process enshrined the power of slaveholders and racist
ideas in the nation's founding document."[10]

Race and racism became the inevitable result of this convergence between
slavery and American "democracy." Slavery, however, had contradictory effects
on poor Southern whites, who comprised at least 30 percent of the white population by 1860;[11] it lowered their wages and generated patterns of extreme inequalities among whites. The small class of slaveholders monopolized the material
benefits of "human property," leaving the white majority in dire economic conditions. As Keri Leigh Merritt has explained:

> Under capitalism, labor power was the commodity of the laborer. . . . The sys-
> tem was predicated on elites coercing individuals to work, often by violent
> means. In the slave South, where laborers were in competition with brutal-
> ized, enslaved labor, the laborers, whether legally free or not, had little to no
> control over their labor power. The profitability and profusion of plantation

slave labor consistently reduced the demand for free workers, lowered their wages, and rendered their bargaining power ineffective, indeed generally (except in the case of specialized skills) worthless.[12]

In the antebellum South, slavery had thus deleterious consequences for poor whites, who were confined to conditions of material destitution that "prevented [them] from enjoying many of the privileges of whiteness."[13] This is not to say that poor whites did not espouse the dominant racism of Southern society, but rather that they represented a separate class from slave owners that "interacted with slaves and free blacks on frequent bases, and likely considered those relationships a routine part of daily life."[14] Obviously, slavery imposed the political and cultural structures of white supremacy, but white unity was a myth.[15] The master class excluded poor whites from its moral community and described them as "'dark and swarthy' ruffians, who served as a constant threat to the plantation system."[16] Deep economic inequalities of income and wealth reinforced this moral and physical exclusion. According to Merritt, in 1860 about a thousand families monopolized half the wealth of the Deep South, while the poorest half accounted for a mere 5 percent.[17] These massive disparities reflected the reality that virtually all slaves were owned by the top 1 percent of antebellum Southern citizens.[18] The class antagonism between poor slaveless whites and wealthy slaveholders endangered the latter's continued rule and contributed to their drive to secession. Slaveless whites may have acquired racist attitudes, but their destitution did not generate an unbridgeable chasm between them and the slaves. In fact, the nearly half a million Southern unionists who fought against the Confederacy included not only African Americans but a large number of whites who tended to be predominantly poor.[19]

Wealth and property fueled the defense of slavery and enhanced the will of the master class to become soldiers in the Confederate army. As Andrew B. Hall, Connor Huff, and Shiro Kuriwaki, have argued,

> Slaveownership increased individuals' propensity to fight . . . because it was a form of wealth directly threatened by the war. Wealthy slaveowners who perhaps would have avoided fighting in other conflicts fought at higher rates in the American Civil War because the stakes of the conflict were high for them. . . . The familiar observation that many soldiers were non-slaveowners largely reflects the fact that most Southerners were not slaveowners, but it does not imply that non-slaveowners supported the Confederacy more enthusiastically—in fact, non-slaveowners were measurably less enthusiastic.[20]

The development and defense of slavery and the establishment of white supremacy was above all the affair of the propertied master class. In the succinct words of Keri Leigh Merritt, "Secession, the Confederacy, and Civil War were all overwhelmingly the creation of one small class of Americans: wealthy south-ern slaveholders."[21] Poor whites were alienated from slave owners and had little stake in the "peculiar institution" from which they derived few if any benefits.

Paradoxically, and yet not surprisingly, it was in the post–Civil War era when slavery had been abolished, and in the aftermath of Reconstruction,[22] that racism intensified among poor whites. As Merritt explains:

> Before the civil war, poor whites had functioned as social pariahs in the Deep South because they had no real place or stake in the slave system, and thus actu-ally stood to threaten it. With the emancipation, however, poor whites were finally granted at least enough of the privileges of whiteness to get them off the bottom rung of society, which would now be occupied by blacks. . . . With the region in economic ruin, poor whites were no longer effectively barred from land ownership. . . . Most importantly, poor white workers were finally able to compete in a free labor economy, which at least provided them with a potential opportunity to improve their economic situation. . . . Because the lower classes were finally able to begin enjoying some of the privileges of whiteness [Jeff] Forret contended, once surprisingly fluid "racial lines hardened."[23]

This is not to say that the development of racism as a system of belief did not predate the Civil War. On the contrary, as Karen Fields and Barbara Fields explain in their masterful book *Racecraft: The Soul of Inequality in American Life*:

> Race is not an idea but an ideology. It came into existence at a discernible his-torical moment for rationally understandable historical reasons and is subject to change for similar reasons. The revolutionary bicentennials that Americans have celebrated with such unction—of independence in 1976 and of the Consti-tution in 1989—can as well serve as the bicentennial of racial ideology, since the birthdays are not far apart. During the revolutionary era, people who favoured slavery and people who opposed it collaborated in identifying the racial inca-pacity of Afro-Americans as the explanation for enslavement. American racial ideology is as original an invention of the Founders as is the United States itself. Those holding liberty to be inalienable and holding Afro-Americans as slaves were bound to end by holding race to be a self-evident truth.[24]

Race and racism became all the more powerful because they generated the material foundation that sustained the *Herrenvolk* democracy. The primitive accumulation that the labor of enslaved people produced cannot be exagger-ated. As Calvin Schermerhorn puts it:

> The cotton bales they made streamed into factories in New and old England, spun into yarn and woven into fabric that clothed people across the globe. Cotton shipped abroad each year increased from just a few thousand bales in 1790 to 4 million by 1860. . . .

Enslaved people became the largest share of property other than the land itself. As property they were worth correspondingly more over time. Between 1770 and 1810, slaves as capital were worth between two and a half and three years of national—not just Southern—income. . . . In 1830, aggregated slave property was worth $577 million or 15 percent of the national wealth. By 1860, the figure reached more than $3 billion or nearly 19 percent of the total US wealth (the equivalent of $12.7 trillion as a share of 2016 gross domestic product). By then slave property was worth more than all the investments in factories and railroads combined.[25]

Slavery was thus a system of economic extraction that fueled America's capitalist development. American exceptionalism, however, has sought to hide or deny the intimate connection between the rise of the "free market" system, "liberal democracy," and slavery. It is only in the past thirty years or so that a new historiography has emerged to define "American economic development as 'slavery's capitalism.'"[26] In fact, far from being some backward mode of production, slavery and the plantation system exhibited not only very Weberian and "rational" forms of accounting, but also cruel methods of labor regimentation that increased productivity dramatically and that generated the modern technologies of management.[27] As Caitlin Rosenthal argues, "The commodization and capitalization of lives made it easier to put numbers to work. Innovation was, in a sense, a by-product of bondage."[28]

Thus, the development of American capitalism is inextricably rooted in enslaved labor and its methods of production and extraction. Sven Beckert and Seth Rockman put it succinctly: "Slave-grown cotton . . . provided the basis for the so-called Great Divergence, thereby making the violence of the plantation central to economic modernity itself. And in this story, no technology was more important than the whip."[29] Slavery, however, was much more than economic production; it was also a property regime in which black bodies were sold, inherited, and capitalized. In the process, it transformed race into the marker of supremacy and servitude. Karen Fields and Barbara Fields are worth quoting again:

> Probably a majority of American historians think of slavery in the United States as primarily a system of race relations—as though the chief business of slavery were the production of white supremacy rather than the production of cotton, sugar, rice, and tobacco. One historian has gone so far as to call slavery "the ultimate segregator." He does not ask why Europeans seeking the "ultimate" method of segregating Africans would go to the trouble and expense of transporting them across the ocean for that purpose, when they could have achieved the same end so much more simply by leaving the Africans in Africa.[30]

Unlike such historians, slave owners knew the economic value of their "institution" and intended to maximize the wealth that it generated. For instance,

American founder Thomas Jefferson, who was the principal author of the Declaration of Independence and wrote that "all men are created equal" and who
later served as the third president of the United States from 1801 to 1809, had a
clear idea of the benefits of slavery. Dubbed by Winthrop Jordan the "grand-
father of American racism,"[31] Jefferson calculated the profits generated by his
slaves and found out that he was making "a 4 percent profit every year on the
birth of black children."[32] As Henry Wiencek explains:

> The enslaved were yielding him a bonanza, a perpetual human dividend at
> compound interest. Jefferson wrote, "I allow nothing for losses by death, but,
> on the contrary, shall presently take credit four per cent. per annum, for their
> increase over and above keeping up their own numbers." In another com-
> munication from the early 1790s, Jefferson takes the 4 percent formula further
> and quite bluntly advances the notion that slavery presented an investment
> strategy for the future.[33]

The combination of "possessive individualism"[34] and racism on which liberalism was founded explains not only the genesis of America's *Herrenvolk* democracy, but also how the "enlightened" European intellectuals of the seventeenth,
eighteenth, and nineteenth centuries and their American disciples could articulate both a strong theoretical aversion to, and a full practical endorsement of,
slavery. In fact, at times, geopolitical and economic interests contributed to tame
white supremacist ideologies.[35] For instance, in 1798, the United States under
President John Adams adopted a law dubbed "Toussaint's Clause" that kept an
embargo—the Non-Intercourse Act—on France but allowed commercial activities with Toussaint's Saint Domingue.[36] The goal of weakening France and
Napoleon's imperial drives overruled the prevailing racist ideology.

Similarly, while in 1801 Thomas Jefferson—Adams's successor as president—
promised the French chargé d'affaires in the United States, Louis-Andre Pichon,
that he would join First Consul Napoleon Bonaparte in "starv[ing] Toussaint,"
by the end of the year he had changed his mind. In a letter to James Monroe
dated November 24, 1801, Jefferson envisaged resolving his own Southern problem of rebellious slaves by sending them to Toussaint's quasi-autonomous Saint
Domingue. As he put it,

> The West Indies offer a more probable & practicable retreat for them. Inhab-
> ited already by a people of their own race & color; climates congenial with
> their natural constitution; insulated from the other descriptions of men;
> nature seems to have formed these islands to become the receptacle of the
> blacks transplanted into this hemisphere. . . . The most promising portion
> of them is the island of St Domingo, where the blacks are established into
> a sovereignty de facto, & have organized themselves under regular laws &
> government. I should conjecture that their present ruler might be willing, on

many considerations, to receive even that description which would be exiled for acts deemed criminal by us, but meritorious perhaps by him.[37]

Thus, for Jefferson the existence of an autonomous black territory could become a place of permanent exile for insurgent slaves and a means of pacifying American slaveholding states. Quarantining these people in Saint Domingue would not threaten the United States, continued Jefferson, "on a contemplation of our relative strength, and of the disproportion daily growing; and it is overweighed by the humanity of the measures proposed, & the advantages of disembarrassing ourselves of such dangerous characters."[38]

In fact, at the end of October 1802, Jefferson contemplated tolerating an independent Saint Domingue under the rule of Toussaint provided that the island posed no military threat. Pichon, the French representative in the United States, reportedly claimed that Jefferson told him,

> Why will France not declare [Saint Domingue] independent under her protection and that of the United States and England? Perhaps that would be wisest. That island needs an oriental [i.e., despotic] government. After General Toussaint another despot will be necessary. Why should not the three powers unite to confine the pest in the island? Provided that the Negroes are not permitted to possess a navy, we can allow them without danger [to ourselves] to exist and we can moreover continue with them very lucrative commercial relations.[39]

Not surprisingly, Jefferson decided to allow Saint Domingue's black revolutionaries to have access to American weapons and goods in their fight against white Frenchmen. Clearly, Jefferson's strategy was opportunistic and indeed duplicitous. On the one hand, it reflected his desire both to bolster the trading interests of American bankers and merchants and to weaken Napoleon's military forces, while on the other hand, it allowed him to pretend that he was supportive of the French intervention in Saint Domingue.[40] Ultimately, the victory of Saint Domingue's slaves compelled Napoleon to negotiate with Jefferson the Louisiana Purchase, which doubled the territory of the United States.[41] Douglas Egerton points out this major historical irony: "Although the . . . Louisiana Purchase is typically regarded as the crowning achievement of Jefferson's first term as president, the truth is that it was Louverture's black army that made the purchase possible. . . . Jefferson's greatest accomplishment came not because of adroit diplomacy, but—just the reverse—because of the courage of half a million black rebels who refused to be subjugated."[42]

To achieve his objective, however, Jefferson had to curb his racist convictions by temporarily allowing American trading with revolutionaries of African descent. La raison d'état prevailed over the instincts of the slaveholder. On the other hand, even in this case, Jefferson's primary goal was to "confine the pest in the island." Once Haiti gained its independence in 1804, American policy changed. Terrified that the new republic would spread black insurrection in the southern states of the United States, Jefferson prohibited the export of weapons to Haiti in 1805 and imposed a total trade embargo against the island a year later. As Douglas Egerton explains, "If Jefferson was resolute on any point, it was regarding his fear that slave rebelliousness in the Caribbean might spread to the Southern mainland. He was particularly concerned that 'black crews & missionaries' from . . . Saint-Domingue could spread word of the uprising under Toussaint Louverture to Virginia."[43]

Paradoxically, in the short and medium term, the Haitian Revolution expanded and increased the violence of slavery in the United States rather than minimizing, let alone challenging, it. In fact, by contributing to the Louisiana Purchase and white Southerners' paranoia about slaves' uprisings, the revolution dramatically expanded the territory of American slavery westward. The fear of such uprisings led to the prohibition of the importation of Caribbean slaves to southern states and invigorated the intra-American slave trade, which acquired a "continental dimension." "Slaves from the Chesapeake were, in growing numbers, sold 'down the river' to territories southward and westward,"[44] write Dillon and Drexler. Moreover, they continue, "the end of the Haitian Revolution marked the advent of . . . the 'second slavery'—a slavery in which labor regimes were intensified as they were integrated with industrial technologies and international capital markets. In the United States, in particular, this took the form of the rapid growth of cotton production, pushing westward along the so-called "cotton frontier."[45]

Thus, it seems clear that in the late eighteenth and early nineteenth centuries virtually all of the major Western rulers who allegedly celebrated the ideas of the Enlightenment never confronted slavery as a system that had to be abolished, and abolished immediately if the promises of the Enlightenment were to be fulfilled. In fact, even those claiming abolitionist sentiments thought in terms of la très longue durée to do away with the "peculiar institution." They always postponed the day of reckoning; in their eyes, ending slavery was always the business of the next generation, as neither slave masters nor slaves were allegedly ready for freedom.[46] In the 1799 congressional debate on "intercourse with France" and the possibility of Saint Domingue's independence, Albert Gallatin, an American statesman and congressman born in Geneva and an opponent of slavery, exposed this conundrum:

> Suppose that island, with its present population, under present circumstances, should become an independent State. What is this population? It is known to consist, almost altogether, of slaves just emancipated, of men who received their first education under the lash of the whip, and who have been initiated to liberty only by that series of rapine, pillage, and massacre that have laid waste

and deluged that island in blood. Of men, who, if left to themselves, if alto-gether independent, are by no means likely to apply themselves to peaceable cultivation of the country, but will try to continue to live, as heretofore, by plunder and depredations. No man wishes more than I do to see an abolition of slavery, when it can be properly effected, but no man would be more unwill-ing than I to constitute a whole nation of freed slaves, who had arrived to the age of thirty years, and thus to throw so many wild tigers on society.[47]

Most "enlightened" Western leaders had thus a hard time resolving the criti-cal problem of slavery and contemplating the possibility of black people acquir-ing their freedom and full independence. Racism, the fear of generalized slave insurgencies, and economic interests in the "peculiar" institution conspired against the principles of the equality of men so loudly proclaimed by the Amer-ican founding fathers and the leaders of the French Revolution of 1789. In fact, when their silence on the matter was not deafening, they largely agreed with Hegel, who while contending that the condition of African slaves was "in and for itself *injustice*," argued in *The Philosophy of History*:

> Bad as this may be, their lot in their own land is even worse, since there a slav-ery quite as absolute exists; for it is the essential principle of slavery, that man has not yet attained a consciousness of his freedom, and consequently sinks down to a mere Thing—an object of no value. Among the Negroes moral senti-ments are quite weak, or more strictly speaking, non-existent. . . . [The Negro] exhibits the natural man in his completely wild and untamed state. We must lay aside all thought of reverence and morality—all that we call feeling—if we would rightly comprehend him; there is nothing harmonious with humanity to be found in this type of character. . . . The gradual abolition of slavery is therefore wiser and more equitable than its sudden removal.[48]

Hegel was obviously not alone in condemning and yet tolerating if not fully embracing slavery. John Locke declared that "slavery is so vile and miserable an estate of Man, and so directly opposite to the generous Temper and Courage of our Nation; that 'tis hardly to be conceived, that an *Englishman*, much less a *Gen-tleman*, should plead for it,"[49] and yet he was involved in two institutions benefit-ing from and viciously regimenting slavery. As an investor in the Royal African Company and a member of the Board of Trade and Plantations for four years,[50] Locke contradicted his high-sounding principles.[51] Similarly, Thomas Jefferson condemned slavery as "this execrable commerce . . . this assemblage of horrors," and a "cruel war against human nature itself, violating its most sacred rights of life and liberties,"[52] but he lived and died as a man who owned hundreds of slaves.

By denouncing slavery, while on the other hand espousing it, Jefferson betrayed liberalism's "macroscopic exclusion clauses"[53] on which rested the circumscribed community of the free. As Losurdo puts it, "The rise of liberalism and the spread of racial chattel slavery are the product of a twin birth." He adds, "Slavery in its most radical form triumphed in the golden age of liberalism and at the heart of the liberal world. This was acknowledged by James Madison, slave-owner and liberal, . . . who observed that 'the most oppressive dominion ever exercised by man over man'—power based on 'mere distinction of colour'— was imposed 'in the most enlightened period of time.'"[54]

While it is true that Madison, Locke, Tocqueville, and Jefferson oscillated about the posited biological inferiority of blacks and the superiority of whites, they unambiguously espoused the belief that cultural differences between races were unbridgeable and that democracy could only flourish in the homogeneous setting of propertied whiteness. This racism found its paradigmatic expression in Jefferson's *Notes on the State of Virginia*, where the principal author of America's Declaration of Independence makes claims about the insurmountable physical, moral, sexual, and mental differences between blacks and whites. As Henry Wiencek explains, "In the infamous passages of *Notes*, Jefferson speculates that blacks were in some ways, possibly inferior to whites, but in any case, were unquestionably *different*, and the difference was 'fixed in nature.' They looked different, they smelled different, they thought, felt, and loved differently from whites."[55]

Jefferson believed that the superior beauty of white people drove black men to covet white women's bodies "as uniformly as is the preference of the Ora-nootan for the black women over those of his own species."[56] Blacks were not only esthetically unappealing; their color transformed them into inscrutable beings because their "immoveable veil of black . . . covers all their emotions."[57] Ultimately, Jefferson had the "suspicion . . . that the blacks, whether originally a distinct race, or made distinct by time and circumstances, are inferior to the whites in the endowments both of body and mind."[58] Not surprisingly, he reviled interracial relations between black and white people, even though he himself engaged in them.[59] In a 1814 letter to Edward Coles, Jefferson expressed his contempt for "amalgamation"; the amalgamation of blacks "with the other color produces a degradation to which no lover of his country, no lover of excellence in the human character can innocently consent."[60]

Like Jefferson, Tocqueville embraced the notion that a cultural chasm between whites and blacks underpinned America's *Herrenvolk* democracy. He contrasted the Anglo-Saxon "spirit of liberty" with "the habit of servitude" that gave blacks "the thoughts and desires of a slave" who "[admired] his tyrants more than he [hated] them, and [found] his joy and his pride in the servile imitation of those who [oppressed] him."[61] And yet, paradoxically, Tocqueville feared that these servile slaves might become a mortal danger to *Herrenvolk* democracy. In fact, he contended that propertied whiteness had to be protected from the lesser civilization of invidious blacks. For Tocqueville, blacks represented "the most formidable evil" threatening the future of the United States. He predicted that a bloody and vicious war between whites and blacks was "more or less distant but inevitable," because it was unthinkable that "white and black races [would] ever be brought anywhere to live on a footing of equality."[62] Tocqueville was thus echoing Jefferson's fears of a war to the death between the races: "Deep rooted prejudices entertained by the whites; ten thousand recollections, by the blacks, of the injuries they have sustained; new provocations; the real distinctions which nature has made; and many other circumstances, will divide us into parties, and produce convulsions which will probably never end but in the extermination of the one or the other race."[63]

Many used this fear of extermination by an inferior race as a justification for the preservation of the white supremacist *Herrenvolk*. It is not only that blacks had to be kept in their place, but that their thoughts of equality and freedom had to be obliterated. Slavery was the means to that end. In 1837, John C. Calhoun put it clearly: "I hold that in the present state of civilization, where two races of different origin, and distinguished by color, and other physical differences, as well as intellectual, are brought together, the relation now existing in the slaveholding states between the two, is, instead of an evil, a good—a positive good."[64]

Always in the background of American life, blacks were the hidden laborers producing the wealth of the *Herrenvolk*. Like the design of Jefferson's Monticello, which "effectively shielded the visitor from any views of industry or enslavement and created an experience of a wild and natural landscape," American exceptionalism radically expunged blacks from its original creed but was haunted by their presence.[65] According to Waldstreicher, America's founding fathers managed "to keep the entire Western world focused on their potential political enslavement, rather than on their African slaves' actual bondage. . . . [And yet] slavery was as important to the making of the Constitution as the Constitution was to the survival of slavery."[66] For most "enlightened"[67] white leaders, this inconvenient fact led them into various forms of tortured reasoning. Their proclaimed attachment to the equality of men clashed with their virulent racism and material dependence on slavery.

In their vain attempts to resolve these contradictions, some American leaders advocated removing African-Americans from their midst and sending them to distant colonies. With such farfetched schemes of colonization amounting to a form of "ethnic cleansing," America's leadership revealed its rejection of a multiracial society where blacks and whites would live together as equal citizens. As Nicholas Guyatt explains, "[Racial] separation was a national preoccupation in the nation's first decades, and it was presented as impeccably liberal in its intention and effects. . . . We have, in other words, to take 'separate but equal' for what it was: a founding principle of the United States."[68]

While America's leaders may have dreamt of creating an American apartheid, they confronted the hard reality that a strict separation of the races was incompatible with the continued viability of the Southern economy. "Separate but equal" may have been a foundational principle of the United States, but it was impossible as policy because enslaved African American labor was too critical to the well-being of white society to be removed from its midst. At best, whites may have expressed a desire to abolish slavery, but they could not hide the fact that the young nation was grounded in the virulent racism of segregationism. Dreams for black invisibility were artificial, a simulacrum that was ultimately incapable of concealing the interests, contradictions, and phobias of white supremacy.

These contradictions are evident not simply in the Declaration of Independence's claim that "all men are created equal" while slavery abounded, but also in the incapacity and unwillingness of the Declaration's authors to do anything to resolve them. In fact, when the American founders ratified the Constitution thirteen years later in 1789, their response to slavery was utter silence. In spite of this deafening silence, American exceptionalism has fabricated the idea that the democratic aspirations of the Declaration and the Constitution embodied a powerful antislavery narrative. The extent of the emancipatory powers of the Declaration and the Constitution is thus at the heart of American exceptionalism, and it has fueled a modern cultural "war"[69] with the 2019 *New York Times'* publication of the "1619 Project."[70] The "1619" in the title is meant to underline the year of the arrival of the first chattel slaves in the colonies and thus to convey the centrality of slavery in the American experience.

As described by the *Times*, the 1619 Project's aim "is to reframe American history by considering what it would mean to regard 1619 as our nation's birth year. Doing so requires us to place the consequences of slavery and the contributions of black Americans at the very center of the story we tell ourselves about who we are as a country."[71] At one level, the 1619 Project and its creator, Nikole Hannah-Jones, challenge American exceptionalism by claiming that "the United States is a nation founded on both an ideal and a lie."[72] The lie is obviously the long and cruel coexistence of slavery and universal claims of human equality. The ideal is the constant and strenuous African American struggle for democracy and freedom. According to Hannah-Jones, the black struggle has expanded democratic rights to all in spite of the war of independence, which was mainly fought to preserve slavery, and in spite of continuous white resistance and violence. In her eyes, African Americans have achieved "astounding progress" even though "anti-black racism runs in the very DNA of this country, as does the belief, so well articulated by Lincoln, that black people are the obstacle to national unity."[73]

Hannah-Jones is thus advancing an ontological racism depicting America as inexorably divided between whites and blacks. The country's conflicts and politics are thus reduced to the African American struggle for full citizenship against the pervasive antiblack racism of white people who seem to be inherently racist. African Americans are thus a cohesive cultural group whose internal differences pale in the face of white racism, and similarly antiblack racism dissolves whatever social and economic fractures might exist among whites. The history of the United States is thus the history of the struggle between two races, with whites always seeking to impose and maintain their supremacy, and blacks continuously seeking their emancipation and democratic rights. Clearly, these claims undermine the exceptionalist narrative; they depict the American Revolution as a fraudulent event bent on preserving slavery rather than expanding freedom and breaking the chains of tyranny.[74] Thus, at inception, the republic was neither democratic nor a promise for the emancipation of African Americans. It embodied a regime of institutionalized racism and white supremacy.

Paradoxically, however, Hannah-Jones's celebration of African Americans as a people totally "disconnected" and "severed" from the world and Africa itself, and yet triumphant in its solitary struggle for freedom, is nothing but a reinvigoration of American exceptionalism. It turns American exceptionalism upside down by espousing a racial reductionism that transforms black Americans into a lonely group that has suffered a unique form of exploitation because of its race and has always fought alone for its liberation. From these exceptional circumstances, African Americans in their solitary struggles for emancipation have expanded the narrow boundaries of American democracy. They have managed to do so, however, because they identify as a race, a cultural group whose divisions have always been thwarted by an ever present systemic racism. In this view, racial identity unifies blacks and trumps their divisions of class or status; it is this racial unity which has made the persistent African American quest for citizenship uniquely American and democratic.

As such, by virtue of their race, African Americans are the truest Americans; they are the embodiment of American exceptionalism. In fact, Hannah-Jones claims that by freeing themselves from bondage and creating America's "most significant original culture," African Americans "became the most American of all." Ultimately, as she emphasizes, "Black people have seen the worst of America, yet, somehow, we still believe in its best."[75] Paradoxically then, in spite of their obdurate limitations, the Declaration of Independence and the Constitution inspired African Americans in their lonely struggle for freedom. Thus, these documents, which supposedly embodied the racist DNA of the American founding itself, are no longer unadulterated white supremacist and proslavery proclamations; they are now contradictory and incomplete narratives of potential emancipation. And it is only when black America seized them to fight for its rights that they gained their democratic vitality.

This is certainly not the position espoused by historians opposed to the 1619 Project who have claimed, using Frederick Douglass's words, that the Constitution was so uniquely democratic that it represented a "glorious liberty document."[76] These historians seem to refuse to acknowledge that full emancipation required a bloody civil war fought eight decades after the Constitution's ratification. If the Constitution was such a "glorious liberty document," why did leaders in both

Southern and Northern states go to the horrific lengths of a fratricidal conflict for abolishing slavery? They could have settled the matter very simply and peacefully in 1789. This is not to agree with Hannah-Jones's contention that the founders "believed that independence was required in order to ensure that slavery would continue."[77] In fact, the founders struggled over the continued legality of slavery,[78] but they ultimately protected it. The point is that the emancipatory aspirations of both the Declaration of Independence and the Constitution were originally designed for the creation of a white *Herrenvolk* regime; they were certainly not meant for African Americans. The founders were all racist, but not all were slave owners or ardent supporters of the "peculiar institution."

There is no reason, however, to accept a modern version of American exceptionalism seeking to absolve the founding fathers from their attachment to slavery. They were not passive observers standing in impotence above impersonal and blind forces over which they had no control. In this new narrative, slaves become resilient heroic figures confronting a world without enslavers and without slave owners. As Henry Wiencek pointedly puts it, "Many writers on slavery today have emphasized the 'agency' of the enslaved people, insisting that we pay heed to the efforts of the slaves to resist their condition and assert their humanity under a dehumanizing system. But as slaves gain 'agency' in historical analyses, the masters seem to lose it. As the slaves become heroic figures, triumphing over their condition, slave owners recede as historical actors and are replaced by a faceless system of 'context' and 'forces.' So, we end up with slavery somehow afloat in a world in which nobody is responsible."[79]

In truth, the American founding fathers were not impotent prisoners of the peculiar institution. Their economic and political interests as well as their racism compelled them to guard and defend the institution and its underlying "forces," which they themselves had created.[80] They instituted the infamous "three-fifths clause" which meant that an enslaved person in any state would count as three-fifths of a person for purposes of taxation and representation in Congress. However, as David Waldstreicher explains, enslaved Africans and their descendants "were not being defined as three-fifths of a person, as is sometimes said, for that would have implied that the men among them deserved three-fifths of a vote, when they had none, or had three-fifths of a person's rights before the law, when they had much less than that, usually. Rather, their presence was being acknowledged as a source of power and of wealth, *for their owners*."[81]

Moreover, slavery crushed interracial solidarity and blurred class interests. It solidified the power of the white ruling class by offering all whites, wealthy or destitute alike, a sense of high status and belonging to a superior and privileged caste of human beings. In 1848, in his "Speech on the Oregon Bill," Vice President John C. Calhoun put it plainly: "With us the two great divisions of society are not the rich and poor, but white and black; and all the former, the poor as well as the rich, belong to the upper class, and are respected and treated as equals, if honest and industrious; and hence have a position and pride of character of which neither poverty nor misfortune can deprive them."[82]

It would be wrong, however, to believe that only Southerners and slave owners like Calhoun entertained such feelings of utter superiority to blacks; in fact, it was John Adams, who was born in Massachusetts and served as the second president of the United States from 1797 to 1801 who, under the pseudonym "Humphrey Ploughjogger," wrote a letter to the *Boston Gazette* in 1765 calling for a rebellion against British rule because the American colonists were neither slaves nor blacks: "Our fore fathers came over here for liberty of conscience, and we have been nothing better than servants to 'em all along this 100 years, and got just enough to keep soul and body together, and buy their goods to keep us from freezing to death, and we won't be their negroes. Providence never designed us for negroes, I know, for if it had it wou'd have given us black hides, and thick lips, and flat noses, and short woolly hair, which it han't done, and therefore never intended us for slaves."[83]

Clearly then, American exceptionalism was based on a claim of equality restricted to a small community of the free that would no longer put up with being the "King's negroes" while remaining determined to continue to marginalize nonpropertied whites, enslave blacks, and liquidate indigenous people. To borrow the words of W. H. Auden, the "wardrobe of excuses," and the "mask of rectitude" did not obscure the horrific underbelly of American exceptionalism.[84]

The wardrobe of excuses is not the only means of dismissing past and current crimes. Exceptionalism is often an ode to innocence[85] and compassionate tolerance, if not absolution, for committed sins. This is especially the case for the history of the indigenous peoples of North America. American exceptionalism barely acknowledges their virtual genocidal liquidation and the systematic taking of their lands by the colonial settlers.[86] The mythology of the founders erases these crimes by claiming that the lands were "unoccupied" or "unused" and thus unpopulated. And if there was just an empty wilderness, there could not have been any genocide. Based on the concept of *res nullius*, the American settlers, against all evidence, simply "disappeared" the indigenous peoples. This disappearance was embedded in a web of contradictions; the Indians of North America existed, but the settlers had "discovered" their land, and thus it was theirs in the name of God for prosperous exploitation. At any rate, by defining the indigenous populations as nothing but "savages," the settlers gave themselves the right to take their territories and indeed exterminate them if they became a "hindrance" to their conquest. As Natsu Taylor Saito explains, "From their initial encounters with the Indigenous peoples of 'New England,' the English settlers began erasing them from history, both literally and figuratively. In the settlers' discourse, north American Indians were often deemed nonexistent; in other instances they were treated as part of nature—animals rather than humans—as therefore not 'occupying' the land."[87]

American exceptionalism offers therefore a panoply of obfuscations to sing the innocence of early colonial settlers in the destruction of indigenous peoples and their societies. The founders' view of Native Americans varied. At best it defined them as uncivilized and primitive people who might be integrated into white society, and at worst they were animals who had to be tamed if not liquidated. Thomas Jefferson saw them as "noble savages" who had the potential to be "acculturated" into white society, but eventually they became the "merciless Indian Savages" he condemned in the Declaration of Independence and who as president he deported to lands west of the Mississippi.[88] As he put it in a letter to William Henry Harrison, governor of the Indiana Territory,

> Our settlements will gradually circumscribe and approach the Indians, and they will in time either incorporate with us as citizens of the United States, or remove beyond the Mississippi. The former is certainly the termination of their history most happy for themselves; but, in the whole course of this, it is essential to cultivate their love. As to their fear, we presume that our strength and their weakness is now so visible that they must see we have only to shut our hand to crush them, and that all our liberalities to them proceed from motives of pure humanity only. Should any tribe be foolhardy enough to take up the hatchet at any time, the seizing the whole country of that tribe, and driving them across the Mississippi, as the only condition of peace, would be an example to others, and a furtherance of our final consolidation.[89]

Clearly, Jefferson was offering indigenous people either the death of their society, or their physical extinction. While George Washington offered them a similar "choice," he called them "beasts" that had to be expeditiously manipulated and exploited until they vanished into oblivion: "I am clear in my opinion, that policy and economy point very strongly to the expediency of being upon good terms with the Indians, and the propriety of purchasing their Lands in preference to attempting to drive them by force of arms out of their Country; . . . when the gradual extension of our Settlements will as certainly cause the Savage as the Wolf to retire; both being beasts of prey tho' they differ in shape."[90]

Thus, the founders and the early Puritans had contempt for the indigenous people; they identified them as animalistic and primitive creatures who ultimately had no rights to their land. American exceptionalism glosses over not only this expropriation of territories but also the "disappearance" of the native population as if it occurred magically. In fact, John Winthrop, the English Puritan lawyer, leading figure in the founding of New England, and first governor of the Massachusetts Bay Colony, hailed divine intervention in the liquidation of American Indians as he exclaimed, "God hath consumed the natives with a miraculous plague, whereby the greater part of the country is left void of inhabitants."[91] Thus, the decimation of the indigenous population had little to do with the wars of conquest and the slaughters inflicted on them by the settlers;

similarly, the deadly epidemics they suffered were nothing but God's wrath.[92] Moreover, the taking of American Indian territory was on a grand scale; by 1890 indigenous peoples retained a mere 2.5 percent of their previous land base.[93] Finally, notes Saito, the magnitude of the "erasure" of Native Americans was devastatingly tragic: "In 1513, there were approximately fifteen million people living in the territory now claimed by the United States and Canada. By 1900 the U.S. Census Bureau reported fewer than 250,000 native people living in the United States. Much of this devastation was the result of diseases introduced by Europeans, with up to 90 percent of some peoples dying within two generations of initial contact. This was often celebrated by the early settlers as evidence that God was on their side."[94]

American exceptionalism has thus always exuded a self-proclaimed and God-given form of innocence. Even when it acknowledges failings and transgressions, it portrays them as inadvertent mistakes, or well-intentioned goals that sadly ended in unintended misdeeds. America is thus always absolved of its crimes. Its leaders simply and arrogantly ignore them. For instance, in the aftermath of the downing of a commercial Iranian airliner that killed 290 civilians by the USS Vincennes on July 3, 1988, then–Vice President George H. W. Bush bluntly declared, "I will never apologize for the United States of America, ever. I don't care what the facts are."[95]

When it tolerates inconvenient facts, American exceptionalism transforms them into unintentional outcomes of virtuous policies. The well-known liberal economist and *New York Times* columnist Paul Krugman, who has lived through the wars in Vietnam, Iraq, Afghanistan, and Libya, illustrates this transformative phenomenon in a 2018 op-ed titled, "Fall of the American Empire":

> Our role in the world was always about more than money and guns. It was also about ideals: America stood for something larger than itself—for freedom, human rights and the rule of law as universal principles.
>
> Of course, we often fell short of those ideals. But the ideals were real, and mattered.... The Pax Americana was a sort of empire; certainly America was for a long time very much first among equals. But it was by historical standards a remarkably benign empire, held together by soft power and respect rather than force.[96]

Thus, in this self-congratulatory statement, Krugman sings the innocence and benevolence of American imperialism while exorcizing its violence and nefarious consequences. Entrapped in American exceptionalism, Krugman is incapable of acknowledging the horrific logic of its hegemony and the simple fact that since its independence in 1776, America has been at war 93 percent of the time–222 out of 239 years.[97] The long American war in Vietnam killed an estimated two million civilians and over one million North Vietnamese and Viet Cong fighters. In addition, according to the U.S. government, between 200,000 and 250,000 South Vietnamese soldiers died in the war.[98] In the recent American-led conflicts in Iraq and Afghanistan, more than 370,000 people were killed in direct violence, and another 800,000 died from the indirect effects of war since 2001.[99] Thus, the imposition of American exceptionalism on others is neither soft nor benign. In spite of preaching some sort of human universalism, American exceptionalism with its very own unique and "God-sanctioned" global mission, has more often than not excluded the "others"—both within and beyond its territorial boundaries—from its moral community. This exclusion is as old as the arrival in North America of the English Puritans. In fact, it is constitutive of both liberalism and liberal democracy. As Anthony Marx explains,

> At the very heart of liberalism is an ugly secret: Supposedly inclusive nationalism was founded on the basis of violent exclusion, used to bound and forge the nation to whom rights would then be selectively granted. Democracy itself was so founded also on exclusions in demarcating the unit to which rights of citizenship would be granted. Founded on this basis, liberal democracy would then eventually serve as a cover, with gradual enfranchisement hiding past exclusions and obfuscating that at the heart of liberalism is an illiberal determination of who is a member of the incorporated community and who is not.[100]

In the next chapter, I will examine the nexus between the racial exclusionism of America's exceptionalism and the radical emancipation of race brought about by Haiti's successful slave revolution.

CHAPTER 3

Exceptionalism and "Unthinkability"

Given their pervasive racism, it is not surprising that American leaders were horrified by history's only successful slave revolution, which created the Haitian republic in 1804.[1] In *Silencing the Past*, Michel-Rolph Trouillot has provocatively but mistakenly argued that Haiti was "unthinkable" because it was the first black independent nation of the modern world. He contended that the West and its intellectuals, and "non-white plantation owners as well," trivialized the Haitian Revolution as a "non-event," as something "unthinkable." In other words, Western historiography and popular narratives consistently portrayed slaves as lacking agency and thus incapable of changing their circumstances, let alone of imagining or fighting for their freedom. Thus, in Trouillot's eyes the Western world had purposefully "silenced" the makers of 1804. As he put it, "The Haitian Revolution thus entered history with the peculiar characteristic of being unthinkable even as it happened. . . . If some events cannot be accepted even as they occur, how can they be assessed later? In other words, can historical narratives convey plots that are unthinkable in the world within which these narratives take place? How does one write a history of the impossible?"[2]

The Haitian Revolution was, however, all too thinkable; it was not only the embodiment of a long held and terrifying specter that white supremacists feared more than anything, but it was also celebrated by enslaved people in the New World as well as radical European thinkers.[3] In fact, in the late 1700s and early 1800s, British authors such as John Thelwall, Percival Stockdale, and Marcus Rainsford defended the violence of the enslaved against their masters as legitimate means to gain their rights and freedom.[4] While the French revolution of 1789 might have inspired the blacks of Saint Domingue to break their chains, it was their own agency which led them to declare their independence in 1804. Stockdale supported the enslaved's revolutionary violence and pointedly asked, "Should we not crown it with eulogium, if they exterminated their tyrants with fire, and sword?"[5] Moreover, Rainsford viewed 1804 as more than a mere revolutionary act; it was an "event which may powerfully affect the condition of the human race."[6] In fact, the Haitian Revolution represented for the radical Thelwall a cataclysmic transformation of the world order that announced the possibility of the worldwide revolt of all downtrodden against the privileged few. It was an anticolonial revolt that could activate workers into insurrection and spread the wings of freedom to Europe itself.[7] Finally, Thelwall reminded those alarmed by the successful emancipation of Haiti that they could not "forget, that slavery is robbery and murder; and that the master who falls by the bondsman's hand, is the victim of his own barbarity."[8]

The creation of Haiti was not trivialized; it embodied not only the enslaved's recovery of their humanity but also the universal aspirations for an egalitarian and classless world trespassing the boundaries of race. Thus, in the eyes of its makers, virulent opponents, and hopeful supporters, the Haitian Revolution was undeniably thinkable; the issue was whether the forces of white supremacy would contain it. Indeed, the two original government-printed versions of the Haitian Declaration of Independence that Julia Gaffield discovered at the National Archives of the United Kingdom in London in 2010 and 2011 clearly indicate that "silenced" was not quite the word defining the impact of the revolution. As Gaffield explains:

> The presence of the documents in London tells a story of international communications in the early months of Haiti's independence. The proclamation announced to the nations and empires of the Atlantic World that the territory was no longer under French authority; instead the new "Haytian" government ruled it. Haitian leaders knew that independence from France could only be complete if foreign governments recognized and supported the new nation.
>
> The document circulated around the Atlantic, and portions of it were reprinted in newspapers in cities like Philadelphia and London, and even as far away as Bombay. . . . Would the revolution spread? was the question on everyone's mind.[9]

What is clear and not farfetched is to agree with Rayford Logan's claim that "the specter of a free Negro Republic that owed its independence to a successful slave revolt frightened slave holding countries as much as the shadow of Bolshevist Russia alarmed capitalistic countries in 1917."[10] It is critical, however, to remember that anxiety about the possibility of slaves revolting against their bondage was not an exclusively white or Western affair. The so-called free people of color, comprising black and "mulatto" slave owners of Saint Domingue,[11] had initially refused to fight for the full emancipation of slaves; they merely sought equality with the white colonists. Their decision to join and, in some instances, lead the revolutionary forces came only after those demands had been rejected.

The paradigmatic figure of this contradictory political trajectory was none other than Toussaint Louverture, an enslaved black man who, upon gaining his freedom, became a slave owner himself and eventually emerged as the emblematic military commander of the Haitian Revolution.[12] Toussaint exemplified the antinomies of property relations in a class-ridden colonial, slave-plantation economy. He did not imagine a world beyond the boundaries of class and the existing system of production. In fact, as Alex Dupuy has argued, "Louverture and most other high-ranking military officers, including [Jean-Jacques] Dessalines acquired several plantations and transformed themselves into a new black propertied class alongside the old class of white and mulatto property owners. Military officers and administrators of the new political order did not only appropriate properties from former French planters; they also pilfered the public treasury."[13]

The class project of the Haitian revolutionaries should not, however, obscure its ideological universalism rooted in the abolition of slavery and the equality of all people irrespective of their race. The pre-independence period of Toussaint's autonomous rule over Saint Domingue (1798–1801), which Sabine Manigat has called the "Louverturian state,"[14] was a promise of racial equality; it guaranteed blacks, whites, and mulattoes the rights to hold both property and public office. The Louverturian state was thus a direct challenge to the dominant white-supremacist world order, but the liberty it promised had limits. In fact, Toussaint's Constitution of 1801 envisaged the possibility of importing "new captives from Africa" to the island to repopulate the labor force that had been decimated by the revolutionary insurrections. While these "captives" would "enjoy legal freedom," they would be compelled to perform regimented and disciplined work on the plantations.[15]

Thus, the multiracial Louverturian state abolished slavery, but it upheld new forms of servitude; it navigated between the revolutionary overthrow and the conservative preservation of *l'ordre des choses*.[16] It mirrored Toussaint's contradictory commitments to achieving complete political autonomy from, and keeping strong ties to, France. In fact, the imperialist "civilizing" values of the French Revolution impregnated Toussaint's ideology. In 1799, according to Hippolyte-Daniel de Saint-Anthoine, Toussaint considered resigning his position as commander in chief of the island to wage a military operation in Africa that would "abolish the slave trade and slavery."[17] At this time, it was in the name of France that Toussaint envisaged launching his colonizing and emancipatory project; his ultimate goal was to make millions of Africans "free and French."

Haitian exceptionalism was thus influenced by French revolutionary ideals, but its essence resided in the quest for liberty ignited by the cruel experience of slavery.[18] Enslaved black bodies did not need the French Revolution to understand the barbarism unleashed against them. In fact, in the Haitian imaginary, it is the Bois-Caïman Vodou ceremony which allegedly took place on the night of August 14, 1791, that set in motion the revolution. It represents the electrifying moment when slaves acquired the insurrectionary will defining the Haitian identity from whose womb was born the Haitian nation in 1804. Haitian lore portrays the event in vivid terms derived from Antoine Dalmas's *Histoire de la Révolution de Saint Domingue*, published in 1814 but supposedly written in 1793.[19] The words of the Haitian diplomat and statesman Dantes Bellegarde are worth quoting at length, because they capture well how Haitians have historically viewed Bois-Caïman:

> During the night of 14 August 1791 in the midst of a forest called Bois-Caïman, on the Morne Rouge in the northern plain, the slaves held a large meeting to draw up a final plan for a general revolt. They consisted of about two hundred slave drivers, sent from various plantations in the region. Presiding over the assembly was a black man named Boukman, whose fiery words exalted the conspirators. Before they separated, they held amidst a violent rainstorm an impressive ceremony, so as to solemnize the undertakings they made. While the storm raged and lightning shot across the sky, a tall black woman appeared suddenly in the center of the gathering. Armed with a long, pointed knife that she waved above her head, she performed a sinister dance singing an African song, which the others, face down against the ground, repeated as a chorus. A black pig was then dragged in front of her and she split it open with her knife. The animal's blood was collected in a wooden bowl and served still foaming to each delegate. At a signal from the priestess, they all threw themselves on their knees and swore blindly to obey the orders of Boukman, who had been proclaimed the supreme chief of the rebellion. He announced as his choice of principal lieutenants Jean Francois Papillon, Georges Biassou, and Jeannot Bullet.[20]

For Haitians therefore, Bois-Caïman is the myth of origin, the event that mixed secular and Vodou forces in the making of their nation. It proudly asserts their Africanness and the triumphant vindication of their culture over the cruel and brutal rule of French colonial slavery. In fact, Boukman, the most prominent revolutionary leader at that time, apparently swore at Bois-Caïman this famous oath: "The God of the Whites commands crimes; ours wants only good deeds. / The Lord in his goodness orders us to rise and avenge ourselves. / He will guide our arms; He will help us. / Let us throw down the picture of the White God who thirsts for our tears. / Let us listen to the voice of freedom shouting in our hearts."[21]

Thus, Bois-Caïman became Haiti's foundational myth, and its oath framed Haitian exceptionalism on the basis of the Africanness of its citizens. Asserting in Article 14 that "all Haitians are black," Jean-Jacques Dessalines's Constitution of 1805 instituted the sovereignty of the republic by excluding from its collectivity the forces of "whiteness." Haitian exceptionalism, like its counterparts elsewhere, had to demarcate itself by a dual and systematic process of exclusion and inclusion; it excluded and denigrated the white supremacist forces of colonial slavery, and it included and celebrated the African "avengers of the new world."[22] In fact, the Haitian revolutionaries called the land they had liberated by the name that its original Taino inhabitants had given it.

Haiti symbolized not merely a triumphant blackness, but it avenged all those who had been the casualties of imperial brutalities and encroachments, irrespective of race. In a letter to Napoleon Bonaparte, Toussaint Louverture called for the unfettered freedom of all human beings: "It is not a liberty of circumstance, conceded to us alone, that we want; it is the *absolute adoption* of the principle that no human being, born red, black, or white, can be the property of his fellow."[23] When Toussaint's call was rejected not only by Napoleon but also by the West in general, Haitians chose to espouse the blackness of their Africanness as the embodiment of their resistance and identity. As Article 14 of Haiti's Constitution of May 20, 1805, stipulated, "The Haytians shall hence forward be known only by the generic appellation of Blacks."[24] Moreover, "no whiteman of whatever nation" could acquire property on the republic's territory as this right was reserved exclusively to Haitians. Article 13, however, granted the Haitian citizenship and its attending rights to white women married to Haitians as well as to the Germans and to Poles who had fought alongside the Haitian revolutionaries in the war of independence.[25]

Thus, the exclusionary nature of Haitian exceptionalism has paradoxically a universalist logic. As Doris Garraway explains, "The universal in post-Revolutionary Haiti was categorically different from the racial particularisms that had previously governed power and prestige in the colony: the universal was derived from an opposition to the logic of (racial) particularism itself, and from the exclusion of the previously dominant group that had defined itself in racial terms."[26] Thus, when the enslaved conquered their liberty and rights of citizenship and created Haiti in 1804, blackness came to symbolize the universal in the dominant and particularistic white supremacist world of the eighteenth and nineteenth centuries.[27] And yet the Bois-Caïman ceremony that sacralized Haitian exceptionalism originated from the text of Dalmas, a white colonist whose "malevolent" purpose, according to French scholar Leon-Francois Hoffman, was to concoct the ceremony in order to denigrate it as the deed of African barbarians who engaged in depraved religious practices.

In Hoffman's account, Bois-Caïman simply did not take place; it was a pure invention of Dalmas, who was bent on stigmatizing the enslaved revolutionaries.[28] Thus, in Hoffman's view, the ceremony does not constitute a historical event but rather a myth in the strongest sense of the term.[29] A myth, however, is not unimportant, and as Hoffman himself emphasizes, it can be more real than history itself if it can inspire a people into resistance and rebellion, as Bois-Caïman effectively did.[30]

While Hoffman may have been right in his understanding of the power of myths, he was wrong in depicting Bois-Caïman as a nonhistorical event. In fact, Bois-Caïman did take place; the question is whether all the instances depicted in the story are accurate and whether the ceremony had the immediate

revolutionary impact that many Haitian scholars claim it had.[31] Without engaging into a long historical debate, suffice it to say that Bois-Caïman is an event
still clouded in mystery. David Patrick Geggus sums up the most convincing
historical evidence concerning the ceremony: "[The] Bois Caïman ceremony
did indeed take place—it is not the case of *barbarisme imaginaire*—but . . . much
of what has been written about it is unreliable. . . . What, then, can be said of
the ceremony's role in the revolt? Principally, that it served to sacralize a political movement that was then reaching fruition."[32]

What seems certain, however, is that Bois-Caïman was the second and perhaps less momentous meeting where Haitian revolutionaries plotted their
uprising. It is likely that it took place on August 21 instead of August 14, which
is the probable date of the first and more decisive gathering of some 200 slave
drivers that occurred at the Lenormand plantation. Bois-Caïman seems to have
been a festive affair and "a predominantly secular occasion."[33] Thus, while Bois-
Caïman has acquired mythical status in Haitian history, it has generally been
mistaken for the more important Lenormand meeting.[34]

Moreover, it is not at all clear that Vodou played a determinant role in the
ceremony or in mobilizing slaves into rebels, as many Haitian scholars would
have it.[35] The existing evidence indicates that Vodou cemented a common slave
identity, but whether it was that identity that galvanized them into becoming
revolutionaries remains a question. As Geggus argues, "From the sixteenth to
the nineteenth century, Afro-American religions provided slave rebellions with
leaders, organization, ideologies, and a community of feeling. During the revolutionary crisis in Saint Domingue, too, magico-religious beliefs helped mobilize resistance and foster a revolutionary mentality. Whether Vodou played a
critical role, however, either as an institution or source of inspiration, particularly in the . . . uprising itself, remains to be proven."[36]

What is beyond doubt, however, is that the enslaved were no longer prepared
to put up with being the victims of a despotic colonialism.[37] To put it simply,
they sought freedom from the barbarism of slavery and the modicum of dignity
that any human being ought to have enjoyed. They had a determined hatred for
both the institution of slavery and racism. As the "Chiefs of the [Slaves'] Revolt"
of 1791, Jean-Francois, Biassou, and Belair[38] explained in a letter to colonial
authorities in July 1792:

> We are black, it is true, but tell us Gentlemen, who are so judicious, what is the
> law that says that the black man must belong to and be the property of the white
> man? Certainly you will not be able to make us see where that exists, if it is not
> in your imagination—always ready to form new [phantasms] so long as they are
> to your advantage. Yes, Gentlemen, we are free like you, and it is only by your
> avarice and our ignorance that anyone is still held in slavery up to this day, and
> we can neither see nor find the right which you pretend to have over us, nor

anything that could prove it to us, set down on the earth like you, all being children of the same father created in the same image. We are your equals then, by natural right, and if nature pleases itself to diversify colors within the human race, it is not a crime to be born black nor an advantage to be white.... For too long we have borne your chains without thinking of shaking them off, but any authority which is not founded on virtue and humanity and which only tends to subject one's fellowman to slavery, must come to end, and that end is yours.... [We demand] General Liberty for all men detained in slavery.[39]

The secretary of Jean-Jacques Dessalines, Boisrond-Tonnerre, shared a similar opinion: "And to you, the slaves of all countries, you will learn from this great man [Dessalines], that every man naturally carries liberty in his heart, and that the keys [to this liberty] are in his hands."[40] In short, Haitian revolutionaries knew intimately the harm caused by French imperialism and the institution of slavery and the vicious wounds they inflicted on them. Boisrond-Tonnerre expressed well the rage and the sadness of the Haitian insurrectionaries when he described the Middle Passage as "ships turned into jails," and the plantations on which he slaved as "forests turned into hanging grounds," where "hundreds of blacks and mulattos [were] being led to their deaths daily."[41]

In sum, slaves themselves understood their predicament and decided they would no longer put up with it. The *philosophes* of the French Enlightenment generated neither the growing communities of Maroons nor the slaves' violent resistance to slavery.[42] In fact, the quest for liberty embodied in both the Maroons and the slaves' violent resistance was hardly voiced by the ideologists of the European Enlightenment, who at best lamented the existence of slavery but had little to do with its abolition.[43] Slaves became Maroons and then revolutionaries because they sought their human dignity and autonomy as well as their freedom from the plantations' horrific labor regimentation, insufficient food, and brutal punishments. As Jean Fouchard points out:

Marooning is the dominant feature of all Haitian history. If it does not explain the birth of our nation, it is undoubtedly the phenomenon which gave its orientation to the history of our nation.... Marooning began in 1503 with the first importation of African slaves into Hispaniola.... Africans' marooning began during, and it continued throughout, the whole colonial period, together with other forms of resistance, such as poisoning, abortions, sabotage, and arson. The maroons first stood up for freedom two centuries before the encyclopedists and the ideologists of the French Revolution had started their work. We preceded the French Revolution by two centuries.[44]

Not surprisingly, the phenomenon of *marronage* occupies a privileged place in Haitian exceptionalism and history even if it has a complicated relation to freedom, resistance, and accommodation to regimes of subjugation.[45] Its practice reflects both the original fleeing of the oppressed from the exploitative domains of slavery, and then from the reach of a despotic state. This fleeing into what might be described as spaces of survival represented simultaneously a form of resistance and a type of accommodation to the existing system of predations. In this sense, rather than embodying the oppressed people's frontal assault against exploitative structures of domination, *marronage* has always been their exit from the reach of those lording it over them,[46] whether it be the white masters of the plantation system or the ruling class of Haiti. It has been their favorite means of resistance and is one of the quintessential "weapons of the weak."[47] It is wrong, however, to "overly romanticize [these weapons]. They are unlikely to do more than marginally affect the various forms of exploitation."[48]

In its appropriation of *marronage*, however, Haitian exceptionalism has tended to transform it into a revolutionary rupture with the white colonial settler plantation. In this perspective, *marronage* and the Maroons embody only eman-cipation. That slaves bravely escaped their captivity and occasionally engaged in guerrilla activities or other forms of resistance against their former masters implied neither that revolution was inevitable nor that Maroon communities were more than isolated spaces of survival in an otherwise enslaved territory. It is clear, however, that *marronage* was and remains the preferred welter of elusive actions devised by oppressed Haitians to avoid extreme forms of predation, state repression, and oppressive class rule. This welter of elusive actions does not, how-ever, amount to any fundamental structural change in the status quo. In fact, *marronage* is not the exclusive preserve of the subordinates; it has also character-ized the patterns of governance of Haiti's rulers since the days of the revolution. They have always been elusive, never taking responsibility for the ills of the republic, and always masking their despotic tendencies in the name of democ-racy and the interests of the masses. While in the early period of independence they asserted their support for emancipation, they imposed a regime of forced labor, and more recently while they proclaimed their attachment to national sov-ereignty, they appealed for imperial support and interference. More importantly, however, while always appealing to social justice, they never tore down the apartheid-like wall separating them from the vast majority. Thus, the uses of *marronage* are multiple and contradictory.

In his book *Ti Difé Boulé Sou Istoua Ayiti*, Michel-Rolph Trouillot makes clear the fundamental difference between *marronage* and revolution in the his-tory of Haiti:

> In 1791, the call for liberty found a fertile soil to grow. The slaves were more numerous and their situation had worsened, they could therefore see more easily the contradictions confronting society. They realized that the liberty they sought would not come by itself. They started understanding that this liberty meant **"cut off the head and burn down the house."** While the call

for liberty of 1791 resembled the maroon's quest for freedom, unlike the latter it went beyond a mere **escape** from the slave quarters; it meant **war against slavery** itself. . . . [The] slaves reached a crossroad where instead of fleeing behind freedom they preferred to **fight** for freedom.[49]

Marronage may thus be resistance, but it is also accommodation to the powers that be. While it may engender a new community with a changed set of values and consciousness, it cannot effect a total rupture with the dominant order of exploitation. It is both in and out of this very order; ultimately it is a fruit of hybridity. As Richard Price has argued:

> For while [Maroons and their communities] were, from one perspective, the antithesis of all that slavery stood for, they were at the same time everywhere an embarrassingly visible part of these systems. Just as the very nature of plantation slavery implied violence and resistance, the wilderness setting of early New World plantations made *marronage* and the existence of organized maroon communities a ubiquitous reality. Throughout Afro-America, such communities stood out as an heroic challenge to white authority, and as the living proof of the existence of a slave consciousness that refused to be limited by the whites' conception or manipulation of it.[50]

To this extent, the enslaved did not need the French Revolution to claim their own freedom and equality; neither did they need it to know that they were full human beings. What 1789 offered them, however, was a strategic and transformational political opening, a critical juncture that intensified preexisting ideological struggles, exacerbated long-standing social tensions, and facilitated their insurrection.[51] Thus, the French Revolution smoothed the terrain on which the slaves seized the opportunity to liberate themselves with the force of arms.[52] In addition, the element of chance—the leadership of Léger-Félicité Sonthonax, the French civil commissioner in Saint Domingue and an abolitionist as well as a radical Jacobin, was critical in starting the process of general emancipation by proclaiming on August 29, 1793, the freedom of the slaves of the north province who would henceforth enjoy the rights of French citizens.[53] While it is true that Sonthonax's proclamation followed the slaves' insurrection of 1791, it nonetheless opened wider the window from which the rebels blew the violent winds of liberty that would ultimately sweep away slavery itself.[54]

As Carolyn Fick argues, the "crucial link" between the French Revolution and the "black revolution in Saint Domingue seems to reside in the conjunctural and complementary elements of a self-determined, massive slave rebellion, on the one hand, and the presence in the colony of a practical abolitionist in the person of Sonthonax, on the other."[55]

Emancipation, however, was not a gift of the French Revolution.[56] This became extremely clear when Napoleon put an end to the universalist pretensions of 1789 and passed the "Law of 20 May 1802" annulling the "Law of 16 Pluviôse," which had ended slavery in all French-held territory. Toussaint came to realize this too late; his faith in the French Republic and its values led to his deceitful capture by French troops in June 1802. Under Napoleon's orders, general Victoire Leclerc engineered a meeting between general Jean-Baptiste Brunet and Toussaint where the *Premier des Noirs* was arrested.[57] Toussaint was then compelled to cross the Atlantic and incarcerated in the Fort de Jous deep in the Jura Mountains and not far from Besançon.

Thus, despite his faith in French universalism, Toussaint could not ultimately escape the hard realities of white supremacy. The world capitalist system at the time of the Haitian Revolution was irrevocably racist. Toussaint the black slave owner was an anomaly. Toussaint the revolutionary general leading an enslaved people toward emancipation was an immense danger. Napoleon knew it, and by incarcerating the revolutionary leader, he sought to decapitate the slaves' revolt. While Toussaint died on April 7, 1803, as a prisoner far from the shores of Saint Domingue, as Napoleon intended, his demise in the Fort de Jous did not stop the slaves' insurrection.[58] In fact, as Toussaint is alleged to have declared to his French captors, "In overthrowing me, you have uprooted in Saint-Domingue only the trunk of the tree of the liberty of the blacks; it will grow back because its roots are deep and numerous."[59]

And indeed, soon afterwards, in 1804, the enslaved of Saint Domingue under the leadership of Toussaint's military heirs, Jean-Jacques Dessalines, Henri Christophe, and Alexandre Pétion, defeated the Napoleonic forces to create Haiti. The fact that Haiti is the first and only nation founded by the successful revolution of enslaved black persons signaled to Haitians that they were exceptional and that their history was equally exceptional. The harsh and long struggle from capture to enslavement and eventual emancipation with the concomitant achievement of nationhood are thus the source of Haitian exceptionalism.[60] As Asselin Charles puts it, "The narrative of the myth of collective origins includes these leitmotivs: the African ancestry of Haitians; the Middle Passage; the plantation; resistance to slavery in all its forms but particularly in its heroic forms of marronnage and mass revolt; the epic war of independence; the spectacular victory of the former slaves against the forces of European colonialism; and the founding of the first Black nation-state in the Americas."[61]

Haitian exceptionalism is thus rooted above all in the heroic and successful struggle against slavery and for a genuinely universal freedom transcending race. It rejected violently the severe limitations of French universalism and embraced a new paradigm that no longer confined human beings to the invented status of a superior or inferior race. It is true that Dessalines's Constitution of 1805 defined Haiti as a black nation, but it was not in celebration of black supremacy; it was in fact an attempt, however vain, to erase color in the new

EXCEPTIONALISM AND "UNTHINKABILITY"

society. As the constitution put it, "Because all distinctions of color among children of the same family must necessarily stop, Haitians will henceforth only be known generically as Blacks."[62]

There is little doubt, however, that defining Haiti as a black nation symbolized also Dessalines's hatred of white planters and French colonialism.[63] Paradoxically, that hatred was compounded by his own class aspirations to become a major plantation owner. Killing white French people while fighting for emancipation just happened to coincide with his class interests. And indeed, the 1804 massacre of white *colons* that he engineered can be understood as the liquidation not of race but of class competitors. As Philippe Girard contends:

> As a slave rebel and revolutionary leader, [Dessalines] sought vengeance on white French planters, but he did not allow his racial agenda to undermine the economic goals he had set for his new regime. The spring 1804 massacre pointedly excluded practitioners of specific trades such as surgeons and priests; it also spared mixed-race descendants of French colonists and all non-French whites, particularly Polish veterans of the Victoire Emmanuel Leclerc expedition and U.S. and British merchants present in Haitian ports. In fact, the massacres so specifically targeted French planters that one could analyze them not as a race-based genocide but as an economic pogrom meant to take over the victims' plantations for the benefit of black and mixed-race officers in Dessalines's army.[64]

Thus, it was not racism per se that led to Dessalines's massacres of whites and proclamation of Haiti as a black republic. In fact, such violence was not new, and whites were not its only victims. In October 1801, Toussaint inflicted his wrath on former slaves who had called for the "death of all the white people" and rebelled against the regime of forced labor he had himself established on the plantations. With the help of Dessalines and Christophe, Toussaint planned and executed a systematic and savage campaign of repression against the rebels, killing up to 5,000 of them.[65] Moreover, General Moïse, who supported the insurrectionists and refused "to be the executioner of my color," was shot on order of Toussaint, his uncle.[66]

Clearly this wave of repression was not an expression of racism, but rather the cruel and despotic idiom of the class project of Haiti's founding fathers, whose respective rule mimicked the authoritarian Louverturian regime. As Claude Moïse contends, this regime failed to "transcend the social contradictions arising from dismemberment of the colonial slave regime. It [could not] reconcile antagonistic interests. It [tended] to enclose them in a repressive and authoritarian system strongly modeled on the absolute personal power that Toussaint institutionalized. The masses [did] not count in the economic and social politics of Toussaint Louverture. Rural laborers [sought] all ways to escape the constraints of the system: fleeing into the hills, refusing to work."[67]

Thus, the Louverturian project, like its immediate successors, was based on the reconsolidation of the plantation economy, which henceforth would be owned and controlled by the founders and their top black and mulatto military lieutenants. In this class project, former slaves would be coerced into new forms of labor servitude, but as early as 1802 and definitely by the spring of 1804 it contained no room for white French *colons*. Liquidating them became a means to an end.

This is not to say that race as a marker and signifier played no role in Dessalines's 1804 "economic pogrom." As a former enslaved African victimized by white masters who lived most of his life in a system where color mattered decisively, how could it have been otherwise? While Dessalines did engage in brutal retributions against *grands et petit blancs* for their crimes, he never sought to establish a black supremacist state. After all, he was himself a general in the French army before he defected in 1802 to lead the enslaved in their successful revolutionary war. The portrayal of Dessalines as a cruel racist lacking the sophistication, diplomatic skills, and cosmopolitan vision of Toussaint is one-sided. Girard offers a convincing rebuttal of this all-too-common depiction of Dessalines:

> Dessalines's record immediately prior to and after Haiti's independence thus forces us to reevaluate one of Haiti's most celebrated founding fathers as a more conservative and multifaceted figure than is usually assumed—or, to use Ira Berlin's term, as a latter-day "Atlantic Creole." Far from being the bloodthirsty brute found in contemporary French accounts or the single-minded advocate of independence and racial pride described in some nationalist Haitian works, he was a cautious, sly, pragmatic individual who sought to safeguard his political and economic interests and settle personal scores while advancing his long-term ideological agenda, bringing Haiti's plantation system back to its prerevolutionary apex, and safeguarding Haiti's sovereignty.[68]

In many ways, Toussaint and Dessalines shared a similar agenda; while the latter ultimately fought successfully for an independent Haiti, the former sought political and economic autonomy from France, and had he not been deported he might well have severed colonial ties altogether.[69] Both men were bent on building an economy based on a restored plantation system that required forced labor and perhaps the reintroduction of slavery with the importation of new enslaved Africans.[70] Like all the founders, both had personal class aspirations to become major planters and thus had an interest in developing commerce and trade with the major white supremacist states.[71] Yet personal relations between Toussaint the *ancien libre* and Dessalines the *nouveau libre* were strained. Moreover, it appears that while he was Toussaint's obedient military subordinate, Dessalines resented his commander to the extent that he might have collaborated with the French in Toussaint's arrest and ultimate deportation to France.[72]

These internecine conflicts, however, have always been more than mere per-sonalistic struggles for power. They have reflected historical divisions dating back to the colonial order and reproduced in new forms during and after the revolutionary periods. The hierarchical structures defining Saint Domingue were primarily racial insofar as *gran blans* and *ti blans* dominated a society whose organizing political, economic, legal, and cultural principles were based on the subjugation and inferiority of enslaved black Africans. This divide, how-ever, was not without its contradictions and fissures. When the revolution began, a small segment of the enslaved population had gained its freedom. They were the so-called *affranchis* or *gens de couleur*—the *free people of color*—composed mainly of mulattoes, though there were black exceptions, as Toussaint's case demonstrates. As freed ex-slaves, the *affranchis* could, and in fact some did, own slaves and plantations, and not surprisingly they were besieged by color and incipient class fragmentations. They were nonetheless given privileges and rights that were obviously denied to the enslaved majority. The enslaved themselves were fractured between the Creoles, those who were born in Saint Domingue, and the Bossales, the African-born majority.[73] The former served in disproportionate numbers as *commandeurs* and thus not only considered themselves superior to the latter, but lorded it over them.

The *commandeurs* were chosen by the white planters to oversee and enforce the harsh discipline of slave labor. In fact, they were the most immediate extension of the white masters' violence. In return, they received preferential treatment; they worked far less and enjoyed better food and clothing than other slaves. Their del-egated power pushed them into the highest stratum of the enslaved community. Gabriel Debien describes well the *commandeur*'s function within this community: "The emblem of his authority was a whip with either a long or short staff which he always carried in his hand or a stick that the blacks mockingly called 'coco macaque.' . . . The commandeur undertook the subsidiary management duties of work, deciding on the jobs and therefore the pace of tasks, reprimanding or whip-ping the lazy and unruly. . . . The prestige of his role made of him an official petty tyrant, someone important. . . . [And] the commandeur more readily than anyone else got la liberté de savane, or even legal emancipation."[74]

Thus, whether enslaved or freed, both *commandeurs* and Creoles played a dif-ferent role and had a higher status than the Bossales in the slave plantations of Saint Domingue. While this is not the place to explain the complicated history of the shifting and contradictory alliances between enslaved, Bossales, Creoles, *affranchis*, *nouveaux libres*, and *ancients libres*, it is clear that what is striking is that they managed, however imperfectly and temporarily, to unite in spite of their deep existential, cultural, material, and color divisions.[75] What fused the disparate groups was their common hatred of slavery, the unreconstructed rac-ism of white *colons* and planters, and the uncertainties concerning the extent and permanence of emancipation once it was proclaimed by Sonthonax. The imperfect unity that ultimately proved strong enough to defeat Napoleon's forces paradoxically began to fall apart with the conquest of independence itself. New conflicts arising from the internecine and intense process of class formation pitting top military officers of the revolutionary armies, *anciens affranchis*, and the exploited rural majority exacerbated the old divisions of color.

Not surprisingly, the unitary state of Haiti quickly disintegrated. David Geggus succinctly explains this disintegration: "A profound social cleavage separated the rural masses, about a quarter of whom had been born in Africa, from the new elite that, despite the hostility expressed in the declaration of independence, remained strongly attracted to French culture. The elite itself was divided between black officers that had risen from slavery, who were numerous in the north, and the *anciens libres* of mixed racial descent, who controlled the center and south. In 1807, the country split along these regional and class lines into two warring states and remained divided until 1820."[76]

The assassination and bodily mutilation of Haiti's founder, Dessalines, in October 1806 presaged this split and is its quintessential incarnation. Moreover, the fact that his body was left unattended in Government Square and received no proper burial for some time signified in Carlo Célius's words "a true rite of desecration."[77] This desecration symbolized also the extremely frail basis on which Haiti's exceptionalism rested. The internecine conflicts besieging the ruling class undermined its national project, which in spite of its claims of solidarity and equality included the masses only as a labor force to be regimented and exploited. Not surprisingly, the ruling class never imposed its hegemony on society, and thus Haitian exceptionalism was anchored more in the romantic imaginary of its citizens than in the reality of their daily struggles for economic survival and political representation.

Thus the profound economic, political, cultural, and moral fissure separating rulers and ruled not only shaped the landscape of the early postcolonial period; it never stopped structuring Haitian society. In fact, with the passage of time, the ruling class would use *Bossal* disparagingly not just to describe, as in colonial Saint Domingue, the newly arrived, "dumb," and bewildered African-born enslaved cultivator, but to offer its modern and all-encompassing depiction of *le peuple* as utterly inferior, ugly, and ignorant. *Bossal* came to mean a horrifying, dangerous, and subhuman alien mass of *moun Ginen*.[78] The racist undertones of such a conception are unmistakable in spite of being uttered by both black and mulatto wings of the fractious ruling class. Thus, while Haitian exceptionalism has consistently proclaimed the principle of racial equality, it has had a very hard time adhering to it in practice. The continued influence of both *noirisme* and *mulatrisme* indicates that Haitian exceptionalism has at the very least coexisted with certain forms of racist ideologies.

Like all exceptionalisms, the Haitian variant has consistently embellished if not altogether rewritten or erased embarrassing historical realities. Thus, Haitian exceptionalism has always sought to mask *noirisme* and *mulatrisme* by celebrating blackness as its very embodiment. In fact, it has represented Haitian blackness as the symbol of the rising of the wretched of the earth against white racism and colonialism. The republic is thus at the center of the universal revolt against injustice; blackness is neither race nor color per se, but a category encompassing anyone opposed to white supremacy and Western imperialism. As Gerald Horne explains, "By 1804 Haiti was moving constitutionally toward a radically new concept of citizenship: that only those denoted as "black" could be citizens, revalorizing what had been stigmatized. Yet 'black' was defined expansively—unlike 'white'—to mean those that rejected both France and slavery, meaning that even a 'white' could be defined as 'black' as long as he or she repudiated the logic of racial slavery that intended that only 'whites' should rule and Africans should serve."[79]

Thus, by proffering Haitian citizenship to the downtrodden, oppressed, and excluded human beings of the dominant "enlightened" liberal Western order, the rulers of the newly independent state were creating a universalizing exceptionalism. "Indians"—the indigenous peoples of the Americas—and all enslaved individuals of African descent were included and celebrated in Haiti's radical political dispensation.[80] As Délide Joseph has explained, "The nationalism imagined by Haitian intellectuals . . . seeks to overcome differences between Haitian citizens and blacks in general, to unify them politically. The quest for a 'black state,' a refuge for all slaves and free blacks discriminated against everywhere, expresses not only the hatred for the servile institution, the socioracial system instituted by the colonialist, and slaveholding powers of the period, but also the desire to prove to whites the capacity of black peoples to establish a government, a national administration."[81]

By proclaiming and establishing racial equality, Haiti was bound to gain the enmity of all Western powers and the backing of those who endured the oppression and indignities of white supremacy. As Abbé Grégoire, the nineteenth-century French bishop and abolitionist, put it, "The Haitian Republic, by the sole fact of its existence, will probably have a great influence over the destiny of the New World Africans. Haiti is a beacon shining down over the Antilles towards which the slaves and their masters, the oppressed and the oppressors, turn their eyes, the former with a sigh, the latter with a howl."[82] And it is precisely because the Haitian Revolution erased "color" and indeed race as markers of human status that the Western howl turned so strident and violent. Haiti came to represent a real and existential threat to the interests of Euro-Americans. Western powers, however, reacted with varying degrees of opposition to the black republic. Some, like Jefferson's America, were determined to isolate it and suffocate it, while others were prepared to maintain profitable economic relations with it without granting it diplomatic recognition as a sovereign nation. In short, they used Haiti for their own strategic purposes. As

Julia Gaffield has pointed out, "The evidence of the first years after the Declaration of Independence leads to the conclusion that foreign governments did not collectively and uniformly stigmatize the new country because they could not imagine a 'black republic' in their midst. Neighboring nations, while refusing to fully recognize Haitian independence, were eager to take advantage of trade opportunities and to use Haiti to their own advantage in influencing the balance of power in European warfare."[83]

The connections between Haiti and the Western world were, however, suffused with racism and clearly rooted in hierarchical terms. White supremacist powers and especially the United States during Thomas Jefferson's presidency sought to strangle Haiti with punitive policies from its very inception. Haiti was thus present in the great powers' geopolitical strategies; racism and slavery were not the exclusive prisms with which these powers viewed the new nation. While these powers would not extend full diplomatic recognition to Haiti for decades to come, they were not uniformly bent on isolating and destroying its struggling economy. Strategic and material interests impinged and created sinews for opportunist connections between Haiti and imperial white supremacist forces, especially England.[84] Haiti was thus clearly "thinkable," albeit as an exceptional, anomalous, and dangerous outpost of sovereign and emancipated former slaves. In fact, it was a thinkable threat even before it became Haiti. David Geggus has argued convincingly that slave owners had "premonitions" about the possibility of a slave rebellion: "Those colonists who gathered in Paris in 1789 were warned by the marquis de Mirabeau that they were sleeping at the foot of a volcano. . . . It is particularly difficult to explain the widespread fears of slave revolt that struck colonists, merchants, and officials at the very beginning of the French Revolution if contemporaries were incapable of imagining a massive or successful rebellion."[85]

The "thinkability" of Haiti was the very reason the United States and European colonists framed it as a monstrous savagery, an anticivilization of barbarians, and sought (in vain) to erase the history of its revolution. It is in this context that the late nineteenth-century words of Henry Adams, the great-grandson of John Adams, must be understood: "The story of Toussaint Louverture has been told almost as often as that of Napoleon, but not in connection with the history of the United States, although Toussaint exercised on their history an influence as decisive as that of any European ruler."[86] An empowered black republic represented an ominous presence that had to be quarantined lest it inspired "savage" revolts against the "civilized" white slaveholding order.[87] As David Brion Davis explains:

> For numerous whites the Haitian Revolution reinforced the conviction that emancipation in any form would lead to economic ruin and to the indiscriminate massacre of white populations. . . . The Haitian Revolution was . . .

a turning point in history.... It demonstrated the possible fate of every slaveholding society in the New World. The Haitian Revolution impinged in one way or another on the entire emancipation debate.... Like the Exodus narrative in the Bible, the Haitian Revolution showed blacks that liberation was a possibility in historical time. Their condition was not an inescapable fate.[88]

It is precisely because the American defenders of slavery feared the Haitian Revolution and its emancipatory impact that they sought to erase awareness of 1804.[89] To further appease their fears, slaveholders invoked a form of American exceptionalism based on the notion that their own system of slavery was uniquely benevolent. Unlike the brutal and exploitative nature of French slavery in the Caribbean and Saint Domingue in particular, Southern slave owners viewed American slavery as protective of the well-being of slaves.[90] Large-scale revolt was thus improbable in the United States.[91] And yet the American masterclass feared that the Haitian Revolution would spread like a contagion or erupt like a volcano in the United States itself.

Such metaphors evoked images of an unpredictable, frightening wave of hordes of African savages massacring innocent white victims. They also dehumanized and objectified enslaved people, likening them to a plague that could gain strength and wipe out white civilization.[92] For most white Southerners, then, Haiti symbolized a specter that could abruptly end their world; it haunted their very existence. The possibility of a black revolution fed their determination to preserve their white supremacist order.[93] As Alan Taylor notes:

> Deriding black rebels as vicious and ignorant brutes, most [American] writers cast them as "unworthy of liberty."
>
> Although Americans had declared revolution a universal right for the oppressed, they shuddered when the enslaved claimed that right. Shocked by the Saint-Domingue revolt, most Americans retreated from radical and universal claims for their own revolution. In 1794, a South Carolina legislator warned that, if colleagues continued to declare that "equality is the natural condition of man," they would produce the "ruin of the country, by giving liberty to the slaves, and the desolating [of] the land with fire and sword in the struggles between master and slave."[94]

Moreover, defenders of slavery defined black bodies as naturally suited for slavery; if freed, these bodies were condemned to self-destruction and barbarism. In fact, Haiti was the paradigmatic example of the incompatibility of black freedom and civilization. After describing the "Negro" as basking in "lazy joys" and in a "life of indolence," the proslavery poet William J. Grayson contended that savagery and decay were the inevitable consequence of an emancipated black society. Only when the white master class enslaved black bodies would progress and civilization flourish. In "The Hireling and the Slave," Grayson takes aim at Haiti:

> Such now the Negro's life, such wrecks appear
> Of former affluence, industry, and care,
> On Hayti's plains, where once her golden stores
> Gave their best commerce to the Gallic shores;
> While yet no foul revolt or servile strife
> Marred the calm tenor of the Negro's life,
> And lured his mind with mimicry elate
> Of titled nobles and imperial state
> From useful labor, savage wars to wage,
> To glut with massacre a demon's rage,
> Forget the Christian in the pagan rite,
> And serve a Negro master for a white.
> But even, in climes like this, a fated power
> In patient ambush waits the coming hour,
> When to new regions war and want shall drive
> Its swarms of hunger from the parent hive,
> And Europe's multitudes again demand
> Its boundless riches from the willing land
> That now, in vain luxuriance, idly lies,
> And yields no harvest to the genial skies,
> Then shall the ape of empire meet its doom,
> Black peer and prince their ancient task resume,
> Renounce the mimicries of war and state,
> And useful labor strive to emulate.
> Why peril, then, the Negro's humble joys,
> Why make him free, if freedom but destroys?[95]

Not all white Americans emulated Grayson's strident racism and doubled down, of course. In fact, a vocal minority were abolitionists who celebrated the Haitian Revolution and its leaders, especially Toussaint Louverture, as embodying the heroic promise of a free, nonracial society.[96] Not surprisingly, slaves and free blacks espoused this counternarrative in which they wrapped their hopes for their own liberation.[97] Clearly, for both whites and blacks opposed to slavery, the Haitian Revolution was not only "thinkable," but it provided them the concrete example with which to imagine their own freedom. As Matthew Clavin has explained:

> Public memory of Louverture and the Haitian Revolution had a profound impact on the United States throughout the first half of the nineteenth century: it inspired bondpeople to strike for freedom and those who claimed

ownership of them to take extraordinary measures to keep them enslaved; it helped widen the sectional gulf that was developing between the North and South at the same time it provided symbols that drew various constituencies in each of these sections close together. . . . [At] the height of the longstanding conflict between North and South, Louverture and the Haitian Revolution were resonant, polarizing, and ultimately subversive symbols, which antislavery and proslavery groups exploited to both provoke a violent confrontation and determine the fate of slavery in the United States.[98]

While the Haitian Revolution played a significant role in the ideological debates that fueled the American Civil War,[99] Americans' interest in the Haitian Revolution waned once slavery was abolished. After the failure of Reconstruction,[100] white America sought national reconciliation by erasing the causes of the bloody internecine conflict between North and South, rather than reviving revolutionary symbols and seeking some measure of equality.[101] "Jim Crow" swiftly implanted a new system of racist oppression that most white Americans perceived as a permanent "final settlement" returning the country to "sanity."[102] For many decades, any significant recollection of the multiracial alternative that the Haitian Revolution had offered was lost. In Clavin's words, "In an era of consensus and compromise, there was little need for the divisive symbols provided by the Haitian Revolution. Public amnesia of this iconic event developed quickly."[103]

In the aftermath of emancipation, Jim Crow and state and vigilante violence continued to support both the *habitus*[104] and legal apparatus of white supremacy,[105] even if the contours of racism acquired a more paternalistic form. African Americans were no longer to be enslaved, but they were to be confined to a subordinate and segregated station in life. They would undergo a long and undetermined period of tutelage before assuming the responsibilities of full citizenship.[106] The United States remained a white *Herrenvolk* republic whose vaunted democratic exceptionalism continued to both exclude a majority of its population and repress African Americans.

In summary, the Haitian Revolution was a pervasive specter haunting white supremacist forces, but this very "thinkability" contributed to its defamation and containment by the major powers of the time. Instead of rehabilitating the black race, 1804 provoked the ire of these powers. Anténor Firmin, the eminent Haitian intellectual, was thus wildly optimistic when in 1885 he penned these words in *De L'Egalité des Races Humaines*: "This lonely small Haitian Republic, placed like some brilliant wreck in the midst of the Antilles archipelago, will have sufficed to resolve the question of the equality of the races in all its fundamental implications."[107] *De L'Egalité des Races Humaines* sought to refute the racist theses of the era, but its refutation had little impact on the dominant white consciousness still deeply attached to Arthur de Gobineau's supremacist text of 1855, *De L'Inégalité des Races Humaines*. In fact, Firmin boldly rejected the very concept of race as unscientific; race in his eyes could only degenerate in an "anti-philosophic doctrine of racial inequality that itself rested on the idea of the exploitation of man by man."[108]

Firmin advanced therefore a universalist twist to Haitian exceptionalism: if Haiti was the proof of racial equality, it was also the promise of the ultimate equality of all human beings. As he put it:

> Recognition of the equality of the races entails a definitive recognition of the equality of all social classes in every nation of the world. The moral principle underlying such a recognition thus acquires a universal import which reinforces and consolidates its authority. Wherever the struggle for democracy is being waged, wherever social inequality is still a cause of conflict, the doctrine of the equality of the races will be a salutary remedy. This will be the last blow struck against medieval ideas, the last step toward the abolition of privileges. Such is actually the direction in which all nations are evolving sociologically; such is the horizon which all enlightened and healthy minds are reaching for; such is the ideal toward which the future is marching.[109]

When Firmin wrote these lines in 1885, American slavery had ended but racism remained virulent in America and Europe.[110] These were the high times of empire and colonial domination, and of the collapse of Reconstruction in the postbellum United States. Haitian exceptionalism stood alone in espousing a universal understanding of human equality. In fact, Firmin argued that while in the nineteenth century European thinkers and rulers engaged in complicated obfuscations about racial differences and objected rhetorically to slavery, they ultimately held the same white supremacist principles that their American counterparts wholeheartedly embraced and carved onto their institutions. In Firmin's words: "Only the American school has shown any honesty and consistency in its support of the doctrine [of inequality of the races], for its tenants have never hidden the interest they had in its promotion. We must therefore pay them this homage: whereas European scientists have been timid, expressing their views through understatements and implications, the Americans have been radical and logical, even in their errors."[111]

Thus, while in Firmin's view Americans were radically mistaken in their embrace of racism, they themselves believed that divine providence had sanctified and ordained white supremacy and the hierarchy of races. In short, American exceptionalism had God on its side; it simply could not be wrong. The white *Herrenvolk* was thus the plan of divine providence.

CHAPTER 4

Manifest Destiny and the American Occupation of Haiti

The foundational relationship between American exceptionalism and the white *Herrenvolk* state is unintelligible without inserting into its constitutive linkage the idea that the United States was God's chosen country and thus had a "manifest destiny."[1] This tenet transformed American territory into a "sacred space providentially selected for divine purposes."[2] For leaders who embraced this notion, American imperialism was simply fulfilling God's destiny and work. This belief in the providential nature of American power has not only shaped the formation and founding of the American republic, but it has also remained a continuous source of inspiration for legitimating modern military interventions and adventures. For instance, in January 2003, a few months before waging war against Iraq, President George W. Bush claimed in his State of the Union,

> If Saddam Hussein does not fully disarm for the safety of our people, and for the peace of the world, we will lead a coalition to disarm him....
>
> Americans are a free people, who know that freedom is the right of every person and the future of every nation. The liberty we prize is not America's gift to the world; it is God's gift to humanity.
>
> We Americans have faith in ourselves, but not in ourselves alone. We do not claim to know all the ways of Providence, yet we can trust in them, placing our confidence in the loving God behind all of life and all of history. May he guide us now, and may God continue to bless the United States of America.[3]

Bush, like many of his predecessors, took his own belief in God's anointment to equate American exceptionalism with both the national interests of the United States and the general welfare of humanity. This is not to say that American providentialism has remained unchanged; it has adapted to new circumstances and historical transformations. It no longer claims God's command for

America's old racist hierarchies or the naturalness of its early and massive geo-graphical expansion. It still claims, however, that it has a worldwide mission to spread liberty, and it continues to make this claim in God's name. In fact, Amer-ica's hegemonic power has given the claim an air of naturalness that cannot hide its bizarre character. As Nicholas Guyatt has pointed out, "The idea that God has directed the history of the United States has become a commonplace in Ameri-can life, a way of imagining America's purpose and history that seems so thor-oughly familiar that one can only overlook its essential oddness."[4] America's oddness in the early days of the republic gave it license to engage in a boundless territorial expansion because God had chosen Americans to carry on a divine design of spreading liberty beyond limits. As Anders Stephanson put it, "Since the United States was the first space where man could really be free, [territorial expansion] was by definition also a step in the liberation of universal man. It added to, in Jefferson's apposite term, the 'empire for liberty.'"[5]

Thus, by virtue of its self-defined exceptionalism, America conferred upon itself the unilateral right to spread its creed across the world. And from the eighteenth century to the mid-1930s, this universal moral mission was grounded in the white supremacist principles on which American exceptionalism rested. Senator Albert J. Beveridge of Indiana, a contemporary of Theodore Roosevelt, explained this divinely sanctioned mission in no uncertain terms:

> God has not been preparing the English-speaking and Teutonic peoples for a thousand years for nothing but vain and idle self-contemplation and self-admiration. No! He has made us the master organizers of the world to establish system where chaos reigns. He has given us the spirit of progress to overwhelm the forces of reaction throughout the earth. He has made us adepts in govern-ment that we may administer government among savage and senile peoples. Were it not for such a force as this the world would relapse into barbarism and night. And of all our race He has marked the American people as His chosen nation to finally lead in the regeneration of the world. This is the divine mis-sion of America, and it holds for us all the profit, all the glory, all the happi-ness possible to man. We are trustees of the world's progress, guardians of its righteous peace. The judgment of the Master is upon us: "Ye have been faithful over a few things; I will make you ruler over many things."[6]

The opening sentence of Beveridge's remarks to the Congress shows how American imperial ventures in the nonwhite world were wrapped in hierarchical notions of racial and cultural superiority. Of course, these notions were not new. They derived from the intellectual inventions legitimizing more than two centu-ries of Western European colonial expansion and conquest.[7] As Immanuel Waller-stein has pointed out, it was the Spanish scholar Juan Gines de Sepulveda who provided one of the earliest ideological justifications for Western imperialism. Writing in the sixteenth century, Sepulveda advanced four major arguments to rationalize Christopher Columbus and Spain's conquest of the Americas. According to Wallerstein, these four arguments, namely, "the barbarity of the others, ending practices that violate universal values, the defense of innocents among the cruel others, and making it possible to spread the universal values . . . have been used to justify all subsequent 'interventions' by the 'civilized' in the modern world into 'noncivilized' zones. But of course, these interventions can only be implemented if someone has the political/military power to do so."[8]

American exceptionalism was thus inspired by the hegemonic project of early European imperialism and came to take it for granted that whites and especially Anglo-Saxons had the right to subjugate and civilize "inferior" races.[9] After all, whites had already conquered the Native Americans' lands or "waste spaces"; now, other territories occupied by "unfit" races had to come under the aegis of the United States.[10] As John Burgess, the law professor who taught Theodore Roosevelt and founded American political science at Columbia University, put it, "The civilized states have a claim upon the uncivilized populations as well as a duty towards them, and that claim is that they shall become civilized." When "backward" people proved to be incapable of achieving civilized status on their own, they would have "to submit to the powers that can do it for them."[11] Embracing this claim, Theodore Roosevelt himself advocated in 1904 that in such instances the United States should be compelled "to the exercise of an international police power."[12] Roosevelt saw the Caribbean as one such region. It was America's "own backyard," the zone that the Monroe Doctrine signaled as early as 1823 for the deployment of the United States' coercive might. To declare this vast zone a protectorate of the United States was not just a matter of a God-anointed civilizing mission; it was also a means of achieving the economic dominance of an increasingly assertive American capitalism. To do so meant policing and pacifying foreign territories and peoples in order to protect and expand the dominion of American capital.

Alleyne Ireland, who was appointed as the University of Chicago's "colonial commissioner" in 1901, described himself as an expert in what he called the "science of imperial administration." This science, he argued, was in reality the science of "race subjection" because its principal objective was the "colonization" of near and far lands for the purpose of commercial gains.[13] Senator Beveridge put it bluntly: "A hundred wildernesses are to be subdued. Unpenetrated regions must be explored. Unviolated valleys must be tilled. Unmastered forests must be felled. Unriven mountains must be torn asunder and their riches of gold and iron and ores of price must be delivered to the world."[14] In Beveridge's eyes, this conquest of territories and natural resources would lead to the "commercial supremacy" of the United States, which would in turn become "the sovereign factor in the peace of the world." God would thus anoint Americans as the "lords of civilization" and the "master organizers of the world." This divine plan compelled the United States to impose order where incivility prevailed, and a "system where chaos reign[ed]."[15]

American exceptionalism thus embraced an expansionary, missionary zeal rooted in a self-proclaimed trinity of God, racism, and capital. By the early twentieth century this zeal was reaching maturity, which helps explain the rising American empire's interest in Haiti. President Theodore Roosevelt unveiled his doctrine of "international police power" and "big stick policy" in 1904.[16] The policy traded on exceptionalist views of American supremacy to ensure a political stability in Latin America and the Caribbean that served American strategic and economic interests. A decade later, President Woodrow Wilson took matters into his own hands when Haiti's political, racial, and class conflicts were intensifying and continuing European intrigues exacerbated these dysfunctional symptoms. Like Roosevelt, he expressed a messianic fervor for promoting America's hegemony abroad. On January 27, 1914, Wilson decided to send the marines into Haiti to establish his own version of law and order.[17]

It was a political order that had little to do with improving the well-being of Haitians, or establishing a democracy; rather, it was a form of governance subservient to American interests and imposed by American weapons. In a letter to Secretary of State William Jennings Bryan dated January 13, 1915, Wilson asserted, "The more I think about [the Haitian] situation, the more I am convinced that it is our duty to take immediate action there such as we took in San Domingo. I mean to send commissioners there who will . . . say to them as firmly and definitely . . . that the United States cannot consent to stand by and permit revolutionary conditions constantly to exist there."[18]

In fact, Wilson and his advisers looked at Haiti with contempt as an area of volatile backwardness that lacked the basic requirements for an orderly democracy. According to them, Haitians had shown "complete political incompetence." "These facts," as understood through the eyes of Assistant Secretary of State William Phillips, "point to the failure of an inferior people to maintain the degree of civilization left them by the French, or to develop any capacity of self-government entitling them to international respect and confidence."[19] Robert Lansing, who succeeded Bryan as secretary of state, summarized bluntly the racist American view: "The experience of Liberia and Haiti show[s] that the African race are devoid of any capacity for political organization and lack genius for government. Unquestionably there is in them an inherent tendency to revert to savagery and to cast aside the shackles of civilization which are irksome to their physical nature. Of course, there are many exceptions to this racial weakness but it is true of the mass, as we know from experience in this country. It is that which makes the Negro problem practically unsolvable."[20]

Given this attitude, what started out as a marine invasion would turn into a long American occupation of Haiti. By November 1914, the U.S. Navy had elaborated a "Plan for Landing and Occupying the City of Port-au-Prince."[21] The plan called for a military intervention in case of chaos or revolution in Haiti. The justification was simply that mob violence and political instability endangered foreign interests. The president of the United States would also claim that the takeover was "solely for the establishment of law and order."[22] In the blunt words of Secretary of State Lansing, the only practical way to "cure the anarchy and disorder" prevailing in Haiti was to have "marines policing" Port-au-Prince, even if this was "high handed."[23]

While the military occupation proceeded in spite of Haitian protestations,[24] it went smoothly and faced little open resistance in its first few days. The United States, however, had no clear idea of how to rule effectively or with any semblance of legitimacy. The problem was how to keep firm control of the country and impose unpopular policies, while at the same time finding Haitian politicians who would be willing to govern as servile clients of racist American forces. The first task was to select a new president who would replace the executed and dismembered Vilbrun Guillaume Sam.[25] The new Haitian president, as Admiral Caperton put it, would have to be someone who "realizes that Haiti must agree to any terms laid down by the United States."[26]

That someone was Philippe Sudre Dartiguenave, who was the choice of the U.S. government. Secretary of the Navy Josephus Daniels cabled to Caperton, "The U.S. prefers election of Dartiguenave"[27] to see to it that Dartiguenave became the new president. On August 12, 1915, the Haitian legislature "chose" Dartiguenave as president in elections "held under protection of marines."[28] Once elected, Dartiguenave, in the approving words of Captain Beach, "repeatedly and publicly made known his intention, without reservation, to do everything the U.S. wishes."[29]

The American claim that the only reason for the marines' landing was "to insure, establish and help to maintain Haitian independence and the establishing of a stable and firm government by the Haitian people," and that U.S. troops would remain in the country "only so long as will be necessary for this purpose,"[30] was specious. In reality, the Americans were there to stay for a long time. They were interested neither in Haitian independence nor in the establishment of a democratic government accountable to its citizens. They simply sought to neutralize European powers and impose their strategic and financial domination on Haiti.[31]

President Wilson's pious injunctions that "it is our duty to insist on constitutional government [in Haiti]" and that the United States "must take charge of elections and see that real government is erected which we can support" were paternalistic and misleading.[32] Under the occupation, Haitians had no choice whatsoever in determining their leaders; it was the Americans who decided which Haitians would help them run the country. For the occupiers, the idea that Haitians could take charge of their own affairs, choose who was to govern them, and decide autonomously what constitutional norms they should follow was simply unthinkable. In fact, American forces were to take full control of the country's military, law enforcement, and financial system. The United States compelled Haiti to become a de facto protectorate. On November 11, 1915, the Haitian parliament voted in favor of a treaty ratifying this new status.

While the majority of Haitians felt humiliated by the treaty and opposed it, a significant minority of the ruling elite reluctantly accepted it. Louis Borno, the foreign minister at the time of the signing of the treaty and the eventual successor to President Dartiguenave, viewed the occupation as a necessity: "When I saw [Haiti] fall, exhausted [and] bloody, I understood, and all that is honest and pure in the country understood, that henceforth we no longer had the choice: either permanent evaporation into abjectness, famine, blood, or else redemption with the help of the United States. I preferred this redemption."[33]

Most Haitians did not share Borno's view of the occupation as redemptive. In fact, the Haitian Senate had opposed the treaty but ultimately gave in. Washington had ordered Caperton to "remove all opposition and to secure immediate ratification,"[34] and directed Dartiguenave to pay off key senators to obtain their support.[35] The repressive and fraudulent measures that led to the ratification of the treaty symbolized what "democracy" and "constitutional rule" would mean under the occupation.

America, moreover, was not satisfied with "legalizing" the occupation. It was also bent on compelling the Haitian National Assembly to adopt a constitution "made in Washington." When the National Assembly refused, and sought instead to write its own constitution, Major Smedley Butler, the commandant of the Gendarmerie d'Haïti, simply dissolved the Assembly. As Butler explained, the latter had become "so impudent that the Gendarmerie had to dissolve [it]," a dissolution that was effected by "genuinely Marine Corps methods."[36] The "impudence" Butler mentions refers to the Assembly's refusal to grant foreigners the right to own property in Haiti. The occupiers found this unacceptable and, for all intents and purposes, waged their own coup d'état to impose the laws of the market. The American minister in Haiti, Bailly-Blanchard, wrote Secretary of State Lansing: "[The] Assembly was in every way reactionary and opposed to the best interests of Haiti, refusing to adopt any article permitting foreign ownership of land in any manner whatsoever, and when matters in the Assembly had proceeded thus far . . . it was decided in a conference held at the legation on June 18 . . . to prevent the Assembly from passing such a Constitution by causing its dissolution, if occasion demanded it, preferably by a Presidential Decree, but if necessary by order of the Commander of the Occupation."[37]

Unless it happened to coincide with U.S. interests, Haitian public opinion was irrelevant to the occupiers' political calculations. This was only logical given that Americans who took over Haiti had inherited a worldview that, as we have seen, was deeply colored by imperial arrogance and racist attitudes. Ultimately, the occupation reflected an autocratic American military force on which rested a collaborating class of authoritarian Haitian rulers. As Hans Schmidt has explained, when Americans took over Haiti they "came equipped with a store of . . . prejudices to go along with their superior firepower. This was a world apart from 'civilized' Western wars and the refinement of European diplomacy."[38] In fact, key figures of the U.S. personnel and a large number of the marines operating in Haiti had served in previous imperial ventures and "banana wars" and were members of segregationist military institutions.[39] They exhibited deeply contemptuous attitudes toward Haitians that betrayed both their experiences and their roots. Racist phobias and stereotypes depicting Haitians as "savages," "cannibals," "gooks," and "niggers" were pervasive among the occupiers.[40]

A few commanders of the occupation differentiated between "bad" and "good" Haitians. They saw the small class-conscious Haitian elites—those "wearing shoes"—negatively, and tended to romanticize the overwhelmingly "shoeless" majority. The former were seen as "crooks" and a "joke."[41] For example, Colonel Littleton Waller, the second in command of the occupation, described the elite as "niggers in spite of the thin varnish of education and refinement. Down in their hearts they are just the same happy, idle irresponsible people we know of."[42] The shoeless on the other hand, as described by Butler, were the "most kindly, generous, hospitable, pleasure-loving people." However, these kind, poor folk could become dangerous and "capable of the most horrible atrocities" when incited by the elite wearing "vici kid shoes with long pointed toes and celluloid collars."[43] The point is that Americans never understood how the apparently docile masses could transform themselves into fierce guerrilla fighters on their own. The "uppity" elites who did not "know their place," were always blamed for provoking any form of resistance from below.

Ultimately, the distinction some American administrators made between shoeless and shoe-wearing Haitians was not widely held. Generally, Americans believed that all Haitians were inferior barbarians "born with a semi-ape's brain."[44] As Brigade Commander Eli K. Cole put it, "Fully 75 percent are of very low mentality and ignorant beyond description. . . . No matter how much veneer and polish a Haitian may have, he is absolutely savage under the skin and under strain reverts to type."[45] Colonel Waller maintained that Haitians were also duplicitous and could not be trusted: "There is not an honest man in the whole of Haiti of Haitian nationality."[46]

To this intense and crude racism must be added an equally pervasive disdain for "Latin" culture, which, in American eyes, contributed to aggravate the "irrational" nature of Haitians. Stuart Grummon, the American chargé d'affaires in Haiti, offered in 1930 a cultural explanation for Haiti's predicament that still resonates today in Washington's contemporary policy discourse and American political science:

In general, while the Anglo-Saxon has a deep sense of the value of social organization and of the obligation of democratic government to assume a large share of responsibility for the social welfare of the masses, and has in

addition a profound conviction of the value of democratic government, the
Latin mind, on the contrary, is apt to scorn democracy and neglect activities
looking to the health and educational welfare of the masses. . . . The Anglo-
Saxon who excels in collective action is apt to be impatient with the Haitian
characteristic of intense individualism inherited from the French regime. . . .
The action common with the Latin in general, is in the main directed by
emotion rather than by reason, which in the main dictates the action of the
Anglo-Saxon.[47]

It is no surprise that, armed with this imperial and cultural arsenal, the
United States failed miserably in its attempt to transform Haiti into a "modern
democratic" society. The occupation generated distinct forms of local accommodation and resistance, however, while accentuating preexisting contradictions of class and color. The next chapter examines the social and political
consequences of the American takeover of Haiti.

CHAPTER 5

The American Occupation and Haiti's Exceptionalism

Whatever may have been the reasons advanced by Washington policy makers for the takeover of Haiti in 1915, it is clear that the American occupation had at best very limited success achieving its transformative goals. In fact, while it introduced modest infrastructural improvements in terms of roads and communications, it was marked by significant repression of local resistance movements.[1] The most important legacy of the occupation was the centralization of power in Port-au-Prince through the creation of a more effective state bureaucracy, and more significantly, a national army. The army circumscribed the powers of regionally based armed bands controlled by "big men" and established a modicum of political order.

Political order, however, did not imply popular acquiescence. It is true that many in the traditional Haitian elites initially collaborated with and even welcomed the occupiers. Many of these collaborators had authoritarian reflexes and shared some of the paternalistic and racist ideology of their American overlords. Convinced that Haitians were not prepared for any democratic form of self-government, these elites believed in the *despotisme éclairé des plus capables* ("enlightened despotism of the most capable"). In fact, *despotisme éclairé* had a double meaning: not only did it allude to intellectual enlightenment, but it also conveyed the veiled racist message that rule by the light-skinned minority was superior to that of the black majority.[2] Thus, from their privileged class status and collaborationist position, Haitian rulers under the American occupation regarded the rest of their black compatriots—especially the peasantry—with contempt. This contempt reflected one of the fundamental contradictions of Haitian exceptionalism; it has always celebrated the blackness and Africanness of its citizens as proud descendants of *Ginen*, and yet it never managed to free its ruling class from powerful remnants of colonial racism, especially the Creole's denigration of the African-born slave as *Bossal* and inferior.

It is only when it experienced the unmitigated racism of the occupying American forces that the Haitian ruling class turned against them and espoused varied forms of nationalist resistance. While not inclined to back the *Cacos* guerrilla insurgents,[3] Haitian elites developed a sense of nationhood that curbed the significance of color but had little impact on the salience of class identities.[4] In the eyes of most Haitians, however, those who had participated actively in the occupation machinery, like President Dartiguenave and his successor, Louis Borno, remained opportunistic collaborators.

While the governing Haitian elite was subordinated to the occupiers' rule, its authoritarian tendencies as well as its class and racial prejudices were accentuated by the dictatorial and white supremacist behavior of the occupiers themselves. Borno, who was president from 1922 to 1930, embodied this complex relationship with American imperialism; he was a dictator, but a dictator under American control. Haitians called his rule *la dictature bicéphale*—the "two-headed despotism" of both American imperialism and its domestic clients. This regime had unintended consequences. It intensified the level of nationalist resistance to the occupation and contributed to a convergence of interests between intellectuals, students, public workers, and peasants.

The growing mobilization against the occupation precipitated the 1929 Marchaterre massacre, near Les Cayes in southern Haiti, when some 1500 peasants protesting high taxation confronted armed marines who then opened fire on the crowd. Twenty-four Haitians died and fifty-one were wounded.[5] The massacre set in motion a series of events that would eventually lead the United States to reassess its policies and presence in Haiti. President Herbert Hoover created a commission whose primary objective was to investigate "when and how we are to withdraw from Haiti." The commission—which took the name of its chair, Cameron Forbes, who served in the Philippines as chief constabulary and then as governor— acknowledged that the United States had not accomplished its mission and that it had failed "to understand the social problems of Haiti." While the commission astonishingly claimed that the occupation's failure was due to the "brusque attempt to plant democracy there by drill and harrow" and to "its determination to set up a middle class," it ultimately recommended the withdrawal of the United States from Haiti.[6]

The commission advised, however, that the withdrawal not be immediate, but rather that it should take place only after the successful "Haitianization" of the public services as well as the gendarmerie. Forbes also understood that President Borno had no legitimacy and could be sacrificed. Borno was forced to retire and arrange the election of an interim successor, who would in turn organize general elections. Sténio Vincent, a moderate nationalist who favored a gradual, negotiated ending to the occupation, thus became president in November 1930. Vincent's gradualism was in tune with the Forbes Commission's recommendation for the accelerated Haitianization of the commanding ranks of the government and the eventual withdrawal of all American troops.[7] While Forbes and Vincent operated on the assumption that the United States' withdrawal would not occur until 1936, the election of Franklin Roosevelt in 1932 altered events.

Roosevelt's new "Good Neighbor" strategy toward Latin America was rooted in the premise that direct occupation through military intervention was expensive, counterproductive, and in most instances unnecessary.[8] It was not that the forceful occupation of another country was precluded; it simply became a last resort. Roosevelt understood that in Latin America and the Caribbean in particular, the United States could impose its hegemony through local allies and surrogates, especially through military corps and officers that it had trained, organized, and equipped. It is this perspective that explains the American decision to withdraw from Haiti. In fact, what Haitians came to call the "second independence" arrived two months earlier than expected. On a visit to Cap Haitien, in the north of the country, Roosevelt announced that the American occupation would end on August 15, 1934.

After close to twenty years of "two-headed despotism," Haitians were left with a changed nation. American rule had contributed to the centralization of power in Port-au-Prince and the modernization of the monarchical presidentialism that had always characterized Haitian politics.[9] With the American occupation, praetorian power came to reside in the barracks of the capital, which had supplanted the regional armed bands that had hitherto been decisive in the making, and unmaking, of political regimes. Moreover, the subordination of the Haitian president to American marine forces had nurtured a politics of military vetoes and interference that would eventually undermine civilian authority and help incite the numerous coups of postoccupation Haiti. To remain in office, the executive would have to depend on the support of the military, which had been centralized in Port-au-Prince. The supremacy of Port-au-Prince also implied the privileging of urban groups, especially the capital's ruling class, to the detriment of the rural population. Workers, peasants, and the unemployed continued to be excluded from the moral community of *les plus capables*. They came under a strict policing regime of law and order.

The occupation never intended to cut the roots of authoritarianism; instead, it planted them in a more rational and modern terrain. By establishing a communication network that became a means of policing and punishing the population, and by creating a more effective and disciplined coercive force, American rule left a legacy of centralized power and reinforced the preexisting patterns of authoritarianism. It suppressed whatever democratic and popular forms of accountability and protests it confronted, and nurtured the old patterns of fraudulent electoral practices, giving the armed forces ultimate veto on who would rule Haiti. Elections during the occupation, and for more than seventy years afterward, were never truly free and fair.[10] In most cases, the outcome of elections had less to do with the actual popular vote than with compromises reached between Haiti's ruling classes and imperial forces. Thus, elections lacked the degree of honesty and openness required to define a democratic order. The occupation imposed its rule through fraud, violence, and deceit, and little changed after it ended.

It is true that the imperial presence from 1915 to 1934 contributed to the building of a modest infrastructure of roads and clinics, but it did so with the most paternalistic and racist energy. American authorities convinced themselves that their mission was to bring development and civilization to Haiti. They presumed that Haitians were utterly incapable of doing so on their own. Not surprisingly, they used methods of command and control to achieve their project, a practice that reinforced the authoritarian *habitus* that had historically characterized Haitian governance as unaccountable and undemocratic.

It is this authoritarian *habitus* that the ideology of Haitian exceptionalism denies. The denial is not completely farfetched. After all, the 1804 Declaration of Independence claimed, "It is not enough to have expelled the barbarians who have bloodied our land for two centuries. . . . We must, with one last act of national authority, forever assure *the empire of liberty* in the country of our birth."[11] Moreover, the declaration promised that the nation would be founded on "laws that . . . [would] guarantee [the] free individuality" of all citizens.[12] Thus, it can certainly be argued that the Haitian Revolution embodied ideals that were more democratic, radical, and universalist than those hitherto produced by any revolution. Toussaint Louverture's Constitution of 1801, as well as the 1804 Declaration of Independence, and the Constitution of 1805 all proclaimed not only the emancipation from slavery but also racial equality. Articles 3, 4, and 5 of the Constitution of 1801, when Saint Domingue was briefly autonomous but still a colony of France, decreed:

> Art 3—There can be no slaves on this territory; servitude has been forever abolished. All men are born, live and die there free and French.
>
> Art 4—All men can work at all forms of employment, whatever their color.
>
> Art 5—No other distinctions exist than those of virtues and talents, nor any other superiority than that granted by the law in the exercise of a public charge. The law is the same for all, whether it punishes or protects.[13]

Clearly these articles went beyond the pronouncements of both the American and French Revolutions; they enshrined the notion that race had no role in any hierarchy of human beings and that a legitimate social order had to guarantee equal opportunity to all. As Susan Buck-Morss contends, "Toussaint Louverture's constitution of 1801, without a doubt, took universal history to the farthest point of progress by extending the principle of Liberty to all residents regardless of race, including political refugees who sought asylum from slavery elsewhere, compelling French Jacobins (at least temporarily) to follow their lead. This end to the condition of slavery cannot be overestimated. The license for torture and physical brutality of all kinds was now denied. Legal status mattered."[14]

Thus, the pronouncements of the Haitian Revolution were truly exceptional. They constituted the most radical and far-reaching celebration of liberty and equality that any polity had envisioned.[15] And yet this radical project was severely constrained by an authoritarian *habitus* based on both the militaristic legacy of the revolution and the realities of the domestic and international political economy.[16] Moreover, as David Geggus has emphasized, "[In the Haitian Revolution] the central pursuit of freedom came to be construed in the profound but narrow sense of freedom from slavery rather than as political rights."[17]

A system of despotic monarchism installed itself at the highest levels of governance. The militaristic and violent legacy of the revolutionary struggle for independence established a pattern of rule firmly rooted in command and control from above. Moreover, the founding fathers exhibited a messianic understanding of their role as leaders of the new nation. They saw themselves as indispensable, predestined rulers. Jean-Jacques Dessalines, the military leader of the successful revolution and "governor for life" of an independent Haiti, firmly established the intolerant, despotic paternalism that has characterized the country's dominant pattern of rule. On the very day of his inauguration as governor for life, Dessalines warned his subjects: "And you, people. Remember that I sacrificed everything to fly to your defense—my parents, children, fortune, and that I am now rich only by dint of your freedom; that my name has become anathema to all those peoples desiring slavery, and that the despots and tyrants pronounce my name only to curse the day that I was born; and if you either refuse or accept with reluctance the laws dictated to me for your well-being by the spirit that watches over your destiny, you will deserve the fate of ungrateful people."[18]

Dessalines's authoritarianism was not new; all the leaders of the revolution, starting with Toussaint himself, exhibited the same proclivity. In fact, Toussaint's Constitution of 1801 left to his successors the heavy legacy of despotic paternalism. Articles 28 and 30 firmly entrenched the type of personal absolutism that has characterized most of Haiti's history:

> Art 28—The Constitution names as governor Citizen Toussaint Louverture, General-in-Chief of the army of Saint-Domingue and, in consideration of the important services that the general has rendered to the colony in the most critical circumstances of the revolution, and per the wishes of the grateful inhabitants, the reins are confided to him for the rest of his glorious life.
>
> Art 30—In order to consolidate the tranquility that the colony owes to the firmness, the activity, the indefatigable zeal, and the rare virtues of General Toussaint Louverture, and as a sign of the unlimited confidence of the inhabitants of Saint-Domingue, the Constitution attributes exclusively to this general the right to choose the citizen who, in the unhappy instance of his death, shall immediately replace him. This choice shall be secret.[19]

It is not surprising that given this absolutist tone, the Constitution of 1805 empowered Jean Jacques Dessalines to become emperor for life with virtually unlimited personal power. As Articles 19 to 26 indicate:

19. The Government of Hayti is entrusted to a first Magistrate, who assumes the title of Emperor and commander in chief of the army.

20. The people acknowledge for Emperor and Commander in Chief of the Army, Jacques Dessalines, the avenger and deliverer of his fellow citizens. The title of Majesty is conferred upon him, as well as upon his august spouse, the Empress.

21. The person of their Majesties are sacred and inviolable.

22. The State will appropriate a fixed annual allowance to her Majesty the Empress, which she will continue to enjoy even after the decease of the Emperor, as princess dowager.

23. The crown is elective not hereditary.

24. There shall be assigned by the state an annual income to the children acknowledged by his Majesty the Emperor.

25. The male children acknowledged by the Emperor shall be obliged, in the same manner as other citizens, to pass successively from grade to grade, with this only difference, that their entrance into service shall begin at the fourth demi brigade, from the period of their birth.

26. The Emperor designates, in the manner he may judge expedient, the person who is to be his successor either before or after his death.[20]

Clearly, this arrogation of political power to a sole individual had little to do with a genuinely democratic order. It denied the basic and minimal premise of the universal franchise and the right of citizens to choose their government and elect their rulers. It is true that calls for authoritarian governance were the norm in that epoch. As Madison Smart Bell writes:

The notion of leadership for life was not so out of tune with the times as it might seem. In France, Napoleon was on a similar course, though he had not yet declared it. It was not so long since the United States had considered crowning George Washington its king. The American Federalist Alexander Hamilton suggested to Toussaint directly that he create a "life-long executive." The civilized world had been deeply dismayed by the catastrophic instability of the various governments-by-committee spawned by the French Revolution; nostalgia for monarchy and/or military dictatorship was in the wind.[21]

That Haiti shared a common political authoritarianism with other countries reflects the reality that claims of exceptionalism based on freedom and liberty should not be accepted at face value simply because they are formally enshrined in constitutions. Claims of exceptionalism, as we have seen, frequently mask autocratic and absolutist forms of governance. In Haiti's case, such forms of governance were merely one aspect of a larger despotic structure of power that marginalized former slaves who sought to become free peasants. Haitian leaders found it extremely difficult to extricate their society from the inherited slave-plantation system that had rendered the country a sugar-producing enclave of the world economy.[22] They needed the revenues generated from the export of sugar to sustain state activities and the reconstruction of their nation after the devastation caused by the fight for independence.

Toussaint Louverture, Dessalines, and their successors confronted the harsh truth that this rebuilding required the reestablishment of the plantation system—the system based on the very form of labor that their own revolution had abolished.[23] They had to devise new methods to enlist and control the work of an emancipated people. They sought to impose on them a type of military discipline that would compel them to stay and labor on the hated plantations. Known as *caporalisme agraire* ("rural despotism"), this coercive system established stark class divisions and the moral and political exclusion of the majority from the national community.[24] As Carolyn E. Fick explains, at the end of Toussaint's regime "general emancipation had, in many ways, become little more than a political abstraction with no meaningful substance in the daily lives of the greater mass of black laborers."[25]

While the *caporalisme agraire* persisted for several decades after independence, the state, despite its militaristic pretensions, lacked the financial means and the bureaucratic apparatus to impose the policy successfully on the population; the majority of Haitians became peasants who sought to elude the control of the state.[26] The tradition of *marronage* (running away) that developed during slavery continued during Toussaint's agrarian authoritarianism. This well-honed practice, compounded by the liberating victory over slavery itself, gave newly freed slaves a powerful capacity to engage in "fugitive political conduct."[27] Evading the exploitative reach of the state did not, however, contribute to the creation of a legitimate and constructive social contract between rulers and citizens. Instead of a social contract, what crystallized was in Fick's words an "unbridgeable gap between the state structure, which was a military one, and the rural agrarian base of the nation."[28]

In fact, the rupture between rulers and peoples is also recorded in Vodou oral tradition. As Laurent Dubois has pointed out, in one version of one of the most famous Vodou songs, "Dessalines is coming to the north / Come see what he is bringing," transcribed by anthropologist Odette Mennesson-Rigaud, Dessalines is remembered not as the great emancipator but as the executioner of a whole nation. According to the song, "Dessalines came from France / carrying a *ouanga nouveau*," but with what intentions? "To kill Jean-Pierre Ibo . . . to kill the Ibo nation / to kill my mother's nation / to kill my father's nation."[29] Clearly then, the end of slavery was not the equivalent of popular freedom; it embodied new forms of servitude and hierarchies. These despotic structures may not have

been inevitable, but they were the most likely product of the inherited plantation system of the emerging world capitalist system. Dessalines, as Aimé Césaire puts it, was "a god caught in a trap."[30] Moreover, when it came to matters of
labor, his views betrayed the prejudices of the old white masters. For him,
"Blacks don't know how to work if you don't force them."[31]

In fact, the *caporalisme agraire* that Dessalines and the other founders sought
to impose on the population was in some measure the consequence of Haiti's
rulers' search for resources with which to defend the country against real and
imagined imperial threats. The defense of the country's independence had always
been a central preoccupation of Haitians; it was enshrined in the first article of
the Constitution of 1805: "The people inhabiting the island formerly called
St. Domingo, hereby agree to form themselves into a free state sovereign and
independent of any other power in the universe, under the name of empire of
Hayti."[32]

Independence from and national resistance to the *blans*—the white foreign
colonialists—became defining elements of Haitian exceptionalism.[33] The victory over Napoleon's army meant that Haiti was *the* revolutionary nation and
that colonialism and racism would not be tolerated in its territory. Moreover,
Haitian leaders avowed that they would not hesitate to use brutal force to preserve their freedom. In fact, at the end of the war of independence and in its
immediate aftermath, Dessalines had ordered the massacre of all white Frenchmen to demonstrate his absolute determination to rid Haiti of the presence of
colonialists and slave owners.[34] Proclaiming himself the "avenger of America,"
Dessalines made it abundantly clear in the Declaration of Independence that
Haiti would unleash cruel violence on foreign enemies:

> Independence or death . . . let these sacred words unite us and be the signal
> of battle and of our reunion. . . . And you, precious men, intrepid generals,
> who, without concern for your own pain, have revived liberty by shedding all
> your blood, know that you have done nothing if you do not give the nations a
> terrible, but just example of the vengeance that must be wrought by a people
> proud to have recovered its liberty and jealous to maintain it let us frighten
> all those who would dare try to take it from us again; let us begin with the
> French. Let them tremble when they approach our coast, if not from the
> memory of those cruelties they perpetrated here, then from the terrible reso-
> lution that we will have made to put to death anyone born French whose
> profane foot soils the land of liberty.[35]

Dessalines and his successors were not only determined to repel any *blans*;
they were also bent on keeping Haitian territory in the exclusive hands of Haitians. Haitian soil acquired a quasi-mystical quality; it was the blood of the
nation, and it would not be spoiled by the presence of foreigners. In fact, the
Constitution of 1805 was explicit on the matter. Article 12 decreed, "No white-

man of whatever nation he may be, shall put his foot on this territory with the title of master or proprietor, neither shall he in future acquire any property therein."[36] Haiti's exceptionalism was thus rooted in the unique experience of its people as slaves who fought white supremacy successfully to establish the first free black nation in the world. As Baron de Vastey, the secretary of King Henry Christophe, put it, Haiti unmasked the vast ugliness of imperialism: "At last, the secret, full of horrors, is known: the Colonial System is the domination of the Whites, It is the Massacre or the Enslavement of Blacks."[37] The magnitude of that achievement gave Haitians a sense of glorious loneliness in a hostile world. They came to believe that they could resist any encroachment on their independence and freedom, and that on their sacred soil they were invincible.

Rooted in a particular interpretation of historical experiences, exceptionalism is part of a powerful collective imaginary that can motivate and inspire. In fact, it can be a sign of divine providence, as Baron de Vastey put it: "Great God! How impressive your works are! Of a flock of slaves you have made the avenging instruments of your divine laws."[38] But exceptionalism is also deceiving and illusionary. Material power and its harsh realities can disfigure it. The continuous imperial interferences that have plagued Haiti's history, that were accentuated by the American occupation (1915–1934), and that persist in myriad ways today clearly indicate that Haitian exceptionalism has lacked the means to enforce its vision.[39]

In the aftermath of independence, the Haitian ruling class has never been able to impose a coherent national project. Its internecine color and regional divisions prevented it from unifying the country. Its deep contempt for the rural majority precluded it from imposing its political and cultural hegemony. Moreover, the ruling class proved incapable of fully restoring the plantation economy. Because its *caporalisme agraire* lacked the state power to proletarianize the peasantry, whatever chances existed for the creation of a productive export-oriented capitalist economy vanished.[40] The development of wage labor—the sine qua non of an effective capitalism—was minimal and insufficient. Equipped with backward technological and educational means, peasants remained both producers and sellers of commodities.[41]

The failure of the Haitian rulers' bourgeois class project cannot be understood, however, without taking into consideration the constraints imposed on them by the world capitalist economy. In fact, this failure was almost inevitable given that Haiti was a pariah nation in a white supremacist international order, continuously subjected to military threats and economic sanctions, and condemned to a thoroughly peripheral role in the global chain of production.[42] One of the most consequential imperial punishments imposed on Haiti was the so-called indemnity of 1825.[43] In the face of French military threats, the regime of Jean-Pierre Boyer agreed to pay an indemnity of 150 million francs to France in return for its recognition of Haiti's independence.[44] While Boyer's decision to pay the indemnity partly reflected his fear of the raw power of French imperialism, Alex Dupuy has convincingly argued that it was also determined by the very class interests Boyer represented. Boyer and the members of the ruling class were determined to secure their newly acquired ownership of the land against any potential imperial encroachments. To ensure this outcome, they desperately needed for France to respect its property laws, and this in turn required France's official recognition of Haiti's national sovereignty. Boyer and his supporters, notes Dupuy, "believed in the bourgeois right to private property ownership, [and] sought to legitimize the redistribution of the properties expropriated from the old colonial property owners to create a new landed class in Haiti."[45] In short, Haitian rulers were defending their own class interests when they accepted to pay the indemnity. In addition, they assumed—and rightly so— that once France had recognized Haiti's independence, other major powers would follow.

Paying the indemnity, however, had harmful effects on the future development of the country. It served the interests of the Haitian ruling class, but it confined the country to the neocolonial orbit of the great powers and their banking institutions. In fact, it is not too farfetched to contend that with the payment of the indemnity, the process of recolonizing the country had begun.[46] Haiti had to accumulate a massive debt to pay the indemnity even though the French government agreed to reduce it to 60 million francs in the so-called 1838 Traité d'Amitié. This did not stop "Haiti's vicious spiral of payment and debt," as Anthony Phillips points out: "The final payment to the French government took place in 1883. Haiti had remitted over 90,000,000F in reparations to its former colonial masters—although the French government disbursed much less than that amount to the colonists themselves. To finance the indemnity payments and the early loans, Haiti borrowed over 166,000,000F between 1875 and 1910. More than half of that money was returned to the lending banks under the rubric of commissions, fees and interest payments."[47]

The history of the indemnity shows clearly how Haitian rulers used the narrative of national unity rooted in Haitian exceptionalism to advance their own class interests. The fact that they sought international recognition from the white supremacist order to defend their own property and set their society into a neocolonial orbit was an early sign of their continued capacity for manipulating Haitian exceptionalism for their own ends. The opportunistic convergence of interests between weak and dependent Haitian rulers and the dominant imperial nations has historically been at the core of Haiti's predicament. It generated pervasive patterns of predatory rule that fueled the underdevelopment and growing poverty of the country. That the marginalized majority of Haiti has managed to endure and survive the ravages of this rule is a testament of its resilience. It is because of these dire conditions that Sidney Mintz exclaimed, "Surely the wonder of the second republic of the Hemisphere is not that it has fared badly, but that it has fared at all."[48]

Ironically, one of the fundamental reasons Haiti survived at all is that the major powers squelched the danger it represented. By undermining its material prosperity, disfiguring its achievement, and denigrating its people, the United States and Europe did everything they could to ensure that Haiti's revolution would not inspire other colonized peoples to rise up. While it remained the embodiment of black liberation, Haiti also became emblematic of a dysfunctional politics and a paradigm of underdevelopment, natural degradation, and grinding poverty. By negating the West, Haiti came to represent the symbolic reversal of the logic of progress and modernity. To that extent, the fact that Haiti "fared at all" served as a warning to all colonies and people of color that revolting against the order of things would have dire, violent, and despoiling consequences.

Haitian leaders knew that their country's exceptionalism could come at a serious cost; they comprehended the severe constraints within which they operated. But they believed that they could safely exist in the world system if they contained their revolutionary zeal within their own borders.[49] It is not surprising therefore that Dessalines expressly declared that the revolution of 1804 was not for export: "Let us ensure . . . that a missionary spirit does not destroy our work; let us allow our neighbors to breathe in peace; may they live quietly under the laws that they have made for themselves, and let us not, as revolutionary firebrands, declare ourselves the lawgivers of the Caribbean, nor let our glory consist in troubling the peace of the neighboring islands."[50] The caution of the Haitian leaders had little effect on the world powers; for most of its history, the country was besieged by military threats, economic sanctions, and financial dependence. Alain Turnier put it succinctly: "External finance succeeded in transferring to the economy the colonialism that was politically defeated on the battlefields of Saint-Domingue, and thus perpetuated the past."[51]

In fact, Haiti's century-old entanglements with external finance precipitated the 1915–1934 American occupation, which in turn eviscerated the legacy of the victory on Saint Domingue's battlefields. With its imperial intervention, the United States signaled to Haitian authorities that they would be forced to pay their debt to American private banks, and to the French and German commercial interests that their dominance of Haiti had to end. To that extent, the occupation of Haiti responded to the material realities of an increasingly assertive American imperialism bent on imposing its hegemony over what it deemed to be its regional and strategic "backyard." It would be wrong, however, to assume that economic factors and geopolitical considerations alone explained American imperial policies.

Racism, and a sense of Anglo-Saxon superiority, drastically restricted the universalist claims of American exceptionalism. When Haitians declared their independence in 1804, Thomas Jefferson dubbed them the "Cannibals of the terrible republic."[52] Fearing the spread of black insurrections, Jefferson unleashed a containment strategy to quarantine the new nation and destroy its ailing economy. As Alan Taylor puts it, "When black people became revolutionaries, white Americans recoiled. They set new, racial limits to the spread of republicanism, retreating from the implicitly universal promises of their revolution."[53]

Jefferson and his political cohort announced the exclusionary nature of American exceptionalism while simultaneously affirming its universalism. Thus, if "all men are created equal," not all men are the same, and not all men are members of the "community of the free." In spite of this contradiction deeply rooted in racism, American exceptionalism had the infrastructural resources to exclude while pretending to remain universal. Given this capacity, Jefferson's America managed to prevent the other major Western powers from formally recognizing Haiti as a sovereign nation for decades.

Power is thus indispensable to make any sort of exceptionalism real and effective. The existence of a national exceptionalism, as the Haitian case proves, does not translate into the capacity to act upon it. The power of the imaginary remains imaginary power; but without it, material power lacks the legitimizing and moral force for its effective deployment. On the other hand, the legitimizing and moral force of exceptionalism simply needs to convince the collectivity of the "chosen"; exceptionalism is often exclusive, as it is a bounded category that demarcates and often denigrates "outsiders" while glorifying "insiders." To transcend the boundary of its national community, exceptionalism has to aspire to universalism, but more crucially it must rest on imperial power. Only an empire can denigrate the exceptionalism of those it conquers while transmogrifying its own into a universalism imposed by force. This is the hard lesson of the American occupation of Haiti.

The occupation exposed the fragility of Haitian exceptionalism; unlike its American counterpart, it never imposed its hegemony on the population. This in turn reflected the ideological contradictions and material limitations of its ruling class. While Haitian exceptionalism has always extolled the revolution of 1804 as a world historical achievement and a radical rupture with Western racism, it failed to mask the inner struggles besieging its ruling class. Divided by color between its mulatto and black factions, but united in its contempt and exploitation of the masses, the ruling class was incapable of co-opting and including the population into a coherent national project. In spite of its pretension, Haitian exceptionalism was at inception exclusionary. Its emancipatory project was undermined by the harsh realities of a white supremacist world order, the internal contradictions of an economy confronting both the *marronage* of an "uncaptured" peasantry and a plantation system that could no longer depend on slave labor.

The material basis of Haitian exceptionalism rested therefore on extremely shaky foundations. With the passage of time, these foundations collapsed under the weight of the ruling class's uninterrupted internecine conflicts, despotic form of governance, and plundering of public resources. The United States took advantage of these fissures to easily justify its occupation of Haiti. In the next chapter, I will show that this occupation was symptomatic of a much larger American imperial project and legitimating construct.

CHAPTER 6

Imperial Exceptionalism at the Turn of the Twentieth Century

American exceptionalism, like that of most empires, rests on the paradoxical belief that not only can it be universalized but also that it has a mission to do so. This mission is partly in the search of *Lebensraum* ("living space") for its free citizens. As Jefferson wrote to Monroe in 1801, "However our present interests may restrain us within our limits, it is impossible not to look forward to distant times, when our rapid multiplication will expand it beyond those limits, and cover the whole northern, if not the southern continent, with a people speaking the same language, governed in similar forms, and by similar laws."[1]

This expanding "empire of liberty" had to exclude Africans, because Jefferson could not "contemplate, with satisfaction, either blot or mixture on that surface."[2] And yet American exceptionalism, which gifted to America itself the right to global expansion on account of divine providence, proclaimed the happy coincidence between the American and the universal interest. In fact, John O'Sullivan, the organic intellectual of nineteenth-century American expansionism, asserted "the right of our manifest destiny to overspread and to possess the whole continent which providence has given us for the development of the great experiment of liberty and federated self government."[3] Since its inception, American leaders have never stopped claiming the "divine destiny" of the republic;[4] President Woodrow Wilson's words capture well this continuous theme of American politics: "I do believe in Providence. I believe that God presided over the inception of this nation. I believe he planted in us the vision of liberty. . . . We are chosen and prominently chosen to show the way to the nations of the world how they shall walk in the paths of liberty."[5]

As the "chosen country," America's worldwide spread of its exceptionalism was nothing but a benevolent and moral mission; if it constituted an empire at all, it was a distinct empire that would allegedly "burst the chains" of despotism and "assume the blessings and security of self-government."[6] Thus, American exceptionalism in the eyes of its rulers was a gift to the world, because as Adams wrote to Jefferson in 1813, "Our pure, virtuous, public spirited, federative republic will last forever, govern the globe and introduce the perfection of man."[7] Echoing these sentiments, O'Sullivan proclaimed that "vigorous and fresh from the hand of God," America had a "blessed mission to the nations of the world" that was "destined to cease only when every man in the world should be finally and triumphantly redeemed."[8]

This redemption of humanity was, however, grounded in the exceptional American civil tranquility brought about by individual property and commerce. As a landowning petty-bourgeois, the typical American citizen in Jefferson's eyes,

> [has] land to labor for himself if he chuses; or, preferring the exercise of any other industry, may exact for it such compensation as not only to afford a comfortable subsistence, but wherewith to provide for a cessation from labor in old age. Every one, by his property, or by his satisfactory situation, is interested in the support of law and order. and such men may safely and advantageously reserve to themselves a wholsome controul over their public affairs, and a degree of freedom, which in the hands of the Canaille of the cities of Europe, would be instantly perverted to the demolition and destruction of every thing public and private.[9]

The empire of liberty rested on property and commerce, and only those who enjoyed them could benefit from the fruits of freedom.

America's unique mission was thus to spread this gospel of possessive individualism worldwide. The self-image of American rulers has always been as benevolent providers of assistance and keepers of international peace;[10] they have taken for granted the proposition that the United States' interests coincided with both the global expansion of capitalism and the universal good. Grounded in this missionary foundation, American exceptionalism has granted itself the right of "benevolent" expansion through diplomatic, economic, and military interventions. Before becoming president and while he was still a mere political scientist, Woodrow Wilson expressed the matter very clearly: "Since trade ignores national boundaries and the manufacturer insists on having the world as a market, the flag of his nation must follow him, and the doors of the nations which are closed against him must be battered down. Concessions obtained by financiers must be safeguarded by ministers of state, even if the sovereignty of unwilling nations be outraged in the process. Colonies must be obtained or planted, in order that no useful corner of the world may be overlooked or left unused."[11]

As president, Wilson was equally emphatic. In an address to the World's Salesmanship Congress in 1916, he declared, "Lift your eyes to the horizons of business ... but let your thoughts and your imaginations run abroad throughout the whole world, and with the inspiration of the thought that you are Americans and are meant to carry liberty and justice and the principles of humanity wherever you go, go out and sell goods that will make the world more comfortable and more happy, and convert them to the principles of America."[12]

President Wilson's belief in the United States' benevolent imperial role spreading market capitalism, justice, and democracy throughout the world has been a constant claim of American rulers. Moreover, these rulers have always interpreted the global expansion of capitalism as a sign of their nation's manifest destiny and inevitable leadership. After all, they believed that spreading markets, democracy, and human rights represented an inevitable and rational drive to modernity—a munificent gift of America to the world. It has always been the essence of American "leadership." As President Bill Clinton affirmed in 1996, "We must continue to bear the responsibility of the world's leadership. . . . Our leadership is essential and that to advance our interests, that leadership must remain rooted in our values, must continue to advance democracy and freedom to promote peace and security, to enhance prosperity and preserve our planet. . . . American leadership is indispensable and that without it our values, our interests, and peace itself would be at risk. . . . We have to assume the burden of leadership. There is simply not another alternative."[13]

Paradoxically, in spite of its long history of territorial expansionism and military interventions in near and faraway lands, most Americans and virtually all their organic intellectuals have espoused Clinton's mythical vision.[14] The shibboleth is America's "indispensable" "global leadership," on which rests allegedly a form of reasonable international peace and governance. While such reasonable and yet very relative peace lasted during the Cold War and its aftermath in the 1990s, the rise of terrorism and the September 11, 2001, al-Qaeda attacks unsettled this supremacy. In the eyes of the American security establishment, the United States had to reassert it. For instance, Charles Kupchan, one of the leading organic intellectuals of the establishment, argued that while America had never been an "imperial state with predatory intent,"[15] the world would spin into chaos and war if it was "not up to the task of providing steady and enlightened leadership."[16] To do so, the United States had to "refurbish its armed forces and remain ready for the full spectrum of potential missions." Thus, the United States had the obligation of maintaining its "military primacy," which had always been a "precious national asset."[17]

Military primacy has indeed been the hallmark of America's imperial project since World War II. This project, which had been hitherto confined to the Caribbean and Latin America and the Philippines, expanded to the world.[18] The spread of American exceptionalism was thus intimately tied to the global projection of military power. In fact, the two became inseparable; militarism and exceptionalism were one. Not surprisingly, the agenda of "regime change," the promotion of democracy, the engagement in "nation building," and the deployment of humanitarian assistance have all become thoroughly militarized. In the aftermath of 9/11, the United States defined itself as a "hyperpower" capable not only of using its unparalleled force to destroy enemies if provoked but also of deciding on its own to unleash it against threats that had not yet materialized. According to the conventional wisdom of most organic intellectuals, this commitment to unilateral anticipatory strikes marked a radical departure from the internationalism that had allegedly characterized the "golden age" of American diplomacy, when the United States advanced its "interests by serving those of others."[19] In September 2002, the Bush administration put an end to this golden age by publishing its official doctrine, *The National Security Strategy of the United States of America*, which made clear that unilateral preemptive strikes and wars were from now on America's agenda:

> Today, the United States enjoys a position of unparalleled military strength and great economic and political influence.... And, as a matter of common sense and self-defense, America will act against such emerging threats before they are fully formed.... The United States has long maintained the option of preemptive actions to counter a sufficient threat to our national security. The greater the threat, the greater is the risk of inaction—and the more compelling the case for taking anticipatory action to defend ourselves, even if uncertainty remains as to the time and place of the enemy's attack. To forestall or prevent such hostile acts by our adversaries, the United States will, if necessary, act preemptively.... In exercising our leadership, we will respect the values, judgment, and interests of our friends and partners. Still, we will be prepared to act apart when our interests and unique responsibilities require.[20]

Exceptionalism and its defense had thus been reduced to a unilateral and anticipatory exercise in raw power. This transformation, however, existed only in the eyes of American rulers and the overwhelming majority of their organic intellectuals; the myth of the anti-imperialist "leadership" of the "city on the hill" dispensing selflessly boundless gifts to the rest of the world has always been dressed in the garbs of exceptionalism. It has always masked the reality of empire and predations. Paradoxically, a "neo-conservative" organic intellectual, Robert Kagan, exposed this myth in a clear and cogent way:

> Americans have cherished an image of themselves as by nature inward-looking and aloof, only sporadically and spasmodically venturing forth into the world, usually in response to external attack or perceived threats. This self-image survives, despite four hundred years of steady expansion and an ever-deepening involvement in world affairs, and despite innumerable wars, interventions, and prolonged occupations in foreign lands. It is as if it were all an accident or odd twist of fate. Even as the United States has risen to a position of global hegemony, expanding its reach and purview and involvement across the continent

and then across the oceans, Americans still believe their nation's natural tendencies are toward passivity, indifference, and insularity. . . . Americans have often not realized how their expansive tendencies—political, ideological, economic, strategic, and cultural—bump up against and intrude upon other peoples and cultures. They are surprised to learn that others hate them, are jealous of them, and even fear them for their power and influence. They have not anticipated, therefore, the way their natural expansiveness could provoke reactions, and sometimes violent reactions, against them.[21]

Kagan's view, however, is neither new nor original; critiques of American imperialism have been numerous especially among leftwing intellectuals in the United States and abroad.[22] What is distinctive about his claim is the historical moment at which it crystallized; the moment when the United States had to get over its "imperial denial"[23] and "be more expansive in [its] goals and more assertive in their implementation."[24] *Oderint dum metuant*—"Let them hate, so long as they fear"—had become the unambiguous American slogan, well captured in the United States' "rapid dominance" military doctrine.

Rapid dominance, as described by Harlan K. Ullman and James P. Wade, the theoreticians of the doctrine, "must be all-encompassing." And they add:

> It will require the means to anticipate and to counter all opposing moves. It will involve the capability to deny an opponent things of critical value, and to convey the unmistakable message that unconditional compliance is the only available recourse. It will imply more than the direct application of force. It will mean the ability to control the environment and to master all levels of an opponent's activities to affect will, perception, and understanding. . . . Deception, misinformation, and disinformation are key components in this assault on the will and understanding of the opponent.[25]

This all-encompassing rapid dominance can only be achieved by the full deployment of "shock and awe," which is "a subset of controlling the enemy's perception" by giving this enemy "the appearance that there are no safe havens from attack, and that any target may be attacked at any time with impunity and force."[26] In Ullman and Wade's words, "Shock and Awe are actions that create fears, dangers, and destruction that are incomprehensible to the people at large. . . . To reach the level required to achieve Rapid Dominance, [Shock and Awe] must also bring fear to those who are in charge. It must be applied quickly, decisively, and preferably with impunity (such as stealth bombing with air superiority). The element of impunity . . . is a key element of this strategy."[27]

While rapid dominance and shock and awe were devised in the 1990s and fully deployed after 9/11, they are hardly new to America's expansionist arsenal. In its eighteenth- and nineteenth-century westward expansion, the United States adopted similar doctrines; Native Americans, occupying their own ancestral land, were to be exterminated if they did not accept the "benevolent" expropriation of their territory and the concomitant gift of Anglo-Saxon civilization. While Jefferson described Native Americans as "merciless Indian Savages,"[28] he believed them to "be in body and mind equal to the whiteman."[29] They could form "one family with the whites, born in the same land with them, and bound to live like brethren, in peace, friendship, & good neighborhood."[30] On the other hand, their lack of civilization made them "children" whose potential bellicosity against revolutionary white Americans would be punished in the most brutal way. As Jefferson put it, "My Children, if you love the land in which you were born, if you wish to inhabit the earth which covers the bones of your fathers, take no part in the war between the English & us, if we should have war. Never will we do an unjust Act towards you. On the contrary we wish to befriend you in every possible way. But the tribe which shall begin an unprovoked war against us, we will extirpate from the Earth, or drive to such a distance, as that they shall never again be able to strike us."[31]

As governor of Virginia, Jefferson had also asserted his potential commitment to the total annihilation of the "red Indians." In 1780, he wrote to George Rogers Clark, a military frontier officer, "We must leave it to yourself to decide on the object of the campaign. If against these Indians, the end proposed should be their extermination, or their removal beyond the lakes or Illinois river. The same world will scarcely do for them and us."[32] Thus, since its inception, the United States has used violence and wars to demonstrate its uncompromising determination to employ what it perceived to be its right to expand "civilization" over "savagery," and "freedom" over "despotism." As James William Gibson explains, "The Indian wars formed a fundamental American myth: to justify taking away Indian lands, first colonists and later 'American' explorers and settlers developed a national mythology in which 'American' technological and logistic superiority in warfare became culturally transmitted as signs of cultural-moral superiority. European and 'American' 'civilisation' morally deserved to defeat Indian 'savagery.' Might made right and each victory recharged the culture and justified expansion—what Slotkin calls 'regeneration through violence.'"[33]

Thus, since the time of the "founders," violence and wars have played a mythical role in the development of American exceptionalism. American rulers have always tended to perceive resistance to their expansionist drives as intolerable challenges to their benevolent civilizing mission—challenges that they had to crush with overwhelming military might. For instance, invoking America's democratic, progressive, and compassionate intentions, President William McKinley and his successor, Theodore Roosevelt, went to war against the Filipinos, who were bent on establishing their independence. They were both espousing what the British poet Rudyard Kipling called for in his famous "The White Man's Burden," subtitled "The United States and the Philippine Islands," which was published in *McClure's Magazine* in February 1899. Kipling urged the United States to annex the Philippines by taking "up the White Man's burden" and sending "forth the best ye breed." The responsibility of empire, he argued, compelled America to civilize "Your new-caught sullen peoples, Half devil and half child."[34] In a Kiplingesque address, McKinley proclaimed that "the mission of the United States is one of benevolent assimilation substituting the mild sway of justice and right for arbitrary rule." Such benevolence required, however, the uncontested imposition of order: "There must be sedulously maintained the strong arm of authority to repress disturbance and to overcome all obstacles to the bestowal of the blessings of good and stable government upon the people of the Philippine Islands under the free flag of the United States."[35]

The Filipinos would have none of it; they fought in vain the occupiers long after President Theodore Roosevelt declared victory and the war ended officially on July 4, 1902. Roosevelt celebrated the American victory as the "triumph of civilization over forces which stand for the black chaos of savagery and barbarism."[36] This triumph of civilization was in fact a horrific slaughter of Filipinos—more than 20,000 insurgents perished in battle, and between 200,000 to 1,000,000 civilians died from famine and illness.[37] The Filipinos were subjected to the infamous "water cure" torture,[38] and they endured resettlements in concentration camps[39] and the burning of their homes and villages.[40]

In the eyes of American imperialists, the destruction and death inflicted on the Filipinos was understandable and indeed necessary. As Senator Albert Beveridge put it, "We are not dealing with Americans or Europeans. We are dealing with Orientals. We are dealing with Orientals who are Malays. We are dealing with Malays instructed in Spanish methods. They mistake kindness for weakness, forbearance for fear. It could not be otherwise unless you could erase hundreds of years of savagery, other hundreds of years of Orientalism, and still other hundreds of years of Spanish character and custom."[41]

Beveridge reasserted the racist foundation of American exceptionalism to justify the brutalities of expansionism. He was not alone in believing that no apology was required for massacres and torture; in fact, many religious leaders and policy makers took it for granted that the military behavior of the United States was sanctioned by the Almighty God. As James Francs Smith, the governor-general of the Philippines put it, "Then for the first time since the world began did a nation, flushed with victory and mistress of the fate of conquered millions, turn her face from earth to heaven, and catching some of that divine charity which inspired the Good Samaritan, set herself to lift a subject people to a higher plane of progress."[42]

This belief in America's God-given expansionist right has legitimized uninterrupted patterns of imperial American interventions to this day. According to different sources, from the end of World War II to the early 2000s, the United States has launched between 153 and 201 overseas military operations.[43] The count "does *not* include covert actions and numerous instances in which US forces were stationed abroad since World War II in occupation forces or for participation in mutual security organizations, base agreements, and routine military assistance or training operations."[44] In fact, the United States has an "Empire of Bases"[45] of some 800 military facilities located on foreign territory. The annual cost of maintaining these facilities is conservatively estimated at $71.8 billion,[46] representing a larger amount than Russia's total military budget. In addition, writes John W. Dowder, "elite US special operation forces were deployed to around 150 countries, and Washington provided assistance in arming and training security forces in an even larger number of nations."[47]

The imperial mission goes unabated, therefore, and while the religious fervor that invigorated America's exceptionalism has diminished,[48] it still nurtures the secular and strategic shibboleth of the "indispensable" nation coined by former Secretary of State Madeleine Albright in 1998.[49] The notion of America's indispensability is, however, neither new nor original; it merely reasserts in novel rhetoric the old notions of manifest destiny and leadership. At its core it reaffirms America's imperial mission, as Albright herself makes clear: "If we have to use force, it is because we are America; we are the indispensable nation. We stand tall and we see further than other countries into the future, and we see the danger here to all of us."[50]

The logic of America's indispensability is symptomatic of what K. J. Holsti has defined as the *exceptionalist syndrome*. The syndrome has five critical attributes:

1. A responsibility, obligation, and mission to "liberate" others, usually defined as entire societies suffering from some evil, exploitation, or fallen status. . . . 2. [The] exceptionalist state is or should be free from external constraints such as rules or norms that govern or influence the relations between "ordinary" states. . . . 3. Exceptionalist states usually see themselves existing in a hostile world. . . . 4. Exceptionalist states develop a need to have external enemies. . . . 5. Exceptionalist states portray themselves as innocent victims.[51]

Had it not been for the dominant power of its military-industrial complex, America's exceptionalist syndrome and Albright's concomitant claim of American indispensability would have sounded delusional and hollow. Exceptionalism resonates only when accompanied by the effective threat and deployment of brute force. And in turn, that reality transforms exceptionalism into what Paul Kramer has defined as "the imperial." Irrespective of whether the imperial professes to embody the worldwide spread of liberty, democracy, or capitalism, it "refers to a dimension of power in which asymmetries in the scale of political action, regimes of spatial ordering, and modes of exceptionalizing difference enable and produce relations of hierarchy, discipline, dispossession, extraction, and exploitation."[52]

While American exceptionalizing of the "other" no longer espouses openly racist categories, it has embraced denigrating cultural stereotypes since the end of World War II. During the Korean and Vietnam wars, American politicians, military, and intellectuals depicted Asian peoples as experiencing pain and death differently from their Western counterparts. In their eyes, Asians had no real appreciation of individual life, which could be easily sacrificed in the name of the collective group. For instance, the American lawyer Telford Taylor, who was the chief counsel for the prosecution at the Nuremberg War Trials, declared, "The traditions and practices of warfare in the Orient are not identical with those that have developed in the Occident. . . . Individual lives are not valued so highly in Eastern mores. And it is totally unrealistic of us to expect the individual Korean soldier . . . to follow our most elevated precepts of warfare."[53]

In similar fashion, Haitians are depicted as undisciplined, lazy, bizarre, and primitive *vodouisants*, and their rulers as uniquely venal and corrupt. For many American politicians, journalists, and public intellectuals, Haitian culture is simply incomprehensible and weird. The country is the paradigmatic "other." In fact, Samuel Huntington—one of the leading American political scientists of his generation and a chaired professor at Harvard University as well as an adviser to presidents until his death in 2008—called Haiti in *The Clash of Civilizations and the Remaking of World Order*, a "lone country" that "lacks cultural commonality with other societies." He asserted, "Haiti's Creole language, Voodoo religion, revolutionary slave origins, and brutal history combine to make it a lone country. . . . Haiti, 'the neighbor nobody wants,' is truly a kinless country."[54]

Huntington was not alone in advancing theses of Haitian cultural backwardness. In the aftermath of the 2010 earthquake, David Brooks, the well-known editorialist of the *New York Times*, sought to explain Haiti's unending political and economic problems by appealing to cultural arguments advanced by Lawrence Harrison and Robert Rotberg.[55] Brooks blamed Haiti's woes on "voodoo" as a persisting manifestation of backward African traditions, and on authoritarian child-rearing practices. As he put it, "Haiti, like most of the world's poorest nations, suffers from a complex web of progress-resistant cultural influences. There is the influence of the voodoo religion, which spreads the message that life is capricious and planning futile. There are high levels of social mistrust. Responsibility is often not internalized. Child-rearing practices often involve neglect in the early years and harsh retribution when kids hit 9 or 10."[56]

Pat Robertson, the host of *The 700 Club* and a former Republican presidential candidate, advanced a different but even more bizarre explanation of Haiti's underdevelopment and recent earthquake. According to CNN, he blamed the tragedy on something that "happened a long time ago in Haiti, and people might not want to talk about it. [The Haitians] were under the heel of the French. You know, Napoleon III and whatever. . . . And they got together and swore a pact to the devil. They said, 'We will serve you if you will get us free from the French.' True story. And so, the devil said, 'OK, it's a deal.'"[57]

Such cultural and mystical explanations of Haiti's predicament are tauto-logical, ahistorical, and ultimately racist even if such racism is unconscious.[58] Comments of this kind reflect the "dangerous and resilient . . . idea that the Haitian political quagmire is due to some congenital disease of the Haitian mind. . . . [They make] Haiti's political dilemma immune to rational explana-tion and therefore to solutions that could be both just and practical."[59] In spite of this gross incapacity to understand the basic dynamics of Haitian society, the United States has never hesitated to meddle in the country's politics and in a few instances to impose its diktat through military interventions and outright occupation. Located in its "backyard," Haiti has always been a prime target of global American "policing." Moreover, since the mid-1990s, the United States has taken the lead in so-called humanitarian and nation-building missions that were intimately linked to the deployment and use of military force.

In the post–Cold War era, whether it be in Bosnia and Kosovo, or Afghani-stan and Iraq, or Haiti and Libya, the coercive role of the United States has been essential in imposing "order" on the chaos that Western interventions themselves created. Similarly, the U.S. military has been critical in "humani-tarian missions" generated by natural catastrophes such as the devastating Hai-tian earthquake that destroyed much of Port-au-Prince and killed more than 200,000 people.

At the dawn of the twenty-first century, the so-called Responsibility to Protect (R2P) doctrine elaborated by the International Commission on Inter-vention and State Sovereignty began to legitimate such imperial military behav-ior.[60] Camouflaged behind the claim of a universal defense of human rights, R2P facilitated new forms of imperial interventions. It eroded further the frag-ile sovereignty of peripheral and outer peripheral states.[61] As John Hobson explains, "In certain key respects R2P is reminiscent of the nineteenth century 'white man's burden,' requiring not just Western paternalist intervention to res-cue Eastern victims, but a subsequent reconstruction of the state along Western lines. In this way R2P reconvenes the conception of Western hyper-sovereignty and conditional Eastern sovereignty."[62]

Yet the R2P doctrine is more than a call to assist victims of brutal regimes and justify the hypersovereignty of major powers; it is also an important ele-ment in the repertoire of these powers' security agenda, which seeks to contain the civil conflicts and violence engendered by the world capitalist economy. The *droit d'ingérence* and the R2P are the core of the so-called new humanitarian-ism, a form of militarized intervention offering a moral cloak to justify impe-rial wars and the overthrow of regimes that are no longer useful to imperial power. The new humanitarianism is not only forceful military overthrows of "rogue" states to allegedly protect defenseless civilians, but also militarized relief operations in zones devastated by natural calamities. This effectively means that the United States, as the undisputed hegemon of the "new western imperium,"[63] gives itself the unilateral right to violate the sovereignty of other nations.

In the words of Costas Douzinas, such unilateralism embodies a "universalist exceptionalism," which is an imperial capacity to opt out from the law while simultaneously being its "sole authoritative interpreter."[64] In other words, the United States exempts itself from international rules, laws, and agreements that it imposes on others.[65] "Exemptionalism" is thus a key element of American exceptionalism that frees the full deployment of its missionary zeal. As Michael Ignatieff argues, "What is exceptional about American messianism is that it is the last imperial ideology left standing in the world, the sole survivor of imperial claims to universal significance. . . . This may help to explain why a messianic ideology, which many Americans take to be no more than a sincere desire to share the benefits of their own freedom, should be seen by so many other nations as a hegemonic claim to interference in their internal affairs."[66]

American exceptionalism is thus unfettered; it shrugs off international constraints to its dominion. While this behavior was taken for granted among weak states in the immediate sphere of U.S. influence, it has now extended to powerful allies in Europe and beyond. For instance, Washington feels free to impose on anyone the extraterritorial application of its own legislation regarding financial and security issues. In 2010, the U.S. Congress, in its efforts to criminalize economic transactions with Iran for its alleged nuclear weapons program, "declared that any foreign bank that maintained a correspondent banking relationship with a designated Iranian bank would forfeit its banking relationships in the United States."[67] In 2012, President Obama signed an executive order authorizing additional sanctions regarding Iran. The executive order extended the prohibition "to make sanctionable knowingly conducting or facilitating significant transactions with a private or public foreign financial institution or other entity for the purchase or acquisition of Iranian oil." Moreover, it expanded sanctions on "Iran's petrochemical industry . . . by making sanctionable significant transactions for the purchase or acquisition of Iranian petrochemical products." Finally, it authorized sanctions "for individuals and entities that provide material support to the National Iranian Oil Company, Naftiran Intertrade Company, or the Central Bank of Iran, or for the purchase or acquisition of U.S. bank notes or precious metals by the Government of Iran."[68]

U.S. exceptionalism bypasses conceptions of sovereignty to impose some of its own laws on other nations; sovereignty is thus at bay. This is particularly the case for weak peripheral or outer peripheral states. For the organic intellectuals of the empire, these states should be "recolonized" in some fundamental ways because they lack stability and are prone to authoritarianism. In such cases, sovereignty would simply be an inconsequential barrier to be willfully violated. In short, the so-called failed states cannot be left to their own devices, lest they become dysfunctional territorial spaces easily taken over by terrorists and drug cartels. Stephen Krasner, the former director of the policy planning staff at the U.S. Department of State during the George W. Bush administration and a professor of political science at Stanford University, put it bluntly: "Collapsed and badly governed states will not fix themselves because they have limited administrative capacity, not least with regard to maintaining internal security. . . . To reduce international threats and improve the prospects for individuals in such polities, alternative institutional arrangements supported by external actors, such as de facto trusteeships and shared sovereignty, should be added to the list of policy options."[69]

Along these lines, another leading American political scientist, Robert Keohane, has argued for a "gradation of sovereignty" designed by the international institutions and their Western patrons. Weak and "troubled" states would thus come under the "responsible" tutelage of advanced, mature, and liberal nations, which would in turn gauge the permissible level of sovereignty of these troubled zones. As Keohane put it, for "troubled societies . . . the classic ideal-type of Westphalian sovereignty should be abandoned even as an aspiration. . . . The concept of sovereignty will need to be unbundled, and the Westphalian fetish of total autonomy from external authority discarded, so that stable domestic authority, and peaceful relations among countries in formerly troubled regions, can be restored."[70]

In such recolonizing formulations, little is said about the role of these very imperial networks of power in creating and fomenting the political and economic crises besieging these "troubled regions."[71] This is especially the case for outer peripheral nations like Haiti.[72] The constant meddling of international actors, principally the United States, in the domestic affairs of the country has exacerbated its deep internal social problems. As already noted, the first U.S. occupation, which lasted almost twenty years (1915–1934), contributed little to Haiti's development. The decades that followed, except for short periods of stability and growth, failed to change the old patterns of authoritarian rule, class privilege, and economic stagnation. While the country had regained its formal independence, it clearly remained deeply subservient to the United States. No regime could ultimately survive for long without the approval and support of Washington, and in several instances it was Washington itself that ultimately chose Haitian rulers. This is not to say that the United States could impose its direct and unilateral political will on Haiti, but rather that Haitians holding high office had to respect as beyond question the geopolitical and strategic interests of the United States.[73]

Thus, while virtually all the Haitian governments that followed the American occupation were autocratic and led by rulers with messianic pretensions, their despotic and venal practices reflected more internecine social conflicts and the local authoritarian *habitus* than the long interventionist hand of the United States.[74] And yet while America professed a preference for democracy, it tolerated, supported, and in some instances instigated the rise of military or civilian dictatorships as long as such regimes remained in its orbit as stable and pliant clients. This attitude became more pronounced during the Cold War when the fear of "communist infection,"[75] particularly in the Third World, guided American foreign policy. It is in this context that Haitian-American relations from the 1950s to 1991, as well as the evolution and political manipulation of Haitian exceptionalism, must be analyzed.

CHAPTER 7

Dictatorship, Democratization, and Exceptionalism

The coming to power of Francois Duvalier, "Papa Doc," in 1957 inaugurated three decades of dictatorship by the Duvalier family.[1] For fourteen years until his death in 1971, Francois Duvalier established a repressive and bloody system of absolute personal rule that his son, Jean-Claude, inherited. While Jean-Claude hesitantly and zigzaggingly liberalized his father's regime, he remained a dictator until his fall in 1986. What persisted too over the years in spite of Washington's repeated rhetorical condemnations of the Duvaliers' grave human rights violations, was American economic, political, and military support for their dynasty.[2] It was not only American exceptionalism with its emphasis on promoting democracy and liberty that was sacrificed on the anticommunist altar of markets and political order; Haitian exceptionalism was also jettisoned as its claims of radical black sovereignty and freedom were consistently falsified by Duvaliers' repressive policies.

The Duvaliers' long autocratic rule would have been unthinkable without the Cold War. On the one hand, the Duvaliers manipulated the conflict between East and West to their advantage. This was especially the case with Papa Doc, who used American fears of the "domino effect" of the Cuban Revolution to obtain Washington's support. On the other hand, the United States, in spite of its self-professed commitment to defend and promote democracy and liberty, tolerated and indeed protected the Haitian dictatorship because of its deep anticommunism. It is true that America's policy toward Francois Duvalier was constantly in flux, varying from unmitigated military, diplomatic, and financial patronage to economic sanctions and veiled threats of regime change. Ultimately, however, it preferred the relative stability of a repressive order headed by Papa Doc rather than the potential uncertainties of political chaos or revolution.[3]

Duvalier knew well that the United States was more concerned about the Cold War and winning it than confronting the deployment of his repressive and corrupt dictatorial system, which he sought to mask by propagating a vulgar form of black nationalism. In his quest to legitimize his rule, Duvalier used the themes of African roots and black cultural identity that are prominent features of Haitian exceptionalism. Not surprisingly, he appealed to the ancestors, particularly Jean-Jacques Dessalines, and to the country's "indigenous" religion, Vodou;[4] in the process, he espoused the *noiriste* ideology to camouflage deep class divisions and demonize the mulatto elite as responsible for all the ills of Haiti. Duvalier thus could claim that he was the first political leader to embody the power of negritude, and of black resistance to Western imperial culture.[5] In Duvalier's view, Vodou represented the "transcendent expression of racial consciousness before the enigmas of the world,"[6] the "raising of national and racial awareness," and "the supreme factor of Haitian unity." In fact, according to him it was from Vodou's entrails that Haiti's revolution and independence were born; as he put it, "1804 originates from Vodou."[7] Duvalier used Vodou to create an aura of black nationalist resistance to the *blans* and the Haitian mulatto elites.[8] As Paul Christopher Johnson explains, Duvalier "marshaled and encompassed for himself Vodou's cachet as a national, indigenous, and *noiriste* religion expressing resistance within an elitist and neocolonial State. . . . The idea of Vodou as resistance to foreign encroachment could become persuasive not only because of the message's repeated iteration, or to the objective fact of Haiti's colonial and neocolonial exploitation, but also because of the worldview of Vodou itself, which invokes a 'constant state of alert' to potential spiritual attack or molestation by rivals."[9]

And indeed, it is through this prism that Duvalier viewed his rule as a permanent state of emergency bent on finding and obliterating real and imagined enemies to establish his personal absolutism. Mixing elements of Catholicism, Vodou, and mysticism, Duvalier projected himself as a divine creature. Jean M. Fourcand, a leading organic intellectual of Duvalierism, celebrated the inauguration of Duvalier's life presidency in 1964 by writing the thoroughly sycophantic pamphlet *Catechism of the Revolution*,[10] which claimed that the life president embodied "the five founders of the nation"—Dessalines, Toussaint, Pétion, Christophe, and Estimé.[11] As the *Catechism* put it, "Who are Dessalines, Toussaint, Christopher, Pétion and Estimé? Dessalines, Toussaint, Christophe, Pétion and Estimé are five founders of the nation who are found within François Duvalier. . . . Is Dessalines for life? Yes, Dessalines is for life in François Duvalier."[12]

The "immaterial" life president, as Duvalier dubbed himself,[13] exploited the messianic and monarchic elements of the Haitian *habitus* to transmogrify his persona into a God deserving a version of the Lord's Prayer. Again, the *Catechism* suggests that there ought to be an *Oraison Dominicale* for Duvalier: "Our Doc, who is in the National Palace, hallowed be Thy name in the present and future generations. Thy will be done at Port-au-Prince and in the provinces. Give us this day our new Haiti and never forgive the trespasses of the anti-patriots who spit every day on our country. Let them succumb to temptation, and under the weight of their venom, deliver them not from any evil."[14] Duvalier had little sympathy for his foes; harsh imprisonment, torture, or execution were his preferred methods rather than pardon. In fact, the *Catechism* recommended *L'Extreme Onction Duvalieriste* for opponents, the so-called *apatrides* and *Camoquins*. *L'Extreme Onction Duvalieriste* was a "sacrament instituted by the people's army, the civil militia, and the Haitian people . . . to crush and annihilate with grenades, mortars, mausers, bazookas, flame-throwers and other weapons" the treacherous enemies of the nation.[15]

Violence was thus an integral part of the Duvalierist system; justified in the name of the revolution, it was in reality the means to ensure the presidential absolutism of Papa Doc. The creation of the militia, the *tontons macoute*,[16] had little to do with empowering peasants or proletarians; it was the terrorist *force de frappe* to intimidate, brutalize, and kill not only the *Camoquins* but also members of the traditional mulatto and black elites. As Duvalier emphasized, "Le groupuscule de mulatres et assimilés noirs [The small group of mulattoes and assimilated blacks] plotting against him could only establish "the inhumanity of their borrowed occidentalism."[17] By using the *noiriste* theme, Duvalier emphasized racial "authenticity" to differentiate between real and fake Haitians; the former were blacks of African descent, and the latter supposedly multiracial and light skinned.[18]

Rooted paradoxically in the racist theory of Joseph Arthur de Gobineau, Duvalier's authenticity espoused the notion of "congenital racial essences" whereby biological factors created particular mentalities.[19] Duvalier and his intellectual colleague Lorimer Denis had written in the late 1930s that it was "by the laws of ancestral heredity that the specific features of the forefathers of the most distant off-spring are preserved in the psychology of their descendants."[20] In this perspective, blacks as a race had their own unique predilection based on a distinctive imaginative creativity; in Denis's and Duvalier's words, "sensibility forms the quintessence of the black soul."[21]

Ultimately, *Noirisme*, which derives from a particular interpretation of Haiti's founding myths and exceptionalism, is a mystification. As René Depestre explained long ago:

> In separating the question of race from the economic development and social history of Haiti, and in giving it an absolute and mythical dimension, [pseudo-sociologists like Francois Duvalier] have reduced Haitian history to a series of chaotic ethnic conflicts between mulattos and blacks, who from the time of our independence became the reigning oligarchy of the country. . . . [The] question of race, far from being a determining factor in the development of Haitian society, has only led to mystification, which in the consciousness of two competing aristocracies has served to hide the real stakes and motivations of class struggle.[22]

Mystification does not imply that *Noirisme* lacks mobilizing power. On the contrary, since it derives from the nation's exceptionalism, it implants itself onto society's collective imaginary; it is thus like an ether bathing the political *habitus*. Moreover, as the president for life of the first black independent nation of the world, Duvalier claimed to embody the spirit of decolonization sweeping black Africa in the late 1950s and early 1960s. While his contribution to Africa's independence movement amounted to little but symbolic gestures and rhetorical flourishes, he managed to burnish his credentials at home as a defender of black power. He celebrated Ethiopia's Haile Selassie and Senegal's Leopold S. Senghor, as well as America's civil rights leader Martin Luther King Jr. Posing as the leader of the Afro-American struggle for equality, he asserted, "We constitute for the negro-African masses of the universe the highest exponent or a kind of common denominator of all national and racial consciousness."[23]

Duvalier's brand of Pan-Africanism was, however, self-serving and purely symbolic; at little cost, it projected him domestically as an international leader of the black power movement and defender of third world decolonization. It nurtured a revolutionary aura around his persona that insulated him to some extent from his own repressive and reactionary policies. In addition, the cultural appeals to blackness resonated with some leaders of newly independent African states and minimized his international isolation. As Arthus explains:

> The opening to Africa, in the name of racial solidarity, also allowed the Haitian president to expand the list of his allies on the international scene. During the 14 years of Duvalier's reign, all statesmen, ranking from minister to president, who visited Haiti—with the notable exception of Trujillo . . . — came from the African continent. These trips, sometimes semi-official, were of great importance for the Duvalier regime. African statesmen landed in Port-au-Prince mostly in the late 1960s which was a period when Duvalier sought to reduce his isolation in the Caribbean and from the United States. Moreover, each visit of African officials, whatever the context of its realization, was a joyful occasion at the national palace.[24]

Duvalier's Pan-Africanism was thus emptied of its radical content to embody a color-based message of cultural unity that sought to mask not only his dictatorial rule, but also the deep structural inequalities of class and power over which he was presiding. As I pointed out earlier, this color-based ideology has always informed Haitian exceptionalism, but Duvalier's brutal extremism debilitated its hold on the country's popular consciousness. Writing in 1968, René Depestre argued that Papa Doc's reign of terror "led Haitians to question the ideas they [had] long had of themselves. In their eyes Haiti [was] no longer fixed as that mythical figure imprinted in school on the consciousness of every Haitian: Haiti, first Black Republic in modern history, homeland and myth to black men, cradle and 'paradise' of Negritude!"[25] Because of their intense suffering, Depestre contended, Haitians came to "realize that power, whether in the hands of blacks, whites, mulattos, or indigenous groups in a semicolonial system, is always a brutal force that dehumanized people and their social and cultural history." And Depestre concluded rather optimistically that "Haitians now realize that the exaltation of any given race is pointless absurdity that always masks violent attacks on the oneness of humankind."[26]

The exaltation of race and color, however, remains a powerful ideological weapon in the struggle to acquire and keep power in Haitian politics. Both *noiristes* and mulattoes have engaged in veiled or open appeals to color to mobilize their constituencies. While the light-skinned minority proclaims the racist slogan "*Le pouvoir au plus capable*"(power to the most competent), black politicians incite the masses against light-skinned privilege and exploitation. In reality, both groups have historically kept the masses in conditions of destitution and marginalization.

In the mid and late 1990s, under the first regime of René Préval, certain factions of the Lavalas movement vying for power brandished the specter of a unified, racist, exploitative, and wealthy mulatto bourgeoisie to mobilize popular support. They singled out three influential light-skinned leaders: Robert Manuel, then the secretary of state for public security; Pierre Denizé, the director of the Police Nationale d'Haiti; and Jean Dominique, the country's leading progressive journalist, who had a vast popular following. While the three had been old allies of Lavalas and Jean-Bertrand Aristide, they became increasingly critical of Aristide himself as well as what they saw as the mounting governmental corruption and the growing presence of the Colombian drug cartels. A series of ominous graffiti began to appear on public spaces in Port-au-Prince denouncing the three men as exploitative "*ti wouj*" and claiming "*Bob Manuel vle touye Titid.*"[27] Eventually Manuel and Denizé were compelled to resign and flee the country, while unknown assassins murdered Dominique.[28] The color card thus became a weapon to discredit adversaries and keep the spoils of political power flowing to a small group of *grands mangeurs*—a rapacious species of office holders who devour public resources for their exclusive private gains.[29] It masked the corruption and exploitative practices of emerging and consolidating black elites.

It is clear, however, that *noiristes* are right to claim that the mulatto elite has historically enjoyed a privileged status and expressed its contempt for the poor black majority. In general, light-skinned Haitians have tended to believe that they are entitled to lord it over the masses because they have a natural right to govern by virtue of their color. For instance, in September 2012 under the presidency of Michel Martelly, Senator Edo Zenny, a light-skinned ally of the president, stormed into a radio station to disrupt an interview with Judge Simonis and allegedly spit on his face while accusing him of corruption.[30] Simonis, who is black, claimed that Zenny yelled at him that he "had to respect a mulatto." Apparently, Zenny shouted at Simonis, "I am White, and you, you are a Negro."[31] Zenny eventually apologized for his behavior, but he defended himself by arguing that he was a "descendant of the Zenny dynasty and that he was very rich."[32] He maintained that he was not a racist because both his "wife and his best childhood friends are dark skinned" and in "France he would be considered a Negro."[33]

This episode illustrates that either remnants or resurgent elements of *mulatrisme*—the doctrine of mulatto superiority that insists that mulattoes "occupy the top of the system and all the positions of command"—are still influencing relationships of power.[34] That the crucible of color remains alive in the Haitian imaginary is testimony to the continued vitality and contradictions of the country's exceptionalism, which has always been anchored in the racial politics of the revolutionary war of independence against slavery and for emancipation.

The contradictions of Haitian exceptionalism are not limited to race; they extend also to the politics of nationalism and anti-imperialism. The unique events surrounding 1804 generated a fervor of nationalistic sentiments and claims of undefeatable resistance to any imperial encroachment on the first liberated black land of the world. Rulers have relentlessly reaffirmed and manipulated such fervor and such claims to downplay both the country's vassalage and the fact that they are opportunistic political hostages of foreign powers. The early and mid-1990s' military overthrow and restoration to power of President Jean-Bertrand Aristide illustrates well the cunning uses of Haitian exceptionalism.

In a landslide victory, the charismatic and prophetic priest Jean Bertrand-Aristide was elected president in 1990. Leading the Lavalas movement—the flood in Creole—an unstoppable flood, Aristide came to embody the aspirations of the huge majority of poor Haitians. He assumed the presidency on February 7, 1991, vowing to empower the *moun en deyo*—the marginalized and excluded majority. Bent on turning the world upside down, he preached that "*tout moun se moun*"—all human beings are human beings—and advocated extraparliamentary methods of popular rule to compel the Haitian elite into accepting a redistribution of wealth and power. Attacking and exposing the deep class divide separating Haitians, and seeking to undermine the decisive role that the military had historically played in determining who occupied the highest public offices, Aristide soon discovered that Haiti's dominant class and armed forces found his brand of politics simply unacceptable. In September 1991, barely seven months after his presidential inauguration, Aristide was overthrown in a bloody coup and forced into exile.

During his presidential campaign and short term in office, Aristide repeatedly celebrated the founders, Toussaint and Dessalines, and the 1804 revolution, as well as Charlemagne Péralte, the guerrilla leader who died resisting the first American occupation. He was an ardent nationalist, and as a priest espousing the radical liberation theology, he was a vocal critique of American imperialism and of capitalism, both of which he described as exploitative of poor countries like Haiti. While the revolutionary canons of Haitian exceptionalism inspired Aristide's rhetoric, the coup of September 29, 1991, denied him whatever opportunity he may have had to implement them.

Forced into exile in Caracas and then Washington D.C., Aristide was compelled to negotiate his return to power with General Raoul Cédras's de-facto regime, the very regime that had overthrown him. After three long years of complicated foreign-led consultations, Aristide accepted an agreement that significantly undermined his initial commitment to radical change. Engineered by the Clinton administration, the compromise veered Haiti into the neoliberal age. The radical tenets of Haitian exceptionalism that Aristide continued to voice upon his restoration to the presidency sounded hollow. In fact, he became a hostage of the conditions the United States imposed on him to guarantee his return. These conditions accentuated Haiti's economic and security dependence on the major powers, especially the United States, France, and Canada, as well as on the United Nations and the international financial institutions.

Aristide's rhetorical flurries about 1804 and Haiti's uncompromising sovereignty no longer resonated with reality. The fact that he regained his presidency by giving his blessing to a full military takeover of the country by 20,000 American troops made a mockery of his relentless nationalist rhetoric. The advocate of liberation theology, the prophet of anticapitalism, and the anti-imperialist leader, capitulated; restoring his presidency compelled him to depend, and depend utterly, on massive American military assistance. The circumstances leading to Aristide's "second coming" changed him immensely. Constrained by the overwhelming American presence and by the demands of the international financial institutions, he was forced to collaborate with former enemies and hesitant allies, as well as to implement policies that he had hitherto rejected. Once again, a radical defender of Haitian exceptionalism foundered in the face of imperial intrusions and his own impotence.

Those who violently overthrew Aristide suffered a similar fate; projecting themselves as impartial protectors of the constitution and of the integrity of the nation, they appealed also to the values of Haitian exceptionalism to legitimize their coup. Invoking threats to democracy, the military conspirators waged their coup and imposed a state of exception to impose their rule. General Cédras, the leader of the junta that overthrew Aristide, declared, "There was a deliberate choice not to respect democratic norms. . . . The situation threatened the country's democratic future; the familiar nightmare of a dictator regulating all national institutions . . . made us fear the worst. . . . [We needed to] liberate the country from apprentice dictators for good."[35] When pressed by the exiled Aristide government, the internal opposition, and the international community to allow the return of the elected president, the junta first proposed new elections, then procrastinated in negotiations requesting that it step down.[36] It appealed also to nationalism to condemn foreign interference in Haiti's own domestic affairs

Eventually, however, the de-facto rulers caved in after the United States threatened to invade the country to depose them. The irony of the coup and of the American intervention that restored Aristide to the presidency, is that the key coup makers were all on the payroll of the U.S. Central Intelligence Agency (CIA). The nationalist pretensions of the junta were all debunked, as its principal figure, General Cédras, and other powerful military officers were informants of the United States and had been members of Service d'Intelligence Nationale (SIN), a Haitian unit created by the CIA in the mid-1980s "to fight the cocaine trade, but [which] evolved into an instrument of political terror whose officers at times engaged in drug trafficking." Eventually, SIN spied on the Aristide administration for the United States, and the CIA supported the junta even while Washington was negotiating with the military dictatorship the restoration of Aristide's presidency.[37]

Thus, the coup that overthrew Aristide in 1991 and its political aftermath totally wiped out the commitments to democracy and sovereignty celebrated in both Haitian and American exceptionalisms. As Morris Morley and Chris McGillion explain:

> Washington's goal of getting Aristide "to see eye to eye" with a "critical mass" of the Haitian elite . . . proved effective as the exiled leader began to tone down his radical theology and class struggle rhetoric. . . . With few, if any, alternatives, [Aristide's] acceptance of IMF–World Bank–AID development blueprints calling for large-scale privatization, major tariff cuts, the elimination of import quotas, and a halving of personnel in the civil bureaucracy had become, in effect, one of the preconditions for his return. . . . As AID Administrator J. Brian Atwood later recalled: "When we first met he was running for president, he [had] a real attitude about the United States and the West. But I think he really has grown. He knows all the practical issues now."[38]

The United States managed therefore to change Aristide's project of social transformation into a typical neoliberal program that would further incorporate Haiti into the outer periphery of the world economy. Moreover, the United States succeeded in protecting its old allies in the coercive apparatus of the Haitian state. In fact, the high officers of the junta never had to account for their violence and brutality, and the United States rewarded them financially. General Cédras obtained from Washington "a million-dollar-plus 'golden parachute' to resign and go into exile, including the rental of three of his houses."[39] Defending the payments, U.S. embassy spokesman Stanley Schrager argued, "Our intent was to smooth the transition to President Aristide . . . to make that come about as smoothly as possible."[40]

Before reaching the agreement that led to the lucrative exile of the key members of the junta, Emile Jonassaint, the provisional Haitian president installed in his office by the military, threatened the international community with Haiti's "ancestral protectors, invisible protectors."[41] Invoking Vodou and the role it played in the revolution of 1804, Jonassaint called for "mobilizing all the resources and strategies of our ancestors," and returning "to the worthy heritage of the famous maroons."[42] Before the United States compelled him to resign from the presidency, Jonassaint made "references to Haiti's traditional, African-inspired religion . . . [boasting] that vodou spells [would] protect his nation from attacking aircraft and that invisible Haitian warriors [would] meet the enemy, haunting their every footstep."[43] He thus appealed to the myths of the Haitian Revolution to "not give in to the injunctions of the foreigner"[44] and to resist the *blans'* military invasion.

This invocation of Haiti's exceptionalism was a desperate sign of impotence and an attempt to mystify Aristide's supporters into accepting the rule of the junta. As Jonassaint himself recognized, the international community and the United States in particular were "a giant crushing us because we are weak and we don't have the atom bomb. If we had the atom bomb then everyone would respect us."[45] Knowing this simple reality, Jonassaint nonetheless advanced the farce that those "invisible" Vodou "protectors" and the corrupt and repressive Haitian military could stop imperial forces. In the process, he undermined further whatever hold Haitian exceptionalism may still have had on the popular imaginary.

In fact, the massive American intervention that restored the presidency of Aristide not only left Aristide himself completely weakened, but it also shook the very foundations of Haitian exceptionalism. Whatever nationalist project of social transformation the Lavalas movement may have had originally, it was ultimately swept away by the overwhelming imperial takeover of the country. Nationalist invocations lost much of their popular resonance; the country was thoroughly dependent economically, and its security was in the hands of the international community. Haiti had become an outer periphery; a territory under the virtual trusteeship of imperial powers and their multinational institutions as well as their nongovernmental organizations.[46] The country's politicians and would-be rulers can no longer convince Haitians of their "exceptionality," lest it imply the opposite of what 1804 had historically stood for.

In this climate, it is not surprising that waves of Haitians are seeking an exit from their country. Looking for an alternative to their desperate conditions, they are not only attempting to migrate to the United States or Canada, but increasingly to two Latin American nations, Chile and Brazil.[47] This Haitian diaspora is absolutely critical to the well-being of a majority of their countrymen. It is true that a "high proportion of Haiti's remittances are spent on consumption rather than savings, investment or services such as education and health care,"[48] but without them, Haiti's poverty would be more acute than it already is. In fact, it is not farfetched to claim that without remittances the economy would simply collapse. The diaspora's remittances are estimated to account for 34 percent of Haiti's gross national product.[49]

It is no wonder that the anti-immigration climate existing in the industrialized Western democracies and particularly in the United States under the "America First" presidency of Donald Trump has distressed Haitians in Haiti and abroad. The next chapter seeks to study the impact of the diaspora on a potential reformulation of Haitian and American exceptionalisms.

CHAPTER 8

The Diaspora and the Transmogrification of Exceptionalism

The Haitian diaspora became alarmed when President Trump claimed just before Christmas 2017 that all Haitian refugees suffered from AIDS. Barely three weeks later, in negotiations about immigration reform, the president was at it again, calling Haiti a "shithole."[1] In addition, the president allegedly rejected a bipartisan proposal to give green cards to Haitians who had been granted Temporary Protected Status (TPS). "Why do we need more Haitians?" Trump asked. His next words were "Take them out," meaning, I presume, that Haitians should be removed from the pool of acceptable immigrants. A month before these declarations, the Trump administration announced that it was ending the TPS of some 60,000 Haitians living in the United States. They were ordered to leave the country within eighteen months. The TPS permitted Haitians without legal residence to work and live in the United States after the devastating earthquake of 2010. According to the U.S. Department of Homeland Security, conditions in Haiti had improved to such an extent that its citizens should now return home. This claim, however, was contradicted by the department's own staff, which expressed deep concerns about terminating TPS because current conditions in Haiti were still very fragile.[2]

Trump's statements and his administration's policies outraged Haitians and people of Haitian descent, in part because the president denigrated their country and ignored the notable contributions of Haitian immigrants to American life.[3] And yet the encounter of the Haitian "other" with white Americans on their own soil has always been fraught with contradictions, tensions, and apprehension. What is it about Haiti that provoked such fury from President Trump?

In answering this question, it is important to emphasize that when Haitians proclaim their nation's exceptionalism and revolutionary tradition, they tend to ignore the ugly realities of deep class divisions and extreme poverty besieging a majority of their countrymen. In fact, there is little doubt that a large number of Haitians would welcome an opportunity to emigrate to escape these distressing conditions. On the other hand, it is also clear, as I have argued previously, that the United States has played a major role in, and bears considerable responsibility for, creating the current state of affairs. For many decades Haiti has been beleaguered by the predatory rule of a series of vain and corrupt elites—most of them supported and financed by the United States. In fact, the United States and other members of the so-called international community have a long and persistent history of interfering in and controlling Haiti's domestic affairs. In turn, unpopular and despotic Haitian leaders sought and obtained external assistance in their quest to conquer or maintain power. Haiti has thus been plagued by a malignant convergence of interests between opportunistic politicians and external forces. Moreover, the country has endured the periodic and ravaging wrath of the gods of nature. The result is a society trapped in a maelstrom of poverty, inequity, and recurring political crises—a society whose predicament compels its citizens to seek an exit from its own territory.

The conditions of permanent crisis besieging Haiti have contributed to the exodus of its citizens to more prosperous shores. As René Préval, the former president of Haiti, put it in a moment of extreme bluntness and desperation, "Cé najé poun soti"—you have to swim away from Haiti to have the opportunity to "make it." Many Haitians have thus sought to exit, like generations of others facing similar predicaments. Like the British, Germans, Italians, and Irish who preceded them, Haitians have made America their preferred destination. They are the new immigrants. And yes, they will continue to come as long as their country remains in dire economic and political straits. And, not surprisingly, they are unlikely to be welcome in their new "home." President Trump's Haitian phobia dating back from the 1980s is an extreme version of this reality.

Trump asserted then that Haitian refugees are an AIDS-infected menace to America's health. This claim was not borne out by the facts. It is probably the legacy of the hysteria generated in 1983 when the American Centers for Disease Control identified homosexuals, hemophiliacs, heroin users, and Haitians as the four transmitters for AIDS, the so-called 4-H club. Of this club, Haitians were singled out as the only nationality to be inherently prone to the then-mysterious illness.[4] Trump, who defines himself as a germaphobe, may have thus developed his unfounded fear of Haitians from this bizarre and now discredited identification.[5] Moreover, the containment of AIDS has been one of the few success stories of Haiti's weak health infrastructure. While it is true that the country has a high prevalence of the disease, the Joint UN program on HIV/AIDS has pointed out that since 2010, new HIV infections have decreased by 25 percent and AIDS-related deaths have decreased by 24 percent.[6]

Finally, the repugnance that President Trump exhibits toward Haitians has deep and complex historical roots. In fact, Haitians have been an integral part of America's history and contributed to its very making. For example, in 1779 free men of color from Haiti joined American revolutionary troops in the siege and battle of Savannah against the British. And as I have already pointed out, it was Haiti's defeat of Napoleon's army in 1804 that facilitated the Louisiana Purchase, which doubled the size of the United States. As the only nation born from a successful slave revolution, Haiti became, however, a terrifying specter for America's founding fathers who owned slaves and defended slavery. It was the symbol of black liberation and was therefore a mortal threat; it had to pay for defying the imperial order. Haiti's demonization by Western powers ultimately served to warn other colonized people of color of the dire consequences of revolting.

While Trump himself may or may not have been aware of this history, he clearly imbibed longstanding racist stereotypes of Haiti. These stereotypes have been reinforced by the recent and dramatic increase in the number of Haitian, African, and Central American immigrants in the United States. In 2016, according to government statistics, half a million people from North, South, and Central America, and the Caribbean, and another 111,000 from Africa became legal permanent residents of the United States. In addition, 440,000 Asians obtained their green cards, but only about 98,000 Europeans were granted the same status.[7] Not surprisingly, this influx of people of color has revived the nativistic and racist phobias expressed in 1924 when the U.S. Congress passed an immigration overhaul that set strict quotas to give preferential treatment to immigrants from Western Europe. President Trump echoed these feelings when he angrily questioned why the United States should grant green cards to immigrants from "shithole countries" over people from places like Norway.

Trump's comments, then, are not an aberration; they are deeply etched in the early formation of American exceptionalism. They also appeal to a large American constituency that has been marginalized from the benefits of globalization. This is the constituency of "middle-class "losers," which has seen its standard of living stagnate and indeed decline over the past four decades.[8] In fact, it has been mercilessly squeezed by neoliberalism. According to the Pew Research Center's report *The American Middle Class Is Losing Ground:*

> After more than four decades of serving as the nation's economic majority, the American middle class is now matched in number by those in the economic tiers above and below it. In early 2015, 120.8 million adults were in middle-income households, compared with 121.3 million in lower- and upper-income households combined, a demographic shift that could signal a tipping point. . . . The share [of the nation's aggregate household income] accruing to middle-income households was 43% in 2014, down substantially from 62% in 1970.
>
> And middle-income Americans have fallen further behind financially in the new century. In 2014, the median income of these households was 4% less than in 2000. Moreover, because of the housing market crisis and the Great

Recession of 2007–09, their median wealth (assets minus debts) fell by 28% from 2001 to 2013.[9]

The hollowing-out of the middle class whereby one-fifth of its members have fallen into lower status,[10] has meant that this large segment of the population lives in fear of continuous economic decline and cultural denigration. In fact, it is mainly composed of skilled and unskilled white working-class people, whom Hillary Clinton described as a "basket of deplorables" in the presidential campaign of 2016. In her eyes, they were "racist, sexist, homophobic, xenophobic, Islamophobic—you name it."[11] While many of these "deplorables" had actually voted for Barack Obama, the first African American president, they became disenchanted with the fruits of his neoliberal rule. They started to espouse the xenophobic message of Donald Trump and increasingly saw the foreigner, the "other" of a different color or ethnic background, as a threat to their overall sense of place and security. For those Americans whose towns and cities are decaying, and whose own sense of worth has shrunk, racist and nationalistic phobias offered false—but easy—explanations. Such phobias can become a pathological haven in a world of grotesque wealth and income inequalities.

Paradoxically, Trump has another constituency—a large section of the American plutocracy that, far from suffering the consequences of globalization, has enjoyed its benefits and gained additional economic gains through the type of tax reforms the president engineered to disproportionately reward the "1 percent." The magnitude of wealth and income disparities is well captured in Chuck Collins and Josh Hoxie's 2015 report, *Billionaire Bonanza: The Forbes 400 and the Rest of Us*:

> Over the last decade, a huge share of America's income and wealth gains has flowed to the top one-tenth of the richest 1 percent, the wealthiest one out of a thousand households.
>
> Within this group, our richest 400 individuals command a dizzying amount of wealth, defined here as total assets minus liabilities. . . . Our wealthiest 400 now have more wealth combined than the bottom 61 percent of the U.S. population, an estimated 70 million households, or 194 million people. . . . The wealthiest 20 individuals in the United States today hold more wealth than the bottom half of the U.S. population combined. These 20 super wealthy—a group small enough to fly together on one Gulfstream G650 private jet—have as much wealth as the 152 million people who live in the 57 million households that make up the bottom half of the U.S. population.[12]

Segments of this plutocracy financed the mobilization of the "deplorables" nurturing ethnocentric and racist undercurrents, which President Trump has fueled to enhance his popularity.

Trump, however, is neither the first nor the last to exploit immigration, nationality, and race to secure political power. As Jedediah Purdy has argued, in the election of 2016 "the nativism and racism that had slunk just outside respectable politics returned full-throated. . . . [The Trumpian] moment is not an anomalous departure but rather a return to the baseline—to the historical norm, one might say."[13] In fact, his immediate predecessor, President Barack Obama was called the "Deporter in Chief."[14] As the organization Freedom for Immigrants reported, "At the end of [Obama's] term, detention numbers [were] at a record high of over 40,000 per day and [his] administration [had] deported over 3 million people, more than all presidents since 1890 combined."[15] Thus, the exploitation of immigration for political purposes is not new, and there is no reason to doubt that it will persist for the foreseeable future, not only in America but in Europe and elsewhere. One has only to observe the treatment of people of Haitian descent in the Dominican Republic to know that the problem goes beyond President Trump's vile comments and policies.[16]

There is a long literature on the history of Haitian migrations to the Dominican Republic (D.R.) and the tensions and conflicts they have generated.[17] Suffice it to say that the uneven economic development of the two countries has transformed Haiti into an economic periphery of the D.R. Not surprisingly, a large influx of cheap Haitian labor has entered the growing Dominican economy. The presence of this labor began during the U.S. occupation of Haiti and the search for sugarcane cutters for American plantations in the D.R. Dominicans considered these Haitians to be inferior human beings. In fact, many D.R. rulers and cultural entrepreneurs have articulated an *antihaitianismo*—an "anti-Haitian credo"—that rejected "blackness" as a sign of primitiveness and espoused a "Hispanic" and white identity. The racial divide separating the Dominican Republic and Haiti is not only the result of the former's struggle to achieve independence from the latter in 1844,[18] but it is also the fabrication of the Dominican *criollo*[19] elites who define themselves and their nation as distinctive and civilized in contrast to their "savage" western neighbors.

The intensity of the D.R.'s *antihaitianismo* was reinforced by the global white supremacist order of the nineteenth century. In fact, the United States and, surprisingly, Frederick Douglass viewed the Dominican Republic as a "non black racial other" originating from a complex *mulataje* far different from the inferior blackness of Haiti.[20] As Lorgia Garcia-Pena explains:

> During the early years of the foundation of the Dominican Republic (1844–65) the United States supported the idea of Dominican racial superiority over Haiti and disavowed Haiti as racially inferior and thus unfit for self-government. This dichotomist view of the two Hispaniola nations shaped the relationship between the Dominican Republic and Haiti. It also shaped how the two nations and the relationship between them were imagined, and continue to be imagined and produced, across the globe. Fear of Haiti combined with Dominican *criollo* colonial desire and the threat of US expansionism impelled nineteenth century

Dominican writers and patriots . . . to produce dominicanidad as a hybrid race that was decidedly other than black, and therefore different from Haiti's blackness. . . . The foundational myth of the Dominican hybrid nation has led to the continuous physical and epistemic violence against Dominican blacks, *rayanos* (border subjects), and Haitian-Dominicans.[21]

The most vicious violence occurred in October 1937 when dictator Rafael Trujillo ordered the army to massacre over twelve thousand Haitian residents in the Dominican Republic.[22] Not surprisingly, this genocidal event and the racist and xenophobic ideology promoted by the state as well as ultranationalist intellectuals and parties have left a legacy of seeing Haitians as the "permanent outsider," the polluting "other."[23] In spite of a moment of hope in the aftermath of the earthquake of 2010, when many Dominicans came to the help of their devastated western sisters and brothers and silenced the ugliness of racism,[24] xenophobia persisted. The increasing numbers of people of Haitian descent and recently arrived Haitian immigrants residing in the D.R.—estimated at about half a million people, or approximately 9 percent of the total population— intensified powerful nativistic sentiments in the country. Beginning in 2013 the D.R. government promulgated a series of rulings that left some 180,000 people "undocumented" and "stateless."[25] Unless they could prove their Dominican citizenship, these people were deported to Haiti.[26] In fact, in 2017, 57,687 Haitians were deported to their home country, and that number had already been matched in the first six months of 2018.[27]

The deported are in limbo; relocated at the frontier inside Haiti to very poorly equipped camps, these Haitian citizens have been marginalized again by their own government. Their plight, as well as the suffering of millions of other refugees, compel us to acknowledge the ugly reality that the "shithole" is in fact a metaphor for our disfigured planet. Exceptionalism in this context seeks to function as an ideological mask hiding such disfiguration. Long ago, in May 1928, under the American occupation, Jacques Roumain, arguably Haiti's greatest literary figure, exposed the country's rulers' opportunistic celebration of the national flag. They were simply living a lie on their annual flag day obser-vance of May 18. As Roumain put it:

Daily greyness on this May 18. The stores open on the customary daily traffic. Misery, misery. Beggars, hungry people, hands reaching out. Some have the characteristic thinness of the poor. The bones of the face puncturing the skin and the eyes enlarged, excessive. . . . The flag. Who is talking about the flag? The flag is not edible. . . . The official cars will go to Arcahaie crowded with traitors. There will be an avalanche of speeches. The drool of governmental authorities will flow freely, so will champagne. Venomous mouths singing the flag will also defile it, but there will be some applause. . . . May 18. Who, but who thinks of May 19? Nobody.

Ah! are the dead therefore dumb? And have their open wounds no lips to cry out, to wake up?[28]

The constant and hollow invocation of exceptionalism leads to its utter banalization and ultimately to its incapacity to mobilize and convince. The invention of reality that rulers deploy from exaggerated claims of exceptionalism becomes so grotesque that they can no longer recreate history by extending its reach and imagining events. In such circumstances, exceptionalism drops its mask; the emperor has no clothes and stands naked, unprotected. Those in power lose their legitimacy, and an overwhelming cynicism overruns society. Not surprisingly, rulers seek to fill the ideological void by either reinvigorating a dying exceptionalism or creating a new one altogether. Whether it is reinvigoration or creation, the old never fully dies. While camouflaged, it is always present, reappearing in new forms to constrain and mold the act of transformation and future imaginings.

This is why old practices and beliefs can be invoked to transmogrify fresh historical events into novel and bizarre rituals. It is therefore not surprising to find out that when President Jonassaint summoned the gods of Vodou to defeat the overwhelming military power of the United States, he was not in reality departing from a common and habitual script—a script that is written not only in Port-au-Prince but also in Teheran as well as in Washington, D.C., and other centers of modernity. In fact, the flight from rationality and the espousal of religious, supernatural, and paranormal beliefs to explain reality are always a major ingredient of exceptionalism. As Michael Schatzberg has pointed out: "Reliance on alternative understandings of causality may be quite universal."[29]

After all, Nancy Reagan used the paid services of astrologer Joan Quigley to schedule President Ronald Reagan's meetings and to plan the day-to-day running of the White House. In the aftermath of the public disclosure that Quigley played a significant role in the making of American policies, the Reagans downplayed their dependence on astrology. The *Los Angeles Times* reported, however, that Quigley maintained that "she issued guidance, for pay, that went far beyond mundane scheduling to matters of diplomacy, Cold War politics and even the timing of the president's cancer surgery." Quigley continued: "I would participate in a more intimate way than the publicly recognized insiders of greatest importance."[30] American evangelicals who idolized Ronald Reagan were not amused with such revelations. The Reverend Robert P. Dugan Jr. of the National Association of Evangelicals declared to the *Washington Post* in 1988, "It's obviously troubling to think of national leadership being influenced by superstition. . . . It seems so medieval." And the *Post* reported that a "local megachurch leader went so far as to call astrologers agents of Satan."[31]

Evangelicals were more charitable in their support of the administration of George W. Bush, which was deeply embedded in Christian fundamentalism and implemented "political agendas that seem[ed] to be driven by religious motivations and biblical worldviews."[32] American exceptionalism has always been deeply anchored in religion and in the idea that the United States was God's country, but a more recent phenomenon of anointing certain presidents as the "chosen one" goes well beyond its traditional frontiers.

Kevin Phillips has pointed out that two peculiarities characterized President George W. Bush: "his salute from several religious-right leaders in 2001 as the national head of their movement and his seeming self-image as someone who spoke for God."[33] American exceptionalism has taken an odd turn not only because it has flirted with this theological extremism, but also because it has embraced the distinctive Christian fundamentalist understanding of economics, wealth, and inequality. As Phillips put it, "The tendency of the Christian right is to oppose regulation and justify wealth and relative laissez-faire, tipping its hat to the upper-income and corporate portions of the Republican coalition., Christian Reconstructionists go even further, abandoning most economic regulation in order to prepare the moral framework for God's return."[34]

In this evangelical version, American exceptionalism morphs into a celebration of unfettered capitalism embraced and financed by a class of right-wing Christian plutocrats. This fusion of religion and wealth is partly responsible for the 2016 election of Donald Trump, the "philandering billionaire and reality TV star," which evangelicals describe as an act of God. In fact, they believe that Trump himself is the "chosen one."[35] Liberty University in Lynchburg, Virginia, one of the prominent intellectual institutions of the Christian-right, produced a movie telling the story of Trump's divine selection. Entitled *The Trump Prophecy*, the movie reveals how Mark Taylor, a retired fireman from Florida, heard the voice of God tell him that Trump was the anointed one. As *The Guardian* reported, "Between graphic nightmares featuring demonic monsters and hellish flames, Taylor received a message from God in April 2011, while he was surfing television channels. As he clicked to an interview with Trump, Taylor heard God say: 'You are hearing the voice of the next president.'"[36]

Trump "the chosen" is not an isolated and fringe phenomenon. In fact, Franklin Graham, the prominent evangelist and son of Billy Graham, who counseled and befriended presidents from the 1970s until his death in 2018, declared after praying and traveling across the United States that he knew "that God was going to do something this year. . . . And I believe that at this election, God showed up." And Graham added in his Facebook page: "Did God show up? In watching the news after the election, the secular media kept asking 'How did this happen?' 'What went wrong?' 'How did we miss this?' Some are in shock. Political pundits are stunned. Many thought the Trump/Pence ticket didn't have a chance. None of them understand the God-factor."[37]

Thus, while the theme of God remains a constant in American exceptionalism, evangelicals are giving it new directions and meanings. On the opposite side of the spectrum, a segment of the so-called millennials is embracing witch-craft in its "resistance" to President Trump and his conservative policies. In fact, some witches have placed the ritual hex on President Trump and U.S. Supreme Court justice Brett Kavanaugh.[38] While this is still a minority move-ment, it has an estimated 1.5 million adherents and is larger than the Presbyte-rian Church (USA). It is difficult to know whether this modern resurgence of witchcraft is symptomatic of an increasingly powerful generational reappraisal of exceptionalism. Clearly, however, the Trump presidency has alarmed not just millennials but also the neo-conservative and liberal establishments; both are now opportunistically united in celebrating American militarism and inter-ventionism against what they perceive as the president's isolationism and sur-render to Russia's Vladimir Putin.[39]

The organic intellectuals of America are indeed fearful that Donald Trump is "hypercharging" the "unraveling" of the post–World War II foreign policy consensus.[40] He is transforming the concepts of "leadership and security part-nerships"[41] that were the pillars of American hegemony into shibboleths and replacing them with a dangerous strategy of "retrenchment" nurtured by a "mix of nationalism, unilateralism and xenophobia."[42] In the eyes of Antony J. Blinken and Robert Kagan, the consequences of Trump's new "isolationism" will be dire, engendering global disorder, anarchy, and pandemonium: "If the United States abdicates its leading role in shaping international rules and institutions—and mobilizing others to defend them—then one of two things will happen: Some other power or powers will step in and move the world in ways that advance their interests and values, not ours. Or, more likely, the world will descend into chaos and conflict, and the jungle will overtake us, as it did in the 1930s."[43]

This fear of an America no longer interested in both remaining "the indis-pensable nation" and projecting its global power appears quite overblown. It is difficult to understand how America is "retrenching" when Congress approved a $716 billion national defense budget for 2019 at the urging of the Trump administration. This budget represented an increase of 2.3 percent in national defense spending over 2018, which itself was a 10.4 percent increase over the budget of 2017.[44] In fact, America spends more on national defense "than China, Russia, Saudi Arabia, India, France, United Kingdom, and Japan combined."[45] Moreover, it is estimated that in 2018, the United States has some "800 formal military bases in 80 countries," and "138,000 soldiers stationed around the globe."[46] The claims of America's retreat from its imperial role are thus at best premature if not entirely hollow.

While the ideology of exceptionalism may change under Trumpism, it is unlikely that its core belief in the unique moral, economic, and strategic virtues of the United States will cease. This is especially the case with America's his-torical embrace of market capitalism, which has become a form of idolatry of both the stock market and the deserving wealth of "risk-taking" entrepreneurs.

For instance, Ruchir Sharma, the chief global strategist and head of the Emerging Markets Equity team at Morgan Stanley Investment Management, attributed the bullish United States stock market of 2018 to how well "America has done," and crediting it to another instance of "American exceptionalism."[47] Similarly the exceptional growth of inequalities[48] at home and abroad[49] is now celebrated as the good work of visionary innovators.[50] These innovators represent at best 1 percent of the population, but they devour an obscenely disproportionate share of the national wealth, leaving very little for the rest. As Chuck Collins reports:

> Since 1975, there have been extraordinary gains in productivity. But over half of US wage earners have not shared in the fruits of their labors. In 1970, the bottom half of wage earners, roughly 117 million adults, made an average of $16,000 a year in current dollars. By 2014, earnings for the bottom half of households had remained virtually unchanged, bumping up slightly to $16,200. Over the same period, the incomes of the top 1 percent tripled, from average annual wages of $400,000 to $1.3 million.
>
> The result is persistent poverty at the bottom, a work treadmill for low-wage workers, and a squeeze on middle-class workers. . . . A growing number of low-wage workers are toiling longer hours and taking on debt to survive economically.[51]

Far from deploring these economic realities, the new gospel of wealth hails them as salutary means to increase competition and provoke losers into doing better. Inequalities generate affluence; they reward risk takers and job creators to remain permanently driven to accumulate, invest, and innovate. The growing chasm between the 1 percent and the "rest" is not the result of a zero-sum economy. On the contrary, that chasm is not a danger but rather an asset for continued prosperity. Edward Conard—author of the best-seller *The Upside of Inequality* and a founding partner at Bain Capital, where he worked and befriended Mitt Romney, the former Republican governor of Massachusetts and presidential candidate—summarized well the *geist* of our current epoch:

> In truth, the outsized success of America's 1 percent has been the chief source of growth exerting upward pressure on domestic employment and wages. The success of America's 1 percent is an asset, not a liability. . . . Scrutinizing only the successful 1 percent (or 0.1 percent, or 0.01 percent) ignores the true cost of success, namely the cost of failure. Ignoring the cost of failure creates a distorted view of the value of success. . . . Success diminishes the status of others. Loss of status drives many status seekers to regain their lost status by taking ill-advised risks. More risk-taking produces innovation that is beneficial to all of us.[52]

This celebration of extreme inequalities indicates the chameleonic nature of exceptionalism. In fact, what is striking about exceptionalism is its extreme plasticity; this is especially the case in times of crisis when embattled rulers invoke, reconfigure, or abjure key pieces of its repertoire to reinvigorate or establish their hegemony. Exceptionalism's plasticity stems from its foundational origins, which are themselves rooted in nebulous and malleable concepts such as uniqueness, nationalism, citizenship, heroism, ancestry, and religion. The meaning of these concepts has clearly changed with the passage of time. Social and political struggles, economic transformations, as well as cultural upheavals and technological revolutions have all contributed to reinterpretations of the original script.

While exceptionalism seems to have a similar repertoire of notes in the United States and Haiti, the critical difference between the two is that the notes of the latter played virtually exclusively on its territory and with decreasing audibility, while the former's were exceedingly loud and overwhelming both at home and abroad. As Haiti found out, its exceptionalism was no match for American power, which the United States exercised at will to assert whatever purposes it espoused. As an empire, the United States has used its exceptionalism to advance multilateral cooperation, unilateral military interventions, humanitarian assistance, and democratic promotion or open and secretive support for dictatorships. It also has the capacity to exempt itself from what it forcefully imposes on others. U.S. rulers of all stripes have condemned others for practices and behavior that they themselves have unabashedly espoused in the name of American exceptionalism. They have given themselves the right to wage unprovoked wars, use weapons of mass destruction, abduct and detain foreign citizens, torture suspected and real enemies, and meddle in other countries' politics and elections.[53]

American "exemptionalism" is thus not only consistent with American exceptionalism, but it systematically nurtures it. In this perspective, Trump's "America First" slogan is not a marked departure from historical precedents and an alleged bygone munificent multilateralism, but a more pronounced and vocal reaffirmation of U.S. imperialism. It rejects external dissent or opposition to what it deems to be its imperial interests and mocks international organizations that pretend to have the capacity to organize the world without its explicit consent. For instance, the United States has welcomed decisions and rulings of the International Criminal Court (ICC) when they corresponded to its interests; otherwise it has ignored and condemned them especially when they addressed its own potential violations. In fact, in a major speech to the Federalist Society, John Bolton, Trump's former national security adviser, designated the ICC a major threat to the United States because it was a "supranational tribunal that could supersede national sovereignties and directly prosecute individuals for alleged war crimes." He attacked the court for "targeting [not only] individual U.S. service members, but [also] America's senior political leadership." Bolton vowed the United States would "use any means

necessary to protect [its] citizens and those of [its] allies from unjust prosecution by this illegitimate court." Moreover, it would "not cooperate with the ICC.
[Instead, the United States would] provide no assistance to the ICC [and would]
not join the ICC." Bolton bluntly concluded that the United States "would let
the ICC die on its own. After all, for all intents and purposes, the ICC is already
dead to us."[54]

It is clear, however, that American exceptionalism can embrace "exemptionalism" not because of its global ideological and ideational hegemony, but rather
because it rests on structures of economic and military power second to none.
The so-called Russia-gate, which dominated American politics during the first
three years of the Trump presidency, illustrates well how the United States
places itself in a special and separate category that allows it to condemn others
for behaving exactly the same way it does. Indeed, as I already pointed out, the
alleged Russian meddling in the 2016 presidential elections—if it occurred at all
as a Kremlin-orchestrated strategy[55]—was typical of the very global policies
enacted by the United States itself to influence the politics of both friends and
foes.[56] In fact, the United States has meddled in world elections on a much more
systematic basis than the Soviet Union/Russia in modern history, as Dov
Levin's research demonstrates:

> Between 1946 and 2000, the US and the Soviet Union/Russia have intervened
> in about one of every nine competitive national-level executive elections.
> Partisan electoral interventions have been found to have had significant
> effects on election results, frequently determining the identity of the winner.
> Overt interventions of this kind have also been found to have significant
> effects on the views of the target public toward the intervener.... Overall,
> 117 partisan electoral interventions were made by the US and the USSR/Russia
> between 1 January 1946 and 31 December 2000. Eighty-one (or 69%) of these
> interventions were done by the US while the other 36 cases (or 31%) were con-
> ducted by the USSR/Russia.[57]

American organic intellectuals recognize this reality but argue that when
the United States intervenes it tends to do so to defend democracy and promote
the "good." Two former CIA figures, Steven L. Hall and Loch K. Johnson, were
interviewed by the New York Times, which reported this: "Russian and American interferences in elections have not been morally equivalent. American
interventions have generally been aimed at helping non-authoritarian candidates challenge dictators or otherwise promoting democracy. Russia has more
often intervened to disrupt democracy or promote authoritarian rule, they said.
Equating the two, Mr. Hall says, 'is like saying cops and bad guys are the same
because they both have guns—the motivation matters.'"[58]

While this incantation to American exceptionalism may resonate with the
American public, it is clear that only states with powerful material structures

can invoke such national myths and ideological convictions to legitimize their illegal making of history in and for other societies. In general, then, it is not exceptionalism as such that is capable of transforming the world, but rather the "infrastructural" strength that sustains it. On the other hand, exceptionalisms can be an invitation to change when the promise they contained is violated by social realities. In other words, when invocations to equality, solidarity, and liberty clash violently with individual experiences and expectations, collective mobilization for change, reform, or revolution may occur.

In times of crisis, aspects of exceptionalism lose their potency, and new interpretations of the dominant script mature underground; they take refuge in what James Scott has called the "infrapolitical" world.[59] This is the "unobtrusive realm of political struggle ... [where no] ... public claims are made, no open symbolic lines are drawn. All political actions take forms that are designed to obscure their intentions or to take cover behind an apparent meaning."[60] A "hidden transcript" of exceptionalism emerges "backstage" to both express in coded words outrage at the chasm between official script and reality and to contest dominant ideological forms. A new or revised exceptionalism is in the making, signaling that those who had hitherto been quiet have finally mustered the means, the resources, and the courage to break their silence. They explode into the public stage as a collective historical actor in one of "those rare moments of political electricity when, often for the first time in history, the hidden transcript is spoken directly and publicly in the teeth of power."[61]

This is not the place to study how political, economic, and geostrategic forces generate the type of systemic crisis that facilitates the emergence of collective action provoking partial or total reinterpretations of exceptionalism. Suffice it to say, however, that the civil rights movement in the United States in the 1960s[62] and the Lavalas insurgency[63] of the late 1980s in Haiti represent moments of such reinterpretations. African Americans and the marginalized majority of Haitians gave new meanings to old concepts of citizenship, equality, and democracy. They appropriated these concepts to expand the boundaries of inclusion to themselves. And yet political change is not caused by what Joseph W. Esherick and Jeffrey N. Wasserstrom call "symbol-laden performances whose efficacy lies largely in their power to move specific audiences."[64] In fact, as Sidney Tarrow has explained, "movements frame their collective action around cultural symbols that are selectively chosen from a cultural toolchest and creatively converted into collective action frames by political entrepreneurs.... For if the struggle between movements and their opponents was primarily symbolic, then a social movement could be understood as no more than a cognitive message center, either reviving old meanings from within a cultural tradition, or spinning new meanings out of leaders' imaginings."[65]

In this perspective, powerful narratives matter, but only when they are activated by a movement armed with a political strategy of collective action.

Without a movement and a strategy such narratives are mere echoes in the wilderness. For example, the blacks' struggle for full citizenship came to espouse the idiom of "rights" so prominently expressed in American exceptionalism but so consistently denied to them. African Americans who had been excluded for so long from the script's self-evident truth about the equality and the rights of human beings seized this old language to frame their own emancipation. The language, however, became effective only when it was "combined with an innovative collective action repertoire."[66] Tarrow is worth quoting again when he argues that there was a strategic reason why "rights became the central frame of the Civil Rights movement":

> Equal opportunity rights were a useful bridge, based on traditional American political rhetoric, between the movement's main internal constituency, the southern black middle class, and the white "conscience constituents" whose support was necessary to bolster it from the outside. Liberals were most easily appealed to by the contradiction between the value that America placed on rights and the denial of equal opportunity to African Americans. Rights had the dual function of building on previous consensus formation and of bridging the white liberals and black middle class from which the core of the movements came. . . . Cultural choices framed the movement around rights at the same time as a tactic was chosen that expanded the meaning of equal opportunity and transformed passivity into activism.
>
> From the 1950s on, the modest equal opportunity rights frame was accompanied by a highly dramatic and confrontational *practice*—nonviolent direct action. . . . It was not the grammar of rights, but the action of peaceful resistance, that turned cultural quiescence into action.[67]

The grammar itself is not only a part of, but it is also decisively shaped by the material structure of society. To that extent, the script of exceptionalism represents a type of *habitus*—what Pierre Bourdieu defines as the system of "dispositions acquired through experience" that shapes particular types of behavior at particular historical moments.[68] As I have argued elsewhere,[69] I interpret the concept of the *habitus* as a dialectical phenomenon that simultaneously structures and is structured by historical realities; it is a "structured structure" grounded in the material realities of a particular period. It engenders habit-forming practices and thoughts that correspond to the strategic possibilities opened to individuals and classes in a given historical moment. The *habitus* frames the field of the socially possible by generating historically determined expectations about "life chances";[70] thus, it erects culturally fabricated limitations to human action and shapes political predispositions. Ultimately, the *habitus* is rooted in society's material matrix. As Bourdieu explains, "Through the habitus, the structure which has produced it governs practice, not by the processes of a mechanical determinism, but through the mediation of the orientations and limits it assigns to the habitus's operations of invention. As an acquired system of generative schemes objectively adjusted to the particular conditions in which it is constituted, the habitus engenders all the thoughts, all the perceptions, and all the actions consistent with those conditions, and no others."[71]

This is not to deny the symbolic power of exceptionalism in habituating people to adopt certain beliefs and forms of behavior, but to emphasize that exceptionalism itself is not a gift from heaven, nor an ingrained and virtually immutable cognitive map of action. To take a cultural artifact and transform it into a causal agent is to ignore the political, economic, and geostrategic conditions that created it in the first place. Rather than explaining the social and historical origins of exceptionalism, the cultural paradigm generates a tautology: people behave according to the norms of exceptionalism because they adhere to the norms themselves. As Peter Hall has pointed out, "Unless cultural theories can account for the origins of . . . attitudes by reference to the institutions that generate and reproduce them, they do little more than summon up a *deus ex machina* that is itself unexplainable."[72]

There is nothing innate or intrinsic about citizens espousing or following the script of exceptionalism. In fact, when people embrace exceptionalism it is not necessarily because it is part of their particular cultural legacy, but rather because it is continuously nurtured to them by civic lessons, educational institutions, organic intellectuals, and a panoply of media platforms. Exceptionalism is thus a fabricated and resilient cognitive map that can adjust to changing times, but in rare occasions it can also be turned upside down and disintegrate. In this perspective, can the impact of large migrations of people from distinct cultures and political traditions have such transformative impact on the dominant script of exceptionalism?

In a paradoxical way, the imperial wars waged by the United States as well as recurring American hegemonic interferences in the politics of other nations have led to a boomerang effect whereby those at the receiving end of such wars and interferences become the new immigrants and citizens of America. Cherríe Moraga, the well-known Chicana feminist, essayist, and activist, explains well these contradictions of empire—how violent or secret interventions abroad create the boat peoples, refugees, and newcomers from the violated territories:

> When U.S. capital invades a country, its military machinery is quick to follow to protect its interests. This is Panama, Puerto Rico, Grenada, Guatemala. . . . Ironically, the United States' gradual consumption of Latin America and the Caribbean is bringing the people of the Americas together. . . . Every place the United States has been involved militarily has brought its offspring, its orphans, its homeless, and its casualties to this country: Vietnam, Guatemala, Cambodia, the Philippines. . . . Third World populations are changing the face of America.[73]

Clearly Haiti belongs in Moraga's list of countries victimized by American imperialism, and not surprisingly its citizens have increasingly sought refuge in America itself. This boomerang effect, as I argued earlier, has been a lifeboat to Haitians enduring unending financial and political crises. Had it not been for the diaspora's remittances, the country's economy would have collapsed. This external financial dependence has in turn transformed the nature of Haitian exceptionalism by diluting notions of sovereignty. While nationalist appeals have some resonance at home, they are increasingly irrelevant to the alarming necessity of survival in an environment of extreme scarcity. At the same time, the diaspora in its new foreign "setting" fabricates a cultural and ideological *bricolage* from both its original home and its imperial host; it sets roots in America while longing for a virtually impossible return to Haiti. For the Haitian émigrés, Haitian exceptionalism has become largely imaginary—a dream of an invented history that eases the sadness of a permanent departure and links past to present struggles in a new land.

Thus, by penetrating America, Haiti has redefined its own exceptionalism, but at the same time it has contributed to a form of creolization of America itself. I use the term "creolization" not in the typical Caribbeanist vein; it is not just a matter of *metissage* or "rhizomatic" connections[74] between African and Euro-American-settler cultures, or of unequal "borrowings" generating changes in that which was borrowed.[75] Following Sidney Mintz and Richard Price, I want to say that such cultural exchanges do not really involve "borrowing" as such but rather a new configuration of habits, practices, and behaviors; and thus, the words "'creating' or 'remodeling' may be more precise."[76] Moreover, this "creating" and "remodeling" is not merely a different form of twenty-first-century acculturation, but it represents a major racial transfiguration of what had hitherto been a white-dominated society. In fact, it embodies the political and demographic effects of the penetration of peripheral cultures and people into the imperial core. In the current era, the former's absorption into the latter is on more equal and voluntary terms; it is a portent of a more cosmopolitan outlook, albeit without fundamental structural changes in the core itself.

America's dominant Euro-culture is thus not a frozen whole but is increasingly becoming a product of accommodation, resistance, and change to the new arrivals from its own "backyard" and beyond. It expresses a disparate and contradictory amalgam of ever-changing experiences and conditions; it can no longer simply absorb, distill, and reject "the other." Thus, the ongoing process of creolization will transform the current white majority into a minority by 2045. At this time, the U.S. Census Bureau projects that "whites will comprise 49.7 percent of the population in contrast to 24.6 percent for Hispanics, 13.1 percent for blacks, 7.9 percent for Asians, and 3.8 percent for multiracial populations."[77] Among the youth—those under eighteen—creolization has already arrived, as in this so-called postmillennial population, "minorities will outnumber whites in 2020."[78]

This demographic revolution may reconfigure if not altogether alter the notions of manifest destiny and civilizing foreign military interventions that have nurtured American exceptionalism. The new "creole" American citizens are unlikely to put up with or defend the racist undertones that such notions entail.

On the other hand, America's creolization is not necessarily subversive of the status quo; when immigrants become Americans, they may repudiate the original racist or xenophobic script of exceptionalism and embrace new cosmopolitan identities, but they may still espouse the hard structures of capitalism and their inevitable imperial vocation. Thus, while the emerging multicultural American exceptionalism may see the demise of its Anglo-Saxon mythologies, it may continue to extol the old tradition of military and economic expansionism. To paraphrase W.E.B. Du Bois, the problem of imperialism in the twenty-first century may not be the "color line." In fact, a revisionist version of the doctrine of the Responsibility to Protect (R2P) could take hold and justify continued imperial interventions in the very countries from which the new creolized American citizens hail from. A revised R2P might well embrace the idea that those in the diaspora have an obligation and mission to save the suffering masses of the departed country from the corruptions and repression of their despotic governments. At first sight this commitment appears noble and rooted in international solidarity, and yet it has all the trappings of imperial principles, which have legitimated wars to allegedly prevent both humanitarian crises and the spread of so-called weapons of mass destruction in "failed" or "rogue" states.[79]

The large American military intervention that restored Jean-Bertrand Aristide's presidency in 1994 illustrates well this paradox. After initially encouraging and supporting the intervention, the vast majority of the Haitian diaspora began to criticize it soon afterward.[80] The view that the intervention was a humanitarian, democratic, and emancipatory mission soon gave way to disparaging condemnations of its disappointing results. In fact, this ambivalence on the use of American force to oust the military junta that had overthrown Aristide was shared by Aristide himself. In the aftermath of the coup, Aristide believed that economic sanctions and international pressure would eventually lead to the fall of General Cédras's regime and to his own return to power.

Thus, publicly and privately, Aristide opposed any U.S. or foreign military intervention to reinstate him. He declared in October 1991 that he rejected such intervention because it raised "ugly memories in Haiti."[81] However, with the passage of time and the continuing refusal of the junta to step down, Aristide changed his mind; in his private pronouncements he became increasingly receptive to an international use of force. In fact, Aristide endorsed the United Nations resolution authorizing the use of force to restore his government in July 1994,[82] only a month after claiming that he was "against a military invasion" and that he would "never, never, and never again" agree to be brought back to power through a foreign intervention.[83]

Aristide's contradictory positions reflected well-founded fears that the massive support the intervention enjoyed initially would soon dissipate, as it would inevitably raise the specter of imperialism. Indeed, the popular euphoria that greeted the U.S. Marines–led return of Aristide was short-lived; both Aristide and his supporters felt hamstringed by the American forces, which were no longer perceived as "liberators" but rather as "occupiers" who were eventually replaced by a "peacekeeping" force of the United Nations. The relationship between Aristide and the foreign community deteriorated to the point that when he was reelected president in 2000, he was perceived by the latter as a dangerous left-wing tyrant. In fact, in 2004 Aristide was compelled to resign from office under strong domestic opposition fueled and financed by his former allies the United States, France, and Canada. He was unceremoniously sent into exile and put on an American plane with no clear destination; he eventually landed in Bangui, in the Central African Republic.[84] This time, Aristide could no longer count on the help of a divided diaspora to influence American foreign policy like it did a decade earlier. American military forces with some additional French troops occupied the country again, and once more they were replaced by a new peacekeeping operation of the United Nations.

It seems clear therefore that the diaspora's policy preferences for Haiti tend to be enacted only when they happen to align with traditional American imperial preferences. In fact, President Clinton's decision to send some 20,000 marines to Haiti to restore Aristide's presidency reflected more geostrategic considerations than domestic public opinion, let alone the Haitian diaspora's demands. When Clinton gave the green light to the military intervention in 1994, his administration had suffered what American policy makers described as a humiliating withdrawal from Somalia. After allegedly caving in to African bands of terrorists, the United States began suffering from a so-called Somalia syndrome. Not surprisingly, a rather "cheap" use of massive force against a weak state as Haiti would offer Clinton the opportunity to restore American will and prestige.[85] As David Malone has argued, "Military intervention in Haiti derived in part from a need by the Clinton administration to demonstrate domestically that the USA retained the will and capacity to act decisively on the international level, in the wake of the USA's withdrawal from Somalia and at a time when the USA was frustrated over the nature of the UN's involvement in the Former Yugoslavia."[86]

There is no reason to believe that the creolization of America will erase such strategic considerations. The "browning" of both the population and the government will change the racial makeup of society, but it will not necessarily change the nature of American capitalism, nor will it guarantee a dramatic, let alone progressive, cultural transformation. To believe in this inevitable progressive cultural transformation is to fall in the trap of a reductionist form of "identity politics."

CHAPTER 9

Identity Politics and Modern Exceptionalism

The conventional assumption among those espousing an unadulterated form of "identity politics" is that race, especially when it has historically been associated with a subordinate and exploited category of people, generates among them a distinctive community united by common beliefs, concerns, and interests. So, for instance, blackness creates a cultural identity among African Americans that transcends their social and economic divisions and thus unites them as a race. Similarly, at the other side of the spectrum, those who have invoked race to legitimize their privileged and dominant position in a social order have created a common supremacist identity among all those sharing their color. Thus, in both cases race becomes the transcendent category mobilizing on the one hand the oppressed struggling to gain their freedom and equality, and on the other the oppressors using their power to maintain the supremacist order or at best reform it in patronizing ways.

And yet as I have already pointed out, neither "blackness" nor "whiteness" as such explains anything; patterns of exploitation and repression have marked the history of both black rule in Haiti and white *Herrenvolk* democracy in the United States. In fact, the exercise of cruel and predatory practices over black populations is not the exclusive monopoly of white overlords; black rulers in Haiti and Africa have been guilty of similar transgressions.

Clearly, however, the history of African enslavement in America that rigidly demarcated "free" white labor from black slave labor generated a particular ideology of race and racism in the United States based in part on the assumption that there is a black American exceptionalism embedded in a black culture that transcends class. As David Wilkins puts it:

Unlike whites, blacks cannot forget for one minute that they have a race; a race that links each individual black to the fate of every other black. . . , Black

107

Americans know that their individual chances for achieving success in America are linked to the advancement of the race as a whole. As a result, blacks have looked to each other for both mutual protection and the kind of love and support that is essential to human flourishing. Not surprisingly, this process has produced distinctive styles and modes of expression, attitudes and beliefs about political and social issues, customs and practices, that are recognized and understood (if not always agreed with or followed) by a broad range of blacks across geographic and social lines.[1]

Seemingly, then, there is a "black culture" that reflects the racial hierarchy inherited from the days of slavery and the period of Reconstruction.[2] By offering whites of all social classes a separate and privileged position over all blacks, both slavery and the failed Reconstruction contributed to create a white "labor aristocracy." This is not to say that interracial class solidarity was impossible, but rather that the political, material, and moral environment of the late nineteenth and early twentieth centuries made it quite implausible. The "wages of whiteness" were quite functional to white ruling classes as they consolidated white unity and supremacy and undermined challenges from below.[3] Race has thus played a vital role in deflecting working-class insurgencies by giving to white labor a superior status and material advantages over their black counterparts. As W.E.B. Du Bois put it in a much celebrated and quoted passage of *Black Reconstruction in America*:

> It must be remembered that the white group of laborers, while they received a low wage, were compensated in part by a sort of public and psychological wage. They were given public deference and titles of courtesy because they were white. They were admitted freely with all classes of white people to public functions, public parks, and the best schools. The police were drawn from their ranks, and the courts, dependent on their votes, treated them with such leniency as to encourage lawlessness. Their vote selected public officials, and while this had small effect upon the economic situation, it had great effect upon their personal treatment and the deference shown them. White schoolhouses were the best in the community, and conspicuously placed, and they cost anywhere from twice to ten times as much per capita as the colored schools. The newspapers specialized on news that flattered the poor whites and almost utterly ignored the Negro except in crime and ridicule.[4]

To Du Bois's "public and psychological wage" must be added the realities of deep and continuing inequalities between whites and African Americans. For those who inflict it on others, racism is not merely the power of contempt and the political and institutional authority to unleash it on its victims; it erects also a material structure of wealth and deprivation that survives well beyond its legal demise. In their report *Dreams Deferred: Enriching the 1 Percent Widens*

the Racial Wealth Divide, Chuck Collins, Dedrick Asante-Muhammed, Emanuel Nieves, Josh Hoxie, and Sabrina Terry have documented well the magnitude
of inequalities facing African Americans in the aftermath of Barak Obama's
presidency—the era that some had naively defined as postracial:

> Between 1983 and 2016, the median Black family saw their wealth drop by
> more than half after adjusting for inflation, compared to a 33 percent increase
> for the median White household. The median Black family today owns
> $3,600—just 2 percent of the $147,000 of wealth the median White family
> owns. In other words, the median White family has 41 times more wealth
> than the median Black family. . . . If the trajectory of the past three decades
> continues, by 2050 the median White family will have $174,000 of wealth,
> while Black median wealth will be $600. The median Black family is on track
> to reach zero wealth by 2082.[5]

Present and future economic trends are thus bleak for African-Americans;
in fact, write Collins, Asante-Muhammed, Nieves, and Hoxie in another
report, if "average Black family wealth continues to grow at the same pace it has
over the past three decades, it would take Black families 228 years to amass the
same amount of wealth White families have today."[6] These racial inequalities
should not mask, however, the growing material gap within the black population. A process of class formation has divided African Americans into a small
"well to do" and a much larger "less well off" segment. Drawing from the
research of William Julius Wilson,[7] Henry Louis Gates Jr., has argued this:

> When adjusted for inflation to 2014 dollars, the percentage of African-
> Americans making at least $75,000 more than doubled from 1970 to 2014, to
> 21 percent. Those making $100,000 or more nearly quadrupled, to 13 percent
> (in contrast, white Americans saw a less impressive increase, from 11 to
> 26 percent). Du Bois's "talented 10th" has become the "prosperous 13 percent."
> But the percentage of Black America with income below $15,000 declined
> by only four percentage points, to 22 percent.
> In other words, there are really two nations within Black America. The
> problem of income inequality . . . is not between Black America and White
> America but between black haves and have-nots, something we don't often
> discuss in public in an era dominated by a narrative of fear and failure and
> the claim that racism impacts 42 million people in all the same ways.[8]

Thus, while racism persists and generates huge racial inequalities, it is clear
that black and white Americas are fraught with their own class divisions and
contradictions. And yet appeals to race and racism remain a pervasive and
effective means of electoral mobilization in American politics. Both the Democratic and Republican parties continue to purposefully ignore the chasm of class
to manipulate race and intensify bonds of cultural identities. By concentrating

on "identities" and "social" issues to the detriment of class, they separate the population into a collection of isolated silos. In fact, the type of identity politics practiced by both parties is a revised and modernized version of Thomas Jefferson's racial exceptionalism. For Jefferson, as Anthony Appiah has argued, race was "*a concept that is invoked to explain cultural and social phenomena . . . the alleged political impossibility of a citizenship shared between white and black races.*"[9] While the idea of the impossibility of a citizenship shared between white and black races and its accompanying quasi-biological determinism are no longer entertained by most Americans, current popular concepts of, on the one hand, "white privilege" and "white supremacy," and on the other, a "postracial" or "color-blind" America, indicate the continued primacy of race in structuring political debate in America.

To avoid the trappings of race confinement, while stressing the decisive role of race in shaping contemporary America, a new perspective based on the "intersectionality" of all types of categories of oppression has crystallized.[10] As people have multiple identities, they are victims of different forms of domination depending on which identity they most saliently adopt and/or is assigned to them by the powers that be. Taking gender and race into consideration, Kimberle Crenshaw thus argues for the specificity of the experience of African American women:

> Black women can experience discrimination in ways that are both similar to and different from those experienced by white women and Black men. Black women sometimes experience discrimination in ways similar to white women's experiences; sometimes they share very similar experiences with Black men. Yet often they experience double discrimination—the combined effects of practices which discriminate on the basis of race, and on the basis of sex. And sometimes, they experience discrimination as Black women—not the sum of race and sex discrimination, but as Black women.[11]

Does intersectionality escape, however, from the ubiquity of race that has always trapped American exceptionalism? To a large degree, intersectionality birthed the Movement for Black Lives (M4BL), which has come to embody a different kind of politics that goes beyond race reductionism while paradoxically rooting its alternative vision of society in the very struggles of the most marginalized sectors of the African American community.[12] M4BL was created in 2013 in the aftermath of the police murder of eighteen-year-old Michael Brown in Ferguson, Missouri, and the acquittal of George Zimmerman, a neighborhood watch volunteer, who killed an African American teenager, Trayvon Martin, in Sanford, Florida.[13] By 2016, M4BL, which was well known for its hashtag "#BlackLivesMatter," developed into a powerful if diffuse radical political force in American politics.

While M4BL was initially a specific response to police brutality against black and LGBT communities, it expanded its vision to challenge not only the forces of order but also the overall carceral system, as well as the deep economic inequalities existing in the United States and the world. In fact, in August 2016, M4BL assembled a collective of more than fifty African American organizations to draft "A Vision for Black Lives: Policy Demands for Black Power, Freedom and Justice."[14] The vision articulates an antiracist, anticapitalist, and anti-imperialist program. It calls for, among other things, defunding the police, restructuring the judicial system, and eradicating mass incarceration and its criminalization of marginalized and poor people. Moreover, it demands both the redistribution of wealth and income through massive taxation of the top "one percent," and the end of American militarism and its war machine. "A Vision for Black Lives" has thus a clear understanding of the intimate connections between American racism, the capitalist economy, and its worldwide spread. It arrives at this conclusion by examining the social, cultural, and material conditions of the most marginalized sectors of society, which are disproportionately black.

Race and racism are thus the lens through which "A Vision for Black Lives" ultimately envisages the initial struggle for creating a new commonwealth no longer anchored in race itself. The liberation of African Americans from the brutal reach of state power, harsh incarceration, confinement to polluted areas, poor working and living conditions, and moral exclusion from the rest of society would liberate all irrespective of color, sexual orientation, and class. In this perspective, the emancipation of the most marginalized opens the door to universal emancipation:

> We believe in elevating the experiences and leadership of the most marginalized Black people, including but not limited to those who are women, queer, trans, femmes, gender nonconforming, Muslim, formerly and currently incarcerated, cash poor and working class, differently-abled, undocumented, and immigrant. There can be no liberation for all Black people if we do not center and fight for those who have been marginalized. While this platform is focused on domestic policies, we know that patriarchy, exploitative capitalism, militarism, and white supremacy know no borders. We stand in solidarity with our international family against the ravages of global capitalism and anti-Black racism, human-made climate change, war, and exploitation.[15]

By positing a marginalized blackness as the most marginalized condition, M4BL can thus see in the emancipation of blackness an inevitable universal emancipation. As some M4BL activists put it, "When Black lives matter, everybody lives better." In this view, the creation of a world devoid of race and racism begins with the acknowledgment of the centrality of race itself. Thus, Black Lives Matter uncovers multiple categories of oppression, including gender and class, but its overwhelming emphasis on race may generate divisions within and between the members of these categories. Ultimately, the centrality of race in the chain of grievances and injuries may well obscure universalist appeals and lead to a retreat into making redistributive demands specific to each group instead of challenging the general system of exploitation. In the process, M4BL, in spite of its calls for radical transformation, may end up trapped in a pattern of racial ontology that can easily be co-opted into the existing political and economic system. It would come as no surprise if the corporate ruling class, public authorities, and the wider white population would embrace the hashtag "#BlackLivesMatter" as a purely symbolic and self-evident emblem of cultural and moral "atonement," leaving untouched the material structures and its massive inequalities. In this sense, the demands of Black Lives Matter would be "normalized" into rather inoffensive proclamations of antiracism and a white flurry of guilt-ridden self-flagellations. At best, radical change would be reduced to the typical reallocation of resources between and within categories of marginalized people, leading to the upward mobility of select individuals from the oppressed themselves. As Adolph Reed has argued:

> Struggles for racial and gender equality have largely divested race and gender of their common sense verisimilitude as bases for essential difference. Moreover, versions of racial and gender equality are now also incorporated into the normative and programmatic structure of "left" neoliberalism. Rigorous pursuit of equality of opportunity exclusively within the terms of given patterns of capitalist class relations—which is after all the ideal of racial liberalism—has been fully legitimized within the rubric of "diversity." That ideal is realized through gaining rough parity in distribution of social goods and bads among designated population categories. As Walter Benn Michaels has argued powerfully, according to that ideal, the society would be just if 1 percent of the population controlled 90 percent of the resources, provided that blacks and other nonwhites, women, and lesbian, gay, bisexual, and transgender (LGBT) people were represented among the 1 percent in roughly similar proportion as their incidence in the general population.[16]

This type of inequality that divides subordinate groups by elevating some of their members to higher status has always been embedded in the logic of American capitalism. Racism in particular continues to fragment class solidarities among white and black workers, but now it can no longer ensure "black unity"—if it ever did—nor prevent the fusion of the white neoliberal bourgeoisie with its emerging black counterpart. Moreover, both the Democratic and Republican parties have manipulated racial identities to mobilize their respective constituencies. On the one hand, Democrats have managed to capture the "black vote" as well as generate a small class of elected black politicians, and on the other hand, Republicans have appealed to the "wages of whiteness" to keep their hold on the white electorate.[17] This is not to say that Democrats have not played the "race card" to attract the "white vote." In fact, on March 1, 1992, a few days before critical Democratic presidential primaries in Georgia, Colorado, and Maryland, Bill Clinton, in his quest to occupy the White House, decided to take a picture in front of Stone Mountain. Stone Mountain, the iconic monument to white supremacy, is described in a *New York Times* article as a "825-foot high granite dome . . . famous for many things: the Rushmore-esque relief of the Confederate leaders Robert E. Lee, Jefferson Davis and Stonewall Jackson; and the birthplace of the modern-day Ku Klux Klan."[18] This most "renowned historical marker" celebrating the Confederacy and slave owners was indeed the site chosen by Bill Clinton to pose for a picture with Georgia's Senator Sam Nunn and Governor Zell Miller in front of a group of mostly black prisoners.[19] Clinton's goal in this racist episode was twofold: to distance himself from the Democrats' "liberal brand" and accusations of being soft on "black criminals," and capture the so-called Reagan Democrats who had abandoned the Democratic Party to join the Republicans. Clinton's calculus proved right; he would get the support of African Americans while strengthening his white base.[20]

Thus, while the legal apparatus of the system of white supremacy is gone, race continues to weigh like a nightmare on the living; its invocation remains pervasive. As Barbara Fields has so poignantly put it, "Nothing handed down from the past could keep race alive if we did not constantly reinvent and re-ritualize it to fit our own terrain. If race lives on today, it can do so only because we continue to create and re-create it in our social life, continue to verify it, and thus continue to need a social vocabulary that will allow us to make sense, not of what our ancestors did then, but of what we ourselves choose to do now."[21]

The continued reinvention of race in American exceptionalism derives from the never-ending delineation of power in terms of identity; as whiteness became the reference to racism and privilege, it provoked the emergence of blackness as both a symbol of persecution and resistance. The injuries of white supremacy activated its victims to adopt the very identities imposed on them by their oppressors. These identities embodied what Wendy Brown called "wounded attachments."[22] Blackness acquired therefore contradictory tendencies; it generated solidarity and the aspirations of emancipation, but at the same time it fueled a false sense of unity and a belief that grievances were overwhelmingly of racial nature. The class-ridden nature of black America is easily dismissed for an "uplift" discourse reveling in the individual achievements of African Americans who "have made it." This erasure of class can therefore morph into a mere exhortation "to celebrate and demand accolades, career opportunities, and material accumulation for black celebrities and rich people—e.g., box office receipts for black filmmakers or contracts and prestigious appointments for other well-positioned black people."[23] Moreover, while black identity has created networks of insurgency among those who espoused it, its manifestation has also taken on a very personal and individualized form. As Judith Butler has pointed out, "Called by an injurious name, I come into social being, and because I have a certain inevitable attachment to my existence, because a certain narcissism takes hold of any term that confers existence, I am led to embrace the terms that injure me because they constitute me socially."[24]

Escape from oppression, humiliation, and subordination in the vessel of identity is thus fraught with contradictions; it can move forward, but it also can stall or regress. The "wounded attachments" of identity make its subjects both victim and insurgent; insurgent in the sense that those who had been excluded from the table wage their struggle to sit at that very table, but in this very act of emancipation they change little in the contours of the table or in its menu. This is not to minimize the mass struggles and victories against institutionalized and legalized white supremacy; in fact, they represented remarkable historical gains for greater justice and human dignity. These struggles alleviated the cruel, deep, and extensive injuries racism had inflicted on its victims, but they did not erase the systemic patterns of oppression, nor did they succeed in fully erasing race or racism. In fact, the benefits of "sitting at the table" were very unequally distributed; only a select group, a black bourgeoisie, could enjoy them. As Wendy Brown has pointed out:

> Identity politics . . . will appear not as a supplement to class politics, not as an expansion of Left categories of oppression and emancipation, not as an enriching augmentation of progressive formulations of power and persons . . . but as tethered to a formulation of justice that reinscribes a bourgeois (masculinist) ideal as its measure. . . . Identity politics may be partly configured by a peculiarly shaped and peculiarly disguised form of class resentment, a resentment that is displaced onto discourses of injustice other than class, but a resentment, like all resentments, that retains the real or imagined holdings of its reviled subject as objects of desire.[25]

Thus, the trajectory of identity politics can easily lead to a retreat from class and the reaffirmation of capitalism, both of which reinforce the fundamental structure of American exceptionalism. This is not to say that race or gender are unimportant markers of inequality and discrimination, but rather that privileging them masks the deep class divisions besieging each of them and ultimately obscures wider structural forms of inequality and oppression. It is not clear why more than fifty years after the civil rights movement, the slogan "I am Black," which assumes "the socially imposed identity," should empower "it as an anchor of subjectivity" and ultimately become "a statement of resistance," as Kimberle Crenshaw would have it. While "I am Black" is obviously "linked to celebratory statements like the Black nationalist slogan 'Black is beautiful,'"[26] there is no reason to believe that it can achieve more than just such a celebration of self. In fact, "I am Black" is now fully integrated into a rather innocuous ideology of "diversity" and co-opted into the repertoire of exceptionalism.[27]

The pursuit of diversity through race-based affirmative policies may, however, have paradoxical outcomes. These policies are bent on letting a black elite crash through the glass ceiling without transforming the deep structures of inequality. As William Darity Jr., Ashwini Deshpande, and Thomas Weisskopf explain, "An important goal of affirmative action is to desegregate and diversify the upper strata of a society. Much evidence suggests that the ability to meet qualifying criteria in desired positions—such as a seat in an elite college or a job in an elite profession—depends significantly on social class position."[28]

Darity and his colleagues, however, draw the conclusion that the increasingly limited application of race-conscious policies enhances the virulence of racism. In their view, adopting class-based instead of race-conscious programs to improve the life chances of *all* subordinate people has adverse consequences for those whose specific ethnic or racial background had historically confined them to marginalized status. As they explain, "Our analysis demonstrates that substituting class-based for group-based, affirmative action can compound the marginalization of a subaltern group by screening out of consideration the more class-advantaged members of the group, who are the ones most likely to qualify for elite positions. Thus, class-based affirmative action is even more likely to reinforce beliefs about the inferiority of the subaltern group than race-based affirmative action."[29]

It is not clear at all, however, that this conclusion is warranted. While African Americans are very poorly represented at the top of the class structure of the United States, their greater presence in these upper echelons is unlikely to diminish the virulence of racism. In fact, the contrary is more plausible. As Ibram Kendi put it, "Everyone who has witnessed the historic presidency of Barack Obama—and historic opposition to him—should know full well that the more Black people uplift themselves, the more they will find themselves on the receiving end of a racist backlash. Uplift suasion, as a strategy for racial progress, has failed."[30] Thus, the ascendancy of Obama to the presidency and the fact that a black family occupied the White House seemed to indicate that significant progress had been achieved in erasing racial discrimination, but this progress has generated strong resentment in certain segments of the white population that still cannot fathom such historical development. The development of antiracism is not unilateral; neither is it inevitably linear. Kendi may be right in asserting that what he saw in the Obama phenomenon was "two distinct historical forces . . . a dual and dueling history of racial progress and the simultaneous progression of racism." He saw "the antiracist force of equality and the racist force of inequality marching forward, progressing in rhetoric, in tactics, in policies."[31]

It is therefore not surprising to discover that a growing white backlash against race-conscious policies has unleashed calls to stop affirmative action, which is likened to "reverse discrimination." Significant segments of the white population perceive these policies as unfairly privileging "undeserving" African Americans. Race-conscious strategies elevating African Americans to the "higher circles" can thus exacerbate racial tensions; in fact, they have been easily manipulated by politicians and white nationalists to stoke the flames of racism. Indeed, some analysts have argued that Trump's election was symptomatic of a strong undercurrent of a white backlash. Tyler T. Reny, Loren Collingwood, and Ali A. Valenzuela have found strong "evidence that a non-trivial number of both working class and non-working-class white voters did switch their votes in the 2016 election and that this vote switching was associated more with racial and immigration attitudes than economic factors."[32]

And yet the racist undercurrent explains only partially why whites and particularly white working-class folks voted for Trump; it does not fully account for the fact that significant numbers of these very folks voted for Obama and then four years later shifted their allegiance to Trump.[33] The point here is that the neoliberal patterns of globalization of the past forty years have caused economic, political, and cultural distress in the white working class, which is now increasingly alienated from established parties and discourses.[34] Feeling thoroughly marginalized and ignored, the folks of the white working-class vote, when they do at all, for candidates who seem to listen to their voices and care about their plight. As Justin Gest explains in *The New Minority: White Working Class Politics in an Age of Immigration and Inequality*:

> Ultimately, contrary to conventional portrayals, white working class voters are rational. They seek representatives who care about their grievances. They seek platforms that act on these grievances. And they respond to parties and organizations that invest in them with time, resources, and candidates. This is not different from any other sector of the electorate. The difference is that . . . social and economic forces have isolated the white working class as a political constituency, to the extent that many in this demographic feel like a peripheral afterthought in a country they once defined. A group with a powerful vote has thus been neglected, and populists are beginning to take notice.[35]

Thus, a convergence of real grievances and an undercurrent of racism, combined with a sense that the Obama years changed little in their depressed conditions,[36] explain why significant segments of the white working class embraced Trump's right-wing populism. The fact that for eight years Obama and his black family called the White House *their* house meant that crude appeals to race resonated with parts of the white population's quest to delegitimize both the election and the power of the first black president. But that in itself should not mask the hard reality that under Obama's rule little changed in the deep structures of inequality characterizing neoliberal capitalist America. Obama symbolized simultaneously the triumphant moment and the crushing defeat of diversity. Thus, at the end of his term in office and after he had appointed one of the most "diverse" administrations in U.S. history, which included an African American attorney general and an African American as cabinet secretary of Homeland

Security, the first black president had failed to redress any of the deep and structural inequalities besieging America. In fact, neither black America nor poor America was really better off when Barack Obama ceded the reins of power to Donald Trump. Diversity had shown its obdurate class limitations, but it remains an increasingly powerful element of American exceptionalism.

Diversity, however, sings its melody with an upper-class accent. Lower classes, whether they are black or white, are increasingly perceived by both liberals and conservatives as dysfunctional, lazy, amoral, and addicted to alcohol and drugs. Hillary Clinton views them as "deplorables" when they are Caucasians, and "super-predators" when they are African Americans. In the era of Donald Trump, the conservative columnist Kevin Williamson's depiction of the white working class is not that different from that of the so-called liberal "resistance," and it echoes the common ruling class's conceptions of the black "underclass":

> If you spend time in hardscrabble, white upstate New York, or eastern Kentucky, or my own native West Texas, and you take an honest look at the welfare dependency, the drug and alcohol addiction, the family anarchy—which is to say, the whelping of human children with all the respect and wisdom of a stray dog—you will come to an awful realization. It wasn't Beijing. It wasn't even Washington, as bad as Washington can be. It wasn't immigrants from Mexico, excessive and problematic as our current immigration levels are. It wasn't any of that.
>
> Nothing happened to them. There wasn't some awful disaster. There wasn't a war or a famine or a plague or a foreign occupation. Even the economic changes of the past few decades do very little to explain the dysfunction and negligence—and the incomprehensible malice—of poor white America.... The white American underclass is in thrall to a vicious, selfish culture whose main products are misery and used heroin needles. Donald Trump's speeches make them feel good. So does OxyContin.[37]

Except when it applies to the denigrated and marginalized victims of society, class is the erased category of American exceptionalism that in turn celebrates cultural and racial diversity and eclipses structural inequalities. In this classless vision, those who "fail to make it" are slothful, dysfunctional, and morally reprehensible. Their failures are of their own making. American exceptionalism, however, extolls everyone else as a normal, responsible member of the nebulous middle class, or as accomplished entrepreneurs of a deserving exclusive small upper elite.

In broad terms, middle class implies being neither from the lower nor the upper 20 percent of the income brackets, according to the Pew Research Center. However, writes Anne Sraders, in terms of income, "Pew Research Center has designated that a middle-class income is between 67% and 200% of the median income.... For the 2017 fiscal year . , , an income range of $41,000 and $132,000 is considered to be middle class. . . . Additionally, [for 2019] other reports using Pew data conclude that a middle class four-person household would be in the range of $46,960 to $140,900 in income."[38] In terms of wealth, Pew also quotes New York University professor Edward Wolff, who claims that those with "$0 to $401,000 are considered middle-class on the wealth spectrum."[39] To add more confusion to the matter, "both President Obama and President Trump have used the figure of $200,000 as the minimum for high-income tax rates," and the latter's "2016 tax plan delineated singles making $37,500 to $112,500 and couples making $75,000 to $225,000 to be middle class."[40]

Clearly the middle-class spectrum is phantasmagoric. How can a family with no wealth whatsoever be in the same category as one with over $400,000? This phenomenon is the effect of what might be defined as "classcraft," a term derived from the theoretical construct "racecraft" formulated by Barbara Fields and Karen Fields:

> [Racecraft] refers to mental terrain and to pervasive belief. Like physical terrain, racecraft exists objectively; it has topographical features that Americans regularly navigate, and we cannot readily stop traversing it. Unlike physical terrain, racecraft originates not in nature but in human action and imagination; it can exist in no other way. . . .
>
> Our term racecraft invokes witchcraft. . . . Far from denying the rationality of those who have accepted either belief as truth about the world, we assume it. . . . The outcome is a belief that "presents itself to the mind and imagination as a vivid truth."[41]

In this perspective, classcraft is an ideological fabrication of widely held beliefs resembling a form of magical thinking about either the absence of class or its subsumption in the nebulous and all-encompassing middle class. By invoking middle class, American exceptionalism denies the class-ridden nature of the United States and deflects attention from deep-seated inequalities to the rather harmless pursuit of diversity.[42] Similarly, by generally rejecting the concept of ruling class, it denies the clear relationship between control and ownership of capital and political preponderance in the making of public policy. As political scientists Benjamin I. Page, Larry M. Bartels, and Jason Seawright have demonstrated, what they call wealthy Americans, economic elites, or affluent citizens, and I dub the ruling class—those who have at least $40 million in net worth—are overwhelmingly opposed to redistributionist policies, higher taxes, and any nationalization of corporate firms. They are significantly more conservative on economic policies, though they may be culturally more liberal, than average Americans.[43] In short, they embrace enthusiastically the ideological slogan of the times: "Growth is a rising tide that lifts all boats."

What wealthy Americans prefer matters greatly, because they are in fact the ruling class; they are the people who enjoy an overwhelming preponderance in governmental decision-making processes. They are actively engaged in politics, finance political campaigns, have easy access to office holders, and frame public issues. They are simply more equal than the average citizen. As Gilens and Page explain:

> When the preferences of economic elites and the stands of organized interest groups are controlled for, the preferences of the average American appear to have only a minuscule, near-zero, statistically non-significant impact upon public policy....
>
> Furthermore, the preferences of economic elites ... have far more independent impact upon policy change than the preferences of average citizens do. To be sure, this does not mean that ordinary citizens always lose out; they fairly often get the policies they favor, but only because those policies happen also to be preferred by the economically-elite citizens who wield the actual influence.[44]

Democracy, the fundamental promise of American exceptionalism, remains therefore largely unfulfilled. Again Gilens and Page: "In the United States ... the majority does not rule—at least not in the causal sense of actually determining policy outcomes."[45] But this is not necessarily a new phenomenon; clearly this was the situation for a long period of American history preceding the introduction of the universal franchise, which itself guarantees neither the rule of the majority nor that its interests will prevail over that of an oligarchic capitalist class. In fact, by virtue of its hegemony, this class has always controlled the general political processes of generating, framing, and enforcing state policies.[46] That the majority of the population may have limited input into the making of, and is disgruntled with, policy outcomes does not mean that it will challenge the structural foundation of the system. In fact, American popular disenchantment with existing institutions is striking; when polled between 2009 and 2019, Americans expressed an extremely low opinion of Congress, the media, and the presidency, ranging from lows in the single digits to highs in the mid-30 percent.[47] Thus, while the legitimacy of the system of governance is under strain, American exceptionalism, even in its current weakened state, can mask the severity of the strain and breathe continued life into the status quo.

Exceptionalism is thus an entrenched and resilient belief structure that can survive and indeed endure times of crisis. This is not to say that it is bound to remain unchanged. On the contrary, rulers can reinvent it to adjust it to new circumstances in order that it continue to cement the existing order. In other words, officeholders, organic intellectuals, the media, and the educational system can formulate new narratives co-opting some elements of emerging demands without affecting the fundamental structures of the reigning exceptionalism. As we noted previously, the celebration of "diversity" eclipsed the old legalized racism, but it does not alter the fundamental substance of political power or the material structures underpinning patterns of class domination.

The vitality of American exceptionalism is also a function of its global hegemony. The question facing the United States is whether it can sustain this global hegemony over the long term. Or more precisely, can it tolerate its relative decline without unleashing massive confrontations with emerging rival powers, especially China? As Larry Summers put it, "Can the US imagine a global system in 2050 in which its economy is half the size of the world's largest? Even if we can imagine it, could a political leader acknowledge that reality in a way that permits negotiation over what such a world would look like?"[48] In other words, is the undisputed military and economic supremacy of the American empire indispensable for the continued strength of its exceptionalism? While this is not the place to discuss whether the United States is facing an inevitable decline, it seems unlikely—if recent history is any guide—that any American leader would abandon the country's "imperial mission." American exceptionalism is simply too imbricated in the fabric of American society and institutions to be negotiated away in a cosmopolitan gesture.

What is striking also is that in spite of Haiti's utter institutional and economic fragility, its exceptionalism still occupies a place in the nation's imaginary. Even if they sound increasingly hollow under the cold facts of extreme dependence and cultural hybridity, old notions of race, blackness, Africanness, and national sovereignty continue to resonate among Haitians and the diaspora. Ironically, Haitian exceptionalism keeps on inspiring Haitians precisely because its main themes are no longer a living reality. Haitian exceptionalism is now a form of magical realism filling the void created by the persistent and debilitating crises afflicting the country. Similarly, President Trump's slogan, "Make America Great Again," inebriates his supporters by appealing to a past that never was and thus is impossible to restore. Trump and his followers, however, are not alone in fabricating narratives that appropriate the nationalistic and chauvinistic elements of American exceptionalism. Their opponents, in their self-styled "resistance," are inventing tales of foreign aggression by manipulating America's Russophobia to impugn Trump's election and the country's deep social, cultural, economic, and racial divisions on Vladimir Putin's sinister machinations.[49] As Friedrich Hegel famously put it in the concluding paragraph of the preface to *The Philosophy of Right*, "The owl of Minerva spreads its wings only with the falling of the dusk."[50]

Thus, in both Haiti and the United States, defenders of exceptionalism have invoked phantasmagoric explanations to rationalize its increasing failings. The most common strategy is to blame alien powers for subverting its content and fragilizing the political and social order. While in Haiti, the *blans* is held responsible for the virtual systemic collapse of the country's institutions, in the United States, the Russophobian hold on the neoconservative and liberal imagination has become the easy explanation for Trump's election and the growth of an increasingly divisive and explosive identitarian movement.[51] This type of scapegoating exaggerates the extent of the malignant impact of foreign forces on domestic affairs and eases the mobilization of despondent constituencies while absolving rulers of their responsibilities. Moreover, it challenges neither the logic nor the parameters of the existing exceptionalist script; it simply tries to give it new life.

In sum, both American and Haitian exceptionalisms are in crisis, albeit in different degrees of decay. The latter is so estranged from the daily struggles and realities facing Haitians that it has entered a quasi-terminal agony relieved only by those seeking solace in imaginary glimpses of a glorious past. The former is ridden by contradictory interpretations but remains resilient; it is capable of co-opting new narratives in spite of the deep cultural fracture and numbing social inequalities that divide Americans. In both instances, the crisis has no predetermined outcome. On the one hand, however, the decomposition of Haiti's state does not seem to have an end, and it is difficult to envisage how its exceptionalism can survive for long except as a mere commemoration of a distant past; on the other hand, Americans are embroiled in a politics of identity that generates conflicting visions of their exceptionalism without offering a rupture with its dominant themes. Calls for an expansive and inclusive credo clash with reactionary counterclaims for the preservation of the status-quo. The question then is which vision will prevail; at best, it is likely to be a mere modernization of American exceptionalism, and at worst a hard reaffirmation of its old exclusionary self. It seems clear, nonetheless, that exceptionalism has a life of its own whether it is upheld by America's formidable material, military, and cultural structures, or by the mere imagination of communities etching a living in Haiti's environment of utter destitution. The question for Haitian exceptionalism is how long can it float in mid-air and continue to hypnotize the consciousness of people? It is dying, but of a very slow death. In fact, it may embody the last remnants of a final hope that Haitians may have for what the renowned intellectual Frankétienne has called *la douloureuse Haiti*. Celebrating the past, however, will do little for current and future generations.

In fact, Haitian exceptionalism is likely to generate nothing but vain appeals to national unity that will fail in the face of the massive chasm separating the small, well-off elite from the overwhelming poor majority. Moreover, nationalist calls against foreign intervention can no longer hide the utter dependency of the country on foreign assistance and the political elites' addiction to external military help when they happen to face popular risings or they seek to reclaim power. It is true that Haitians will continue to look at their revolutionary past with pride and sing the praises of the Avengers of the New World. They will continue to extol 1804 as the most radical emancipation that history had hitherto known, but the mere rhetorical exhortation of their exceptionalism will not suffice to cement their nation's multiple fractures,

CHAPTER 10

Conclusion

In this comparative study of American and Haitian exceptionalisms, I have sought to establish the contradictory significance of invented national narratives. They devise the "others" to create the "chosen"; the latter bar the former from their midst to fabricate an exclusive moral and cultural community. I have argued that while exceptionalisms are rooted in old materials, they are not frozen constructs; rulers—especially in conditions of crisis—adjust them to new historical circumstances. The powerful and their ideologues can change their idioms, and enlarge or restrict the circles of the "included." Barring a revolution, such transformations are a reconfiguration rather than a rupture with the original forms of exceptionalism. Thus, in times of relative normalcy, exceptionalist tropes and rationales are likely to persist.

When their power is endangered, rulers may effect what Antonio Gramsci called a "passive revolution,"[1] which involves crafting a "reconfiguration strategy" to reassert exceptionalism's hegemonic grip over society. Not all reconfiguration strategies are successful. Some fail, leaving a profound ideological vacuum in which no clear alternative crystallizes, while others engender unintended outcomes and thus pose potential perils for the continued effectiveness of exceptionalism. What is clear, however, is that insofar as such reconfigurations tend to enlarge the parameters of inclusion, they represent a concession on the part of the power holders. While reconfigurations are designed to mitigate the demands of those who had hitherto been marginalized, they nonetheless offer new opportunities to challenge patterns of injustice and the powers that be. Thus, reconfigurations alter the political and cultural landscape; they are reforms that are more than mere sham.

In general, only hegemonic ruling classes can manage this type of reconfiguration, because they have the political, material, and cultural capacity to relinquish or minimize the use of brute force and co-opt new groups into the system by universalizing their ideological claims. To that extent, a nation's exceptionalism may become more inclusive, and yet the exceptionalism's foundational logic remains unchanged. This is precisely why such reconfigurations should be viewed as successful passive revolutions; they require minimal concessions on the part of rulers. In the process, the governing class absorbs into the old order the masses' call for new social dispensations and policies. Ultimately, it is under the control of the dominant class that such reforms are enacted, and not surprisingly, they tend to be symbolic gestures to appease popular demands rather than ruptures with the status quo.

In this book I have argued that the material, cultural, and military arsenal at the disposal of the American ruling class has enabled it to adjust its exceptionalism to changing circumstances without altering its foundational principles or giving up much of its privilege. When marginalized groups claimed full citizenship and equal treatment under the law—whether it was the extension of the franchise to women in 1920 or to African Americans in 1965—exceptionalism became elastic and incorporated them into an amended dispensation. Diversity, without much attention paid to class hierarchies and the injuries they inflict, became the new shibboleth to co-opt and pacify ethnic minorities and gender insurrectionists. Exceptionalism was thus serving its old mission of transforming America into a unique and ever-changing imaginary utopia. For instance, in the Trump era, close to half the voting population chose to "make America great again," and the defeated other half—the self-proclaimed "resistance"—has been seeking to retake power by invoking both a return to America's old morality and odd Russophobian slogans. The continued vitality of American exceptionalism has accommodated these conflicting claims without ever challenging the structures of capitalism or the missionary and imperial nature of the republic.

American exceptionalism has always made America the virtuous nation in warfare or in peace, and branded America's lies as a necessary ethical choice to defend the higher interests of the state, not to mention freedom-loving people across the globe. Two former directors of the CIA, President George H. W. Bush, and Secretary of State Michael R. Pompeo, expressed at different times such self-congratulatory beliefs. In his 1992 State of the Union, Bush declared, "Much good can come from the prudent use of power. And much good can come from this: A world once divided into two armed camps now recognizes one sole and preeminent power, the United States of America. And this they regard with no dread. For the world trusts us with power, and the world is right. They trust us to be fair, and restrained. They trust us to be on the side of decency. They trust us to do what's right."[2]

If American power was the righteous force combatting "universally" condemned "rogue" nations, state deception was necessary to achieve this noble task. American lies have thus underwritten the grandeur of American exceptionalism. In 2019, in a moment of utter sincerity, Secretary of State Pompeo received the applause of an academic audience at Texas A&M University when he declared, "I was the CIA director. We lied, we cheated, we stole. It's—it was like—we had entire training courses. It reminds you of the glory of the American experiment."[3]

In contrast, Haiti's exceptionalism no longer embodies the lived experiences of its citizens even if it continues to resonate in their imaginary. The chasm between the celebrated national narrative and reality is such that it is difficult to conceive of Haitian exceptionalism as anything more than an escape from the country's current predicament and a longing for a glorious revolutionary past. Haitian rulers are now incapable of invoking the notions of national sovereignty, let alone what Jean Casimir has called "the sovereign people in the political structure."[4] Long gone are the days when Haitians could proclaim with Dessalines, "We must live independent or die."[5] Independence is not the only casualty of Haiti's persistent political, institutional, and economic crisis. The moral fabric of society is at stake, as officeholders, private agents, and firms succumb to the temptations of corruption and easy money, going well beyond Dessalines's famous admonition to simply "pluck the chicken, but make sure it does not cry out."[6] The process of "gangsterization" has not spared any sector of Haitian society; it reflects the elites' increasing dependence on privatized security forces for protecting life and property, on the one hand, and the difficulties of their weak domestic police surrogates and "outsourced" international "peacekeepers" in preventing a precarious social order from imploding, on the other hand. In fact, the state in an outer periphery such as Haiti has virtually lost the capacity to regulate and control its territory, even if it remains the central site for the illicit appropriation of public funds.[7]

These conditions of utter distress expose the material, political, and cultural fragility of the Haitian ruling class, which is incapable of offering a coherent national project that would reinvigorate the old scripts of an increasingly hollow exceptionalism. The viability of exceptionalism as a unifying myth mitigating social divisions and preserving the dominance of the ruling class is thus dependent on the hegemonic reach of the ruling class itself. In turn, to achieve this reach, the ruling class requires a real degree of autonomous material power with which to build a consensual cultural landscape upon which exceptionalism can germinate and flourish. Unlike the United States, Haiti has none of these attributes, and its exceptionalism no longer resonates with its citizens except as a memory of the epic struggles leading to 1804.

More than two hundred years afterward, Haitians are fleeing their country in search of an escape from their destitute conditions. Their plight echoes the famous Vodou song, "Sou Lan Me" ("On the Ocean"), that evokes the indignities and injuries that their ancestors suffered during the Middle Passage and now conjures the hardship of the "boat people" taking to the high seas in search of improved life chances:

On the ocean we are sailing
Agwé in Oyo
There will come a time when they'll see us
On the ocean we are sailing
They took our feet
They chained our two wrists
They dropped us in the bottom

Slave ship under the water
The ocean is bad
The ship is broken
It's ready to sink

Slave ship under the water
At the bottom of the ocean
It's covered in water
It's ready to sink

In the bottom of the ship
We are all one

In the bottom of the slave ship
If it sinks
No one will be saved
Agwe in Oyo
We're all on board
Don't you see we're trapped

We're trapped, papa, trapped
We're trapped Lasirèn, trapped[8]

The tragedy of being trapped in a sinking ship is a grim metaphor that resonates today in Haiti, as I have argued elsewhere.[9] And yet hope persists, as "Sou
Lan Me" insists that "there will come a time when they'll see us." This ability to
survive in the most depressing and injurious conditions is at the very roots of
Haitian history. In fact, it is the peoples' past and present, and most likely their
immediate future. The Vodou song "Depi m soti nan Ginen" ("Since I Left
Africa") tells this seemingly unending tale of struggles and strength:

Since I left Africa, people have been testing me
I am the root
Since I left Africa, people have been testing me
I am a great rock
I came from under the water, I fly up into the sky
When they thought they captured me, I turned to smoke

When they find out who I serve, the earth will tremble
When they learn my real name, the storm will thunder
I am the root
I am a great rock[10]

From the days of slavery to the present, survival has demanded the incon-
ceivable, like a rock flying and vaporizing, to elude capture. It has meant a form
of *marronage* to evade subjugation, abscond the reach of a predatory state, and
escape the deprivations of destitution. Thus, "being a great rock" has always
entailed negotiating survival in a hostile environment rather than simply living
in poverty. In a paradoxical way, "being a great rock" is a metaphor that is
deeply rooted in Haitian exceptionalism; it is the reverse side of the triumpha-
list celebration of the revolution of 1804. It reflects the hard and uninterrupted
struggles of a people first enslaved, then emancipated, and yet unremittingly
trapped in successive historical structures of oppression.

Exceptionalism can thus be both an exaltation of an invented glorious past,
or a heroic mask hiding national failure. What is also clear is that glory is portrayed as the inherent product of a people's unique genius, whereas failure is
caused not by the community's own deficiencies but rather by the interference
of nefarious external forces. Moreover, exceptionalism is full of silences and
obfuscations; so for instance, the American founders produced a constitution
that asserted the people's right to freedom and equality and celebrated their
revolutionary break from colonial oppression, while never mentioning slavery
as the mode of production fueling the prosperity of the new white *Herrenvolk*
they had themselves created.[11] Exceptionalism is important for what it narrates
and highlights, but also for what it ignores and masks. It erases the stains of
national history or reduces them to "paradoxes" and "contradictions" that
people dismiss as not truly constitutive of that history but merely as "unintended" or accidental products of otherwise "well intentioned policy-makers."
In this perspective, exceptionalism can transform criminal rulers into innocent victims of their own involuntary and unplanned actions.[12]

In both Haiti and America, those in power have manipulated exceptionalism to mask the authoritarian roots, the class rule, and the exclusionary
practices of their respective regimes. Whereas the impact of Haiti's exceptionalism has rarely extended much beyond its own small territorial space,
that of the United States has stretched globally, expressing a hegemonic
logic. This logic has, however, its pitfalls. As the ancient Greek historian
Diodurus Siculus warned long ago, "Those who wish to achieve hegemony
acquire it with valour and intelligence, increase it with moderation and
benevolence, and maintain it with fear and paralysing terror."[13] In fact, Siculus may have exaggerated the heroic origins of hegemony and downplayed
the cunning, the brute force, and the demonization of the "other" that makes

hegemony at all possible. In the succinct words of Aimé Césaire, "No one colonizes innocently."[14]

Far from acknowledging this reality, American exceptionalism denies it and transforms its own aggressions into innocent and noble acts of self-defense in the name of the universal interest and the well-being of humankind. America's exceptionalist syndrome thus allows it to embrace fully and unashamedly its imperial role, as if it were an unambiguous moral obligation.[15] However, as I have argued in this book, a powerful belief system cannot by itself sustain this global missionary zeal; the task also requires a massive material and military infrastructure. Moreover, the remanence of exceptionalism can generate behavioral habits that may no longer correspond to the realities of infrastructural dominance and can lead to the miscalculated use of a declining and no longer hegemonic American power. Thus, the continued and uncritical belief in the exceptionalist narrative may outlast America's imperial capacities and unleash international catastrophes.

As I have contended in this book, exceptionalism and power are intertwined; they constitute an organic whole. This does not imply, however, that myth and power cannot be analytically and conceptually separated. On the contrary, exceptionalism and power are independent entities—indeed, this is precisely why they can reinforce each other, or collide in a contradiction. Exceptionalism's invented narrative is an elaborate attempt at legitimizing power, and its continued effectiveness is dependent on the relative strength of that very power.

This comparative study of Haitian and U.S. exceptionalisms exposes their role in both uniting and excluding distinct sectors of society. Exceptionalism has been elastic in its capacity to incorporate or marginalize people on the basis of race, gender, class, or nationality. In fact, the impact of certain exceptionalisms can resonate beyond the confines of their own territoriality. The flow of people and ideas between different zones of distinct political economies has always generated contradictory and mutually reinforcing patterns of resistance, revolt, and repression. For instance, enslaved people moving in the Caribbean seas in the nineteenth century could end up being captured and emancipated by an independent Haiti, or they could land on the shores of slave-owning societies and remain with their chains,[16] and defeated plantation owners could flee Haiti with some of their slaves to seek exile in other Caribbean islands still governed by the "peculiar institution." Abolitionist and revolutionary thoughts coexisted with proslavery and white supremacist ideologies. Thus, during the extended period of the Haitian Revolution, the circulation of ideas, emancipated individuals, enslaved Africans, and white plantation owners created a Caribbean full of social contradictions, radical possibilities, and reactionary counterattacks.

Julius S. Scott has highlighted the narratives and activities generated by the complicated grids connecting freed blacks, enslaved people, and slave owners:

Prior to, during, and following the Haitian Revolution, regional networks of communication carried news of special interest to Afro-Americans all over the Caribbean and beyond. Before the outbreak in Saint-Domingue, British and Spanish officials were already battling rampant rumors forecasting the end of slavery. Such reports gathered intensity in the 1790s. While planters viewed with alarm the growing prospect of an autonomous black territory, fearing that a successful violent black uprising might tempt their own slaves to revolt, the happenings in Saint-Domingue provided exciting news for slaves and free coloreds, increasing their interest in regional affairs and stimulating them to organize conspiracies of their own. By the end of the decade, rulers in slave societies from Virginia to Venezuela moved to short-circuit the network of black rebellion by building obstacles to effective colony-to-colony communication.[17]

The Haitian Revolution had therefore Janus-faced effects on the wider Caribbean system of slavery. On the one hand, it brought to the enslaved of the region a wind of freedom that allowed them to imagine an alternative to their chained existence; on the other hand, fearing that it posed an existential threat to their property and way of life, the master classes redoubled their determination to defend and expand the plantation economy and slavery itself.[18] Thus, while Haiti's emancipation inspired a "revolution in black consciousness"[19] among the enslaved of the New World, it brought about an unintended opportunity for plantation owners to intensify slave labor and maximize both sugar production and economic gains. This contradictory phenomenon was clearly at work in Cuba in the aftermath of Haiti's creation.

The massive disruption generated by Haiti's war of independence drastically weakened the country's productive capacity and left a void in the global economy, which Cuba rapidly filled. Operating in an imperial zero-sum regime, Haiti's abolition of slavery nurtured a more ferocious "second slavery"[20] throughout the Caribbean region. As Ada Ferrer has pointed out, "The Haitian Revolution thus hastened and hardened Cuba's sugar revolution and the brutal practices of enslavement that came with it. Two decades after Haitian independence, Cuba had emerged as the world's largest producer of sugar and one of the greatest consumers of enslaved Africans in the nineteenth-century world."[21] Dale Tomich and Michael Zeuske argue convincingly that the impact of the Haitian Revolution in restructuring slavery and the plantation economy was profound and extended beyond the Caribbean:

> Haiti's victorious slave revolution and the foundation of a new state destroyed France's American empire and Great Britain's imperial ambition. It removed the world's richest colony and largest producer of sugar, coffee, and cotton from international commerce. The revolution also transformed the politics and economics of slavery and the slave trade throughout the Americas in

myriad ways. In this regard, it is perhaps the pivot on which the new zones
of slave production emerged. The transfer of Florida and Louisiana to the
United States was also a consequence of the Haitian Revolution, as, in certain
sense, was the undermining of export slave economies in the *tierra firme* of
Venezuela during the wars of independence, 1810–21.[22]

Thus, while Haiti came to symbolize the radical antislavery movement of the
times and created among the enslaved of the region an imagined community of
the free, it lacked the means to make that community real and ultimately fueled
the "second slavery." Moreover, it is precisely because Haiti revolutionized prevailing liberal notions of property anchored in the commodification of African
bodies that imperial powers perceived it as an existential threat that had to be
quarantined as a deadly disease. The connections between freed Haitians and
the enslaved of the black Atlantic generated a "history from below" feeding
"rumors of emancipation" and Maroon revolts.[23] Rebelling against the infernal
plantation system was not merely a matter of "symbolic discourse"; it was a very
real danger confronting slave owners. Haiti's revolution could not be "silenced";
it was a specter haunting white supremacist forces. Ferrer captures well its
thunderous significance: "After 1804, Haiti stood not only as a symbol of liberty, but literally as free soil—a place in which freedom, enshrined in the law,
could be real for black persons in their own lifetimes. Whether the people in
question were enslaved fugitive sailors from Jamaica or hundreds of Africans
held captive on a vessel about to deliver them as slaves, their freedom now
found institutional and philosophical support in the constitution of a sovereign
and antislavery black state."[24]

Not surprisingly, the creation of Haiti simultaneously galvanized and strength-
ened the abolitionist movement, but it fueled panic among white supremacists
who faced slave revolts or imagined conspiracies between England and Haiti to
end slavery.[25] This panic led to both Haiti's isolation from the world capitalist
system and vilification as a republic of backward uncivilized black savages.
Haiti's political instability and economic woes—partly caused by this very
capitalist system but also driven by the predatory practices of its dominant
classes—reinforced this vilification. In fact, imperial powers came to use Haiti's dysfunctional politics to defend their continuous rule over their colonies.
For instance, as Matthew Smith explains:

> In Jamaica more than any other British colony, Haiti was presented as a
> warning of what the island could become without British rule. This popular
> idea relied on proximity, the close resemblance in post emancipation econo-
> mies, and racial distribution in both places. In the wake of the Morant Bay
> rising, imperial commentators and their local supporters in Jamaica argued
> more forcefully than before that the island's saving grace was British colo-
> nialism, which protected it from becoming "a second Haiti." The term was

intended to conjure a fearsome image of Jamaica beset with endless revolutions and race wars.[26]

Outside of its territory, Haiti has had multiple representations; in the eyes of the enslaved, it symbolized the revolutionary road to emancipation and the overcoming of white supremacy; for plantation owners it embodied the antithesis of early liberal civilization—an existential threat that had to be contained and demonized. Thus, Haiti's emancipatory exceptionalism nurtured the imagination of the enslaved of the Caribbean and beyond with dreams and possibilities of freedom, but ultimately the young republic lacked the diplomatic and military sway to compel white supremacist rulers into abandoning the commodification and exploitation of black bodies. Great Britain and the United States abolished the slave trade in 1807, but the transport of captured Africans to Brazil and Cuba continued until the 1860s, and slavery itself persisted for many generations, while its racist legacy endures and haunts us to this day.

Finally, within its boundaries, Haiti's radical rupture with racial enslavement failed to deliver the revolutionary promise of social solidarity and equality; instead, Haiti developed an authoritarian *habitus* that accentuated class and color divisions.[27] In fact, as I have argued in this book, unlike the United States, Haiti confronted a hostile Western imperial world system and lacked a hegemonic and productive ruling class as well as the material resources to make its exceptionalism truly effective.

Thus, the sway of both American and Haitian exceptionalisms has been a function of the hegemonic strength of their respective ruling classes; in turn, that strength has reflected their infrastructural power. Not surprisingly, American exceptionalism has managed to be far more inclusive than its Haitian counterpart. Groups that had been historically marginalized were gradually incorporated and co-opted as full citizens into the American polity. In Haiti, in spite of their repeated attempts, the so-called *moun andeyo* have largely failed to gain their basic social and economic rights.[28] The claims of Haitian exceptionalism have little resonance with them except as increasingly demagogic nationalistic appeals. The current Haitian predicament requires abandoning exceptionalist narratives; rooted in an epic struggle and radical aspirations, the original national script is majestic but empty. What I am suggesting here resonates with what Manuel, an ordinary Haitian "guide and fixer," told anthropologist Greg Beckett, who became his friend. In 2002 in the midst of one of the recurring crises that has historically plagued the country, Manuel exclaimed, "Haiti is dead. There is no more Haiti."[29] Initially shocked by this thoroughly bleak and defeatist statement, Beckett eventually understood it to mean something quite different. As he put it:

It is easy to mistake his comment that Haiti is dead as fatalistic resignation. Yet, when I think of Manuel, when I remember his smile, remember running through the market with him, remember all the other things he said and did, the things he hoped for and dreamed about, I hear him saying something terribly sad and yet also profoundly hopeful. I hear him trying to come to terms with the fact that the future is radically open, that even if it is full of crisis, it is also full of possibility. . . .

And then I imagine him saying something he did not say. Haiti is dead. Long live Haiti.[30]

In contrast, everything seems to indicate that American exceptionalism will enjoy a longer life. While facing challenges, it has shown flexibility and managed to be culturally and politically inclusive, albeit slowly and without drastically changing its deep capitalist structures of privilege and inequality. For over two hundred years, exceptionalist thinking has sustained the founding tropes of the American republic and withstood the changing circumstances of history. Organic intellectuals have tweaked the original script without damaging it. That the script remains a cluster of invented narratives has not seemed to bother anyone or weakened people's support for it. As I have argued above, the significance of exceptionalism is neither its plausibility nor its veracity, but rather that it continues to command people's allegiance.

Continually reinventing their exceptionalism, Americans have developed varied interpretations of their country's uniqueness, and yet they have always posited this singularity as a central truth. These interpretations have not moved in a uniform linear, progressive trajectory; the steps forward to greater inclusiveness and democratic justice have coexisted with a simultaneous backward slide, or more precisely, a defense of portions of the original script that carry racist stains and class injuries. As we have seen, in spite of its universalistic claims, exceptionalism is by definition a strike against "others" that can easily become a celebration of national and ethnic purity. Thus, exceptionalism is Janus-faced; it has invented the bonds of the past that have forged the imagined national fellowship of the chosen, but it has also constructed the belief system spouting racial supremacy, class dominance, and imperial hegemony. A cosmopolitan world genuinely committed to human solidarity, equality, and social justice has little room for any form of exceptionalism. One could argue that exceptionalism contains reservoirs of strength built on the inherited routines, identities, and practices of the past. But can these rather chauvinistic claims to uniqueness really move us forward? Instead, as Marx acknowledged long ago, "The tradition of all the dead generations weighs like a nightmare on the brains of the living."[31]

Notes

PREFACE AND ACKNOWLEDGMENTS

1. *Blan* is the Creole word for foreigners and white people.

2. Donald J. Trump (@realDonaldTrump), "So Interesting to See 'Progressive' Democrat Congresswomen," Tweet, July 14, 2019, https://twitter.com/realDonaldTrump.

3. "Karl Marx to Arnold Ruge, September 1843," in *Letters from the Deutsch-Französische Jahrbücher*, https://www.marxists.org/archive/marx/works/1843/letters/43_09.htm.

4. Barack Obama, "President Barack Obama's Inaugural Address," speech, Washington, DC, January 21, 2009, White House, https://obamawhitehouse.archives.gov/blog/2009/01/21/president-barack-obamas-inaugural-address.

5. Natsu Taylor Saito, *Meeting the Enemy* (New York: New York University Press, 2010), 54–66.

6. For instance, in his book *The Rise of Afrikanerdom: Power, Apartheid, and the Afrikaner Civil Religion* (Berkeley: University of California Press, 1975), Dunbar Moodie explains well how Afrikaner organic intellectuals invented their own exceptionalism by combining race, religion, and ethnicity to legitimate the establishment of the South African white supremacist state. They thus created the ideological framework for the racist exclusion of Africans from white-dominated South Africa.

7. Robert Fatton Jr., *The Roots of Haitian Despotism* (Boulder, CO: Lynne Rienner Publishers, 2007).

8. Theodore Roosevelt, "Expansion and Peace," *The Independent*, December 21, 1899, https://www.bartleby.com/58/2.html.

9. Julie Hirschfeld Davis, Sheryl Gay Stolberg, and Thomas Kaplan, "Trump Alarms Lawmakers with Disparaging Words for Haiti and Africa," *New York Times*, January 11, 2018, https://www.nytimes.com/2018/01/11/us/politics/trump-shithole-countries.html; see also Jina Moore and Catherine Porter, "'Don't Feed the Troll': Much of the World Reacts in Anger at Trump's Insult Image," *New York Times*, January 12, 2018, https://www.nytimes.com/2018/01/12/world/africa/africa-trump-shithole.html.

10. Hillary Clinton, "Why America Is Exceptional," *Time*, October 13, 2016, https://time.com/collection-post/4521509/2016-election-clinton-exceptionalism.

11. David Morgan, "Clinton Says U.S. Could 'Totally Obliterate' Iran," Reuters, April 22, 2008, https://www.reuters.com/article/us-usa-politics-iran/clinton-says-u-s-could-totally -obliterate-iran-idUSN2224332720080422.

12. BBC News, "Trump Warns Iran of 'Obliteration' in Event of War," last modified June 22, 2019, https://www.bbc.com/news/world-us-canada-48728465.

13. Robert Fatton Jr., *Haiti: Trapped in the Outer Periphery* (Boulder, CO: Lynne Rienner Publishers, 2014).

14. Branko Milanovic, *The Haves and the Have-Nots* (New York: Basic Books, 2011), 120–123.

CHAPTER 1 — INTRODUCTION

1. Eric Hobsbawm, "Introduction: Inventing Traditions," in *The Invention of Tradition*, ed. Eric Hobsbawm and Terence Ranger (Cambridge: Cambridge University Press, 1983), 2–6. Here I seek to convey the idea that, like "traditions," exceptionalisms are "invented." To appropriate Eric Hobsbawm's wording, invented exceptionalisms are "responses to novel situations which take the form of reference to old situations, or which establish their own past by quasi-obligatory repetition." In this sense, while an invented exceptionalism comes into being for "novel purposes," it is rooted in the "ancient materials" of an earlier dominant exceptionalism or tradition. Again, Hobsbawm writes: "A large store of such materials is accumulated in the past of any society, and an elaborate language of symbolic practice and communication is always available. Sometimes new traditions could be readily grafted on old ones, sometimes they could be devised by borrowing from well-supplied warehouses of official ritual, symbolism and moral exhortation."

2. Michel-Rolph Trouillot, "The Odd and the Ordinary: Haiti, the Caribbean, and the World," *Cimarrón: New Perspectives on the Caribbean* 2, no. 3 (1990): 4.

3. Ibid., 6. Moreover, as I have argued elsewhere (Fatton, *Haiti: Trapped in the Outer Periphery*, 5):

Haiti is continuously described as the "poorest nation of the Western Hemisphere." Its citizens are seen as lacking the discipline to work, its rulers are deemed venal and corrupt, and its culture is perceived as incomprehensible and weird. Haiti is simply the paradigmatic "Other." In fact, Samuel Huntington [*The Clash of Civilizations and the Remaking of World Order* (New York: Simon & Schuster, 1996), 136–137] calls Haiti a "lone country" that "lacks cultural commonality with other societies." He says that "Haiti's Creole language, Voodoo religion, revolutionary slave origins, and brutal history combine to make it a lone country. . . . Haiti, 'the neighbor nobody wants,' is truly a kinless country." This tale of Haitian exceptionalism explains nothing; it assumes that Haitians are so unique—or bizarre—that their history is incomprehensible and their predicament is beyond any solution. It is as if Haitian poverty were inexplicable, vodou unfathomable, and the slave-led revolution unconceivable. In such a view, Haiti remains an impenetrable enigma.

Haiti has its own unique history. But Haiti is also like any other nation; it confronts similar problems and shares common experiences. While understanding the causes of poverty, corruption, religion, revolution, and violence is difficult, these phenomena are not exceptional. They are as explicable in Haiti as in any other place on earth. To claim Haitian exceptionalism when it comes to intelligibility is to claim unintelligibility *tout court*.

4. Perry Anderson (*American Foreign Policy and Its Thinkers* [London: Verso, 2015], 3–6) describes these contradictory tendencies in what he defines as the "ideological repertoire" of American nationalism:

> This repertoire afforded seamless passage to an American imperialism, characterized by a *complexion oppositorum* of exceptionalism and universalism. The United States was unique among nations, yet at the same time a lodestar for the world: an order at once historically unexampled and ultimately a compelling example to all. . . . From the beginning, exceptionalism and universalism formed a potentially unstable compound. Conviction of the first allowed for belief that the United States could preserve its unique virtues only by remaining a society apart from a fallen world. Commitment to the second authorized a messianic activism by the United States to redeem that world.

5. On the notion of "organic intellectuals," see Antonio Gramsci, *Selections from the Prison Notebooks*, ed. and trans. Quintin Hoare and Geoffrey Nowell Smith (London: Lawrence and Wishart, 1971). Organic intellectuals are those intellectuals who are connected politically, materially, and ideologically to a rising class and articulate the collective consciousness of that class. They are not only of great significance in guiding a particular class to power, but also in establishing the cultural terrain justifying and legitimating this class's continued rule. This is especially the case during the complicated process of nation-making.

In the United States, the organic intellectuals par excellence are lawyers and judges because they are the anointed authorities and living interpreters of the American Constitution, which has played and continues to play an exceptionally powerful role in shaping and disciplining the politics, thoughts, and behavior of citizens. To that extent, American exceptionalism has been subjected to the legal parameters of the Constitution.

As Bertell Ollman has explained (introduction to *The United States Constitution 200 Years of Anti-Federalist, Abolitionist, Feminist, Muckraking, Progressive, and Especially Socialist Criticism*, ed. Bertell Ollman and Jonathan Birnbaum [New York: New York University Press, 1990], 5–6.]:

> [The] Constitution has been a way of understanding reality as much as it has served to effect it. . . . In sum, an important part of the Constitution's work is ideological. As ideology, the Constitution provides us with a kind of bourgeois fairy tale in which claims to equal rights and responsibilities are substituted for the harsh realities of class domination. Through the Constitution, the struggle over the legitimacy of any social act or relationship is removed from the plane of morality to that of law. Justice is no longer what is fair but what is legal, and politics itself is transformed into the technical wrangling of lawyers and judges. The Constitution organizes consent not least by its manner of organizing dissent. The fact that two-thirds of the world's lawyers practice in the United States is not, as they say, a coincidence.

See also Noam Chomsky, *Towards a New Cold War* (New York: Pantheon Books, 1982), 60–114.

6. Karen E. Fields and Barbara J. Fields, *Racecraft: The Soul of Inequality in American Life* (London: Verso, 2012), 135.

7. Fatton, *Haiti: Trapped in the Outer Periphery.*

8. Edward E. Baptist, *The Half Has Never Been Told* (New York: Basic Books, 2014), 433.

9. Elizabeth Maddock Dillon and Michael J. Drexler, "Introduction: Haiti and the Early United States, Entwined," in *The Haitian Revolution and the Early United States*, ed. Elizabeth Maddock Dillon and Michael J. Drexler (Philadelphia: University of Pennsylvania Press, 2016), 1.

10. Angelica Maria Bernal, *Beyond Origins: Rethinking Founding in a Time of Constitutional Democracy* (New York: Oxford University Press, 2017), 75–103.

11. Rogers M. Smith, "Beyond Tocqueville, Myrdal, and Hartz: The Multiple Traditions in America," *American Political Science Review* 87, no. 3 (1993): 549–563. Writing in 1993, Smith noted, "For over 80% of U.S. history, its laws declared most of the world's population to be ineligible for full American citizenship solely because of their race, original nationality, or gender. For at least two-thirds of American history, the majority of the domestic adult population was also ineligible for full citizenship for the same reasons." Smith added:

> State policies prior to 1789 on the whole made nonwhites and women ineligible for full citizenship. Women could always formally be U.S. citizens, but they were almost universally denied the vote until 1920, making them clearly second-class citizens. Other overt legal discriminations on their political and economic rights continued through the 1960s. Naturalization was confined to whites from 1790 through 1868 and closed to most Asian nationals until 1952. By then, the national origins quota system of immigration restrictions, enacted in the 1920s, prevented most Asians and many southern Europeans from coming to the United States and becoming permanent residents or citizens, explicitly because of their original nationality or ethnicity. That system was not repealed until 1965. Despite formal constitutional guarantees enacted in the mid-1860s, blacks were also widely denied basic rights of citizenship until the 1964 Civil Rights Act and the 1965 Voting Rights Act. Thus, though the specifics changed, denials of access to full citizenship based explicitly on race, ethnicity, or gender always denied large majorities of the world's population any opportunity for U.S. citizenship up to 1965. That represents about 83% of the nation's history since the Constitution, 88% since the Declaration of Independence. If, controversially, one assumes that women became full citizens with the vote in 1920, then a majority of the domestic adult population became legally eligible for full citizenship then. This still means that a majority of domestic adults were ineligible for full citizenship on racial, ethnic, or gender grounds for about two-thirds of U.S. history.

12. According to Pierre Van den Berghe (*Race and Racism* [New York: John Wiley & Sons, 1967], 29) whose work derived from the South African experience, *Herrenvolk* democracy is "a parliamentary regime in which the exercise of suffrage is restricted, de facto and often de jure, to the dominant group; a regime democratic for the master race but tyrannical for the subordinate groups." This definition describes well the political system of the United States from the time of its foundation to arguably the pre-1960s civil rights era.

13. See Fatton, *Roots of Haitian Despotism*.

14. Julius S. Scott, *The Common Wind: Afro-American Currents in the Age of the Haitian Revolution* (New York: Verso, 2018), 118–201.

15. Fatton, *Roots of Haitian Despotism*; Sibylle Fischer, *Modernity Disavowed* (Durham, NC: Duke University Press, 2004), 260–271.

16. Marlene L. Daut, *Tropics of Haiti* (Liverpool: Liverpool University Press, 2015), 605–611.

17. Bruce Cumings has argued convincingly that American expansionism became a truly global imperialism in the aftermath of the Korean war of the 1950s. As he explains in *The Korean War: A History* (New York: Modern Library Edition, 2010), 191–201:

> The Korean conflict was the occasion for transforming the United States into a very different country than it had ever been before: one with hundreds of permanent military

bases abroad, a large standing army and a permanent national security state at home. . . . In the second half of the twentieth century an entirely new phenomenon emerged in American history, namely, the permanent stationing of soldiers in a myriad of foreign bases across the face of the planet, connected to an enormous domestic complex of defense industries. For the first time in modern history the leading power maintained an extensive network of bases on the territories of its allies and economic competitors— Japan, Germany, Britain, Italy, South Korea, all the industrial powers save France and Russia—marking a radical break with the European balance of power and the operation of realpolitik, and a radical departure in American history: an archipelago of empire.

18. Anders Stephanson, *Manifest Destiny* (New York: Hill and Wang, 1995), 21–24.

19. It is clear that Jefferson welcomed the expansion of American territory; he stated the following in a letter to James Monroe ("Jefferson to James Monroe," November 24, 1801, Quotes by and about Thomas Jefferson, Thomas Jefferson Foundation, http://tjrs .monticello.org/letter/1743): "However our present interests may restrain us within our own limits, it is impossible not to look forward to distant times, when our rapid multiplication will expand itself beyond those limits, & cover the whole Northern, if not the Southern continent with a people speaking the same language, governed in similar forms, & by similar laws."

20. Ibid.

21. Ibid.

22. Stephanson, *Manifest Destiny*, 23.

23. Sidney Lens, *The Forging of the American Empire* (London: Pluto Press, 2003), 14.

24. Fatton, *Haiti: Trapped in the Outer Periphery.*

CHAPTER 2 — AMERICAN EXCEPTIONALISM

1. See the classic argument developed by Louis Hartz, *The Liberal Tradition in America* (New York: Harcourt, Brace, and World, 1955).

2. Alexis de Tocqueville, *Democracy in America*, From the Henry Reeve Translation, revised and corrected, 1899. http://xroads.virginia.edu/~Hyper/DETOC/preface.htm.

3. Ibid.

4. Ibid.

5. Gramsci, *Selections from the Prison Notebooks*. Perry Anderson (*American Foreign Policy and Its Thinkers*, 155–235) offers a panoramic assessment of what he calls the *Consilium*—the American security elite—of the early twenty first century. The *Consilium* comprises select members of the academy and foundations as well as the media; while tensions exist in its midst, its members are all committed to formulate a grand strategy for the continued "primacy" of American power.

6. Tocqueville, *Democracy in America*, 339.

7. Ibid. As Achille Mbembe (*Critique of Black Reason*, trans. Laurent Dubois [Durham, NC: Duke University Press, 2017], 82) has pointed out, "For Tocqueville, the Black slave embodies all the traits of debasement and abjection. He arouses aversion, repulsion, and disgust. A herd animal, he is the symbol of castrated and atrophied humanity from which emanates poisoned exhalations: he is a kind of constitutive horror. To encounter the slave is to experience an emptiness that is as spectacular as it is tragic. What characterizes him is the impossibility of finding a path that does not always return to servitude as its point of departure." See also Elise Marienstras, *Les Mythes Fondateurs de la Nation Americaine: Essai sur le Discours Ideologique aux Etats-Unis a l'epoque de L'independence (1763–1800)* (Paris: François Maspéro, 1976), 209–275. Marienstras put it very succinctly (275):

"Théoriquement reconnu comme membre de l'espèce humaine, le Noir d'Amérique n'obtient aucune des prerogatives que l'idéologie en vigueur reconnaît universellement à l'humanité."

8. Quoted in George Fredrickson, *The Black Image in the White Mind* (Middletown, CT: Wesleyan University Press, 1987), 62.

9. David Waldstreicher, *Slavery's Constitution: From Revolution to Ratification* (New York: Hill and Wang, 2009), 9.

10. Ibram X. Kendi, *Stamped from the Beginning: The Definitive History of Racist Ideas in America* (New York: Bold Type Books, 2016), 116.

11. Keri Leigh Merritt, *Masterless Men: Poor Whites and Slavery in the Antebellum South* (New York: Cambridge University Press, 2017), 16.

12. Ibid., 23.

13. Ibid., 19.

14. Ibid., 28.

15. Merritt points out that

poor whites unquestionably resented, and at times even hated, wealthy slaveholders. But perhaps more importantly to the larger narrative of American history is the realization of slaveholders' fears of poor whites. These often transient people received no benefits from slavery, and increasingly they came to realize that their own livelihoods were somehow intertwined with those of the slaves themselves. Although the overwhelming brunt of slaveholder brutality and cruelty fell upon the backs of African Americans, slavery was also a deeply injurious institution for a significant number of southern whites. These masterless men and women greatly threatened the existing southern hierarchy, and undoubtedly helped push the slaveholders towards secession. (Ibid., 26)

16. Ibid., 254.

17. Ibid., 45.

18. Ibid., 8.

19. Ibid., 306.

20. Andrew B. Hall, Connor Huff, and Shiro Kuriwaki, "Wealth, Slaveownership, and Fighting for the Confederacy: An Empirical Study of the American Civil War," *American Political Science Review* 113, no. 3 (2019): 672.

21. Merritt, *Masterless Men*, 300.

22. Eric Foner, *The Second Founding* (New York: W. W. Norton & Co., 2019), xix. Reconstruction (1865–1877) was the period following the Civil War when the federal government sought in vain to erase the heavy white supremacist legacy of the defeated slaveholding southern states. In spite of this failure, the period marks what Eric Foner has called "the Second Founding." As he argues:

During Reconstruction, the United States made its first attempt, flawed but truly remarkable for its time, to build an egalitarian society on the ashes of slavery. Some of the problems of those years haunt American society today—vast inequalities of wealth and power, terrorist violence, aggressive racism. But perhaps the era's most tangible legacies are the Thirteenth, Fourteenth, and Fifteenth Amendments to the United States Constitution. The Thirteenth irrevocably abolished slavery. The Fourteenth constitutionalized the principles of birthright citizenship and equality before the law and sought to settle key issues arising from the war, such as the future political role of Confederate leaders and the fate of Confederate debt. The Fifteenth aimed to secure black male suffrage throughout the reunited nation.

While these amendments did not prevent the rise of Jim Crow and the disenfranchise-ment of African Americans, they created a constitutional basis for the future development of the civil rights movement of the 1950s and 1960s. As Foner put it (xxix), "The movement did not need a new Constitution; it needed the existing one enforced." In short, the legacy of Reconstruction demonstrates well the flexibility of American exceptionalism; a flexi-bility that shows, in turn, that history moves neither in a progressive linear, nor in a regressive counterrevolutionary direction.

23. Merritt, *Masterless Men*, 326–327.

24. Fields and Fields, *Racecraft*, 121.

25. Calvin Schermerhorn, *Unrequited Toil A History of United States Slavery* (New York: Cambridge University Press, 2018), 1–2. See also Sven Beckert and Seth Rockman, eds., *Slavery's Capitalism: A New History of American Economic Development* (Phila-delphia: University of Pennsylvania Press, 2016); Greg Grandin, *The Empire of Neces-sity: Slavery, Freedom, and Deception in the New World* (New York: Metropolitan Books, 2014); David Brion Davis, "Free at Last: The Enduring Legacy of the South's Civil War Victory," *New York Times*, August 26, 2001, http://www.nytimes.com/2001/08/26/weekinreview/free-at-last-the-enduring-legacy-of-the-south-s-civil-war-victory.html. In a similar fashion, Edward E. Baptist emphasizes the significance of cotton and thus slavery in the early making of industrial capitalism in America (*Half Has Never Been Told*, xxiii): "The returns from cotton monopoly powered the moderniza-tion of the rest of the American economy, and by the time of the Civil War, the United States had become the second nation to undergo large-scale industrialization. In fact, slavery's expansion shaped every crucial aspect of the economy and politics of the new nation—not only increasing its power and size, but also, eventually, dividing US poli-tics, differentiating regional identities and interests, and helping to make civil war possible."

26. Sven Beckert and Seth Rockman, "Introduction: Slavery's Capitalism," in *Slavery's Capitalism: A New History of American Economic Development*, ed. Sven Beckert and Seth Rockman (Philadelphia: University of Pennsylvania Press, 2016), 1.

27. Caitlin Rosenthal, "Slavery's Scientific Management: Masters and Managers," in *Slavery's Capitalism: A New History of American Economic Development*, ed. Sven Beckert and Seth Rockman (Philadelphia: University of Pennsylvania Press, 2016), 62–86.

28. Ibid., 62–63; see also Baptist, *Half Has Never Been Told*.

29. Beckert and Rockman, "Introduction: Slavery's Capitalism," 15.

30. Fields and Fields, *Racecraft*, 117.

31. Winthrop D. Jordan, *White over Black: American Attitudes toward the Negro, 1550–1812* (Chapel Hill: University of North Carolina Press, 1968).

32. Henry Wiencek, *Master of the Mountain: Thomas Jefferson and His Slaves* (New York: Farrar, Straus, and Giroux, 2012), 8.

33. Ibid. Caitlin Rosenthal points out that the plantation economy contributed to a very capitalist mode of management of slave labor bent on maximizing profits. It announced industrial capitalism's forms of worker control under the famous "Tay-lorist" regime of production. As she explains (*Accounting for Slavery: Masters and Man-agement* [Cambridge, MA: Harvard University Press, 2018], 203–205):

The portrait that emerges from plantation records is that of a society where precise management and violence went hand in hand. Spared many of the challenges faced by manufacturers relying on wage labor ... slaveholders built large and complex organizations, conducted productivity analysis akin to scientific management, and developed an array of ways to value and compare human capital. The limited rights and opportunities of the men, women, and children laboring beneath them facilitated these efforts. Put differently, slavery encouraged the development of sophisticated management practices. Like other entrepreneurs, slaveholders strove to mobilize capital and motivate labor, regularly turning to numbers as an aid to profits. But on plantations the soft power of quantification supplemented the driving force of the whip.... Slaveholders ... built an innovative, global, profit-hungry labor regime that contributed to the emergence of the modern economy.... [Their] manipulation of human capital compounded it into massive fortunes—both through financial maneuvering and through human reproduction. The power of capital to control labor was rarely more acutely felt than where labor was capital.

34. C. B. Macpherson, *The Political Theory of Possessive Individualism* (Oxford: Oxford University Press, 1962); see also Domenico Losurdo, *Liberalism: A Counter-History* (London: Verso, 2014).

35. Gordon Brown, in his book *Toussaint's Clause* (Jackson: University Press of Mississippi, 2005), 6–7, argues that the United States forged its relations with Haiti primarily on the basis of economic motivations:

Economic interests ... determined the main lines of the debate over America's Haitian policy. Specifically, it was a clash between the shipping and merchant interests, largely from the North, and the slaveholding interests in the South, and it was an exemplar of the fundamental North-South divide that characterized the nation's politics at the time. Oversimplified, the maritime centers wanted to trade with the Haitian rebels, while the plantation owners wanted to isolate them or squelch them, and the direction of our fluctuating policy was determined by which of the groups had the current administration's ear. Successive American administrations supported first the French then the Haitian rebels—even flirting with encouraging their independence— and then again (although with reservations) the French.

36. Ibid., 136–143. Brown explains (138):

The bill advanced by the [Adams] administration proposed to extend the embargo against France for the duration of the new Congress, with one major change: it would allow the president to suspend its effect to selected French territories, and under certain conditions. The language eventually negotiated was vague; it simply authorized the president to discontinue the restrictions of the act "either with respect to the French republic, or to any island, port, or place, belonging to the said republic, with which a commercial intercourse may safely be renewed." The intent of this clause, however, was very clear to Congress; it was intended to reopen the trade with St. Domingo. It quickly was named the Toussaint Clause.

37. Thomas Jefferson, *Notes on the State of Virginia*, ed. Frank Shuffelton (New York: Penguin Books, 1999), 278. As Peter S. Onuf explains (*Jefferson's Empire: The Language of American Nationhood* [Charlottesville: University Press of Virginia, 2000], 179–180), "Thus, in deporting slaves to Haiti, Jefferson would not ... transform enemies, or the children of enemies, into friends. But the removal of a dangerous internal enemy would enhance the security (and improve the morals) of Virginia and its sister states. Fighting for their freedom, rebellious slaves might well overthrow a demoralized master class; but deportation would render them harmless, as they became members of a weak, unrecog-

nized nation that would risk its very freedom by any belligerent move against the United States."

38. Jefferson, *Notes on the State of Virginia*, 278.

39. Quoted in Rayford W. Logan, *The Diplomatic Relations of the United States with Haiti, 1776-1891* (Chapel Hill: University of North Carolina Press, 1941), 125-126.

40. Gordon Brown explains (*Toussaint's Clause*, 212):

> Jefferson was embarking on a policy that involved carrying water on both shoulders. He would have to keep the French satisfied that the American government was not assisting the St. Domingo rebels, while at the same time allowing the private sector to do exactly that—and conniving implicitly with the bankers to avoid every appeal for help from Leclerc as he strove to solve his supply and financial difficulties. The policy was also expedient domestically, as it protected American security while keeping the merchant interests quiet. But for sheer diplomatic duplicity, it rivaled the work of the master, Talleyrand.

See also Robert L. Paquette, "Revolutionary Saint Domingue in the Making of Territorial Louisiana," in *A Turbulent Time: The French Revolution and the Greater Caribbean*, ed. David Barry Gaspar and David Patrick Geggus (Bloomington: Indiana University Press, 1997), 204-225; Carolyn Fick, "Revolutionary St. Domingue and the Emerging Atlantic: Paradigms of Sovereignty," in *The Haitian Revolution and the Early United States*, ed. Elizabeth Maddock Dillon and Michael J. Drexler (Philadelphia: University of Pennsylvania Press, 2016), 23-41; and David Geggus, "The Louisiana Purchase and the Haitian Revolution," in *The Haitian Revolution and the Early United States*, ed. Elizabeth Maddock Dillon and Michael J. Drexler (Philadelphia: University of Pennsylvania Press, 2016), 117-129.

41. Geggus, "The Louisiana Purchase." Paquette argues ("Revolutionary Saint Domingue," 210), "Not only was revolutionary process in Saint Domingue conspicuously shaped by European balance-of-power politics; it shaped them as well in some cases decisively. The interconnectedness of Louisiana and Saint Domingue existed not just in Napoleon's mind. By heroically defending the gains of the French Revolution, the rebels of Saint Domingue had drastically limited Napoleon's capacity to fulfill his western design and to project power in the Americas."

In an editorial published in the *New-York Evening Post* on July 5, 1803, Alexander Hamilton articulated a similar view ("Hamilton on the Louisiana Purchase: A Newly Identified Editorial from the *New-York Evening Post*," *William and Mary Quarterly* 12, no. 2 [1955]: 274):

> On the part of France the short interval of peace had been wasted in repeated and fruitless efforts to subjugate St. Domingo; and those means which were originally destined to the colonization of Louisiana, had been gradually exhausted by the unexpected difficulties of this ill-starred enterprize.
>
> To the deadly climate of St. Domingo, and to the courage and obstinate resistance made by its black inhabitants are we indebted for the obstacles which delayed the colonization of Louisiana, till the auspicious moment, when a rupture between England and France gave a new turn to the projects of the latter, and destroyed at once all her schemes as to this favourite object of her ambition.

See also Robin Blackburn, *The American Crucible: Slavery, Emancipation, and Human Rights* (London: Verso 2013), 242-246.

42. Douglas R. Egerton, "Race and Slavery in the Era of Jefferson," in *The Cambridge Companion to Thomas Jefferson*, ed. Frank Shuffleton (Cambridge: Cambridge University Press, 2009), 76. In 1803, Alexander Hamilton, Jefferson's nemesis, put it succinctly ("Hamilton on the Louisiana Purchase," 274–275): "The real truth is, Bonaparte found himself absolutely compelled by situation, to relinquish his darling plan of colonizing the banks of the Mississippi."

43. Egerton, "Race and Slavery," 75.

44. Dillon and Drexler, "Introduction: Haiti and the Early United States," 9.

45. Ibid.

46. While Thomas Jefferson's views "were reactionary even by eighteenth century standards," they illustrate well the "slavery question" haunting the Enlightenment. As Egerton puts it ("Race and Slavery in the Era of Jefferson," 73), "As a young politician, Jefferson insisted that abolishing slavery was the task of senior statesmen, but even after retiring from the presidency, when he had nothing left to lose apart from his reputation among Virginia planters, he rebuffed Edward Coles's request to endorse a plan to liberate slaves in the West. Jefferson now insisted that it was the duty of the 'younger generation' to advance the hour of emancipation." By 1814, he claimed that he had "ceased to think" about black liberation, as it was "not to be the work of my day."

47. Representative Albert Gallatin, speaking on intercourse with France (U.S. Congress, *Annals of Congress*, 5th Congress, 3rd session, 2752, https://memory.loc.gov/cgi-bin/ampage?collId=llac&fileName=009/llac009.db&recNum=169.

48. Georg Wilhelm Friedrich Hegel, *The Philosophy of History*, ed. Eduard Gans, trans. John Silbee (London: George Bell and Sons, 1902), https://www.marxists.org/reference/archive/hegel/works/hi/introduction-lectures.htm. Hegel's contradictory position on the emancipation of slaves is quite clear when he mentions Haiti, maintaining at one and the same time that slaves could fight successfully for their freedom, but that this freedom was ultimately impossible because they were of African descent. As he explains in *The Philosophy of Subjective Spirit*, vol. 2, *Anthropology* (ed. and trans. Michael John Petry [Netherlands: D. Reidel Publishing Co., 1978] 54–55):

> [Negroes] cannot be said to be ineducable, for not only have they occasionally received Christianity with the greatest thankfulness and spoken movingly of the freedom they have gained from it after prolonged spiritual servitude, but in Haiti they have even formed a state based on Christian principles. In their homeland the most shocking despotism prevails; there, they have no feeling for the personality of man, their spirit is quite dormant, remains sunk within itself, makes no progress, and so corresponds to the compact and *undifferentiated* mass of the African terrain.

In the same text, Hegel blatantly expresses his racism (47): "One can speak of the objective superiority of the colour of the Caucasian race as against that of the Negro." He thus denies black people the capacity for full emancipation by affirming their inferiority to the "world-historical" West. Not surprisingly, Teshale Tibebu writes (*Hegel and the Third World: The Making of Eurocentrism in World History* [Syracuse, NY: Syracuse University Press, 2011], p. xxi), "Hegel's paradigm, including his philosophy of world history, lays the foundation for systemic Eurocentrism predicated on the claim of the absolute superiority of the 'West' over the 'non-West.' *All Eurocentrism is thus essentially a series of footnotes to Hegel*." See also Susan Buck-Morss, *Hegel, Haiti, and Universal History* (Pittsburgh: University of Pittsburgh Press, 2009); John M. Hobson, *The*

Eurocentric Conception of World Politics (Cambridge: Cambridge University Press, 2012); and Losurdo, *Liberalism*.

49. Quoted in Robin Blackburn, *The Making of New World Slavery* (London: Verso, 1997), 263.

50. The Royal African Company was founded in 1672 by the British King Charles II and City of London merchants. It was a joint stock trading firm that had monopoly over British commerce with West Africa until 1698. While the acquisition of gold was its main concern initially, it became involved in the profitable slave trade. According to Alan Price, "The Royal Africa Company could buy an enslaved African with trade goods worth £3 and have that person sold for £20 in the Americas. The Royal Africa Company was able to make an average profit of 38% per voyage in the 1680s" ("The Economic Basis of the Slave Trade," Revealing Histories: Remembering Slavery, The Manchester Museum et al., last modified 2007, http://revealinghistories.org.uk/africa-the-arrival-of-europeans-and-the-transatlantic-slave-trade/articles/the-economic-basis-of-the-slave-trade.html). In addition, Blackburn (*Making of New World Slavery*, 255) points out that between 1672 and 1713, the Royal African Company was "responsible for buying 125,000 slaves on the African coast, losing a fifth of them on the 'Middle Passage' and selling the remainder, about 100,000, to the English West Indian planters." See also K. G. Davis, *Royal African Company* (London: Longmans, Green and Co., 1957).

The Board of Trade and Plantations made no objections to Virginia's 1691 "Act for Suppressing of Outlying Slaves." The act asserted the legality of killing and destroying "negroes, mulattoes and other slaves" if they engaged in any form of *marronage*. The same act prohibited any interracial union to prevent "that abominable mixture." See Blackburn, *Making of New World Slavery*, 264.

51. Blackburn, *Making of New World Slavery*, 263-266, 329.

52. Quoted in Wiencek, *Master of the Mountain*, 6.

53. Losurdo, *Liberalism*, 124.

54. Ibid., 37.

55. Wiencek, *Master of the Mountain*, 46.

56. Jefferson, *Notes on the State of Virginia*, 145. See also W. Jordan, *White over Black*, xii, 455-459, 490, 494.

57. Jefferson, *Notes on the State of Virginia*, 145.

58. Ibid., 150-151.

59. For instance, Jefferson's sexual involvement with his enslaved black woman, Sally Hemings, is well documented in Annette Gordon-Reed, *Thomas Jefferson and Sally Hemings: An American Controversy* (Charlottesville: University of Virginia Press, 1997).

60. Thomas Jefferson to Edward Coles, August 25, 1814, The Letters of Thomas Jefferson, 1743-1826, American History: From Revolution to Reconstruction and Beyond, http://www.let.rug.nl/usa/presidents/thomas-jefferson/letters-of-thomas-jefferson/jefl232.php.

61. Tocqueville, *Democracy in America*, chap. 18.

62. Ibid.

63. Jefferson, *Notes on the State of Virginia*, 145.

64. Quoted in George Fredrickson, *White Supremacy* (Oxford: Oxford University Press, 1981), 154.

65. Sara Bon-Harper, "Contrasting Worlds: Plantation Landscapes at Monticello," presentation at the annual meeting of the Society for Historical Archaeology, Amelia Island, Fla., 2010, 4.

66. Waldstreicher, *Slavery's Constitution*, 13–17.

67. Nicholas Guyatt, *Bind Us Apart: How Enlightened Americans Invented Racial Segregation* (New York: Basic Books, 2016).

68. Ibid., 12.

69. Alex Lichtenstein, "From the Editor's Desk: 1619 and All That," *American Historical Review* 125, no. 1 (2020): xv–xxi; Victoria Bynum, James M. McPherson, James Oakes, Sean Wilentz, and Gordon S. Wood, "Letter to the Editor: Historians Critique the 1619 Project," *New York Times Magazine*, December 29, 2019, https://www.nytimes .com/2019/12/20/magazine/we-respond-to-the-historians-who-critiqued-the-1619 -project.html; Leslie M. Harris, "I Helped Fact-Check the 1619 Project. The *Times* Ignored Me," *Politico*, March 6, 2020, https://www.politico.com/news/magazine/2020 /03/06/1619-project-new-york-times-mistake-122248; Niles Niemuth, Tom Mackaman, and David North, "*The New York Times*' 1619 Project: A Racialist Falsification of American and World History," September 6, 2019, https://www.wsws.org/en/articles/2019/09 /06/1619-s06.html.

70. Jake Silverstein, "Why We Published the 1619 Project," *New York Times Magazine*, December 20, 2019, https://www.nytimes.com/interactive/2019/12/20/magazine/1619 -intro.html. The Project used the year 1619 to mark the four-hundredth anniversary of the beginning of slavery in what would become the United States.

71. Ibid.

72. Nikole Hannah-Jones, "The Idea of America," *New York Times Magazine*, August 14, 2019, https://www.nytimes.com/interactive/2019/08/14/magazine/black-history-american -democracy.html.

73. Ibid.

74. Jake Silverstein, the editor of the *New York Times*, has sought to revise the contention that the 1619 Project posited "that one primary reason the colonists fought the American Revolution was to protect the institution of slavery." And yet he basically reasserted this very contention by stating, "We stand behind the basic point, which is that among the various motivations that drove the patriots toward independence was a concern that the British would seek or were already seeking to disrupt in various ways the entrenched system of American slavery." It is unlikely that this "revision" will assuage those historians who were outraged by the initial claim; they will still see it as an assault on American exceptionalism. See Jake Silverstein, "An Update to the 1619 Project," *New York Times Magazine*, March 11, 2020, https://www.nytimes.com/2020/03 /11/magazine/an-update-to-the-1619-project.html.

75. Ibid.

76. Bynum et al., "Letter to the Editor: Historians Critique."

77. Hannah-Jones, "Idea of America."

78. For an excellent and sympathetic review of the 1619 Project, see Harris, "I Helped Fact-Check the 1619 Project." For a scathing critique of the 1619 Project that views the whole initiative as a "politically motivated falsification of history" promoting the Democratic Party's "identity politics," see Niemuth, Mackaman, and North, *New York Times' 1619 Project*. Niemuth, Mackaman, and North claim that the Project is "irrational and scientifically absurd" because it posits that white people are possessed of a racist

DNA and thus "blacks and whites are hostile and incompatible species." For an account that stresses the role of the American Revolution in stimulating the emancipatory aspirations of African Americans, see Benjamin Quarles, *The Negro in the American Revolution* (Chapel Hill: University of North Carolina Press, 1996).

79. Wiencek, *Master of the Mountain*, 272.

80. In *No Property in Man: Slavery and Antislavery at the Nation's Founding* (Cambridge, MA: Harvard University Press, 2018), Sean Wilentz seeks to demonstrate that instead of enshrining slavery, the American Constitution created the philosophical and political spaces that ultimately abolished slavery itself (1–2):

> Descriptions of the Constitution as proslavery have misconstrued critical debates inside the convention. They have slighted the anti-slavery impulses generated by the American Revolution, to which the delegates, for better or worse, paid heed. They have missed the crucial subtlety, which is this: although the framers agreed to compromises over slavery that blunted antislavery hopes and augmented the slaveholders' power, they also deliberately excluded any validation of property in man.
>
> This exclusion, insisted upon by a majority of delegates, was of profound and fateful importance. It rendered slavery solely a creation of state laws. It thereby opened the prospect of a United States free of slavery—a prospect some delegates deeply desired and many more believed was coming to pass. Above all, it left room for the new federal government to hinder slavery's expansion, something which, after the Constitution's ratification, slavery's opponents struggled to achieve.

Wilentz's argument is flawed. For one thing, the antislavery path could only be opened by a brutal civil war decades after the ratification of the Constitution in 1789. And while the racist undercurrents of the founders may not be as virulent, they persist in twenty-first-century America. Moreover, Wilentz's *No Property in Man* fails to account for the massive growth of slavery after 1789 and the Constitution's infamous "three-fifths clause." In a friendly but forceful refutation of Wilentz's thesis, Nicholas Guyatt ("How Proslavery Was the Constitution?" *New York Review of Books* 66, no. 10 [2019], https://www.nybooks.com/articles/2019/06/06/how-proslavery-was-the-constitution) argues convincingly:

> Beyond the three-fifths rule, the international slave trade was exempted from regulation by the federal government, which otherwise oversaw foreign commerce. Congress was banned from abolishing the trade until 1808 at the earliest. The federal government was prevented from introducing a head tax on slaves, and free states were forbidden from harboring runaways from slave states. The Founders obliged Congress to "suppress insurrections," committing the national government to put down slave rebellions. The abolitionist Wendell Phillips . . . summarized the work of the Founders in 1845: "Willingly, with deliberate purpose, our fathers bartered honesty for gain, and became partners with tyrants, that they might share in the profits of their tyranny."
>
> The effectiveness of constitutional protections for slavery can be measured in the growth of the institution between the formation of the federal government in 1789 and the secession of South Carolina in 1860. Across these seven decades, the number of enslaved people in the United States increased from 700,000 to four million. . . .
>
> [The] Constitution allowed proslavery forces to use the power of the federal government to support appalling measures. With the Dred Scott decision of 1857, which denied the possibility of black citizenship in America and invited slaveholders to take

their property into any state of the Union, slavery's domination of national politics seemed absolute.

81. Waldstreicher, *Slavery's Constitution*, 4–5.

82. John C. Calhoun, "Speech on the Oregon Bill," United States Senate, Washington, D.C., June 27, 1848, http://online.hillsdale.edu/file/constitution-courses-library/constitution -101/week-6/Speech-on-the-Oregon-Bill.pdf. Similarly, President John Adams told de Tocqueville that slavery "is the root of almost all the troubles of the present and fears for the future. Slavery has modified the whole state of society in the South. Every white man in the south is an equally privileged being whose destiny it is to make the Negroes work without working himself." Alexis de Tocqueville, *Journey to America*, rev. ed., trans. George Lawrence, ed. J. P. Mayer (New York: Anchor, 1971), 49–50.

83. John Adams, "Humphrey Ploughjogger to the *Boston Gazette*, October 14, 1765," October 14, 1765, Adams Papers: Digital Edition, Massachusetts Historical Society, https://www.masshist.org/publications/apde2/view?id=ADMS-06-01-02-0057.

84. W. H. Auden, "In Memory of Sigmund Freud," in *W.H. Auden Collected Poems*, ed. Edward Mendelson (New York: Vintage, 1991), 274.

85. Roberto Sirvent and Danny Haiphong, *American Exceptionalism and American Innocence: A People's History of Fake News—From the Revolutionary War to the War on Terror* (New York: Skyhorse Publishing, 2019). As Sirvent and Haiphong put it (5–6):

American exceptionalism has always presumed national innocence despite imposing centuries of war and plunder. The U.S. has been at war for over ninety percent of its existence. These wars have all been justified as necessary ventures meant to defend or expand America's so-called founding values and beliefs. A consequence of centuries of endless war has been the historical tendency of the U.S. to erase from consciousness the realities that surround American domestic and international policy, not to mention the system of imperialism that governs both.

86. Saito, *Meeting the Enemy*, 60–66.

87. Ibid., 62.

88. Peter S. Onuf, "'We Shall All Be Americans': Thomas Jefferson and the Indians," *Indiana Magazine of History* 95, no. 2 (1999), 103–141. Onuf contends (116), "Jefferson's celebration of Indian society and his moral indictment of European despotism thus gave way to his more profound identification with the great struggle of civilization against savagery." The power of exceptionalism is such that a contemporary account (Christian B. Keller, "Philanthropy Betrayed: Thomas Jefferson, the Louisiana Purchase, and the Origins of Federal Indian Removal Policy," *Proceedings of the American Philosophical Society* 144, no. 1 [2000], 39–66) of Jefferson's affection for the "noble savage" is transformed into a "philanthropic ideal of acculturation" that he had to abandon because he "had set unrealistic expectations for himself and for the Indians."

89. Thomas Jefferson to William Henry Harrison, Governor of the Indiana Territory, February 21, 1803, Digital History, http://www.digitalhistory.uh.edu/active_learning /explorations/indian_removal/jefferson_to_harrison.cfm.

90. George Washington to James Duane, September 7, 1783, Founders Online, National Archives, https://founders.archives.gov/documents/Washington/99-01-02-11798.

91. Quoted in Jayme A. Sokolow, *The Great Encounter: Native Peoples and European Settlers in the Americas, 1492–1800* (London: M. E. Sharpe, 2003), 155.

92. In fact, the governor of the Carolina colony declared, "The hand of God was eminently seen in thin[ning] the Indians, to make room for the English." Quoted in Saito, *Meeting the Enemy*, 63.

93. Ibid., 108.

94. Ibid., 63.

95. Jeremy R. Hammond, "The 'Forgotten' US Shootdown of Iranian Airliner Flight 655," *Foreign Policy Journal*, July 3, 2017, https://www.foreignpolicyjournal.com/2017/07/03/the-forgotten-us-shootdown-of-iranian-airliner-flight-655%C2%AD. While George Bush did not apologize, and the U.S. government lied about the circumstances of the airline downing, it eventually compensated the victims' families in 1996. It paid them $61.8 million and "expressed deep regret" about the downing of the airline. Moreover, as Hammond contends:

> [The] incident is, of course, something that the people of Iran well remember. Americans who rely on the US mainstream media, on the other hand, would have to be forgiven for never having heard about it. Furthermore, in the rare instances when the media do mention it, to this day they tend to maintain official US government falsehoods about what occurred and otherwise omit relevant details that would inform Americans about what really happened. . . . In the case of the media, the preconceived notion is that the US is an exceptional nation whose government is sometimes capable of "mistakes," but only ever acts out of benevolent intent.

96. Paul Krugman, "Fall of the American Empire," *New York Times*, June 18, 2018, https://www.nytimes.com/2018/06/18/opinion/immigration-trump-children-american-empire.html.

97. Global Research, "America Has Been at War 93% of the Time—222 out of 239 Years–since 1776," *Washington's Blog*, Centre for Research on Globalization, February 20, 2015, updated January 20, 2019, https://www.globalresearch.ca/america-has-been-at-war-93-of-the-time-222-out-of-239-years-since-1776/5565946.

98. Ronald H. Spector, "Vietnam War 1954–1975," in *Encyclopaedia Britannica*, updated June 21, 2019, https://www.britannica.com/event/Vietnam-War.

99. John Byron, "We Have Been at War a Long Time," *Proceedings* 143, no. 8 (2017), https://www.usni.org/magazines/proceedings/2017/august/we-have-been-war-long-time.

100. Anthony W. Marx, *Faith in Nation: Exclusionary Origins of Nationalism* (Oxford: Oxford University Press, 2003), 200.

CHAPTER 3 — EXCEPTIONALISM AND "UNTHINKABILITY"

1. Alfred N. Hunt, *Haiti's Influence on Antebellum America* (Baton Rouge: Louisiana State University Press, 1988), 107–146.

2. Michel-Rolph Trouillot, *Silencing the Past* (Boston: Beacon Press, 1995), 73.

3. David Brion Davis, *Inhuman Bondage: The Rise and Fall of Slavery in the New World* (New York: Oxford University Press, 2006), 169–172; J. S. Scott, *Common Wind*; Raphael Hormann, "Thinking the 'Unthinkable'? Representations of the Haitian Revolution in British Discourse, 1791 to 1805," in *Human Bondage in the Cultural Contact Zone*, ed. Raphael Hormann and Gesa Mackenthun (New York: Waxmann 2010), 137–170.

4. Marcus Rainsford, *An Historical Account of the Black Empire of Hayti. Comprehending a View of the Principal Transactions in the Revolution of Saint Domingo. With Its Antient and Modern State* (London: James Cundee, 1805); Percival Stockdale, *A Letter*

from Percival Stockdale to Granville Sharp Esq. Suggested to the Authour, by the Present Insurrection of the Negroes, in the Island of St. Domingo (Durham: L. Pennington, n.d.); John Thelwall, *The Daughter of Adoption: A Tale of Modern Times in Four Volumes* (London: R. Philipps, 1801); John Thelwall, *The Politics of English Jacobinism: Writings of John Thelwall*, ed. Gregory Claeys (University Park: Pennsylvania State University Press, 1995).

5. Quoted in Hormann, "Thinking the 'Unthinkable,'" 139.

6. Quoted in Hormann, "Thinking the 'Unthinkable,'" 155.

7. Ibid., 159–161.

8. Quoted in Hormann, "Thinking the 'Unthinkable,'" 161.

9. Julia Gaffield, preface to *The Haitian Declaration of Independence: Creation, Context, and Legacy*, ed. Julia Gaffield (Charlottesville: University of Virginia Press, 2016), viii.

10. Logan, *Diplomatic Relations of the United States with Haiti*, 72.

11. Jeremy D. Popkin, *A Concise History of the Haitian Revolution* (West Sussex: Wiley-Blackwell, 2012), 22–24.

12. Louverture became a freedman in 1776 at the age of thirty-three; the year after, he was already a slave owner. See Marie-Antoinette Menier, Gabriel Debien, and Jean Fouchard, "Toussaint Louverture avant 1789: Légendes et Réalités," in *Toussaint Louverture et l'Indépendance d'Haïti*, ed. Jacques de Cauna (Paris: Karthala, 2004), 61–67, previously published in *Conjonction, Revue de l'Institut Français d'Haïti*, no. 134 (1977). See also Madison Smart Bell, *Toussaint Louverture: A Biography* (New York: Pantheon Books, 2007), 70–77. In spite of owning a small farm and a dozen slaves, Toussaint did not accumulate any significant wealth. According to Jeremy D. Popkin (*Concise History of the Haitian Revolution*, 70), "In contrast to the wealthy members of the mixed-race elite . . . who often received inheritances from a white ancestor, Toussaint did not manage to accumulate much of a fortune before the revolution. He seems to have sold his own property and taken a job on his former owner's plantation, where his wife and children continued to be listed as slaves until the revolution."

13. Alex Dupuy, *Haiti: From Revolutionary Slaves to Powerless Citizens* (New York: Routledge, 2014), 46.

14. Sabine Manigat, "Les Fondements Sociaux de l'état Louverturien," in *La Révolution Française et Haïti: Filiations, Ruptures, Nouvelles Dimensions*, vol. 1, ed. Michel Hector (Port-au-Prince: Société Haïtienne d'histoire et de géographie et Éditions Henri Deschamps, 1995), 130–142.

15. Popkin, *Concise History of the Haitian Revolution*, 98.

16. Pierre Pluchon, *Toussaint Louverture: Un Révolutionnaire Noir d'Ancien Régime* (Paris: Fayard, 1989).

17. J.-Hippolyte-Daniel de Saint-Anthoine, *Notice sur Toussaint Louverture* (Paris: A. Lacour, 1842), 28–29. See also Victor Schoelcher, *Vie de Toussaint Louverture* (Paris: Karthala, 1982), 400–402; C.L.R. James, *The Black Jacobins: Toussaint L'Ouverture and the San Domingo Revolution* (London: Allison and Busby, 1980), 265; Doris L. Garraway, "'Légitime Défense': Universalism and Nationalism in the Discourse of the Haitian Revolution," in *Tree of Liberty: Cultural Legacies of the Haitian Revolution in the Atlantic World*, ed. Doris L. Garraway (Charlottesville: University of Virginia Press, 2008), 74–76.

18. Jean Fouchard, *Les Marrons de la Liberté* (Port-au-Prince: Editions Henri Deschamps, 1988).

19. Antoine Dalmas, *Histoire de la Révolution de Saint Domingue* (Paris: Chez Mame Frères, 1814).

20. Dantes Bellegarde, *Histoire du Peuple Haïtien (1492–1952)* (Port-au-Prince: Fardin, 1953), 63, quoted and trans. by David Patrick Geggus, *Haitian Revolutionary Studies* (Bloomington: Indiana University Press, 2002), 81.

21. Quoted in and translated by Asselin Charles, "Haitian Exceptionalism and Caribbean Consciousness," *Journal of Caribbean Literatures* 3, no. 2 (Spring 2002): 118.

22. Laurent Dubois, *Avengers of the New World* (Cambridge, MA: Harvard University Press, 2004).

23. Schoelcher, *Vie de Toussaint Louverture*, 264 (my translation).

24. Haiti Constitution of 1805 (superseded 1806), Article 14, http://faculty.webster.edu /corbetre/haiti/history/earlyhaiti/1805-const.htm.

25. Ibid.

26. Garraway, "'Légitime Défense,'" 82.

27. As Jeremy Popkin puts it (*You Are All Free: The Haitian Revolution and the Abolition of Slavery* [Cambridge: Cambridge University Press, 2010], 379–380):

The constitution [Dessalines] promulgated in 1805 proclaimed that "slavery is abolished forever" and that "because all distinctions of color among children of the same family must necessarily stop, Haitians will henceforth only be known generically as Blacks." The principles of liberty and equality first articulated in the struggles in France and in Saint Domingue in the early 1790s thus became part of the heritage of the new nation, although the constitution of 1805 also specified that "no white man, regardless of his nationality, may set foot in this territory as a master or landowner," and the installation of Dessalines's regime in 1804 was accompanied by systematic massacres of most of the remaining whites in the island. Meanwhile, in France, the ideals of racial equality and freedom were repudiated altogether. A Napoleonic decree of 13 An X (July 2, 1802) forbade the entry of blacks and people of color in France, and those who were already living there suffered increasing legal discrimination. A spate of overtly racist literature, claiming that blacks were inherently inferior, accompanied these legal measures; the violence in Saint Domingue was frequently cited as evidence of their savage nature. Slavery was reintroduced in the colony of Guadeloupe and Cayenne, where it had been abolished in the 1790s, and it was maintained in Martinique.... Not until the second French abolition decree of April 27, 1848 would the slaves in these French colonies gain their freedom.

28. It is clear that Dalmas was a racist convinced that Africans and their descendants were ignorant, brutal savages. His description of Bois-Caïman confirms this fact (quoted and translated by David Geggus in *The Haitian Revolution: A Documentary History* [Indianapolis: Hackett Publishing Co., 2014], 79):

The elements of this plan had been worked out a few days before by the main leaders on the Lenormand plantation at Morne Rouge. Before carrying it out, they held a sort of celebration or sacrifice in the middle of an uncultivated, wooded area on the Choiseul plantation called Le Caïman, where the Negroes gathered in great number. An entirely black pig, surrounded with fetishes and loaded with a variety of bizarre offerings, was sacrificed to the all-powerful spirit of the black race. The religious ceremonies that accompanied the killing of the pig were typical of the Africans, as was their eagerness to drink its blood and the value they placed on getting some of its hairs as a sort of talisman that they thought would make them invulnerable. It was natural that such a primitive and ignorant caste would begin the most terrible attack with superstitious rites of an absurd and bloodthirsty religion.

29. Léon-Francois Hoffman, "Un mythe national: la cérémonie du Bois-Caïman," in *La République Haitienne: Etat des Lieux et Perspectives,* ed. Gérard Barthélémy and Christian Girault (Paris: Karthala, 1993), 434–448.

30. Léon-Francois Hoffman, "Débat," in *La République Haïtienne: Etat des Lieux et Perspectives,* ed. Gérard Barthelemy and Christian Girault (Paris: Karthala, 1993), 448.

31. Hérard Dumesle, *Voyage dans le Nord d'Haiti* (Cayes: Imprimerie du Gouvernement, 1824), 85–90; C. Ardouin, *Essais sur l'histoire d'Haiti* (Port-au-Prince: Bouchereau, 1865), 16–18; Frank Sylvain, *Le Serment du Bois-Caïman et la Premiere Pentecôte* (Port-au-Prince: Éditions Henri Deschamps, 1979), 15–21.

32. Geggus, *Haitian Revolutionary Studies,* 82, 86–87, and 90–91; originally published as "The Bois Caiman Ceremony," *Journal of Caribbean History* 25, nos. 1–2, 1991): 41–57.

33. Ibid., 77.

34. Ibid., 77, 92.

35. Hénock Trouillot, *Introduction à une Histoire du Vaudou* (Port-au-Prince: Fardin, 1970); Emmanuel C. Paul, *Panorama du Folklore Haitien: Presence Africaine en Haiti* (Port-au-Prince: 1962); Jean Price-Mars, *Ainsi Parla l'Oncle* (Port-au-Prince: Imprimerie de Compiègne, 1928).

36. Geggus, *Haitian Revolutionary Studies,* 80. Laurent Dubois (*Avengers of the New World,* 43) offers a very plausible summary of the role of Vodou in Saint Domingue:

African religions . . . put down roots in the soil of plantations, changing in the process. They entered into dialogue with the practices of Catholicism, whose saints were imbued with a new meaning by worshipers in both Africa and the Americas. In Saint-Domingue the Arada slaves from the Bight of Benin, who were the majority during the first decades of the eighteenth century, brought the traditions of the Fon and Yoruba peoples, which were joined by those brought by the Kongo slaves who eventually became the island's majority. In a world organized to the production of plantation commodities, where slaves were meant to be laborers and nothing more, religious ceremonies provided ritual solace, dance and music, but most importantly a community that extended beyond the plantation. They also provided an occasion for certain individuals to provide advice and guidance. Out of the highly industrialized and regimented plantations, then, emerged a powerful set of religious practices that celebrated and reflected the human struggles of those who participated in them. Religion was, in some sense, a space of freedom in the midst of a world of bondage, and helped lay the foundation for the revolt that ultimately brought complete freedom to the slaves.

37. Gabriel Debien ("Marronage in the French Caribbean," in *Maroon Societies: Rebel Slave Communities in the Americas,* ed. Richard Price, 3rd ed. [Baltimore: Johns Hopkins University Press, 1996], 118–119) describes some of the horrifying punishments invented by the white masters:

[The] most common punishment was a few "days" detention "at the bar." Here, the legs of the offender were held fast between two small beams fixed to the foot of the plank on which he slept at the plantation "hospital" [which often doubled as prison]. . . . Then the whip would be the prelude to such measures as the chain, the collar, and the *nabot.* . . . The *nabot* (a large, iron, circular device weighing six, eight, or even ten pounds) was the severest punishment of all. It was cold-riveted to the foot. . . . The *cachots effrayants* were also an invention of the last twenty years before the Revolution. As their name indicates, they were tiny maximum-security cells, which were probably totally without light.

Leg amputations to prevent escape as well as atrocities like castration and being slowly roasted to death were integral parts of the white masters' arsenal of terror against rebelling slaves. See Richard Price, introduction to *Maroon Societies*, ed. Richard Price, 3rd ed. (Baltimore: Johns Hopkins University Press, 1996), 3.

38. Belair's name is likely to have been used "as a screen" for Toussaint Louverture; see M. Bell, *Toussaint Louverture*, 42–43.

39. Quoted and translated by M. Bell, *Toussaint Louverture*, 39–41.

40. Louis Boisrond-Tonnerre, *Mémoire pour Servir à l'Histoire d'Haïti* (Port-au-Prince: Fardin, 1804), 95; translated by Marlene Daut, "Un-Silencing the Past: Boisrond-Tonnerre, Vastey, and the Re-Writing of the Haitian Revolution," *South Atlantic Review* 74, no. 1 (Winter 2009): 50.

41. Ibid., 70, as translated by Daut, "Un-Silencing the Past," 47.

42. Michèle Duchet, *Anthropologie Et Histoire Au Siècle Des Lumières* (Paris: Albin Michel, 1995), 139–177.

43. As Louis Sala-Molins (*Dark Side of the Light: Slavery and the French Enlightenment* [Minneapolis: University of Minnesota Press, 2006], 13) puts it,

Among the very best of the philosophes, the emphasis was on the "feasibility" of making a subject out of the slave, a human being out of the Negro through the adoption of two different approaches: different and yet—in the mind of their proponents and in terms of the results they expected—convergent. The slave trade had to be abolished, and a schedule of emancipation established. It goes without saying that between the drying up of the market as a result of the desired abolition and the end of the moratorium—in other words, between the elevation of the slave from "movable asset" to "subject"—the cultivation of the sugarcane, indigo, cotton, and tobacco fields had to continue, the mills had to keep grinding; in short, the inescapable economic imperatives of metropolitan France had to remain unquestioned.

It thus became necessary to work out a "royal path" from slavery to emancipation. One that was slow, clear in its layout, and protected from start to finish. The black man would no longer be hunted in Africa; he would be bred and raised on the spot.

44. Jean Fouchard, interviewed by Mohamed B. Taleb-Khyar, *Callaloo* 15, no. 2 (1992), 322.

45. See R. Price, ed. *Maroon Societies*; Gabriel Debien, *Les Esclaves aux Antilles Françaises, XVIIe et XVIIIe Siècles* (Basse-Terre: Société d'Histoire de la Guadeloupe, 1974); Fouchard, *Les Marrons de la Liberté*; Carolyn E. Fick, *The Making of Haiti: The Saint-Domingue Revolution from Below* (Knoxville: University of Tennessee Press, 1990); Geggus, *Haitian Revolutionary Studies*, 69–80.

46. I use the term "exit" in the way it was explored and explained in Albert O. Hirschman, *Exit, Voice, and Loyalty* (Cambridge, MA: Harvard University Press, 1970).

47. James C. Scott, *Weapons of the Weak* (New Haven, CT: Yale University Press, 1985).

48. Ibid., 29–30.

49. Michel-Rolph Trouillot, *Ti Difé Boulé Sou Istoua Ayiti* (Brooklyn: Koleksion Lakansiel, 1977), 75–76 (emphasis in the original). This book, written entirely in Creole is a major intervention in Haitian history, but unfortunately it is poorly circulated. Jean Jonassaint helped me translate the original Creole:

An 1791, modòd libèté-a té jouinn tè gras pou l-té pousé. Esklav yo té pi konsantré sitiya-son yo té pi rèd, yo té pi fasil ouè kontradiksion sosiété-a. Nan Nò-a sitou, anpil té kòmansé konprann libèté yo té bézouin an pat ap janm vini poukont li. Yo té kòmansé konprann libèté sila-a té vlé di: **koupé tèt boulé kay.** Modòd la té sanblé ak modòd ans-yin maron yo, min angiz libèté té égal **sové,** pou ésklav 1791 yo, nan Nò-a sitou, libèté té égal **goumin.**

An vérité, 2 modòd sa yo sanblé min yo pa minm. Jouroumou pa donnin kalbas, min pitit Jan pa Jan. Sé sètin, maronnay la sé youn fason pou youn group protésté, youn fason pou l-di li pa dakò ak system nan. Min mak fabrik maronnay la sé sové. Sové al nan mòn, sové pou travay jading osnon fè travay la mal, sové pou loua klas anro yo, sové pou sèvis yo, pou langaj yo, osnon sové pou lavi-a.... Min gin youn kafou youn klas rive, soua li **pa kapab** fè maronnay ankò, soua li **pa bézouin** fè maronnay ankó, soua li **pa vlé** fè maronnay ankó. Nan Nó-a sitou, an 1791 ésklav yo té rive nan youn kafou koté, angiz yo té **sové** dèyè libèté yo té pito **goumin** pou libèté.

50. R. Price, introduction to *Maroon Societies*, 2.

51. As Ruth Berins Collier and David Collier explain in *Shaping the Political Arena* ([Princeton, N.J.: Princeton University Press, 1991], 29): "A critical juncture may be defined as a period of significant change, which typically occurs in distinct ways in dif-ferent countries . . . and which is hypothesized to produce distinct legacies."

52. As Dale Tomich has argued ("Thinking the 'Unthinkable': Victor Schoelcher and Haiti," *Review [Fernand Braudel Center]* 31, no. 3 [2008]: 413):

The Haitian and French Revolutions influenced one another because they were related. They were not related because they influenced one another. The ideas of the Enlightenment and the French Revolution did not travel to Haiti to exert their influ-ence. Ideas, movements, and institutions reverberated across the Atlantic and inter-acted with one another because they were part of the same complex of trans-atlantic relations. In different ways, conditions were ripe for them at each pole of the metropolitan-colonial complex. The same ideas could have very different consequences in each par-ticular context. Different groups appropriated, adapted, and mobilized them in distinct ways in particular social and geographical locations. The same Rights of Man could be interpreted differently in each location and each set of conditions, and people could appropriate, interpret, and apply them in original and surprising ways to speak to their immediate situations.

See also Fick, *Making of Haiti*, 237–244.

53. On Sonthonax's contribution to both the abolition of slavery and the Haitian Rev-olution, see M. Bell, *Toussaint Louverture*, 46–192; Popkin, *You Are All Free*, 212–213.

54. As Nick Nesbitt has pointed out ("The Idea of 1804," *Yale French Studies* no. 107 [2005]: 37):

We know that when Sonthonax declared the abolition of slavery on August 29, 1793, the first article of his decree stipulated that "The Declaration of the Rights of Man and Citizen will be printed, published, and displayed wherever need be." Though we will never know how many Afro-Haitians read these postings or had someone else read them, enough testimony remains to be certain that the declaration was discussed, analyzed, critiqued, and internalized by the hundreds of thousands of members of this public sphere. No censure of revolutionary texts even attempted to limit their flow into Saint-Domingue until December of 1789.

55. Carolyn E. Fick, "The French Revolution in Saint Domingue: A Triumph or a Failure?" in *A Turbulent Time: The French Revolution and the Greater Caribbean*, ed. David Barry Gaspar and David Patrick Geggus (Bloomington: Indiana University Press, 1997), 69.

56. The conflicting interpretations of the social origins of the Haitian Revolution are succinctly and critically analyzed in David Geggus, "The Haitian Revolution: New Approaches and Old," *Proceedings of the Meeting of the French Colonial Historical Society* 19 (1994): 141–155.

57. There is evidence that General Leclerc had the assistance of Dessalines in arresting Toussaint; see Philippe R. Girard, "Jean-Jacques Dessalines et l'arrestation de Toussaint Louverture," *Journal of Haitian Studies* 17, no. 1 (2011): 123–138. The history of betrayals and personalistic divisions among the Haitian founders is critical in understanding the incapacity of the Haitian ruling class to impose its hegemony, a theme that I will develop in this and following chapters.

It is clear, however, that Napoleon had a Machiavellian plan to feint support for Toussaint, draw him further into his orbit, and then neutralize and arrest him. As Carolyn Fick ("The Saint Domingue Slave Revolution and the Unfolding of Independence, 1791–1804," in *The World of the Haitian Revolution*, ed. David Geggus and Norman Fiering [Bloomington: Indiana University Press, 2009], 185–186) explains:

> Before the expedition set sail from Brest on December 14, 1801, Bonaparte gave its commander, General Victor-Emmanuel Leclerc, his brother-in-law, a set of secret instructions. The captain-general was first to deal with Toussaint and grant his every request in order to enter the colony and capture the strategic positions. The black generals, especially Toussaint Louverture, should be reassured of the good intentions of the metropolis. They should know that the 20,000 regular troops, the elite of the Napoleonic army; the 50-some ships and frigates; and the division generals, brigade generals, and the whole array of lesser-ranking officers had come to Saint-Domingue simply to protect the colony from its enemies, preserve order, and suppress the few rebels that might emerge here and there. Above all, Leclerc should reassure Toussaint and the blacks that their freedom was safeguarded by France: "Never will the French nation place chains upon men whom she has recognized to be free." These were Bonaparte's instructions, and the language was a masterpiece of duplicity. Leclerc had come to bring peace and security to the island, but at the point of bayonets. In Bonaparte's own threatening words, "Whosoever should refuse the authority of the captain-general shall be a traitor to the fatherland, upon whom the wrath of the Republic will descend just as swiftly as fire devours dry cane."

58. Schoelcher, *Vie de Toussaint Louverture*, 347–361. See also Philippe Girard, *Toussaint Louverture* (New York: Basic Books, 2016), 242–251.

59. Schoelcher, *Vie de Toussaint Louverture*, 249 (my translation).

60. See Hannibal Price, *De la Réhabilitation de la Race Noire par la République d'Haiti* (Port-au-Prince: Imprimerie Verollot, 1900).

61. Charles, "Haitian Exceptionalism and Caribbean Consciousness," 117.

62. Translated and quoted in Popkin, *You Are All Free*, 379.

63. It is important to note that this was not only the sentiment of Dessalines; all the major founders of Haiti signed in approval of the constitution: H. Christophe, Clerveaux, Vernet, Gabart, Petion, Geffard, Toussaint, Brave, Raphael, Roamin, Lalondridie, Capoix, Magny, Daut, Conge, Magloire, Ambrose, Yayou, Jean Louis Franchois, Gerin, Mereau, Fervu, Bavelais, Martial Besse.

64. Philippe R. Girard, "Jean-Jacques Dessalines and the Atlantic System: A Reappraisal," *William and Mary Quarterly* 69, no. 3 (July 2012): 579.

65. Girard, *Toussaint Louverture*, 226; Dubois, *Avengers of the New World*, 247.

66. Claude Moïse, *Le projet national de Toussaint Louverture* (Port-au-Prince: Les Editions Memoire, 2001), 102 (my translation); Claude Moïse, ed., *Dictionnaire Historique de la Révolution Haïtienne 1789–1804* (Montréal: Editions du Cidihca, 2003), 235–237.

67. Moïse, *Le projet national de Toussaint Louverture*, 47.

68. Girard, "Jean-Jacques Dessalines and the Atlantic System," 581.

69. Philippe R. Girard has uncovered evidence that prior to his arrest and deportation, Toussaint had clearly committed himself to renew his war against the French; see "Jean-Jacques Dessalines et l'arrestation de Toussaint Louverture," 123–138.

70. On Toussaint's flirtation with importing slaves, see Popkin, *Concise History of the Haitian Revolution*, 98, and Dubois, *Avengers of the New World*, 247. David Geggus puts it clearly (*Haitian Revolutionary Studies*, 22–23):

Although fiercely committed to the liberty of the blacks, [Toussaint] believed it essential that the plantation regime be revived in order to restore Saint Domingue's prosperity. With no export economy, there would be no revenue to maintain his army of 20,000 to 40,000 men. And without the army, the gains of the revolution would be at the mercy of France's unstable politics. Toussaint therefore continued with the schemes of Commissioner Sonthonax, whereby the ex-slaves were compelled to work on the plantation in return for a share of the produce. It was a difficult policy to implement, for increasingly the blacks preferred to establish smallholdings of their own and had little desire to work for wages. . . . Toussaint, however, refused to break up the great estates. He used the army to impose the regime of forced labor and sanctioned the use of corporal punishment; he even supported the reintroduction of the slave trade to make up the loss of manpower.

According to Girard ("Jean-Jacques Dessalines and the Atlantic System," 576), Dessalines had similar inclinations:

On January 17, 1804, while meeting Corbet during his first visit to Haiti, Dessalines suddenly asked whether British slave traders in Jamaica would be willing to sell some of their human cargo in Haiti (where imported slaves would presumably have worked under the semifree cultivator status). Corbet, startled by a proposal that did not feature in his instructions and did not fit his understanding of Dessalines's worldview, could offer no response. But Dessalines formally requested that a clause promoting the slave trade be included in the proposed treaty of commerce, then brought up the matter again—twice—during Corbet's second mission in February. The proposal was passed on to Nugent and ultimately to the British government, both of whom rejected it because they preferred not to strengthen Dessalines's regime with potential soldiers but also because British policy was rapidly moving toward an overall abolition of the slave trade.

71. Gordon Brown, *Toussaint's Clause* (Jackson: University Press of Mississippi, 2005), 233; see also Girard, "Jean-Jacques Dessalines and the Atlantic System," 554–569, 573–574.

72. Girard, "Jean-Jacques Dessalines et l'arrestation de Toussaint Louverture," 123–138.

73. Dubois, *Avengers of the New World*, 42.

74. Debien, *Les Esclaves Aux Antilles Françaises*, 124–126 and 133 (my translation).

75. Thomas Ott, *The Haitian Revolution* (Knoxville: University of Tennessee Press, 1973); James, *Black Jacobins*; Popkin, *You Are All Free*; Dubois, *Avengers of the New World*.

76. David Patrick Geggus, *The Haitian Revolution: A Documentary History* (Indianapolis: Hackett Publishing Company, 2014), xxxi.

77. Carlo Célius, "Neoclassicism and the Haitian Revolution," in *The World of the Haitian Revolution*, ed. David Geggus and Norman Fiering (Bloomington: Indiana University Press, 2009), 368.

78. While celebrated in Haitian exceptionalism and particularly in Vodou, the words *moun Ginen*, "African people," or *pitit Ginen*, "the sons and daughters of Africa," are in some instances used pejoratively to invoke inferiority. In spite of their ancestry, the ruling classes, particularly the mulatto faction, has tended to identify the word *moun Ginen* with *Bossale*.

79. Gerald Horne, *Confronting Black Jacobins* (New York: Monthly Review Press, 2015), 102. See also Garraway, "'Légitime Défense,'" 63–88. Similarly, Sibylle Fischer (*Modernity Disavowed* [Durham, NC: Duke University Press, 2004], 233) contends,

> Disrupting any biologistic or racialist expectations, they make "black" a mere implication of being Haitian and thus a political rather than a biological category. In both cases, liberation from oppression is imagined through a complete break with the inherited past. . . . The very act of calling all Haitians black, regardless of their phenotype, would for a long time be recognized as a racial break from the entrenched practice of distinguishing, at the very least, between mulattoes, blacks, and whites. . . . Calling all Haitians, regardless of skin color, black is a gesture like calling all people, regardless of their sex, women: it both asserts egalitarian and universalist intuitions and puts them to a test by using the previously subordinated term of the opposition as the universal term.

80. Délide Joseph, *L'État Haitien et ses Intellectuels* (Port-au-Prince: Imprimerie Le Natal, 2017), 257–298.

81. Ibid., 258 (my translation):

> Le nationalisme imaginé par les intellectuels Haitiens . . . cherche à dépasser les différences existant entre les citoyens de l'État haïtien et les Noirs en général, pour les unifier politiquement. Vouloir créer un "État noir," refuge pour tous les esclaves et les Noirs libres discriminés un peu partout, exprime le mécontentement envers l'institution servile, le système socio-racial institué par les puissances colonialistes et esclavagistes de la période, mais également un désir de leur prouver la capacité des peuples noirs à instaurer un gouvernement, une administration nationale et à s'autogérer.

82. Abbé Grégoire, *De la Liberté de Consciences et de Culte a Haïti* (Paris: Baudoin Frères, 1821), 42; translated and quoted in Jean-François Brière, "Abbé Grégoire and Haitian Independence," *Research in African Literatures* 35, no. 2 (2004): 38. See also Alyssa Goldstein Sepinwall, *The Abbé Grégoire and the French Revolution: The Making of Modern Universalism* (Berkeley: University of California Press, 2005).

83. Julia Gaffield, *Haitian Connections in the Atlantic World: Recognition after Revolution* (Chapel Hill: University of North Carolina Press, 2015), 183.

84. Ibid. As Gaffield puts it (58–60):

> Neither the Haitian state nor individuals abroad were successful in implementing their espoused goals: Haiti was not able to secure the complete confidence of the

international community, nor was the country uniformly isolated, even after different governors prohibited trade to Haiti. . . . Over the course of the first two years of Haitian independence, British representatives figured out a way to incorporate a de facto foreign island into their colonial system. In this sense, British policy with respect to nascent Haiti was dramatically different from every other nation of the Atlantic.

85. David Patrick Geggus, "Saint Domingue on the Eve of the Haitian Revolution," in *The World of the Haitian Revolution*, ed. David Geggus and Norman Fiering (Bloomington: Indiana University Press, 2009), 3–4. In addition, Marlene L. Daut has exhaustively demonstrated that there was no literary "silence" about the Haitian Revolution in the eighteenth and nineteenth centuries, and that the revolution was quite thinkable during that period. See *Tropics of Haiti*, 1–48, and "Un-Silencing the Past," 35–64. See also Alyssa Goldstein Sepinwall, "The Specter of Saint Domingue: American and French Reactions to the Haitian Revolution," in *The World of the Haitian Revolution*, ed. David Geggus and Norman Fiering (Bloomington: Indiana University Press, 2009), 317–338; Alyssa Goldstein Sepinwall, "Still Unthinkable? The Haitian Revolution and the Reception of Michel-Rolph Trouillot's 'Silencing the Past,'" *Journal of Haitian Studies* 19, no. 2 (2013): 75–103; and Tomich, "Thinking the 'Unthinkable.'"

86. Quoted in Matthew J. Clavin, *Toussaint Louverture and the American Civil War* (Philadelphia: University of Pennsylvania Press, 2010), 184.

87. In spite of being the instigator of the doctrine that has his name, President Monroe was bent on excluding Haiti from the moral community of the Western Hemisphere. As Tim Matthewson explains (*A Proslavery Foreign Policy: Haitian-American Relations during the Early Republic* [Westport: CT: Praeger Publishers, 2003], 145):

During the Monroe administration, President Boyer of Haiti had requested formal recognition. But President Monroe directed that the letter from Boyer should not be answered, saying later, in a formal address to Congress, that the Haitians constituted a "separate interest" or a threat to the United States. In doing so, Monroe cast doubt on the common humanity of the former slaves, stigmatized them as social pariahs, and consigned them to a social netherworld, shifting to Haitians the onus for aggressive behavior against the United States. In 1823, therefore, when he issued his famous Doctrine, Monroe omitted reference to Haiti, thus tacitly approving of the publicly declared French intention to restore French power in their former colony of Saint Domingue.

88. Davis, *Inhuman Bondage*, 158.

89. As Tim Matthewson put it ("Jefferson and Haiti," *Journal of Southern History* 61, no. 2 [May 1995]: 237):

From the start of the Haitian Revolution, the example of the slave revolt had become an effective tool in the hands of southerners for checking discussion of slavery, the slave trade, and related issues, including Haiti. Firmly rooted in the interests and culture of the planter class, defenders of slavery felt compelled to deny recognition to the new order of things in Haiti. Haitian independence was a compelling rejection of the legitimacy of slavery and the southern way of life, which left slaveholders with the realization that they could never again feel confident of their claims that slaves were contented with bondage. One historian suggested that the South sought to "banish the reality of St. Domingo."

90. The arrival of white exiles from Haiti further consolidated this belief in American exceptionalism. The presence of these exiles activated the debate about whether Ameri-

can democracy was compatible with slavery and the slave trade. As Ashli White (*Encountering Revolution: Haiti and the Making of the Early Republic* [Baltimore: Johns Hopkins University Press, 2010], 204–205) put it:

> In coming to grips with the Saint-Dominguans, Americans articulated, in both word and deed, competing visions of their republic. These notions were unstable; the latest turn of revolution brought new trials and new responses. Nevertheless, the Haitian Revolution helped forge this crucial moment in U.S. nation building. Despite the ambivalence that marked U.S. attitudes toward the revolution, the result was a bolstering of the slaveholding republic, as white Americans used the exiles as a foil in arguing for their nation's exceptionalism. Because they differed from their Saint-Dominguan counterparts the reasoning went, white Americans could prevent a similar fate in the United States, or at least had time to find another, more acceptable solution to the national paradox. In their selective reading of events, white Americans were of sounder character and were better republicans than the French creoles and black Americans were content under a more benign version of slavery. As best they could, African Americans (and a few white abolitionists) invoked the Haitian Revolution to fight the status quo, yet not until shortly before the Civil War would their rhetoric resonate and lead to decisive action.

91. Ibid., 125–130 and 204–205.

92. Ibid., 124–125.

93. Clavin, *Toussaint Louverture and the American Civil War.*

94. Alan Taylor, *American Revolutions* (New York: W. W. Norton & Co., 2016), 421.

95. William J. Grayson, *The Hireling and the Slave, Chicora, and Other Poems* (Charleston, SC: McCarter & Co. Publishers, 1856), 70–71.

96. Clavin, *Toussaint Louverture and the American Civil War*; White, *Encountering Revolution*, 130–154.

97. Clavin, *Toussaint Louverture and the American Civil War*, 121–143; Hunt, *Haiti's Influence on Antebellum America*, 147–188.

98. Clavin, *Toussaint Louverture and the American Civil War*, 4–5.

99. Clavin, *Toussaint Louverture and the American Civil War*, 144–180.

100. Eric Foner, *Reconstruction: America's Unfinished Revolution 1863–1877* (New York: Harper Perennial, 2014).

101. Clavin, *Toussaint Louverture and the American Civil War*, 184–185; David Blight, *Race and Reunion: The Civil War in American Memory* (Cambridge, MA: Harvard University Press, 2001), 389.

102. C. Vann Woodward, *The Strange Career of Jim Crow* (New York: Oxford University Press, 2002), 29; see also Michelle Alexander, *The New Jim Crow: Mass Incarceration in the Age of Colorblindness*, rev. ed. (New York: New Press, 2011), 20–35.

103. Clavin, *Toussaint Louverture and the American Civil War*, 184–185.

104. Pierre Bourdieu, *The Logic of Practice* (Stanford, CA: Stanford University Press, 1980), 52–65. Bourdieu defines *habitus* as "systems of durable, transposable dispositions, structured structures predisposed to function as structuring structures." The *habitus* is itself produced by the "conditionings associated with particular class of conditions of existence" (53). See also Pierre Bourdieu, *In Other Words: Essays Toward a Reflexive Sociology* (Stanford, CA: Stanford University Press, 1990), 9, 61, and 77.

105. Alexander, *New Jim Crow*, 26–35.

106. Ibid.

107. Anténor Firmin, *De L'Egalité des Races Humaines* (Montréal: Mémoire D'Encrier, 2005), 267 (my translation).

108. Ibid., 124.

109. Anténor Firmin, *The Equality of the Human Races*, trans. Asselin Charles (Champaign: University of Illinois Press, 2002), 438.

110. It is important to note, however, that slavery in the Americas was ultimately abolished in 1888 with Brazil's so-called Golden Law.

111. Firmin, *Equality of the Human Races*, 140.

CHAPTER 4 — MANIFEST DESTINY AND THE AMERICAN OCCUPATION OF HAITI

1. Seymour Martin Lipset, *American Exceptionalism* (New York: W. W. Norton & Co., 1996), 13. Lipset argues that from the very beginning of their republic, Americans have felt the protective "hand of providence." See also Nicholas Guyatt, *Providence and the Invention of the United States, 1607–1876* (Cambridge: Cambridge University Press, 2007).

2. Stephanson, *Manifest Destiny*, 5.

3. George W. Bush, "State of the Union Address" (speech, Washington, D.C., January 28, 2003), *Washington Post*, https://www.washingtonpost.com/wp-srv/onpolitics /transcripts/bushtext_012803.html.

4. Guyatt, *Providence and the Invention of the United States*, 1–2.

5. Stephanson, *Manifest Destiny*, 22.

6. Albert J. Beveridge, "In Support of an American Empire," January 9, 1900, 56th Congress, 1st session, *Congressional Record* 33, pt. 1.

7. Immanuel Wallerstein, *European Universalism: The Rhetoric of Power* (New York: New Press, 2006).

8. Ibid., 6.

9. Reginald Horsman, *Race and Manifest Destiny* (Cambridge, MA: Harvard University Press, 1981); Losurdo, *Liberalism*, 95–125.

10. As Henry Cabot Lodge claimed, the United States had "a record of conquest, colonization, and territorial expansion unequalled by any people in the nineteenth century." Quoted in Stephanson, *Manifest Destiny*, 104.

11. Quoted in Stephanson, *Manifest Destiny*, 84. Burgess was a clear advocate of colonialism. According to him, Teutonic nations—"the English, French, Lombards, Scandinavians, Germans, and North Americans"—had an obligation to "carry the political civilization of the modern world into those parts of the world inhabited by unpolitical and barbaric races; *i.e.* they must have a colonial policy." Quoted in Robert Vitalis, *White World Order, Black Power Politics* (Ithaca, NY: Cornell University Press, 2015), 35. Albert Lawrence Lowell, another major American political scientist and academic figure, who eventually became president of Harvard University, believed also in a racist hierarchy of human beings. In his view, inferior races were "not sufficiently trained in habits of self-government," and thus the "theory of universal political equality does not apply to tribal Indians, to Chinese, or to negroes under all conditions." Quoted in Vitalis, *White World Order, Black Power Politics*, 40.

12. Quoted in Stephanson, *Manifest Destiny*, 107.

13. Quoted in Vitalis, *White World Order, Black Power Politics*, 44.

14. Quoted in Stephanson, *Manifest Destiny*, 99.

15. Quoted in Stephanson, *Manifest Destiny*, 100.

16. Walter LaFeber, *The Cambridge History of American Foreign Relations* (Cambridge: Cambridge University Press, 1993), 188.

17. This section on the American occupation of Haiti draws heavily from my book, *The Roots of Haitian Despotism*, 131–192, and my article "Killing Haitian Democracy," *Jacobin*, July 22, 2015, https://www.jacobinmag.com/2015/07/monroe-doctrine-1915-occupation -duvalier/.

18. Quoted in David Healy, *Gunboat Diplomacy in the Wilson Era: The U.S. Navy in Haiti, 1915–1916* (Madison: University of Wisconsin Press, 1976), 34.

19. Quoted in Hans Schmidt, *The United States Occupation of Haiti, 1915–1934* (New Brunswick, NJ: Rutgers University Press, 1995), 63.

20. Quoted in Schmidt, *United States Occupation of Haiti*, 62–63.

21. Ibid., 64–65.

22. Ibid.

23. Quoted in Healy, *Gunboat Diplomacy in the Wilson Era*, 131.

24. The Comité Révolutionaire de Port-au-Prince, which was set up to fill the vacuum left by the murder of Sam, told Captain Beach that there was no reason to have American troops on Haitian soil since order had been reestablished. According to the British ambassador in Haiti, the Comité agreed to the landing of the marines for the sole purposes of protecting foreign legations. See Roger Gaillard, *Les Blancs Débarquent (1914–1915): Les Cent-Jours de Rosalvo Bobo* (Port-au-Prince: Presses Nationales, 1973), 104–105.

25. Facing a violent insurrection, President Vilbrun Guillaume Sam sought safety at the French embassy, only to be caught, lynched, and dismembered by an enraged militia of supporters of Rosalvo Bobo. Sam's brutal murder was an act of revenge and retaliation for ordering the killing of 167 political prisoners. Bobo, who led the insurrection against Sam, was on the verge of capturing the presidency, but Washington vetoed him. Seeing Bobo as an unacceptable, radical revolutionary nationalist, the occupying forces opposed him and sent him into exile. See François Blancpain, *Haïti et les États Unis, 1915–1934* (Paris: L'Harmattan, 1999), 46–56, and Gaillard, *Les Blancs Débarquent*.

26. Quoted in Arthur C. Millspaugh, *Haiti under American Control 1915–1930* (Boston: World Peace Foundation, 1931), 38.

27. Quoted in Schmidt, *United States Occupation of Haiti*, 73.

28. These were the words of American chargé d'affaires R. B. Davis, quoted in Millspaugh, *Haiti under American Control*, 41.

29. Quoted in Schmidt, *United States Occupation of Haiti*, 74.

30. Quoted in Millspaugh, *Haiti under American Control*, 38.

31. In a 1915 memorandum to President Wilson, Secretary of State Lansing spelled out clearly the objectives of American policy in the Caribbean (quoted in Schmidt, *United States Occupation of Haiti*, 59): "The opposition to European control over American territory is not primarily to preserve the integrity of any American state.... The essential idea is to prevent a condition which would menace the national interests of the United States.... I make no argument on the ground of the benefit which would result to the peoples of these republics by the adoption of this policy."

32. Quoted in Healy, *Gunboat Diplomacy in the Wilson Era*, 129.

33. Quoted in François Blancpain, *Haïti et les États Unis*, 64–65 (my translation): "Tant que j'ai cru que notre malheureuse patrie pouvait se délivrer elle-même, j'ai

repoussé le concours étranger. Mais quand je l'ai vue tomber, épuisée, saignée à blanc, dans la boue . . . j'ai compris, et tout ce qu'il y a d'honnête et pur dans le pays a compris que nous n'avons plus désormais que le choix: ou bien la disparition définitive dans l'abjection, dans la famine, dans le sang, ou bien la Rédemption avec l'aide des États-Unis. J'ai préféré cette Rédemption."

34. Healy, *Gunboat Diplomacy in the Wilson Era*, 180.

35. Ibid.

36. Quoted in Schmidt, *United States Occupation of Haiti*, 97.

37. Ibid., 98.

38. Ibid., 7.

39. Ibid., 8–9. Schmidt writes:

Major Smedley D. Butler, first commandant of the American-sponsored Gendarmerie d'Haïti, had previously campaigned in the Philippines, China, Honduras, Nicaragua, Panama, and Mexico; and Colonel Littleton W. T. Waller, commander of the Marine Expeditionary Forces in Haiti in 1915, had commanded the marine landing in Cuba in 1906 and before that had achieved notoriety in connection with the Samar atrocities in the Philippines. Many American civilian administrators also came to Haiti with previous colonial experience; three of the four financial advisers, the most important civilian officials, had held similar posts in Peru, Persia, and Liberia, and the head of the agricultural-technical service had held a similar position in Indochina. (8)

If the Southern heritage and the imperial mindset were dominant among the most prominent marines, there does not seem to be strong evidence showing a Southern preponderance among marines enlisted in the corps and serving in Haiti (see Schmidt, 144–145). For instance, while General Waller and High Commissioner Russell were both Southerners, Commandant Butler was a Quaker born in Pennsylvania. The occupiers' racism was all-pervasive; regional appurtenance had little effect on its intensity and viciousness. As Schmidt argues shrewdly, "Whether or not there was a disproportionately large number of Southern marines in Haiti, the fact that many observers felt that this was the case indicates that Southerners and Southern racial codes were conspicuous." (145).

40. Schmidt, *United States Occupation of Haiti*; see also Healy, *Gunboat Diplomacy in the Wilson Era*, 216–220.

41. Major Smedley Butler, quoted in Healy, *Gunboat Diplomacy in the Wilson Era*, 219.

42. Quoted in Schmidt, *United States Occupation of Haiti*, 79.

43. Quoted as cited in Healy, *Gunboat Diplomacy in the Wilson Era*, 219.

44. Quoted in Schmidt, *United States Occupation of Haiti*, 147.

45. Ibid., 146.

46. Ibid., 70.

47. Ibid., 145–146.

CHAPTER 5 — THE AMERICAN OCCUPATION AND
HAITI'S EXCEPTIONALISM

1. Schmidt, *United States Occupation of Haiti*, 199–200; Suzy Castor, *L'Occupation Américaine D'Haïti* (Port-au-Prince: Imprimerie Henri Deschamps, 1988), 168–173.

2. David Nicholls, *From Dessalines to Duvalier: Race, Colour and National Independence* (New Brunswick, NJ: Rutgers University Press, 1996), 101–141.

3. The Cacos were peasants organized as guerrillas who first emerged in the 1870s in the north of the country. They supported Rosalvo Bobo, whom the American occupiers pre-

vented from succeeding the murdered President Sam. Eventually they became a violent resistance movement opposed to the U.S. occupation; they joined the larger guerrilla insurgency led by the nationalist Charlemagne Péralte. With the American killing of Péralte in 1919, the country was "pacified." See Schmidt, *United States Occupation of Haiti*, 199–200; Castor, *L'Occupation Américaine D'Haïti*; Fatton, *Roots of Haitian Despotism*, 159–165.

4. As David Nicholls emphasizes (*From Dessalines to Duvalier*, 142): "The clumsy actions of the Americans who insisted on treating all Haitians of whatever colour as 'niggers', contributed to this growing solidarity. Paradoxically the Americans unintentionally succeeded, where Dessalines had failed, in uniting all Haitians under the name 'black'. The twenties saw a growing solidarity among Haitians; collaborators like Presidents Dartiguenave and Borno found themselves virtually isolated from national life, being maintained in office solely by United States military support."

5. See Schmidt, *United States Occupation of Haiti*, 199–200; Castor, *L'Occupation Américaine D'Haïti*; Fatton, *Roots of Haitian Despotism*, 173–175. The massacre followed a period of intense resistance to the occupation that began with student protests in October 1929 and culminated in a nationwide strike.

6. Schmidt, *United States Occupation of Haiti*, 207–214; Robert Spector, *W. Cameron Forbes and the Hoover Commissions to Haiti* (New York: University Press of America, 1985), 39–156.

7. Millspaugh, *Haiti under American Control*, 187. See also Blancpain, *Haïti et les États Unis*, 326.

8. Walter LaFeber, *Inevitable Revolutions* (New York: W. W. Norton & Co., 1984), 78–83; see also Schmidt, *United States Occupation of Haiti*, 5–14.

9. Fatton, *Roots of Haitian Despotism*, 81–130.

10. Fatton, *Roots of Haitian Despotism*; Robert Fatton Jr., *Haiti's Predatory Republic* (Boulder, CO: Lynne Rienner Publishers, 2002); Michel-Rolph Trouillot, *Haiti: State against Nation* (New York: Monthly Review Press, 1990).

11. Jean-Jacques Dessalines, "Haitian Declaration of Independence," 1804 (emphasis added), https://today.duke.edu/showcase/haitideclaration/declarationstext.html.

12. Ibid.

13. Haiti Constitution of 1801 (superseded 1804), https://www.marxists.org/history/haiti/1801/constitution.htm.

14. Buck-Morss, *Hegel, Haiti, and Universal History*, 94–95.

15. Ibid., 94–107; Fischer, *Modernity Disavowed*, 260–271. David Patrick Geggus puts it well ("The Caribbean in the Age of Revolution," in *The Age of Revolutions in Global Context, c. 1760–1840*, ed. David Armitage and Sanjay Subrahmanyam (New York: Palgrave Macmillan, 2010), 87):

> Of all the Atlantic revolutions, Saint-Domingue's most fully embodied the contemporary struggle for freedom, equality and independence, and it produced the greatest degree of economic and social change. Beginning as a home-rule movement among wealthy white colonists it quickly spread to militant free people of colour seeking political rights and then gave rise to the largest slave uprising in the history of the Americas. Its narrative is a succession of major precedents: colonial representation in a metropolitan assembly, the ending of racial discrimination, the first abolition of slavery in a major slave society, and the creation of a Latin American state. By 1804 colonialism and slavery, the defining institutions of the Caribbean, were annihilated precisely where, for three hundred years of unchecked growth, they had most prospered.

16. Fatton, *Roots of Haitian Despotism*, 13–130.

17. Geggus, "Caribbean in the Age of Revolution," 100.

18. Quoted in Claude Moïse, *Constitutions et luttes de pouvoir en Haiti: Tome 1—La faillite des classes Dirigeantes (1804–1915)* (Montreal: CIDIHCA, 1988), 30 (my translation).

19. Haiti Constitution of 1801.

20. Haiti Constitution of 1805 (superseded 1806), http://faculty.webster.edu/corbetre /haiti/history/earlyhaiti/1805-const.htm.

21. M. Bell, *Toussaint Louverture*, 212.

22. Alex Dupuy, *Haiti in the World Economy: Class, Race, and Underdevelopment since 1700* (Boulder, CO: Westview Press, 1989).

23. Claude Moïse's description of Toussaint's authoritarian regime is equally valid for the first rulers of an independent Haiti (*Le projet national de Toussaint Louverture: La Constitution de 1801* (Port-au-Prince: Editions Mémoire, 2001), 47):

> Le projet social louverturien ne transcende pas les contradictions sociales issues du démembrement du régime colonial esclavagiste. Il ne peut concilier les intérêts antagoniques. Il tend à les enfermer dans un régime autoritaire et répressif fortement modelé par le pouvoir personnel absolu que Toussaint a fait institutionnaliser. . . .
>
> [Les] masses ne trouvent pas leur compte dans la politique économique et sociale de Toussaint Louverture. Les cultivateurs cherchent par tous les moyens à échapper aux contraintes du système: fuite dans les mornes, refus de travailler. C'est une assez longue histoire qui va de la résistance passive a la résistance active et qui se confond avec celle de la colonisation et de l'esclavage.

> The Louverturian social project does not transcend the social contradictions arising from dismemberment of the colonial slave regime. It cannot reconcile antagonistic interests. It tends to enclose them in a repressive and authoritarian regime strongly modeled on the absolute personal power that Toussaint institutionalized.
>
> The masses do not count in the economic and social politics of Toussaint Louverture. Rural laborers seek all ways to escape the constraints of the system: escape into the hills, refusal to work. It is a rather long story that goes from passive to active resistance and which gets mixed up with the story of colonization and slavery.

24. Toussaint's labor decree of October 12, 1800, makes it clear that he believed, like most Haitian leaders of the early and mid-nineteenth century, that a form of agrarian despotism was necessary for economic prosperity:

> [Field-negroes] are forbidden to quit their respective plantations without a lawful permission. This is by no means attended to, since they change their place of labour as they please, go to and fro, and pay not the least attention to agriculture, though the only means of furnishing sustenance to the military, their protectors. They even conceal themselves in towns, in villages, and mountains, where, allured by the enemies of good order, they live by plunder, and in a state of open hostility to society.
>
> Whereas, since the revolution, labourers of both sexes, then too young to be employed in the fields, refuse to go there now under pretext of freedom, spend their time in wandering about, and give a bad example to the other cultivators. . . .
>
> Art. 1. All overseers, drivers and field-negroes are bound to observe, with exactness, submission, and obedience, their duty in the same manner as soldiers.

Art. 2. All overseers, drivers, and field-labourers, who will not perform with assiduity the duties required of them, shall be arrested and punished as severely as soldiers deviating from their duty. . . .

Art. 3. All field-labourers, men and women, now in a state of idleness, living in towns, villages, and on other plantations than those to which they belong, with an intention to evade work, even those of both sexes who have not been employed in field labour since the revolution, are required to return immediately to their respective plantations. . . .

All those who shall be found in contravention hereto, shall be instantly arrested, and if they are found guilty they shall be drafted into one of the regiments of the army. . . . Liberty cannot exist without industry. (Quoted in Geggus, *Haitian Revolution*, 153–154.]

25. Fick, *Making of Haiti*, 222; see also François Blancpain, *La Condition des Paysans Haitiens* (Paris: Karthala, 2003), 103; Dupuy, *Haiti: From Revolutionary Slaves to Powerless Citizens*, 46–50.

26. Fatton, *Roots of Haitian Despotism*, 43–79.

27. J. C. Scott, *Weapons of the Weak*, xii.

28. Fick, *Making of Haiti*, 23. Alex Dupuy (*Haiti: From Revolutionary Slaves to Powerless Citizens*, 54–62) argues convincingly that the evasive capacity of the peasantry was ultimately a "Pyrrhic victory" in that it undermined whatever possibility Haiti might have had to generate a more productive form of capitalism.

29. Laurent Dubois, "Thinking Haitian Independence in Haitian Vodou," in *The Haitian Declaration of Independence: Creation, Context, and Legacy*, ed. Julia Gaffield (Charlottesville: University of Virginia Press, 2016), 207.

30. Aimé Césaire, *The Tragedy of King Christophe*, trans. Ralph Manheim (New York: Grove Press, 1970), 78–79 (act 3, scene 2).

31. Quoted in M. Bell, *Toussaint Louverture*, 204.

32. Haiti Constitution of 1805.

33. *Blans* is a complicated Creole word; its literal translation is "white," but when used in the Constitution of 1805 it implied foreign colonialists. Indeed, the Polish and Germans who fought alongside the Haitian revolutionary army were considered full citizens of the new republic. Color or race did not define citizenship.

34. Popkin, *Concise History of the Haitian Revolution*, 137.

35. Jean-Jacques Dessalines, "Haitian Declaration of Independence," 1804, https://today.duke.edu/showcase/haitideclaration/declarationstext.html. See also Laurent Dubois, "Avenging America: The Politics of Violence in the Haitian Revolution," in *The World of the Haitian Revolution*, ed. David Geggus and Norman Fiering (Bloomington: Indiana University Press, 2009), 111–124.

36. Haiti Constitution of 1805.

37. Quoted and translated by Daut in "Un-Silencing the Past," 51.

38. Quoted and translated by Charles in "Haitian Exceptionalism and Caribbean Consciousness," 119.

39. Fatton, *Haiti: Trapped in the Outer Periphery*.

40. Eugene Genovese, *From Rebellion to Revolution* (Baton Rouge: Louisiana State University Press, 1979), 88–89; see also Dupuy, *Haiti: From Revolutionary Slaves to Powerless Citizens*, 54–62.

41. Dupuy, *Haiti: From Revolutionary Slaves to Powerless Citizens*, 56–57.

42. Ibid., 59–60; Fatton, *Haiti: Trapped in the Outer Periphery.*

43. The ordinance that established the terms of the indemnity was signed by King Charles X on April 17, 1825 (quoted in Liliana Obregón, "Empire, Racial Capitalism, and International Law: The Case of Manumitted Haiti and the Recognition Debt," *Leiden Journal of International Law* 31, no. 3 [2018]: 610):

> Article I. The ports of the French part of St. Domingo shall be open to the commerce of all nations. The duties levied in these ports either on ships or on goods, both at entry and exit, shall be equal and uniform for all flags except the French flag in favour of which such charges shall be Reduced by half. Article 2. The present inhabitants of the French part of Santo Domingo shall pay to the Caisse des Depots and consignations of France in five equal terms from year to year, the first due to 31 December 1825, the sum of one hundred and fifty million francs intended to compensate the former settlers who demanded an indemnity. Article 3. We grant these conditions by the present Ordinance to the present inhabitants of the French part of Santo Domingo, the full and complete independence of their government. And shall be the present seal of the great seal. Given at Paris, at the Chateau des Tuileries, on the 17th of April, in the year of 1825, and of our reign first.

44. The indemnity represented a colossal sum; as Liliana Obregón notes ("Empire, Racial Capitalism, and International Law," 610], it "amounted to five times France's total annual budget and ten times as much as the United States paid Napoleon for the Louisiana Purchase (F50 million)." The process leading to Haiti's decision to pay the indemnity involved a complicated, decadelong negotiation between three different Haitian rulers—Alexandre Petion, Henry Christophe, and Jean-Pierre Boyer—and the French government. This history is well recounted in Jean-François Brière, *Haiti et la France, 1804–1848: Le Rêve Brisé* (Paris: Karthala, 2008); Louis-Philippe Dalembert, "Haïti, la dette originelle," *Liberation,* March 25, 2010, http://www.liberation.fr/planete/2010/03/25/haitila-dette-originelle_617159; Alex Dupuy, *Rethinking the Haitian Revolution* (London: Rowman and Littlefield, 2019), 91–133; Obregón, "Empire, Racial Capitalism, and International Law"; and Anthony Phillips, "Haiti, France, and the Independence Debt of 1825," Canada-Haiti Information Project, 2008, canada-haiti.ca/sites/default/files/Haiti,%20France%20and%20the%20Independence%20Debt%20of%201825_0.pdf.

45. Dupuy, *Rethinking the Haitian Revolution,* 114.

46. In the words of Liliana Obregón ("Empire, Racial Capitalism, and International Law," 610–614):

> King Charles X of France delivered a unilateral ultimatum. The purpose of France's final proposal, or rather imposition, was to grant recognition while at the same time humiliating Haiti and destroying her capital by making her into a dependent commercial colony for France. Much like the manumitted slaves who had to continue working for their former owners, Haiti was made an offer that was already unconscionable on its face.... Though "neo-colonialism" was a term coined in the 1960s to refer to European (and particularly French) foreign capital control of the newly decolonized African states, Haiti was the first "African" state where creditors built a practice of economic imperialism.

47. A. Phillips, "Haiti, France, and the Independence Debt," 6.

48. Sidney Mintz, *Caribbean Transformations* (Chicago: Aldine Publishing, 1974), 263.

49. Jean Casimir, "From Saint Domingue to Haiti: To Live Again or to Live at Last," in *The World of the Haitian Revolution,* ed. David Geggus and Norman Fiering (Blooming-

ton: Indiana University Press, 2009), xvii–xviii; Philippe R. Girard, "Did Dessalines Plan to Export the Haitian Revolution?" in *The Haitian Declaration of Independence: Creation, Context, and Legacy*, ed. Julia Gaffield (Charlottesville: University of Virginia Press, 2016), 136–157.

50. Dessalines, "Haitian Declaration of Independence." In a personal communication, Alex Dupuy reminded me that there was an important exception to this principle of Haitian noninterference. When President Boyer invaded and annexed Spanish Santo Domingo in 1822, he abolished slavery in the territory. Not surprisingly, Spain, the Santo Domingo planter class, and the United States did not welcome Haiti's act of emancipation.

51. Alain Turnier, *La Société des Baïnnettes* (Port-au-Prince: Imprimerie Le Natal, 1985), 40 (my translation).

52. Thomas Jefferson to Aaron Burr, February 11, 1799, in *The Thomas Jefferson Encyclopedia*, Thomas Jefferson Foundation, https://www.monticello.org/site/research-and -collections/st-domingue-haiti#footnote27_xj2co5c. Arthur Scherr, however, seeks to situate Jefferson in the racist spectrum of the eighteenth and nineteenth centuries as having a more nuanced view on the matter than most of his contemporaries. In addition, he contends that Jefferson's description of Haitians as "Cannibals of the terrible republic" was in fact intended for the French Jacobins. Jefferson's words, according to Scherr, were borrowed from Edmund Burke's writings on the *Regicide Directory of France*. See Arthur Scherr, "Cannibals" Revisited: A Closer Look at His Notorious Phrase," *Journal of Southern History* 77, no. 2 (2011): 251–282. See also Arthur Scherr, *Thomas Jefferson's Haitian Policy: Myths and Realities* (Lanham, MD: Lexington Books, 2011).

53. Taylor, *American Revolutions*, 9.

CHAPTER 6 — IMPERIAL EXCEPTIONALISM AT THE TURN
OF THE TWENTIETH CENTURY

1. Thomas Jefferson to James Monroe, November 24, 1801.

2. Ibid.

3. Quoted in Stephanson, *Manifest Destiny*, 42.

4. Walter A. McDougall, *The Tragedy of U.S. Foreign Policy: How America's Civil Religion Betrayed the National Interest* (New Haven, CT: Yale University Press, 2016).

5. Quoted in McDougall, *Tragedy of U.S. Foreign Policy*, 144–145.

6. Thomas Jefferson to Roger C. Weightman, June 24, 1826, quoted in Onuf, *Jefferson's Empire*, 2.

7. John Adams to Thomas Jefferson, November 15, 1813, Founders Online, National Archives, https://founders.archives.gov/documents/Adams/99-02-02-6198.

8. John O'Sullivan, quoted in Stephanson, *Manifest Destiny*, 40.

9. Thomas Jefferson to John Adams, October 28, 1813, Founders Online, National Archives, https://founders.archives.gov/documents/Jefferson/03-06-02-0446.

10. William Appleman Williams, *Empire as a Way of Life* (New York: Oxford University Press, 1980), 111–142.

11. Quoted in Richard W. Van Alstyne, "Woodrow Wilson and the Idea of the Nation State," *International Affairs* 37, no. 3 (1961): 300.

12. Woodrow Wilson, "Address to the Salesmanship Congress in Detroit, Michigan" (speech, Detroit, July 10, 1916), American Presidency Project, http://www.presidency .ucsb.edu/ws/?pid=117701.

13. William J. Clinton, "Remarks at a Freedom House Breakfast," speech, Washington, DC, October 6, 1995, American Presidency Project, http://www.presidency.ucsb.edu/ws /?pid=50612.

14. Anderson, *American Foreign Policy and Its Thinkers*.

15. Charles Kupchan, *The End of the American Era: US Foreign Policy and the Geopolitics of the Twenty-First Century* (New York: Vintage Books, 2003), 228.

16. Charles Kupchan, "Grand Strategy: The Four Pillars of the Future," *Democracy: A Journal of Ideas*, no. 23 (2012), https://democracyjournal.org/magazine/23/grand -strategy-the-four-pillars-of-the-future/.

17. Ibid.

18. Williams, *Empire as a Way of Life*.

19. Josef Joffe, *Uberpower: The Imperial Temptation of America* (New York: W. W. Norton & Co., 2006), 237.

20. White House, *The National Security Strategy of the United States of America* (Washington, DC: White House, 2002), i, 15, 31, https://2009-2017.state.gov/documents /organization/63562.pdf.

21. Robert Kagan, *Dangerous Nation: America's Foreign Policy from Its Earliest Days to the Dawn of the Twentieth Century* (New York: Vintage Books, 2007), 5.

22. Williams, *Empire as a Way of Life*; William Appleman Williams, *The Tragedy of American Diplomacy* (New York: World Publishing Co., 1959); Gabriel Kolko, *The Roots of American Foreign Policy* (Boston: Beacon Press, 1969); Harry Magdoff, *The Age of Imperialism* (New York: Monthly Review Press, 1969); Chomsky, *Towards a New Cold War*; Lens, *Forging of the American Empire*; Chalmers Johnson, *The Sorrows of Empire: Militarism, Secrecy, and the End of the Republic* (New York: Metropolitan Books, 2004).

23. Niall Ferguson, "An Empire in Denial: The Limits of US Imperialism," *Harvard International Review* 25, no. 3 (2003): 64-69.

24. Max Boot, "The Case for American Empire," *Weekly Standard*, October 15, 2001, https://www.weeklystandard.com/max-boot/the-case-for-american-empire.

25. Harlan K. Ullman, James P. Wade, L. A. Edney, Fred M. Franks, Charles A. Horner, Jonathan T. Howe, and Keith Brendley, *Shock and Awe: Achieving Rapid Dominance* (Washington, DC: National Defense University Press, 1996), xxvii.

26. Ibid., 83.

27. Ibid., 110-112.

28. Thomas Jefferson, "The Declaration of Independence," July 4, 1776, https://www .constitutionfacts.com/us-declaration-of-independence/read-the-declaration/.

29. Thomas Jefferson to Chastellux, June 7, 1785, Avalon Project, Yale Law Library, http://avalon.law.yale.edu/18th_century/let27.asp.

30. Thomas Jefferson to Indian Nations, January 10, 1809, Founders Online, National Archives, https://founders.archives.gov/documents/Jefferson/99-01-02-9516.

31. Ibid.

32. Thomas Jefferson to George Rogers Clark, January 1, 1780, Founders Online, National Archives, https://founders.archives.gov/documents/Jefferson/01-03-02-0289.

33. James William Gibson, "American Paramilitary Culture and the Reconstitution of the Vietnam War," in *Vietnam Images: War and Representation*, ed. Jeffrey Walsh and James Aulich (London: Macmillan Press, 1989), 14.

34. John Bellamy and Robert W. McChesney, "Kipling, the 'White Man's Burden,' and U.S. Imperialism," *Monthly Review Press*, November 1, 2003, https://monthlyreview.org/2003/11/01/kipling-the-white-mans-burden-and-u-s-imperialism/.

35. William McKinley, "Executive Order, December 21, 1898," American Presidency Project, http://www.presidency.ucsb.edu/ws/?pid=69309. Appeals to Kipling's missionary calls are still celebrated by some contemporary scholars supporting the imperial interventions of the United States. For instance, while Niall Ferguson (*Empire: The Rise and Demise of the British World Order and the Lessons for Global Power* [New York: Basic Books, 2004], 316) writes that "no one would dare use such politically incorrect language today," he asserts, "The reality is nevertheless that the United States has—whether it admits it or not—taken up some kind of global burden, just as Kipling urged. It considers itself responsible not just for waging a war against terrorism and rogue states, but also for spreading the benefits of capitalism and democracy overseas. And just like the British Empire before it, the American Empire unfailingly acts in the name of liberty, even when its own self-interest is manifestly uppermost."

36. Theodore Roosevelt, "Memorial Day Address, Arlington National Cemetery," May 30, 1902, http://www.theodore-roosevelt.com/images/research/txtspeeches/11.txt.

37. According to John Bellamy and Robert W. McChesney ("Kipling, the 'White Man's Burden,' and U.S. Imperialism"), "Major Edwin Glenn saw no reason to deny the charge that he had made a group of forty-seven Filipino prisoners kneel and 'repent of their sins' before bayoneting and clubbing them to death. General Jacob Smith ordered his troops to 'kill and burn,' to target 'everything over ten,' and to turn the island of Samar into 'a howling wilderness.' General William Shafter in California declared that it might be necessary to kill half the Filipino population in order to bring 'perfect justice' to the other half."

38. Paul Alexander Kramer, "The Water Cure: Debating Torture and Counterinsurgency—a Century Ago," *New Yorker*, February 17, 2008, https://www.newyorker.com/magazine/2008/02/25/the-water-cure/amp. Kramer quotes A. F. Miller of the Thirty-Second Volunteer Infantry Regiment, who explained how American soldiers inflicted the "water cure" on Filipinos: "[We] lay them on their backs, a man standing on each hand and each foot, then put a round stick in the mouth and pour a pail of water in the mouth and nose, and if they don't give up pour in another pail. They swell up like toads. I'll tell you it is a terrible torture."

39. Paul Alexander Kramer, *The Blood of Government: Race, Empire, the United States, and the Philippines* (Chapel Hill: University of North Carolina Press, 2006), 152–154.

40. See Bellamy and McChesney, "Kipling, the 'White Man's Burden,' and U.S. Imperialism"; McDougall, *Tragedy of U.S. Foreign Policy*, 126–127; Angel Velasco Shaw and Luis H. Francia, *Vestiges of War: The Philippine-American War and the Aftermath of an Imperial Dream, 1899–1999* (New York: New York University Press, 2002).

41. Beveridge, "In Support of an American Empire."

42. Quoted in McDougall, *Tragedy of U.S. Foreign Policy*, 128. Many influential Protestant religious leaders believed in the providential nature of American expansionism. For instance, the view of Pastor L. B. Hartman was shared by many: "Thus without the least consciousness of presumption or extravagance we recognize our republic as the politico-religious handmaid of Providence in the aggressive civilization of the world" (quoted in McDougall, 123; for more on this matter, see pp. 117–129).

43. Brian Bogart, "US Conflicts Abroad since World War II America Declassified," *Institute for Policy Research and Development*, Intelligent Future (Eugene, OR, 2004); Carl Herman, "Earth: 248 Armed Conflicts after WW2; US Started 201 (81%), Killing 30 Million So Far. Arrests Are When Now?" *Washington Blogs*, May 17, 2014, http://washingtonsblog.com/2014/05/earth-248-armed-conflicts-ww2-us-started-201-81-killing-30-million-far-arrests-now.html; Therese Pettersson and Peter Wallensteen, "Armed Conflicts, 1946–2014," *Journal of Peace Research* 52, no. 4 (2015): 536–550; Barbara Salazar Torreon, *Instances of Use of United States Armed Forces Abroad, 1798–2017*, R42738 (Washington, DC: Congressional Research Service, 2017), https://fas.org/sgp/crs/natsec/R42738.pdf; William H. Wiist, Kathy Barker, Neil Arya, et al., "The Role of Public Health in the Prevention of War: Rationale and Competencies," *American Journal of Public Health* 104, no. 6 (2014): 34–47, https://www.ncbi.nlm.nih.gov/pmc/articles/PMC4062030/pdf/AJPH.2013.301778.pdf.

44. Bogart, "US Conflicts Abroad since World War II."

45. Johnson, *Sorrows of Empire*, 151–186; see also John W. Dowder, *The Violent American Century* (Chicago: Haymarket Books, 2017), 8–15.

46. David Vine, *Base Nation: How U.S. Military Bases Abroad Harm America and the World* (New York: Metropolitan Books, 2015), 4–9.

47. Dowder, *Violent American Century*, 9.

48. While reasserting the supremacy of the United States in the world order and invoking God, both Presidents George Bush and Barack Obama lessened the predestined nature of American power. For instance, in his Second Inaugural Address, following the terrorist attacks of 9/11, Bush stated, "We go forward with complete confidence in the eventual triumph of freedom, not because history runs on the wheels of inevitability— it is human choices that move events; not because we consider ourselves a chosen nation— God moves and chooses as He wills" (George W. Bush, "Inaugural Address," speech, Washington, DC, January 20, 2005, American Presidency Project, http://www.presidency.ucsb.edu/ws/?pid=58745). Similarly, in his Second Inaugural Address (January 21, 2013), Barack Obama proclaimed, "We will support democracy from Asia to Africa, from the Americas to the Middle East, because our interests and our conscience compel us to act on behalf of those who long for freedom." He then asserted, "The oath I have sworn before you today, like the one recited by others who serve in this Capitol, was an oath to God and country, not party or faction." Finally, he exhorted Americans to "answer the call of history and carry into an uncertain future that precious light of freedom," and he concluded by invoking God to "forever bless these United States of America" (Barack Obama, "Inaugural Address by President Barack Obama," speech, Washington, DC, January 21, 2013, Office of the Press Secretary, White House, https://obamawhitehouse.archives.gov/the-press-office/2013/01/21/inaugural-address-president-barack-obama).

49. Jeet Heer, "Donald Trump Killed the 'Indispensable Nation.' Good!" *New Republic*, May 15, 2017, https://newrepublic.com/article/142571/donald-trump-killed-indispensable-nation-good.

50. Ibid. At the end of his second term, President Obama warned his successor, Donald Trump, that he should never forget that "the United States really is an indispensable nation in our world order" (Shawn Donnan and Andres Schipani, "Obama Urges Trump to Regard US as an 'Indispensable Nation,'" *Financial Times*, November 20, 2016, https://www.ft.com/content/643f6c9c-af84-11e6-a37c-f4a01f1b0fa1.

51. K. J. Holsti, "Exceptionalism in American Foreign Policy: Is It Exceptional?" *European Journal of International Relations* 17, no. 3 (2011): 384.

52. Paul Alexander Kramer, "Power and Connection: Imperial Histories of the United States in the World," *American Historical Review* 116, no. 5 (2011): 1349.

53. Cumings, *Korean War*, 28.

54. Huntington, *Clash of Civilizations and the Remaking of World Order*, 136–137.

55. Lawrence E. Harrison, "Voodoo Politics," *Atlantic Monthly* 271, no. 6 (1993): 101–107; Lawrence E. Harrison and Samuel Huntington, eds., *Culture Matters: How Values Shape Human Progress* (New York: Basic Books, 2000); Lawrence E. Harrison, *The Central Liberal Truth* (Oxford: Oxford University Press, 2006); Robert Rotberg with Christopher Clague, *Haiti: The Politics of Squalor* (Boston: Houghton Mifflin, 1971).

56. David Brooks, "The Underlying Tragedy," *New York Times*, January 4, 2010, http://www.nytimes.com/2010/01/15/opinion/15brooks.html.

57. CNN, "Pat Robertson Says Haiti Paying for 'Pact to the Devil," January 13, 2010, http://www.cnn.com/2010/US/01/13/haiti.pat.robertson/index.html.

58. Fatton, *Roots of Haitian Despotism*, 13–42.

59. Michel-Rolph Trouillot, "Haiti's Nightmare and the Lessons of History," in *Haiti: Dangerous Crossroads*, ed. NACLA (Boston: South End Press, 1995), 121–122.

60. International Commission on Intervention and State Sovereignty, *The Responsibility to Protect* (Ottawa, Ont.: International Development Research Centre, 2001). See also Michael Barnett and Thomas G. Weiss, *Humanitarianism Contested* (London: Routledge, 2011), 70–104; Costas Douzinas, *Human Rights and Empire* (New York: Routledge-Cavendish, 2007), 177–196.

61. Fatton, *Haiti: Trapped in the Outer Periphery*.

62. Hobson, *Eurocentric Conception of World Politics*, 301.

63. Ignatieff, *Empire Lite*, 112.

64. Douzinas, *Human Rights and Empire*, 195.

65. Michael Ignatieff, "Introduction: American Exceptionalism and Human Rights," in *American Exceptionalism and Human Rights*, ed. Michael Ignatieff (Princeton, NJ: Princeton University Press, 2005), 3–7.

66. Ibid., 16.

67. Richard Goldberg, "Europe's Sanctions-Blocking Threats Are Empty," *Foreign Policy*, February 20, 2018, https://foreignpolicy.com/2018/02/20/europes-iran-deal-threats-are-empty-trump-iran-eu/.

68. White House, "Fact Sheet: Sanctions Related to Iran," Office of the Press Secretary, July 31, 2012, https://obamawhitehouse.archives.gov/the-press-office/2012/07/31/fact-sheet-sanctions-related-iran.

69. Stephen D. Krasner, "Sharing Sovereignty: New Institutions for Collapsed and Failing States," *International Security* 29, no. 2 (Fall 2004): 86, 119.

70. Robert Keohane, "Political Authority after Intervention: Gradations in Sovereignty," in *Humanitarian Intervention: Ethical, Legal, and Political Dilemmas*, ed. J. Holzgrefe and R. Keohane (Cambridge: Cambridge University Press, 2003), 276, 298.

71. Robert Fatton, "Development and the Outer Periphery: The Logic of Exclusion," in *The Palgrave Handbook of Critical International Political Economy*, ed. Alan Cafruny, Leila Simona Talani, and Gonzalo Pozo Martin (London: Palgrave Macmillan, 2016), 119–137.

72. Fatton, *Haiti: Trapped in the Outer Periphery*.

73. Wien Weibert Arthus (*Duvalier a l'Ombre de la Guerre Froide* [Port-au-Prince: Alexandre Fritz Arios, 2014], 339) argues convincingly that Francois Duvalier used the Cold War to establish a foreign policy that remained at the service of his successful quest to monopolize political power domestically:

> Duvalier met sa politique étrangère complètement au service de sa politique intérieure. Tout ce qu'il entreprend vise un seul objectif: conserver le pouvoir de manière réelle et effective. Dans un pays qui a une grande tradition de président de doublure ou dépendant de l'étranger, particulièrement des Etats-Unis, Duvalier est une rare exception. C'est lui qui définit et conduit sa politique étrangère, en toute indépendance. Il garde les mains libres en toute chose. Comme en politique intérieure, il utilise la menace, la peur, le chantage, l'insensibilité et la méfiance comme des piliers de ses relations internationales. (Duvalier puts his foreign policy completely at the service of his domestic policy. Everything he does has one single goal: retain power in a real and effective way. In a country that has a long tradition of having presidents whose power is dependent on a moneyed elite, or on foreign powers, particularly the United States, Duvalier is a rare exception. It is he who defines and conducts foreign policy, in complete independence. He always keeps his freedom of maneuver. Like in the conduct of his domestic politics, he uses threats, fear, blackmail, callousness and mistrust as pillars of his international relations.)

Arthus, however, may go too far in asserting that Duvalier was conducting his foreign policy "en toute indépendance"; in fact, the United States tolerated Duvalier because his ferocious anticommunism coincided with Washington's Cold War objectives and geopolitical interests. As long as Duvalier operated within these parameters, he was utile to the United States. In fact, as Arthus himself points out, Duvalier's autonomy was always circumscribed by the presence of U.S. marines in the country as well as by his dependence on U.S. foreign economic assistance.

74. Fatton, *Roots of Haitian Despotism*.

75. Odd Arne Westad, *The Global Cold War* (Cambridge: Cambridge University, 2007).

CHAPTER 7 — DICTATORSHIP, DEMOCRATIZATION, AND EXCEPTIONALISM

1. Fatton, *Haiti's Predatory Republic*; Michel-Rolph Trouillot, *Haiti: State against Nation* (New York: Monthly Review Press, 1990).

2. Arthus, *Duvalier a l'Ombre de la Guerre Froide*.

3. Ibid., 245–337. As Robert Newbegin, the American ambassador in Haiti, put it in a memorandum to the U.S. State Department (quoted on p. 265): "En cas de chute de Duvalier, on pourrait se retrouver face à un chaos organisé résultant de la lutte de pouvoir entre les individus en qui nous pourrons avoir peu de confiance. De plus, Castro ou Trujillo pourrait tenter d'y intervenir de manière à mettre en péril notre intérêt national et même nous forcer d'y intervenir militairement." (Should Duvalier fall, there is a decided danger of chaos and a struggle for power among individuals in whom we would have little confidence. Such a situation might well tempt Castro or Trujillo to intervene in such a way as to jeopardize our national interests, possibly even forcing military intervention.)

4. As Paul Christopher Johnson ("Secretism and the Apotheosis of Duvalier," *Journal of the American Academy of Religion* 74, no. 2 [2006]: 437) explains, "Duvalier chose Dessalines—first Emperor, black indigenist par excellence, Kreyol nationalist warrior,

returning warrior spirit—as the ancestor to possess him. When Duvalier compelled all Vodou centers to hang his portrait from the center pole (*poteau mitan*), the conduit along which the spirits descend to mount the bodies of the living during possession rituals, he must have hoped that another *loa* would be in the making."

5. Nicholls, *From Dessalines to Duvalier*, 229.

6. Ibid., 170 (my translation).

7. Francois Duvalier, *Oeuvres Essentielles I: Eléments d'une Doctrine* (Port-au-Prince: Presses Nationales d'Haiti, 1966), 167–177 (my translations).

8. As Laënnec Hurbon has pointed out (*Comprendre Haïti: Essai sur l'État, la nation, la culture* [Paris: Les Éditions Karthala, 1987], 146–147, http://chf-ressourceshaiti.com /data/chfressources/media/ouvrage/Comprendre-Haiti-Essai-sur-lEtat-la-nation-la -culture-Hurbon-Laennec.pdf):

> Les observateurs étrangers, en particulier américains, mais aussi une fraction non né- gligeable de la bourgeoisie haïtienne, ont cru que le pouvoir de Duvalier se fondait réel- lement sur la volonté de promouvoir le vodou et la « race noire ». C'était pure illusion . . . L'on sait assez qu'il n'a jamais été porté que par une seule visée: celle de son maintien au pouvoir. Loin d'envisager une quelconque promotion du vodou ou de la culture popu- laire, Duvalier travaillait—comme les autres chefs d'État—à exercer le plus strict con- trôle sur le vodou . . . Le régime de Duvalier a travaillé au contrôle du vodou, en disposant de son propre réseau d'ougan, en organisant ses propres cérémonies, et sur- tout en cherchant à faire manipuler les aspects les plus réprouvés du vodou, c'est-à-dire les croyances et pratiques de sorcellerie, par les vodouisants eux-mêmes. (Foreign observers, especially Americans, but also a significant fraction of the Haitian bour- geoisie, believed that Duvalier's power was really based on the desire to promote voo- dou and the "black race." It was pure illusion. . . . We know well enough that it was never carried by one objective: that of maintaining power. Far from considering any promotion of voodou or popular culture, Duvalier worked—like other heads of state— to exercise the strictest control over voodou. . . . The Duvalier regime worked to control voodou, by having its own network of ougans, by organizing its own ceremonies, and above all by seeking to manipulate the most condemned aspects of voodou, that is to say the beliefs and practices of witchcraft, by the vodouisants themselves.)

9. Johnson, "Secretism and the Apotheosis," 424.

10. The full French title of Jean M. Fourcand's pamphlet is *Catéchisme de la révolu- tion: En l'honneur du docteur François Duvalier, président constitutionel à vie de la république d'Haïti et de madame Simone O. Duvalier, première Marie-Jeanne d'Haïti* (Port-au-Prince: Edition Imprimerie de l'Etat, 1964).

11. Ibid., 17.

12. Ibid.

13. Bernard Diederich and Al Burt, *Papa Doc* (New York: McGraw-Hill, 1969), 217.

14. Fourcand, *Catéchisme de la révolution*, 37 (my translation).

15. Ibid., 32.

16. Laënnec Hurbon (*Comprendre Haïti*, 165) offers a succinct definition of the Tonton Macoute: "Personnage du folklore, se dit de l'oncle (tonton) qui se promène la nuit, portant une 'macoute' (sac) dans laquelle il met les enfants qui ne sont pas 'sages.' Le tonton-macoute est censé 'manger' les enfants qu'il emmène avec lui. Vers les années 1958–60, les tonton-macoutes sont des cagoulards qui rentrent de nuit chez les opposants à Duvalier, pour les piller, les torturer et les tuer. Jusqu'à la chute de Jean-Claude Duvalier, ils constituaient un corps de police parallèle pour défendre le Président" (The *Tonton*

Macoute is a character from folklore—the uncle who walks at night, carrying a "Macoute" [bag] in which he puts children who are disobedient. The uncle-macoute is supposed to "eat" the children he takes with him. Around 1958–60, hooded *tonton-macoutes* broke into Duvalier's opponents' houses at night, to loot, torture and kill them. Until the fall of Jean-Claude Duvalier, they formed a parallel police force to defend the President.)

17. Quoted in Nicholls, *From Dessalines to Duvalier*, 235.

18. The critical literature on *Noirisme* is abundant; see Micheline Labelle, *Idéologie de couleur et classes sociales en Haïti* (Montreal: Presses de l'Université de Montréal, 1978); René Depestre, "The Winding Course of Negritude," in *Souffles-Anfas: A Critical Anthology from the Moroccan Journal of Culture and Politics*, ed. Olivia C. Harrison and Teresa Villa-Ignacio, trans. Laura Reeck (Stanford, CA: Stanford University Press, 2016), 120–125. This text was originally a public address delivered by Depestre at the January 1968 Cultural Congress in Havana and was published in that same year by the Moroccan journal *Souffles*; it can be accessed at http://pastandfuturepresents.blogspot .com/2015/12/the-winding-course-of-negritude-rene.html. See also Fields and Fields, *Racecraft*, for a masterful critique of race as a social category in the American context. For the moment, suffice it to say, as I have argued elsewhere (*Haiti: Trapped in the Outer Periphery*, 118–119): "*Noirisme* is little more than a strategy for unseating and preventing mulatto supremacy without transforming the exploitative foundations of Haiti's political economy. Far from being the emancipatory medium of the black masses, this racialist ideology is a moralistic mask hiding the aspirations of a small black middle-class to capture wealth, privilege, and power for itself. To a large degree, the charged, but non-transformative rhetoric of *Noirisme* is the legacy of three corrupt and dictatorial decades of Duvalierism."

In his important book *Comprendre Haïti*, Laënnec Hurbon made a similar argument, but he added a critical aspect to *Noirisme*: its power in the imaginary of Haitians and thus the difficulties in dislodging it from the country's political culture (105):

> La permanence de l'opposition Noir/mulâtre, dans l'écriture de l'histoire d'Haïti, semble prendre sa source dans le désir de la petite bourgeoisie intellectuelle d'exercer le pouvoir comme tel, hors de toute perspective réelle de changement de la condition des masses et de réalisation d'une démocratie.
>
> On le voit bien, toute attaque frontale contre la négritude en Haïti ne peut que relancer et alimenter le colorisme, puisque nous sommes en présence d'un thème de l'imaginaire, semblable à celui de la sorcellerie. L'agitation de ce thème auprès des couches populaires a indéniablement quelque succès, dans la mesure où il leur fournit une homogénéité nationale, à son tour imaginaire, qui laisse dans l'oubli des divisions sociales et culturelles bien réelles. (The persistence of the Black / Mulatto conflict, in the writing of the history of Haiti, seems to have its source in the desire of the intellectual petty bourgeoisie to exercise raw power, outside of any real perspective of change in both the condition of the masses and the achievement of democracy. It is obvious that any frontal attack against negritude in Haiti can only revive and fuel colorism, since we confront a theme of the imaginary, similar to that of witchcraft. The agitation of this theme among the popular strata has undeniably some success, insofar as it provides them with a sense of national homogeneity, albeit imaginary, that masks very real social and cultural divisions.)

19. In his article "Biology and Politics in Haiti" (*Race and Class* 13, no. 2 [1971]: 203–214), David Nicholls summarizes well Duvalier's intellectual connection to Gobineau:

> Duvalier ... accepted Gobineau's contentions that it is possible to distinguish certain races in the history of mankind, that in spite of racial mixtures these groups have retained a specifiable identity, and that there are a number of psychological characteristics which are peculiar to the races. He further agreed that the black races are distinguished by the importance which they attach to the senses, and by their practice of understanding by association with, rather than by detachment from, the external world. He disagreed, of course, with Gobineau's belief that the black races are inferior. (208).

20. Nicholls, *From Dessalines to Duvalier*, 169.

21. Ibid.

22. Depestre, "Winding Course of Negritude."

23. Quoted in Nicholls, *From Dessalines to Duvalier*, 235.

24. Arthus, *Duvalier a l'Ombre de la Guerre Froide*, 239 (my translation).

> L'ouverture vers l'Afrique, au nom de la solidarité raciale, permet aussi au président haïtien d'étendre la liste de ses alliés sur la scène internationale. Pendant les quatorze années de règne de Duvalier, les hommes d'Etat de rangs de ministre et président qui visitent Haïti—à l'exception notable de Trujillo ... —viennent tous du continent africain. Ces voyages, parfois semi-officiels, sont d'une grande importance pour le régime de Duvalier. Les hommes d'Etat africains débarquent à Port-au-Prince à la fin des années 1960. C'est une période où Duvalier cherche à réduire son isolement dans la Caraïbe et par les Etats-Unis. Aussi, chaque visite d'officiels africains, quelque soit le contexte de sa réalisation, est une occasion de réjouissances au palais national.

25. Depestre, "Winding Course of Negritude."

26. Ibid.

27. In Creole, *ti wouj* is a slur to describe mulattoes as "little reds," and *Bob Manuel vle touye Titid* means "Bob Manuel wants to kill Aristide." The use of color in this political instance is depicted well in Michael Deibert, *Notes from the Last Testament: The Struggle for Haiti* (New York: Seven Stories Press, 2005), 89–96.

28. Ibid., 97–98; see also Michèle D. Pierre-Louis, "Pourquoi Tuer Jean Dominique?" *Chemins Critiques* 5, no. 1 (2001): 105–111.

29. The term *grands mangeurs* became very popular in the 1997 Carnival. See "Carnaval Grands Mangeurs," *Haiti en Marche*, February 12–18, 1997, 1–8; "Carnaval Grands Mangeurs," *Haiti en Marche*, February 19–25, 1997, 12. During the 1997 Carnival, huge dancing crowds chanted accusatory songs against the Haitian political class for "getting fat" at the expense of the poor majority. Vilified as obese characters who had been deformed by the corruptions of power, the *grands mangeurs* became the target of popular mockery and insults: "Gad grosé kravat yo," "Gad grosé tét bèf yo," "Gad grosé bank yo," and "Yo manje jistan yo gonfle" ("Look at their huge ties," "Watch their humongous sport utility vehicles," "Look at their fat bank accounts," "They eat to the point of ballooning"). Thus, *grands mangeurs* refers not only to the voracious appetite for the personal consumption of state resources; it symbolizes also the intimate relationship between the acquisition of power and growing physical corpulence. In a country where malnourishment and hunger are a permanent predicament for the vast majority, the conquest of public office is a meal ticket to corpulence, a sign of growing status and privilege.

30. La Redaction, "Edo Zenny crache au visage d'un juge," *Radio Television Caraibes*, September 9, 2012, http://www.radiotelevisioncaraibes.com/nouvelles/haiti/edo_zenny _crache_au_visage_d_un_juge.html.

31. Claudy Bélizaire, "Tu dois respecter un mulâtre, Edo Zenny te connais, mais pas le sénateur Zenny: Je suis blanc, et toi tu es nègre," *Tout Haiti*, September 11, 2012, http:// www.touthaiti.com/touthaiti-actualites/853-tu-dois-respecter-un-mulatre-edo-zenny -te-connais-mais-pas-le-senateur-zenny-je-suis-blanc-et-toi-tu-es-negre.

32. Eddy Jackson Alexis, "L'amnésie d'Edo Zenny," *Le Matin*, September 9, 2012, http://www.lematinhaiti.com/contenu.php?idtexte=32535.

33. La Redaction, "Edo Zenny: Je ne suis pas raciste, ma femme, mes amis d'enfance ont leur peau foncée," *Radio Television Caraibes*, September 15, 2012, http://www .radiotelevisioncaraibes.com/nouvelles/haiti/je_ne_suis_pas_raciste_ma_femme_mes _amis_d_enfance_ont_leur_peau.html.

34. Claude Moïse, *Constitutions et luttes de pouvoir en Haïti: Tome 2—De l'occupation etrangère à la dictature Macoute (1915–1987)* (Montreal: CIDIHCA, 1990), 264 (my translation).

35. Michael Norton, "Coup Leader Says Uprising Necessary to Stop 'Apprentice Dictator,'" Associated Press, October 2, 1991, https://www.apnews.com/eeddff991e9a0c410491 ed2d183cea6e.

36. Anonymous, *Haiti: Efforts to Restore President Aristide, 1991–1994*, Report no. 95-602 F (Washington, D.C.: Congressional Research Service, 1995), https://www.everycrsreport .com/files/19950511_95-602_6c19769dbf2c82c7a1d4458d505c45cfa9990234.pdf. See also Kate Doyle, "Hollow Diplomacy in Haiti," *World Policy Journal* 11, no. 1 (1994): 53–55; Mark Danner, "The Fall of the Prophet," *New York Review of Books* 40, no. 20 (1993), http://www .markdanner.com/articles/the-fall-of-the-prophet.

37. Tim Weiner, "C.I.A. Formed Haitian Unit Later Tied to Narcotics Trade," *New York Times*, November 14, 1993, https://www.nytimes.com/1993/11/14/world/cia-formed -haitian-unit-later-tied-to-narcotics-trade.html. The covert involvement of the CIA in Haiti went beyond SIN; its support for the military and its opposition to Aristide are well documented in Brian Latell's 1992 memorandum, "Impressions of Haiti," to the agency's former director Robert Gates. Declaring that "the Haitian regime barely resembles Latin American dictatorships I have known," Latell, the CIA's senior analyst for Latin America, went on to contend that he "saw no evidence of oppressive rule" during his July 1992 visit to Port-au-Prince. In fact, Latell described the coup leader and army chief, Raoul Cédras, as "a conscientious military leader who genuinely wishes to minimize his role in politics, professionalize the armed services, and develop a separate and competent civilian police force." On the other hand, Latell portrayed Aristide as an erratic and even demented individual bent on fomenting mob violence against his opponents. Latell's view of the situation closely resembled that of the Haitian military and privileged classes, who favored "an elite-dominated leadership to stabilize Haiti and begin a process of economic development." Quoted in Doyle, "Hollow Diplomacy in Haiti," 52; see also Tim Weiner, "Key Haitian Military Leaders Were on The CIA's Payroll," *New York Times*, November 1, 1993, A1–A8, https://timesmachine.nytimes.com/timesmachine /1993/11/01/issue.html.

The CIA was also involved in the creation of the violent paramilitary organization Front for the Advancement and Progress of Haiti (FRAPH). In the eyes of the CIA, FRAPH would constitute a political front that "could balance the Aristide movement [and do] intelligence against it." For a comprehensive report on the linkage between the CIA and FRAPH, see Alan Nairn, "Our Man in FRAPH," *The Nation* 259, no. 13 (1994): 458–461; and Alan Nairn, "He's Our S.O.B.," *The Nation* 259, no. 14 (1994): 481–482.

The ambiguities of American foreign policy toward Haiti are well summarized in Jane Regan, "A.I.D.ing U.S. Interests in Haiti," *Covert Action*, no. 51 (Winter 1994–1995): 7–13, 56–58. See also Nicolas Jallot and Laurent Lesage, *Haiti: Dix Ans d'Histoire Secrète* (Paris: Editions du Felin, 1995).

38. Morley and McGillion, "'Disobedient' Generals and the Politics of Redemocratization," 378.

39. Kenneth Freed, "US Gives Cédras a Lucrative Deal to Get Out of Haiti," *Los Angeles Times*, October 14, 1994, http://articles.latimes.com/1994-10-14/news/mn-50281_1 _white-house; see also Morley and McGillion, "'Disobedient' Generals and the Politics of Redemocratization," 363–384.

40. Quoted in ibid.

41. TFI, "Emile Jonassaint Veut Combattre Les américains Avec La Magie Noire," December 17, 2020, YouTube video, https://www.youtube.com/watch?v=cxnw-kH4_gk.

42. Quoted in Howard W. French, "Port-au-Prince Journal: Is Voodoo the Weapon to Repel the Invaders?" *New York Times*, June 24, 1994, https://www.nytimes.com/1994/06 /24/world/port-au-prince-journal-is-voodoo-the-weapon-to-repel-the-invaders.html.

43. Ibid.

44. Associated Press, "Military Backed Leader Declares State of Emergency in Haiti," June 12, 1994, https://www.apnews.com/e50463dd4bc17af24d2a3e1c65c90276.

45. Ibid.

46. Fatton, *Haiti: Trapped in the Outer Periphery*. In this book I define the outer periphery as follows:

> [In] the last two decades the neo-liberal regime has engendered a new zone of catastrophe that tumbled out of the existing periphery to become a new outer periphery, a zone integrated into the margins of the margin of the global economy.
>
> This outer periphery is at the very bottom of the production process of the world system; its states are virtual trusteeships of the "international community" and the large majority of its population lives in abject poverty. It is a zone that has suffered not only from the economic devastation of neo-liberalism, but also from the "shocks" and "after-shocks" of politics, nature, and wars. Broadly speaking, the outer periphery is a de-facto "occupied territory" under the surveillance of foreign "peacekeepers" and under the control of International Financial Institutions (IFIs), and Non-Governmental-Organizations (NGOs). Not surprisingly, the ruling classes in the states of the outer periphery are continuously negotiating the terms of their countries' subservience to the core. This degree of subservience depends not only on the global strategic location of the country in question, but also on the nature of the particular political system and domestic constellation of power within which it operates.
>
> The typical state of the outer periphery is a simulacrum of democracy with extremely limited sovereignty over its territory, domestic policies, and electoral processes (14).

47. In a study on remittances to Latin America and the Caribbean, Manuel Orozco reports (*Remittances to Latin America and the Caribbean in 2017* [Washington, DC: Inter-American Dialogue, 2018], 3, https://www.thedialogue.org/wp-content/uploads /2018/01/Remittances-2017-1.pdf) that "an outmigration . . . has occurred years after the

2010 earthquake of people who went to Brazil and then over the past three years have gradually been moving to Chile. . . . Haitians in Chile were less than 5,000 in 2010, and the number has increased exponentially to more than 100,000.

48. David Carment and Rachael Calleja, "Diasporas and Fragile States—beyond Remittances Assessing the Theoretical and Policy Linkages," *Journal of Ethnic and Migration Studies* 44, no. 8 (2018): 1271, https://doi.org/10.1080/1369183X.2017.1354157; see also Jeb Sprague-Silgado "Global Capitalism in the Caribbean," *NACLA Report on the Americas* 50, no. 2 (2018), 139–147, https://doi.org/10.1080/10714839.2018.1479465.

49. Orozco, *Remittances to Latin America and the Caribbean in 2017*, 1.

CHAPTER 8 — THE DIASPORA AND
THE TRANSMOGRIFICATION OF EXCEPTIONALISM

1. Davis, Stolberg and Kaplan, "Trump Alarms Lawmakers with Disparaging Words"; see also Moore and Porter, "'Don't Feed the Troll.'"

2. Miriam Jordan, "Trump Administration Ends Temporary Protection for Haitians," *New York Times*, November 20, 2017, https://www.nytimes.com/2017/11/20/us/haitians-temporary-status.html. The situation of Haitians facing deportation was not only critical for those concerned, but it affected the well-being of Haiti itself. As Manuel Orozco explains (*Remittances to Latin America and the Caribbean in 2017*, 8):

> The current political landscape regarding migration policy in the United States, and even in countries like Chile, where a rhetoric to reduce immigration is translating in drastic policies, may have an adverse effect to several countries in the near future. For one, the debate over the termination of the Temporary Protected Status to four Latin American and Caribbean immigrants in the US would affect these country's economies. . . . One can think that the effect on Haiti . . . would devastate its economy. Haitians on TPS are 6% of all Haitian migrants.

3. Leon D. Pamphile, *Haitians and African Americans: A Heritage of Tragedy and Hope* (Gainesville: University Press of Florida, 2001); Tanael Joachim, "What Makes a Country Great? Meet Haiti's People," *New York Times*, January 12, 2018, https://www.nytimes.com/2018/01/12/opinion/what-makes-a-country-great-meet-haitis-people.html. Two historic figures who immediately come to mind are Jean Du Sable, the founder of Chicago, and W.E.B. Du Bois, the towering civil rights activist and intellectual, as well as one of the founders of the NAACP.

4. Paul Farmer, *The Uses of Haiti* (Monroe, ME: Common Courage Press, 1994), 274–281 and 339–344.

5. As a bachelor, Trump is reported to have asked his dates to take an AIDS test at his doctor's clinic. See Asawin Suebsaeng, "Stay Classy: Trump Used to Test His Dates for AIDS," *Daily Beast*, July 25, 2015, https://www.thedailybeast.com/stay-classy-trump-used-to-test-his-dates-for-aids?ref=scroll. Moreover, according to Trump, shaking hands is repugnant; he described it as "barbaric" and a portent of diseases and "all sorts of things." In his book *The Art of the Comeback*, Trump wrote, "One of the curses of American society is the simple act of shaking hands, and the more successful and famous one becomes the worse this terrible custom seems to get. . . . I happen to be a clean hands freak. I feel much better after I thoroughly wash my hands, which I do as much as possible." Quoted in Ben Guarino, "Shaking Hands Is 'Barbaric': Donald Trump, the Germaphobe in Chief," *Washington Post*, January 12, 2017, https://www

.washingtonpost.com/news/morning-mix/wp/2017/01/12/shaking-hands-is-barbaric
-donald-trump-the-germaphobe-in-chief/?utm_term=.04a2bcfc5e44.

6. UNAIDS, "Haiti," United Nations, 2019, http://www.unaids.org/en/regionscountries
/countries/haiti.

7. Office of Immigration Statistics, *Yearbook of Immigration Statistics: 2016* (Washington, DC: U.S. Department of Homeland Security, 2017), https://www.dhs.gov/sites
/default/files/publications/2016%20Yearbook%20of%20Immigration%20Statistics
.pdf.

8. Pew Research Center defines "middle-income" households as "those with an income
that is two-thirds to double that of the U.S. median household income, after incomes
have been adjusted for household size. For a three-person household, the middle-
income range was about $42,000 to $126,000 annually in 2014 (in 2014 dollars)." Pew
Research Center, *The American Middle Class Is Losing Ground: No Longer the Majority
and Falling Behind Financially* (Washington, DC: Pew Research Center, 2015), 2. See
also Anne Case and Angus Deaton, *Deaths of Despair and the Future of Capitalism*
(Princeton, NJ: Princeton University Press, 2020).

9. Pew Research Center, *American Middle Class Is Losing Ground*, 4. See also Branko
Milanovic, *Global Inequality: A New Approach for the Age of Globalization* (Cambridge,
MA: Harvard University Press, 2016), 194–211.

10. Milanovic, *Global Inequality*, 195.

11. BBC News, "Clinton: Half of Trump Supporters 'Basket of Deplorables,'" September 10, 2016, https://www.bbc.com/news/av/election-us-2016-37329812/clinton-half-of
-trump-supporters-basket-of-deplorables.

12. Chuck Collins and Josh Hoxie, *Billionaire Bonanza: The Forbes 400 and the Rest of
Us* (Washington D.C.: Institute for Policy Studies, 2015), 2–3, https://ips-dc.org/wp
-content/uploads/2015/12/Billionaire-Bonanza-The-Forbes-400-and-the-Rest-of-Us
-Dec1.pdf. See also Milanovic, *Global Inequality*, and Thomas Piketty, *Capital in the
Twenty-First Century* (Cambridge, MA: Harvard University Press, 2014).

13. Jedediah Purdy, "Normcore," *Dissent*, Summer 2018, https://www.dissentmagazine
.org/article/normcore-trump-resistance-books-crisis-of-democracy.

14. See Carroll Dansereau, "Whose Moral Stain? Obama's Immigration Atrocities Led
to Trump's," self-published paper, September 28, 2018, https://www.dropbox.com/s
/4603lpfx6y97ohm/WhoseMoralStainReport9.28.18.pdf?dl=0.

15. Freedom for Immigrants, "A Short History of Immigration Detention," 2018,
https://www.freedomforimmigrants.org/detention-timeline/.

16. See Richard Lee Turits, "A World Destroyed, a Nation Imposed: The 1937 Haitian
Massacre in the Dominican Republic," *Hispanic American Historical Review* 82, no. 3
(2002): 599–600.

17. Lorgia Garcia-Pena, *The Borders of Dominicanidad* (Durham, NC: Duke University Press, 2016); Richard Lee Turits, *The Foundations of Despotism: Peasants, the Trujillo Regime, and Modernity in Dominican History* (Stanford, CA: Stanford University
Press, 2003); Eric Paul Roorda, "Genocide Next Door: The Good Neighbor Policy, the
Trujillo Regime, and the Haitian Massacre of 1937," *Diplomatic History* 20, no. 3 (Summer 1996): 301–319; R. Michael Malek, "Dominican Republic's General Rafael Trujillo
and the Haitian Massacre of 1937: A Case of Subversion in Inter-Caribbean Relations,"
SECOLAS Annals 11 (March 1980): 137–155.

18. Garcia-Pena, *Borders of Dominicanidad*, 28–30.

19. I follow Garcia-Pena's use of the term *criollo* "to refer to the descendants of the Spanish colonial caste whose ancestry is white European—not to be confused with the Creole definitions of racial and cultural mixing" (ibid., 216n16).

20. Ibid., 9.

21. Ibid., 7.

22. Ibid., 93–126; Roorda, "Genocide Next Door"; Malek, "Dominican Republic's General Rafael Trujillo."

23. Ernesto Sagás, *Race and Politics in the Dominican Republic* (Gainesville: University of Florida Press, 2000).

24. Garcia-Pena, *Borders of Dominicanidad*, 129–169.

25. Ezequiel Abiu Lopez and Danica Coto, "Dominican Ruling Strips Many of Citizenship," Associated Press, September 26, 2013; Agence France Presse, "La République dominicaine 'dénationalise' des milliers d'Haïtiens," France24, October 3, 2013, http://www.france24.com/fr/20131003-haiti-republique-dominicaine-nationalite-dechenace-transit-immigrants; Lis Bell, "Rép. Dominicaine: La 'dénationalisation' des Dominicains d'origine haïtienne planifiée par le PLD et la FNP depuis 2008," *AlterPresse*, December 13, 2013, http://www.alterpresse.org/spip.php?article15624#.Uv2Xgv2_2os; GARR-Haiti, "Position de la Plateforme GARR autour du dossier de la dénationalisation des Dominicains/Dominicaines d'ascendance haïtienne," ReliefWeb, January 31, 2014, http://reliefweb.int/report/dominican-republic/position-de-la-plateforme-garr-autour-du-dossier-de-la-d-nationalisation.

26. RFK Center, "RFK Center Welcomes Landmark Ruling on Dominican Nationality in Inter-American Court," October 24, 2014, http://rfkcenter.org/rfk-center-welcomes-landmark-ruling-in-inter-american-court; GARR-Haiti, "Le GARR se prononce sur la déclaration de la 2ème rencontre binationale entre Haïti et la République Dominicaine Spécial," ReliefWeb, February 5, 2014, http://reliefweb.int/report/dominican-republic/le-garr-se-prononce-sur-la-d-claration-de-la-2-me-rencontre-binationale. See also Garcia-Pena, *Borders of Dominicanidad*, 203–209.

27. Amelie Baron, "Inequality Drives Migration Crisis for Haiti, Dominican Republic," Agence France Presse, July 4, 2018, https://www.yahoo.com/news/inequality-drives-migration-crisis-haiti-dominican-republic-215318549.html; Amnesty International, "Haiti/Dominican Republic: Reckless Deportations Leaving Thousands in Limbo," June 15, 2016, https://www.amnesty.org/en/latest/news/2016/06/haiti-dominican-republic-reckless-deportations-leaving-thousands-in-limbo; Editors, "How a Broken Migration Policy Has Divided Haiti and the Dominican Republic," *World Politics Review*, March 23, 2018, https://www.worldpoliticsreview.com/trend-lines/24431/how-a-broken-migration-policy-has-divided-haiti-and-the-dominican-republic.

28. Jacques Roumain, *Oeuvres complètes: Édition critique*, Léon-François Hoffmann, Coordinateur (Paris: Allca XX, 2003), 472–473 (my translation):

> Ce 18 Mai, grisaille quotidienne. Les magasins s'ouvrent sur une circulation de tous les jours. Misère, misère. Des mendiants, des affamés, des mains qui se tendent. Certains ont la maigreur caractéristique des pauvres. Les os du visage crevant la peau et les yeux agrandis, démesurés. . . . Le drapeau. Qui parle de drapeau? Le drapeau n'est pas comestible. . . . Les autos officiels iront à l'Arcahaie bondées de traîtres.

> Il y aura une avalanche de discours. La bave gouvernementale coulera à flots, le champagne aussi. Des bouches venimeuses chantant le drapeau, le souilleront aussi, mais il y aura quelques applaudissements. . . . 18 mai. Qui, mais qui pense au 19 mai? Personne.

Ah! les morts sont-ils donc muets? Et leurs blessures ouvertes n'ont-elles point de lèvres pour crier, réveiller?

29. Michael G. Schatzberg, *Political Legitimacy in Middle Africa: Father, Family, Food* (Bloomington: Indiana University Press, 2001), 205.

30. Shelby Grad and David Colker, "Nancy Reagan Turned to Astrology in White House to Protect Her Husband," *Los Angeles Times*, March 6, 2016, http://www.latimes.com /local/lanow/la-me-ln-nancy-reagan-astrology-20160306-story.html. See also Steven V. Roberts, "White House Confirms Reagans Follow Astrology, up to a Point," *New York Times*, May 4, 1988, https://www.nytimes.com/1988/05/04/us/white-house-confirms -reagans-follow-astrology-up-to-a-point.html; Cynthia Gorney, "The Reagan Chart Watch: Astrologer Joan Quigley, Eye on the Cosmos," *Washington Post*, May 11, 1988, https://www .scribd.com/doc/303989261/The-Reagan-Chart-Watcher#fullscreen&from_embed; Lou Cannon, "Nancy Reagan, an Influential and Protective First Lady, Dies at 94," *New York Times*, March 6, 2016, https://www.nytimes.com/2016/03/07/us/nancy-reagan-a-stylish-and -influential-first-lady-dies-at-94.html?module=ArrowsNav&contentCollection=U.S .&action=keypress&region=FixedLeft&pgtype=article.

31. Julie Zauzmer, "Meet the Astrologer Who Brought the Cosmos into the Reagan White House," *Washington Post*, March 11, 2016, https://www.washingtonpost.com /news/acts-of-faith/wp/2016/03/11/meet-the-astrologer-who-brought-the-cosmos-into -the-reagan-white-house/?noredirect=on&utm_term=.05ab65eb5c5c.

32. Kevin Phillips, *American Theocracy* (New York: Viking, 2006), ix.

33. Ibid., 234.

34. Ibid., 238.

35. Harriet Sherwood, "The Chosen One? The New Film That Claims Trump's Election Was an Act of God," *The Guardian*, October 9, 2018, https://www.theguardian.com/us -news/2018/oct/03/the-trump-prophecy-film-god-election-mark-taylor; see also Harriet Sherwood, "Christian Leader Jerry Falwell Urges Trump Support: 'He's a Moral Person,'" *The Guardian*, October 9, 2018, https://www.theguardian.com/us-news/2018/oct/09 /christian-leader-jerry-falwell-urges-trump-support-hes-a-moral-person?CMP=Share _iOSApp_Other.

36. Sherwood, "The Chosen One?"

37. Lindsey Bever, "Franklin Graham: The Media Didn't Understand the 'God-Factor' in Trump's Win," *Washington Post*, November 10, 2016, https://www.washingtonpost .com/news/acts-of-faith/wp/2016/11/10/franklin-graham-the-media-didnt-understand -the-god-factor/?noredirect=on&utm_term=.77821b330310.

38. Rachel Ray, "Witchcraft Moves to the Mainstream in America as Christianity Declines—and Has Trump in Its Sights," *The Telegraph*, December 21, 2018, https:// www.telegraph.co.uk/news/2018/12/21/witchcraft-moves-mainstream-america -christianity-declines. Ray reports:

As Christianity declines across the country, paganism has swung to the mainstream, with witchcraft paraphernalia for sale on every high street and practises normalised across popular culture. In the past two years, it has also become darkly politicised.

Dakota Bracciale, a 29-year-old transgender/queer witch and co-owner of Catland Books and witch shop in Brooklyn, is pleased with the outcome of the ritual hex placed on US Supreme Court Justice Brett Kavanaugh in October. The curse, carried out from Catland Books, was well attended by witches, atheists and humanists—and was followed around the country on social media

Millennials, says Bracciale, are looking for spiritualism outside traditional religion. "The hex centres on the notion that we live in a universe of chaos, entropy, destruction, death, decay with a final ending of oblivion—scientists are telling us. So the witch does everything for themselves—there is no other help in this universe of decay and chaos. If you don't get in the driver's seat things will just get worse," the witch said. . . .

Bracciale is "absolutely" willing to cause physical harm through a hex—"no issue with that." And while Bracciale would have been just as pleased with the new Supreme Court Justice's death, resignation or physical disfigurement, the main goal of the Kavanaugh hex, and the three hexes on President Donald Trump from Catland Books this summer, was to "let them be exposed for who they are—especially as impotent men."

The curse began with a recitation of the Biblical scripture Psalm 109:8: "let his days be few, let another take his office." . . . Witchcraft is powerful, according to Bracciale, because of the "intersectionality of feminism, sexuality, gender, the fight for freedom, eschewing the patriarchy and having sort of a vitriolic response towards it."

39. The best analysis of the current American Russophobia is Stephen F. Cohen, *War with Russia: From Putin and Ukraine to Trump and Russiagate* (New York: Hot Books, 2018). The official American intelligence report (CIA, FBI, NSA, "Assessing Russian Activities and Intentions in Recent US Elections," ICA 2017-01D [Washington, DC: Office of the Director of National Intelligence, 2017], https://www.dni.gov/files /documents/ICA_2017_01.pdf) claimed that Vladimir Putin instigated a vast operation to influence the 2016 presidential elections (ii):

Russian efforts to influence the 2016 US presidential election represent the most recent expression of Moscow's longstanding desire to undermine the US-led liberal democratic order, but these activities demonstrated a significant escalation in directness, level of activity, and scope of effort compared to previous operations.

We assess Russian President Vladimir Putin ordered an influence campaign in 2016 aimed at the US presidential election. Russia's goals were to undermine public faith in the US democratic process, denigrate Secretary Clinton, and harm her electability and potential presidency. We further assess Putin and the Russian Government developed a clear preference for President-elect Trump. . . .

Moscow's influence campaign followed a Russian messaging strategy that blends covert intelligence operations—such as cyber activity—with overt efforts by Russian Government agencies, state-funded media, third-party intermediaries, and paid social media users or "trolls." Russia, like its Soviet predecessor, has a history of conducting covert influence campaigns focused on US presidential elections that have used intelligence officers and agents and press placements to disparage candidates perceived as hostile to the Kremlin.

While the establishment media, particularly the *Washington Post*, the *New York Times*, CNN, and MSNBC, have blindly followed the security and intelligence agencies of the U.S. government in claiming that Vladimir Putin's Russia "meddled" in and "hacked" the presidential elections of 2016 and may even have caused Donald Trump's victory, the evidence is at best scant if not utterly unconvincing (see Cohen, *War with Russia*, 84–88). If Russia meddled, it was with extremely limited resources. As Jeffrey St. Clair put it ("They Came, They Saw, They Tweeted," *Counterpunch*, February 23, 2018, https://www.counterpunch.org /2018/02/23/99972/):

Let's try to put the troll offensive in context. The 2016 presidential elections were the most expensive in history, with both parties spending a combined $2.4 billion. Of this, the Clinton and Trump campaigns bought $81 million worth of advertising on Facebook. Contrast this with the $100,000 the Russians spent on Facebook ad buys. In the battleground states, Russian Facebook ad buys totaled $300 in Pennsylvania, $832 in Michigan, and $1979 in Wisconsin, all but $54 of that before the primary. If this amounted to subversion, it was definitely subversion on the cheap.

While the official Mueller report (Robert S. Mueller III, *Report on the Investigation into Russian Interference in the 2016 Presidential Election*, vol. 1 [Washington, DC: Department of Justice, 2019]) claimed (1) that the "Russian government interfered in the 2016 presidential election in sweeping and systematic fashion" through the alleged "hacking" of the Democratic National Committee by the Russian intelligence service known as the Main Intelligence Directorate of the General Staff of the Russian Army (GRU), the scope of Russian meddling was in fact quite modest. As the Mueller report itself acknowledged (25), "To reach larger U.S. audiences, the IRA [the Russian Internet Research Agency] purchased advertisements from Facebook that promoted the IRA groups on the newsfeeds of U.S. audience members. According to Facebook, the IRA purchased over 3,500 advertisements, and the expenditures totaled approximately $100,000." That sum was minute compared to the more than $2 billion spent by the Trump and Clinton campaigns. Moreover, the quality of these advertisements was at best mediocre and exhibited some bizarre if not altogether lunatic content. For instance, the Mueller Report states (32), "The IRA also recruited moderators of conservative social media groups to promote IRA-generated content, as well as recruited individuals to perform political acts (such as walking around New York City dressed up as Santa Claus with a Trump mask)." The report contends that the activities of the IRA tended to support the candidacies of Trump and Bernie Sanders because they were deemed less anti-Putin than Clinton, who espoused a determined anti-Russian strategy. To support this claim, the report argues that the IRA asked Trump partisans to endorse and participate in pro-Trump rallies (25): "Throughout 2016, IRA accounts published an increasing number of materials supporting the Trump Campaign and opposing the Clinton Campaign. For example, on May 31, 2016, the operational account 'Matt Skiber' began to privately message dozens of pro-Trump Facebook groups asking them to help plan a "pro-Trump rally near Trump Tower." Whatever one may think of Russian meddling, it appears that its significance was grossly exaggerated.

In similar fashion, the idea that Donald Trump was in "collusion" with Russia and became Putin's "pawn" was not only farfetched but ultimately unsubstantiated. As the Mueller report conclusively stated (2), "The investigation did not establish that members of the Trump Campaign conspired or coordinated with the Russian government in its election interference activities." And the report added (9), "While the investigation identified numerous links between individuals with ties to the Russian government and individuals associated with the Trump Campaign, the evidence was not sufficient to support criminal charges. Among other things, the evidence was not sufficient to charge any Campaign official as an unregistered agent of the Russian government or other Russian principal." For a short, incisive summary of the Mueller report's findings, see Glenn Greenwald, "Robert Mueller Did Not Merely Reject the Trump/Russia Conspiracy Theories. He Obliterated Them," *The Intercept*, April 18, 2019, https://theintercept.com/2019/04/18/robert-mueller-did-not-merely-reject-the-trumprussia-conspiracy-theories-he-obliterated-them/. See also Davis Richardson, "Glenn Greenwald on Sucker Journalists—and Why There's No Silver Bullet Coming for Trump," *The Observer*, December 20, 2018, https://observer.com/2018/12/glenn-greenwald-on-sucker-journalists-and-why-theres-no-silver-bullet-coming-for-trump/; Aaron Maté, "Don't Let Russophobia Warp the Facts on Russiagate," *The Nation*, December 14, 2018, https://www.thenation.com/article/russiagate-russophobia

182

-mueller-trump/; Aaron Maté, "New Studies Show Pundits Are Wrong about Russian Social-Media Involvement in US Politics," *The Nation*, December 28, 2018, https://www .thenation.com/article/russiagate-elections-interference/; Mike Whitney, "Where's the Beef? The Senate Intel Committee and Russia," *Counterpunch*, October 12, 2017, https:// www.counterpunch.org/2017/10/12/wheres-the-beef-the-senate-intel-committee-and -russia/; Rob Urie, "Why 'Russian Meddling' Is a Trojan Horse," February 9, 2018, https:// www.counterpunch.org/2018/02/09/why-russian-meddling-is-a-trojan-horse/; Carl Boggs, "Russophobia and the Specter of War," *Counterpunch*, December 19, 2018, https://www .counterpunch.org/2018/12/19/russophobia-and-the-specter-of-war/; Daniel Lazare, "Concord Management and the End of Russiagate?" *Consortium News*, July 12, 2019, https:// consortiumnews.com/2019/07/12/concord-management-and-the-end-of-russiagate/.

40. Steven Metz, "Why 2019 May Be the Year America's Global Strategy Finally Unravels," *World Politics Review*, January 4, 2019, https://www.worldpoliticsreview.com /articles/27100/why-2019-may-be-the-year-america-s-global-strategy-finally-unravels.

41. Ibid.

42. Antony J. Blinken and Robert Kagan, "'America First' Is Only Making the World Worse. Here's a Better Approach," *Order out of Chaos* (blog), Brookings Institution, January 4, 2019, https://www.brookings.edu/blog/order-from-chaos/2019/01/04/america -first-is-only-making-the-world-worse-heres-a-better-approach/?utm_campaign =Brookings%20Brief&utm_source=hs_email&utm_medium=email&utm_content =68759211, 1.

43. Ibid., 5.

44. Jim Garamone, "President Signs Fiscal 2019 Defense Authorization Act at Fort Drum Ceremony," U.S. Department of Defense, August 13, 2018, https://dod.defense .gov/News/Article/Article/1601016/president-signs-fiscal-2019-defense-authorization -act-at-fort-drum-ceremony/; Lara Seligman, "In Reversal, Trump Signals Further Boost in Defense Spending," *Foreign Policy*, December 27, 2018, https://foreignpolicy .com/2018/12/27/in-reversal-trump-signals-further-boost-in-defense-spending -pentagon-iraq.

45. Peter G. Peterson Foundation, "U.S. Defense Spending Compared to Other Countries," May 7, 2018, https://www.pgpf.org/chart-archive/0053_defense-comparison.

46. Alice Slater, "The US Has Military Bases in 80 Countries. All of Them Must Close," *The Nation*, January 24, 2018, https://www.thenation.com/article/the-us-has-military -bases-in-172-countries-all-of-them-must-close/.

47. Michelle Fox, "Morgan Stanley: Belief in 'American Exceptionalism' among Global Investors Has Never Been Higher," CNBC, October 8, 2018, https://www.cnbc.com/2018 /10/08/morgan-stanley-global-investors-are-betting-on-us-exceptionalism.html.

48. Chuck Collins gives a summary of current inequalities in the United States ("Is Inequality in America Irreversible?" Inequality.org, April 2, 2018, https://inequality.org /great-divide/inequality-america-irreversible-2/):

Between 1980 and 2013, the richest 1 percent saw their average real income increase by 142 percent, with their share of national income doubling from 10 percent to 20 percent. But most economic gains during this period have flowed to the top 0.1 percent—the top one-tenth of 1 percent—whose real income increased by 236 percent. Their share of national income almost tripled, from 3.4 percent to 9.5 percent. Since the economic meltdown of 2008, an estimated $91 of every $100 in increased earnings have gone to the top 1 percent. The bottom 99 percent of wage earners split the remaining 9 percent in gains.

Wealth has increasingly concentrated at the top. The wealthiest 1 percent of households now hold roughly 42 percent of private wealth, up from 33 percent in 1983. At the very pinnacle of US wealth is the Forbes 400, all of whom are billionaires, with a combined net worth of $2.3 trillion. Together, this group has more wealth than the bottom 62 percent of the US population combined. The 20 wealthiest billionaires— who could all fit into a Gulfstream 650 luxury jet—have more wealth than the entire bottom half of the US population.

See also Pew Research Center, *American Middle Class Is Losing Ground*; Piketty, *Capital in the Twenty-First Century*.

49. A 2015 report from Credit Suisse (Jill Treanor, "Half of World's Wealth Now in Hands of 1% of Population," *The Guardian*, October 13, 2015, https://www.theguardian .com/money/2015/oct/13/half-world-wealth-in-hands-population-inequality-report) points out:

Global inequality is growing, with half the world's wealth now in the hands of just 1% of the population. . . . The middle classes have been squeezed at the expense of the very rich. . . . Tidjane Thiam, the chief executive of Credit Suisse, said: "Middle class wealth has grown at a slower pace than wealth at the top end. This has reversed the pre-crisis trend which saw the share of middle-class wealth remaining fairly stable over time." The report shows that a person needs only $3,210 (£2,100) to be in the wealthiest 50% of world citizens. About $68,800 secures a place in the top 10%, while the top 1% have more than $759,900. The report defines wealth as the value of assets including property and stock market investments, but excludes debt.

About 3.4 bn people—just over 70% of the global adult population—have wealth of less than $10,000. A further 1bn—a fifth of the world's population—are in the $10,000– $100,000 range. Each of the remaining 383m adults—8% of the population—has wealth of more than $100,000. This number includes about 34m US dollar millionaires. About 123,800 individuals of these have more than $50m, and nearly 45,000 have more than $100m. . . . The report said: "Wealth inequality has continued to increase since 2008, with the top percentile of wealth holders now owning 50.4% of all household wealth." At the start of 2015, Oxfam had warned that 1% of the world's population would own more wealth than the other 99% by next year.

50. Edward Conard, *The Upside of Inequality* (New York: Penguin, 2016).

51. Collins, "Is Inequality in America Irreversible?"

52. Conard, *Upside of Inequality*, 13, 28, 35.

53. F. William Engdahl, *Manifest Destiny: Democracy as Cognitive Dissonance* (Wiesbaden, Germany: mine.books, 2018); Alfred W. McCoy, *In the Shadows of the American Century* (Chicago: Haymarket Books, 2017).

54. John Bolton, "Protecting American Constitutionalism and Sovereignty from International Threats," *Lawfare*, September 10, 2018, https://www.lawfareblog.com /national-security-adviser-john-bolton-remarks-federalist-society.

55. See Cohen, *War with Russia*.

56. The list of documented American interferences in the domestic affairs of other countries is too long to enumerate here. Suffice it to say that such interferences have encompassed a panoply of policies ranging from outright military invasions and coups, to electoral manipulations and economic strangulations. See John A. Tures, "United States Military Operations in the New World Order," *American Diplomacy*, April 2003,

http://www.unc.edu/depts/diplomat/archives_roll/2003_01-03/tures_military/tures
_military.html; Hugh Gusterson, "Empire of Bases," *Bulletin of the Atomic Social Scientists*, March 10, 2009, http://www.thebulletin.org/web-edition/columnists/hugh-gusterson /empire-of-bases; Eric Hobsbawm, *On Empire* (New York: Pantheon Books, 2008).

57. Dov H. Levin, "Partisan Electoral Interventions by the Great Powers: Introducing the PEIG Dataset," *Conflict Management and Peace Science* 36, no. 1 (2019): 89 and 94, https://journals.sagepub.com/doi/pdf/10.1177/0738894216661190.

58. Scott Shane, "Russia Isn't the Only One Meddling in Elections. We Do It, Too," *New York Times*, February 17, 2018, https://www.nytimes.com/2018/02/17/sunday-review /russia-isnt-the-only-one-meddling-in-elections-we-do-it-too.html.

59. James C. Scott, *Domination and the Arts of Resistance* (New Haven, Conn.: Yale University Press, 1990).

60. Ibid., 183, 199.

61. Ibid., xiii.

62. Sidney Tarrow, *Power in Movement* (Cambridge: Cambridge University Press, 1994), 129–131.

63. Fatton, *Roots of Haitian Despotism*; Fatton, *Haiti's Predatory Republic*, 51–106.

64. Joseph W. Esherick and Jeffrey N. Wasserstrom, "Acting Out Democracy: Political Theater in Modern China," *Journal of Asian Studies* 49, no. 4 (1990): 839.

65. Tarrow, *Power in Movement*, 119.

66. Ibid., 130.

67. Ibid., 129–130. The significance of the language of rights in the struggle for black citizenship has a long history, which Martha S. Jones describes in her book *Birthright Citizens* ([New York: Cambridge University Press, 2018], 3–4). She traces it back to William Yates's 1838 celebrated legal treatise, *Rights of Colored Men to Suffrage, Citizenship, and Trial by Jury*. For Yates, law was Janus-faced; it could be a powerful bulwark of oppression, but it could also be the vehicle of emancipation. According to Jones:

> Yates provides a window onto the position that some activists—black and white— took on race and citizenship at the end of the 1830s. Law was an instrument of change, and Yates forthrightly explained his objective: to understand prejudice against color. Racism had led to "legal disability": exclusion from militia service, naturalization, suffrage, public schooling, ownership of real property, office holding and courtroom testimony.... Assembling evidence from legal culture, he believed, would help establish the rights and citizenship of free black people.... Most powerful was Yates's argument about how law, though suffering from amnesia, could be made right. The same instruments that had woven racism into the nation's legal fabric—courts, conventions, and legislatures—could now be used to recraft it. Legal culture was also capable of reform, of itself and of the status of black Americans.

68. Bourdieu, *In Other Words*, 9, 61, and 77.

69. Fatton, *Roots of Haitian Despotism*, 13–42.

70. Ralf Dahrendorf, *Life Chances* (Chicago: University of Chicago Press, 1979). According to Dahrendorf (29–30), "Life chances are not attributes of individuals. Individuals have life chances in society; their life chances may make or break them; but their lives are a response to these chances. Life chances are a mould. They may be too big for individuals and challenge them to grow; or they may be too restricted and challenge them to resist. Life chances are opportunities for individual growth, for the real-

ization of talents, wishes and hopes, and these opportunities are provided by social conditions."

71. Pierre Bourdieu, *Outline of a Theory of Practice* (Cambridge: Cambridge University Press, 1977), 95.

72. Peter Hall, *Governing the Economy: The Politics of State Intervention in Britain and France* (New York: Oxford University Press, 1986), 34.

73. Cherríe Moraga, "Art in America con Acento," in *In Other Words: Literature by Latinas of the United States*, ed. Roberta Fernandez (Houston: Arte Publico, 1994), 301–302.

74. Edouard Glissant, *Poetics of Relation* (Ann Arbor: University of Michigan Press, 1997); Edouard Glissant, *Caribbean Discourse* (Charlottesville: University of Virginia Press, 1989); Pascale De Souza and H. Adlai Murdoch, "Caribbean Textuality and the Metaphors of Métissage," *Journal of Caribbean Literatures* 4, no. 2 (2006): vii-xvi; Sanyu Ruth Mulira, "Edouard Glissant and the African Roots of Creolization," *Ufahamu: A Journal of African Studies* 38, no. 2 (2015): 115–128; Melville J. Herskovits, *The Myth of the Negro Past* (Boston: Beacon Press, 1990).

75. Sidney Mintz and Richard Price, *The Birth of African-American Culture* (Boston: Beacon Press, 1992), 42–60.

76. Ibid., 83.

77. William H. Frey, "The US Will Become 'Minority White' in 2045, Census Projects. Youthful Minorities Are the Engine of Future Growth," *The Avenue* (blog), Brookings Institution, March 14, 2018, https://www.brookings.edu/blog/the-avenue/2018/03/14/the-us-will-become-minority-white-in-2045-census-projects.

78. Ibid.

79. See Lee Feinstein and Anne-Marie Slaughter, "A Duty to Prevent," *Foreign Affairs* 83, no. 1 (2004), https://www.foreignaffairs.com/articles/2004-01-01/duty-prevent. Feinstein and Slaughter defend the idea of both R2P and their proposed "duty to prevent" so-called rogue states from acquiring weapons of mass destruction. In their view the major powers have to develop the international institutions and norms allowing them to "protect" and "prevent," while legitimating these powers' monopoly of such weapons. The imperial undertones of such proposals are striking, especially after the fabricated reasons for the U.S. destruction of Iraq by the George W. Bush administration. Feinstein and Slaughter put it bluntly:

> [R2P] holds that today UN member states have a responsibility to protect the lives, liberty, and basic human rights of their citizens, and that if they fail or are unable to carry it out, the international community has a responsibility to step in. . . . We propose a corollary principle in the field of global security: a collective "duty to prevent" nations run by rulers without internal checks on their power from acquiring or using WMD. . . .
>
> "The Responsibility to Protect" . . . took on nothing less than the redefinition of sovereignty itself. The Evans-Sahnoun Commission argued that the controversy over using force for humanitarian purposes stemmed from a "critical gap" between the unavoidable reality of mass human suffering and the existing rules and mechanisms for managing world order. To fill this gap, the commission identified an emerging international obligation—the "responsibility to protect"—which requires states to intervene in the affairs of other states.

80. Philippe R. Girard, *Clinton in Haiti: The 1994 US Invasion of Haiti* (New York: Palgrave Macmillan: 2004), 63, 79–101.

81. Quoted in Girard, *Clinton in Haiti*, 97.

82. Ibid., 99.

83. Ibid.

84. For a pro-Aristide explanation of his departure into exile, see Peter Hallward, *Damming the Flood: Haiti, Aristide, and the Politics of Containment* (London: Verso, 2007), and Randall Robinson, *An Unbroken Agony: Haiti, From Revolution to the Kidnapping of a President* (New York: Basic Civitas Books, 2007). For the U.S. government's point of view, see Press Secretary, "Statement on Haiti," The White House: President George W. Bush, February 28, 2004, https://georgewbush-whitehouse.archives.gov/news/releases/2004/02/20040228-2.html.

85. On May 13, 1994, Richard Haass, who served in the National Security Council in the George H. W. Bush administration, joined former Democratic congressman Stephen Solarz in publishing an influential editorial in the *Washington Post* calling for a U.S.-led intervention in Haiti. They argued (quoted in Roland I. Perusse, *Haitian Democracy Restored—1991–1995* [New York: University Press of America, 1995], 88–89), "U.S. policy toward Haiti is not working. As a consequence, both Haitian democracy and American credibility are on the line. . . . Defeating the small, lightly armed and poorly trained Haitian military would not be hard. If Desert Storm took six weeks, "Caribbean Hurricane" would take six hours.

86. David Malone, *Decision-Making in the UN Security Council: The Case of Haiti* (Oxford: Oxford University Press, 1998), 162.

CHAPTER 9 — IDENTITY POLITICS AND MODERN EXCEPTIONALISM

1. Quoted in K. Anthony Appiah and Amy Gutman, *Color Conscious: The Political Morality of Race* (Princeton, NJ: Princeton University Press, 1996), 22–23.

2. Foner, *Reconstruction*.

3. David Roediger, *The Wages of Whiteness: Race and the Making of the American Working Class* (London: Verso, 2007); David Roediger, *Class, Race, and Marxism* (London: Verso, 2017).

4. W.E.B. Du Bois, *Black Reconstruction in America* (New York: Harcourt, Brace and Co., 1935), 700–701.

5. Chuck Collins, Dedrick Asante-Muhammed, Emanuel Nieves, Josh Hoxie, Sabrina Terry, *Dreams Deferred: Enriching the 1 Percent Widens the Racial Wealth Divide* (Washington, DC: Institute for Policy Studies, 2019), 5, https://ips-dc.org/wp-content/uploads/2019/01/IPS_RWD-Report_FINAL-1.15.19.pdf. See also Douglas Massey and Nancy Denton, *American Apartheid: Segregation and the Making of the Underclass* (Cambridge, MA: Harvard University Press, 1993), and Melvin Oliver and Thomas Shapiro, *Black Wealth/White Wealth: A New Perspective on Racial Inequality* (New York: Routledge, 1995).

6. Chuck Collins, Dedrick Asante-Muhammed, Emanuel Nieves, Josh Hoxie, *The Ever-Growing Gap: Failing to Address the Status Quo Will Drive the Racial Wealth Divide for Centuries to Come* (Washington, DC: Institute for Policy Studies, 2016), 5, https://ips-dc.org/report-ever-growing-gap/. See also Adolph L. Reed and Merlin Chowkwanyun, "Race, Class, Crisis: The Discourse of Racial Disparity and Its Analytical Discontents," *Socialist Register* 48 (2012): 149–175.

7. William Julius Wilson, "The Declining Significance of Race: Revisited and Revised," *Daedalus*, 140, no. 2 (2011): 55–70; William Julius Wilson, *The Declining Significance of Race: Blacks and Changing American Institutions*, 3rd ed. (Chicago: University of Chicago Press, 2012).

8. Henry Louis Gates Jr., "Black America and the Class Divide," *New York Times*, February 1, 2016, https://www.nytimes.com/2016/02/07/education/edlife/black-america -and-the-class-divide.html.

9. Appiah and Gutman, *Color Conscious*, 43.

10. Kimberle Crenshaw, "Demarginalizing the Intersection of Race and Sex: A Black Feminist Critique of Discrimination Doctrine, Feminist Theory, and Antiracist Practice," *University of Chicago Legal Forum* 1989, no. 1 (1989): 139–167.

11. Ibid., 149.

12. Jamilah King, "How Black Lives Matter Has Changed US Politics," *New Internationalist*, February 2018, https://newint.org/features/2018/03/01/black-lives-matter-changed -politics; Robin G. Kelley, "What Does Black Lives Matter Want?" *Boston Review*, August 17, 2016, http://bostonreview.net/books-ideas/robin-d-g-kelley-movement-black-lives-vision.

13. Jelani Cobb, "The Matter of Black Lives," *New Yorker*, March 7, 2016, https://www .newyorker.com/magazine/2016/03/14/where-is-black-lives-matter-headed.

14. The Movement for Black Lives, "A Vision for Black Lives: Policy Demands for Black Power, Freedom and Justice," August 2016, https://neweconomy.net/sites/default /files/resources/20160726-m4bl-Vision-Booklet-V3.pdf.

15. Ibid.

16. Adolph L. Reed Jr., "Marx, Race, and Neoliberalism," *New Labor Forum* 22, no. 1 (2013): 53–54.

17. Kenneth O'Reilly, *Nixon's Piano: Presidents and Racial Politics from Washington to Clinton* (New York: Free Press, 1995). O'Reilly shows convincingly that all presidents— at least from Washington to Clinton—have always played the so-called Southern strategy (10–12):

> Southern strategy in our time remains what it has always been: the gut organizing principle of American politics. At root it is nothing more than a belief that presidential elections can be won only by following the doctrines and rituals of white over black. The pecking order has stayed that way through the death of slavery and Jim Crow, and notwithstanding Lincoln and Johnson our presidents have in nearly every other case made it their job to keep that order.
>
> All three of the nation's two-party systems have accommodated white over black and respected White House responsibilities to ensure that the nation's politics remains organized according to that dictate. . . . Segregation was not a time-honored tradition even in the deep South but a relatively recent construct of the late nineteenth and early twentieth centuries. In the history of American racism, stateways have influenced folkways far more deeply than the reverse; and the men who came to the Oval Office were as responsible for seeing to this as any Jamestown slaveowner or Jim Crow architect or practitioner of the segmented racial politics that dominates presidential elections today.

18. Somini Sengupta, "Georgia Park Is to Hail 'Southern Spirit,'" *New York Times*, October 8, 2000, https://www.nytimes.com/2000/10/08/us/georgia-park-is-to-hail-southern -spirit.html.

19. Ibid. See also Christopher Petrella, "On Stone Mountain: White Supremacy and the Birth of the Modern Democratic Party," *Boston Review*, March 30, 2016, https://bostonreview.net/us/christopher-petrella-stone-mountain-white-supremacy-modern-democratic-party; Nathan J. Robinson, "Bill Clinton's Stone Mountain Moment," *Jacobin*, September 16, 2016, https://www.jacobinmag.com/2016/09/stone-mountain-kkk-white-supremacy-simmons/.

20. In fact, the celebrated novelist Toni Morrison called Bill Clinton "the first black President." As she put it in an ironic 1998 *New Yorker* comment ("On the First Black President, *New Yorker*, September 28, 1998, https://www.newyorker.com/magazine/1998/10/05/comment-6543):

> White skin notwithstanding, [Clinton] is our first black President. Blacker than any actual black person who could ever be elected in our children's lifetime. After all, Clinton displays almost every trope of blackness: single-parent household, born poor, working-class, saxophone-playing, McDonald's-and-junk-food-loving boy from Arkansas. And when virtually all the African-American Clinton appointees began, one by one, to disappear, when the President's body, his privacy, his unpoliced sexuality became the focus of the persecution, when he was metaphorically seized and body-searched, who could gainsay these black men who knew whereof they spoke? The message was clear: "No matter how smart you are, how hard you work, how much coin you earn for us, we will put you in your place or put you out of the place you have somehow, albeit with our permission, achieved. You will be fired from your job, sent away in disgrace, and—who knows?—maybe sentenced and jailed to boot. In short, unless you do as we say (i.e., assimilate at once), your expletives belong to us.

21. Fields and Fields, *Racecraft*, 147–148.

22. Wendy Brown, *States of Injury* (Princeton, NJ: Princeton University Press, 1995), 52–76.

23. Adolph L. Reed Jr., "The Trouble with Uplift," *The Baffler*, no. 41 (September 2018), https://thebaffler.com/salvos/the-trouble-with-uplift-reed.

24. Judith Butler, *The Psychic Life of Power* (Stanford, CA: Stanford University Press, 1997), 104.

25. W. Brown, *States of Injury*, 59–60.

26. Kimberle Crenshaw, "Mapping the Margins: Intersectionality, Identity Politics, and Violence Against Women of Color," *Stanford Law Review* 43, no. 6 (1993): 1247.

27. Walter Benn Michaels, *The Trouble with Diversity: How We Learned to Love Identity and Ignore Inequality* (New York: Holt Paperbacks, 2006); see also Toure F. Reed, *Toward Freedom* (New York: Verso, 2020).

28. William Darity Jr., Ashwini Deshpande, and Thomas Weisskopf, "Who Is Eligible? Should Affirmative Action Be Group- or Class-Based?" *American Journal of Economics and Sociology* 70, no. 1 (2011): 264.

29. Ibid.

30. Kendi, *Stamped from the Beginning*, 505.

31. Ibid., x.

32. Tyler T. Reny, Loren Collingwood, and Ali A. Valenzuela, "Vote Switching in the 2016 Election: How Racial and Immigration Attitudes, Not Economics, Explain Shifts in White Voting," *Public Opinion Quarterly* 83, no. 1 (2019): 4, https://www.dropbox.com/s/qphz9lxy6pxni1k/final_submission_reny_etal_poq_public.pdf?dl=0; Cornell Belcher, *A Black Man*

in the White House: Barack Obama and the Triggering of America's Racial-Aversion Crisis (New York: Water Street Press, 2016); Matthew W. Hughey, "White Backlash in the 'Post-Racial' United States," *Ethnic and Racial Studies* 37, no. 5 (March 2014): 721–730, https://www.tandfonline.com/doi/pdf/10.1080/01419870.2014.886710?needAccess=true; Vann R. Newkirk II, "Five Decades of White Backlash," *The Atlantic,* January 15, 2018, https://www.theatlantic.com/politics/archive/2018/01/trump-massive-resistance-history-mlk/550544/.

33. Adolph L. Reed Jr., "What Materialist Black Political History Actually Looks Like," *Nonsite,* January 8, 2019, https://nonsite.org/editorial/what-materialist-black-political-history-actually-looks-like.

34. Case and Deaton, *Deaths of Despair and the Future of Capitalism.*

35. Justin Gest, *The New Minority: White Working Class Politics in an Age of Immigration and Inequality* (New York: Oxford University Press, 2016), 200.

36. Adolph L. Reed Jr., "Obama No," *The Progressive,* April 28, 2008, https://progressive.org/magazine/obama/. In this prescient article, Reed states that Obama's "fundamental political center of gravity, beneath an empty rhetoric of hope and change and new directions, is neoliberal." See also T. Reed, *Toward Freedom,* 101–158.

37. Kevin D. Williamson, "The Father-Führer," *National Review,* March 28, 2016, https://www.nationalreview.com/magazine/2016/03/28/father-f-hrer/; see also Charles Murray, *Coming Apart: The State of White America, 1960–2010* (New York: Random House, 2012).

38. Anne Sraders, "What Is Middle Class, Really? Income and Range in 2019," *The Street,* January 18, 2019, https://www.thestreet.com/personal-finance/what-is-middle-class-14833259.

39. Ibid.

40. Ibid.

41. Fields and Fields, *Racecraft,* 18–19. The quote is from W. E. H. Lecky, *History of the Rise and Influence of the Spirit of Rationalism in Europe,* with an introduction by C. Wright Mills (New York: George Braziller, 1955), 38.

42. Michaels, *Trouble with Diversity,* 6–20.

43. Benjamin I. Page, Larry M. Bartels, and Jason Seawright, "Democracy and the Policy Preferences of Wealthy Americans," *Perspectives on Politics* 11, no. 1 (2013): 51–73.

44. Martin Gilens and Benjamin I. Page, "Testing Theories of American Politics: Elites, Interest Groups, and Average Citizens," *Perspective on Politics* 12, no. 3 (2014): 575–576.

45. Ibid., 576–577.

46. Ralph Miliband, *The State in Capitalist Society* (New York: Basic Books, 1969); Ralph Miliband, *Marxism and Politics* (Oxford: Oxford University Press, 1977); Nicos Poulantzas, *Political Power and Social Classes* (London: NLB, 1973).

47. RealClearPolitics, "Congressional Job Approval," March 30, 2019, https://www.realclearpolitics.com/epolls/other/congressional_job_approval-903.html.

48. Larry Summers, "Washington May Bluster but Cannot Stifle the Chinese Economy," *Financial Times,* December 3, 2018.

49. Cohen, *War with Russia.*

50. Georg Wilhelm Friedrich Hegel, *Hegel's Philosophy of Right,* trans. T. M. Knox (New York: Oxford University Press, 1967), 13.

51. Jeremy Kuzmarov and John Marciano, *The Russians Are Coming, Again: The First Cold War as Tragedy, the Second as Farce* (New York: Monthly Review Press, 2018).

CHAPTER 10 — CONCLUSION

1. Gramsci, *Selections from Prison Notebooks*, 178–81 and 206–276. See also Anne Showstack Sassoon, "Passive Revolution and the Politics of Reform," in *Approaches to Gramsci*, ed. Anne Showstack Sassoon (London: Writers and Readers, 1982), 127–148. Paradoxically, Gramsci's notion of passive revolution stems from Burkean conservatism, which asserted that "society had to change in order to stay the same, i.e., to preserve its most essential features" (15). Accordingly, a passive revolution is a preemptive response from "on high" to the disorganized but potentially revolutionary demands of dominated classes. Gramsci's concept denotes the specific peaceful means of survival of a ruling class in conditions of "organic crisis."

2. George H. W. Bush, "State of the Union," speech, Washington, DC, January 28, 1992, http://stateoftheunion.onetwothree.net/texts/19920128.html.

3. Michael R. Pompeo, "Why Diplomacy Matters," speech, Texas A&M University, April 15, 2019, https://www.state.gov/secretary/remarks/2019/04/291144.htm.

4. Jean Casimir, "The Sovereign People of Haiti during the Eighteenth and Nineteenth Centuries," in *The Haitian Declaration of Independence: Creation, Context, and Legacy*, ed. Julia Gaffield (Charlottesville: University of Virginia Press, 2016), 198.

5. Jean-Jacques Dessalines, "Haitian Declaration of Independence," 1804, https://today.duke.edu/showcase/haitideclaration/declarationstext.html.

6. The Creole version is "Plimen poul la pinga li kriye," and the French is "Plumer la poule, mais éviter de la faire crier."

7. Fatton, *Haiti: Trapped in the Outer Periphery*.

8. Transcribed and translated by Laurent Dubois, "Thinking Haitian Independence in Haitian Vodou," in *The Haitian Declaration of Independence: Creation, Context, and Legacy*, ed. Julia Gaffield (Charlottesville: University of Virginia Press, 2016), 213–214. A recording of the song appears on Wawa and Rasin Kanga, *Haitian Roots*, vol. 1, audio recording (General Records and Productions, 1996). A YouTube version of the song can be accessed at WAWA & Rasin Kanga, "Sou Lanmè," https://www.youtube.com/watch?v=MEMI8M3YHzw. See also Joan Dayan, *Haiti, History, and the Gods* (Berkeley: University of California Press, 1995); Karen McCarthy Brown, *Mama Lola: A Vodou Priestess in Brooklyn* (Berkeley: University of California Press, 1991); Karen E. Richman, *Migration and Vodou* (Gainesville: University Press of Florida, 2005).

9. Fatton, *Haiti: Trapped in the Outer Periphery*.

10. Transcribed and translated by Dubois, "Thinking Haitian Independence in Haitian Vodou," 211–212.

11. David Waldstreicher, *Slavery's Constitution: From Revolution to Ratification* (New York: Hill and Wang, 2009), 13–17.

12. Sirvent and Haiphong, *American Exceptionalism and American Innocence*. As Sirvent and Haiphong put it (5–6):

American exceptionalism has always presumed national innocence despite imposing centuries of war and plunder. The U.S. has been at war for over ninety percent of its existence. These wars have all been justified as necessary ventures meant to defend or expand America's so-called founding values and beliefs. A consequence of centuries of endless war has been the historical tendency of the U.S. to erase from consciousness the realities that surround American domestic and international policy, not to mention the system of imperialism that governs both.

13. Quoted in Perry Anderson, *The H-Word: The Peripeteia of Hegemony* (New York: Verso, 2017), 182–183.

14. Aimé Césaire, *Discourse on Colonialism* (New York: Monthly Review Press 2001), 39.

15. K. J. Holsti, "Exceptionalism in American Foreign Policy: Is It Exceptional?" *European Journal of International Relations* 17, no. 3 (2011): 384.

16. Ada Ferrer, *Freedom's Mirror: Cuba and Haiti in the Age of Revolution* (New York: Cambridge University Press, 2014), 329–330.

17. J. S. Scott, *Common Wind*, xvi–xvii.

18. Ibid., 160–173.

19. Eugene Genovese, *From Rebellion to Revolution* (Baton Rouge: Louisiana State University Press), 96.

20. Dale Tomich and Michael Zeuske provide a useful definition of the "second slavery" ("Introduction, the Second Slavery: Mass Slavery, World-Economy, and Comparative Microhistories," *Review [Fernand Braudel Center]* 31, no. 2, part 1 [2008], 91):

> The term "second slavery" . . . suggests an analogy with the "second serfdom." It refers to the systemic redeployment and expansion of Atlantic slavery during the nineteenth century. It is opposed to the more common view that chattel slavery was in one way or another an archaic institution, incompatible with modernity, that was condemned to extinction after the advent of industrial capitalism, modern political regimes, and liberal ideologies. In contrast, the concept of the second slavery calls attention to the world-historical processes that transformed the Atlantic world between the 1780's and 1888, when slavery was abolished in Brazil. These processes resulted in the decline of old zones of colonial slavery and the formation of highly productive new zones of slave commodity production.

21. Ferrer, *Freedom's Mirror*, 10. Tomich and Zeuske emphasize how the new technologies increased further the productivity of the slave mode of production ("Introduction, the Second Slavery," 92): "By 1830, Cuba emerged as the world's leading sugar producer and doubled its output every 10 years until the 1860's. The railroad made possible the expansion of the Cuban sugar zone. The Cuban *ingenio* produced sugar on an unprecedented scale and incorporated the new technologies of steammill, vacuum pan, and centrifuge. Cuban sugar producers increased the quantity and quality of sugar placed on the market and set world prices."

22. Tomich and Zeuske, "Introduction, the Second Slavery," 93.

23. J. S. Scott, *Common Wind*.

24. Ferrer, *Freedom's Mirror*, 338.

25. Ibid., 288–296.

26. Matthew J. Smith, *Liberty, Fraternity, Exile: Haiti and Jamaica after Emancipation* (Chapel Hill: University of North Carolina Press, 2014), 5.

27. Fatton, *Roots of Haitian Despotism*.

28. *Moun andeyo* is the Creole term for the "outsiders," those who are not part of the nation and are excluded from its benefits and recognition. See Gérard Barthélémy, *Le Pays en Dehors* (Port-au-Prince: Editions Henri Deschamps, 1989).

29. Greg Beckett, *There Is No More Haiti: Between Life and Death in Port-au-Prince* (Oakland: University of California Press, 2019), 6. The Creole version of "Haiti is dead. There is no more Haiti" is *Ayiti fini* or *Ayiti mouri*.

30. Ibid., 238.

31. Karl Marx, "The Eighteenth Brumaire of Louis Bonaparte," in *Karl Marx: Selected Writings*, ed. David McLellan (Oxford: Oxford University Press, 1977), 300.

Bibliography

Adams, John. Humphrey Ploughjogger to the *Boston Gazette*. October 14, 1765. In *Papers of John Adams*, vol. 1, *September 1755–October 1773*, edited by Robert J. Taylor, Mary-Jo Kline, Gregg L. Lint. Cambridge, MA: Harvard University Press, 1977. Adams Papers: Digital Edition. Massachusetts Historical Society. https://www.masshist.org/publications/apde2/view?id=ADMS-06-01-02-0057.

Adams, John. John Adams to Thomas Jefferson. November 15, 1813. Founders Online. National Archives. https://founders.archives.gov/documents/Adams/99-02-02-6198.

Agence France Presse. "La République dominicaine 'dénationalise' des milliers d'Haïtiens." *France24*, October 3, 2013. http://www.france24.com/fr/20131003-haiti-republique-dominicaine-nationalite-dechenace-transit-immigrants.

Alexander, Michelle. *The New Jim Crow: Mass Incarceration in the Age of Colorblindness*. Rev. ed. New York: New Press, 2011.

Alexis, Eddy Jackson. "L'amnésie d'Edo Zenny." *Le Matin*, September 9, 2012. http://www.lematinhaiti.com/contenu.php?idtexte=32535.

Amnesty International. "Haiti/Dominican Republic: Reckless Deportations Leaving Thousands in Limbo." Amnesty International, June 15, 2016. https://www.amnesty.org/en/latest/news/2016/06/haiti-dominican-republic-reckless-deportations-leaving-thousands-in-limbo/.

Anderson, Perry. *American Foreign Policy and Its Thinkers*. London: Verso, 2015.

Anderson, Perry. *The H-Word: The Peripeteia of Hegemony*. New York: Verso, 2017.

Anonymous. *Haiti: Efforts to Restore President Aristide, 1991–1994*. Report no. 95-602 F. Washington, DC: Congressional Research Service, 1995. https://www.everycrsreport.com/files/19950511_95-602_6c19769dbf2c82c7a1d4458d505c45cfa9990234.pdf.

Appiah, K. Anthony, and Amy Gutman. *Color Conscious: The Political Morality of Race*. Princeton, NJ: Princeton University Press, 1996.

Ardouin, C. *Essais sur l'histoire d'Haiti*. Port-au-Prince: Bouchereau, 1865.

Arthus, Wien Weibert. *Duvalier a l'Ombre de la Guerre Froide*. Port-au-Prince: Alexandre Fritz Arios, 2014.

Associated Press. "Military Backed Leader Declares State of Emergency in Haiti." June 12, 1994. https://www.apnews.com/e50463dd4bc17af24d2a3e1c65c90276.

Auden, W. H. "In Memory of Sigmund Freud." In *W. H. Auden: Collected Poems*, edited by Edward Mendelson, 274. New York: Vintage, 1991.

Baptist, Edward E. *The Half Has Never Been Told*. New York: Basic Books, 2014.

Barnett, Michael, and Thomas G. Weiss. *Humanitarianism Contested*. London: Routledge, 2011.

Baron, Amelie. "Inequality Drives Migration Crisis for Haiti, Dominican Republic." Agence France Presse, July 4, 2018. https://www.yahoo.com/news/inequality-drives -migration-crisis-haiti-dominican-republic-215318549.html.

Barthélémy, Gérard. *Le Pays en Dehors*. Port-au-Prince: Editions Henri Deschamps, 1989.

BBC News. "Clinton: Half of Trump Supporters 'Basket of Deplorables.'" September 10, 2016. https://www.bbc.com/news/av/election-us-2016-37329812/clinton-half-of-trump -supporters-basket-of-deplorables.

BBC News. "Trump Warns Iran of 'Obliteration' in Event of War." Last modified June 22, 2019. https://www.bbc.com/news/world-us-canada-48728465.

Beckert, Sven, and Seth Rockman. "Introduction: Slavery's Capitalism." In *Slavery's Capitalism: A New History of American Economic Development*, edited by Sven Beckert and Seth Rockman, 1–27. Philadelphia: University of Pennsylvania Press, 2016.

Beckett, Greg. *There Is No More Haiti: Between Life and Death in Port-au-Prince*. Oakland: University of California Press, 2019.

Belcher, Cornell. *A Black Man in the White House: Barack Obama and the Triggering of America's Racial-Aversion Crisis*. New York: Water Street Press, 2016.

Bélizaire, Claudy. "Tu dois respecter un mulâtre, Edo Zenny te connais, mais pas le sénateur Zenny: Je suis blanc, et toi tu es nègre." *Tout Haiti*, September 11, 2012. http:// www.touthaiti.com/touthaiti-actualites/853-tu-dois-respecter-un-mulatre-edo -zenny-te-connais-mais-pas-le-senateur-zenny-je-suis-blanc-et-toi-tu-es-negre.

Bell, Lis. "Rép. Dominicaine: La 'dénationalisation' des Dominicains d'origine haïtienne planifiée par le PLD et la FNP depuis 2008." *AlterPresse*, December 13, 2013. http://www.alterpresse.org/spip.php?article15624#.Uv2Xgv2_20s.

Bell, Madison Smart. *Toussaint Louverture: A Biography*. New York: Pantheon Books, 2007.

Bellamy, John, and Robert W. McChesney. "Kipling, the 'White Man's Burden,' and U.S. Imperialism." *Monthly Review Press*, November 1, 2003. https://monthlyreview.org /2003/11/01/kipling-the-white-mans-burden-and-u-s-imperialism/.

Bellegarde, Dantes. *Histoire du Peuple Haïtien (1492–1952)*. Port-au-Prince: Fardin, 1953.

Bernal, Angelica Maria. *Beyond Origins. Rethinking Founding in a Time of Constitutional Democracy*. New York: Oxford University Press, 2017.

Bever, Lindsey. "Franklin Graham: The Media Didn't Understand the 'God-Factor' in Trump's Win." *Washington Post*, November 10, 2016. https://www.washingtonpost .com/news/acts-of-faith/wp/2016/11/10/franklin-graham-the-media-didnt -understand-the-god-factor/?noredirect=on&utm_term=.77821b330310.

Beveridge, Albert J. "In Support of an American Empire." January 9, 1900. 56th Congress, 1st session. *Congressional Record* 33, pt. 1.

Blackburn, Robin. *The American Crucible: Slavery, Emancipation, and Human Rights*. London: Verso 2013.

Blackburn, Robin. *The Making of New World Slavery*. London: Verso, 1997.

Blancpain, François. *Haïti et les États Unis, 1915–1934*. Paris: L'Harmattan, 1999.

Blancpain, François. *La Condition des Paysans Haitiens*. Paris: Karthala, 2003.

Blight, David. *Race and Reunion: The Civil War in American Memory*. Cambridge, MA: Harvard University Press, 2001.

Blinken, Antony J., and Robert Kagan. "'America First' Is Only Making the World Worse. Here's a Better Approach." *Order out of Chaos* (blog). Brookings Institution, January 4, 2019. https://www.brookings.edu/blog/order-from-chaos/2019/01/04/america-first-is-only-making-the-world-worse-heres-a-better approach/?utm_campaign=Brookings%20Brief&utm_source=hs_email&utm_medium=e mail&utm_content=68759211.

Bogart, Brian. "US Conflicts Abroad since World War II America Declassified," Institute for Policy Research and Development, Intelligent Future (Eugene, OR, 2004).

Boggs, Carl. "Russophobia and the Specter of War." *Counterpunch*, December 19, 2018. https://www.counterpunch.org/2018/12/19/russophobia-and-the-specter-of-war/.

Boisrond-Tonnerre, Louis. *Mémoire pour Servir à l'Histoire d'Haïti*. Port-au-Prince: Fardin, 2004.

Bolton, John. "Protecting American Constitutionalism and Sovereignty from International Threats." *Lawfare*, September 10, 2018. https://www.lawfareblog.com/national-security-adviser-john-bolton-remarks-federalist-society.

Bon-Harper, Sara. "Contrasting Worlds: Plantation Landscapes at Monticello." Presentation at the annual meeting of the Society for Historical Archaeology, Amelia Island, Fla., 2010.

Boot, Max. "The Case for American Empire." *Weekly Standard*, October 15, 2001. https://www.weeklystandard.com/max-boot/the-case-for-american-empire.

Bourdieu, Pierre. *In Other Words: Essays towards a Reflexive Sociology*. Stanford, CA: Stanford University Press, 1990.

Bourdieu, Pierre. *The Logic of Practice*. Stanford, CA: Stanford University Press, 1980.

Bourdieu, Pierre. *Outline of a Theory of Practice*. Cambridge: Cambridge University Press, 1977.

Brière, Jean-François. "Abbé Grégoire and Haitian Independence." *Research in African Literatures* 35, no. 2 (Summer 2004): 34–43.

Brière, Jean-François. *Haiti et la France, 1804–1848: Le Rêve Brisé*. Paris: Karthala, 2008.

Brooks, David. "The Underlying Tragedy." *New York Times*, January 4, 2010. http://www.nytimes.com/2010/01/15/opinion/15brooks.html.

Brown, Gordon. *Toussaint's Clause*. Jackson: University Press of Mississippi, 2005.

Brown, Wendy. *States of Injury*. Princeton, NJ: Princeton University Press, 1995.

Buck-Morss, Susan. *Hegel, Haiti, and Universal History*. Pittsburgh: University of Pittsburgh Press, 2009.

Bush, George H. W. "State of the Union Address." Speech, Washington, DC, January 28, 1992. http://stateoftheunion.onetwothree.net/texts/19920128.html.

Bush, George W. "Inaugural Address." Speech, Washington, DC, January 20, 2005. American Presidency Project. http://www.presidency.ucsb.edu/ws/?pid=58745.

Bush, George W. "State of the Union Address." Speech, Washington, DC, January 28, 2003. *Washington Post*. https://www.washingtonpost.com/wp-srv/onpolitics/transcripts/bushtext_012803.html.

Butler, Judith. *The Psychic Life of Power*. Stanford, CA: Stanford University Press, 1997.

Bynum, Victoria, James M. McPherson, James Oakes, Sean Wilentz, and Gordon S. Wood. "Letter to the Editor: Historians Critique the 1619 Project." *New York Times*

Magazine, December 29, 2019. https://www.nytimes.com/2019/12/20/magazine/we
-respond-to-the-historians-who-critiqued-the-1619-project.html.

Byron, John. "We Have Been at War a Long Time." *Proceedings* 143, no. 8 (August 2017).
https://www.usni.org/magazines/proceedings/2017/august/we-have-been-war-long
-time.

Calhoun, John C. "Speech on the Oregon Bill." Washington, DC, June 27, 1848. Constitut-
ing America. https://constitutingamerica.org/speech-on-the-oregon-bill-by-john-c
-calhoun-reprinted-from-the-u-s-constitution-a-reader-published-by-hillsdale-college/.

Cannon, Lou. "Nancy Reagan, an Influential and Protective First Lady, Dies at 94."
New York Times, March 6, 2016. https://www.nytimes.com/2016/03/07/us/nancy-reagan
-a-stylish-and-influential-first-lady-dies-at 94.html?module=ArrowsNav&contentCol-
lection=U.S.&action=keypress&region=Fixed Left&pgtype=article.

Carment, David, and Rachael Calleja. "Diasporas and Fragile States—beyond Remittances Assessing the Theoretical and Policy Linkages." *Journal of Ethnic and Migration Studies* 44, no. 8 (2018): 1270–1288. https://doi.org/10.1080/1369183X.2017.1354157.

"Carnaval Grands Mangeurs." *Haiti en Marche,* February 12–18, 1997, 1–8.

"Carnaval Grands Mangeurs." *Haiti en Marche,* February 19–25, 1997, 12.

Case, Anne, and Angus Deaton. *Deaths of Despair and the Future of Capitalism.* Princeton, NJ: Princeton University Press, 2020.

Casimir, Jean. "From Saint Domingue to Haiti: To Live Again or to Live at Last." In *The
World of the Haitian Revolution,* edited by David Geggus and Norman Fiering,
xi–xviii. Bloomington: Indiana University Press, 2009.

Casimir, Jean. "The Sovereign People of Haiti during the Eighteenth and Nineteenth
Centuries." In *The Haitian Declaration of Independence: Creation, Context, and Legacy,* edited by Julia Gaffield, 181–200. Charlottesville: University of Virginia Press,
2016.

Castor, Suzy. *L'Occupation Américaine D'Haïti.* Port-au-Prince: Imprimerie Henri Deschamps, 1988.

Célius, Carlo. "Neoclassicism and the Haitian Revolution." In *The World of the Haitian
Revolution,* edited by David Geggus and Norman Fiering. Bloomington: Indiana University Press, 2009.

Césaire, Aimé. *Discourse on Colonialism.* New York: Monthly Review Press, 2001.

Césaire, Aimé. *The Tragedy of King Christophe.* Translated by Ralph Manheim. New
York: Grove Press, 1970.

Charles, Asselin. "Haitian Exceptionalism and Caribbean Consciousness." *Journal of
Caribbean Literatures* 3, no. 2 (Spring 2002): 115–130.

Chomsky, Noam. *Towards a New Cold War.* New York: Pantheon Books, 1982.

CIA, FBI, and NSA. "Assessing Russian Activities and Intentions in Recent US Elections." ICA 2017-01D. Washington, DC: Office of the Director of National Intelligence, 2017. https://www.dni.gov/files/documents/ICA_2017_01.pdf.

Clavin, Matthew J. *Toussaint Louverture and the American Civil War.* Philadelphia:
University of Pennsylvania Press, 2010.

Clinton, Hillary. "Why America Is Exceptional." *Time,* October 13, 2016. https://time
.com/collection-post/4521509/2016-election-clinton-exceptionalism.

Clinton, William J. "Remarks at a Freedom House Breakfast." Speech, Washington,
DC, October 6, 1995. American Presidency Project. http://www.presidency.ucsb.edu
/ws/?pid=50612.

CNN. "Pat Robertson Says Haiti Paying for 'Pact to the Devil.'" January 13, 2010. http://www.cnn.com/2010/US/01/13/haiti.pat.robertson/index.html.

Cobb, Jelani. "The Matter of Black Lives." New Yorker, March 7, 2016. https://www.newyorker.com/magazine/2016/03/14/where-is-black-lives-matter-headed.

Cohen, Stephen F. War with Russia: From Putin and Ukraine to Trump and Russiagate. New York: Hot Books, 2018.

Collier, Ruth Berins, and David Collier. Shaping the Political Arena. Princeton, NJ: Princeton University Press, 1991.

Collins, Chuck. "Is Inequality in America Irreversible?" Inequality.org, April 2, 2018. https://inequality.org/great-divide/inequality-america-irreversible-2/.

Collins, Chuck, and Josh Hoxie. Billionaire Bonanza: The Forbes 400 and the Rest of Us. Washington, DC: Institute for Policy Studies, 2015. https://ips-dc.org/wp-content/uploads/2015/12/Billionaire-Bonanza-The-Forbes-400-and-the-Rest-of-Us-Dec1.pdf.

Collins, Chuck, Dedrick Asante-Muhammed, Emanuel Nieves, and Josh Hoxie. The Ever-Growing Gap: Failing to Address the Status Quo Will Drive the Racial Wealth Divide for Centuries to Come. Washington, DC: Institute for Policy Studies, 2016. https://ips-dc.org/report-ever-growing-gap/.

Collins, Chuck, Dedrick Asante-Muhammed, Emanuel Nieves, Josh Hoxie, and Sabrina Terry. Dreams Deferred: Enriching the 1 Percent Widens the Racial Wealth Divide. Washington, DC: Institute for Policy Studies, 2019. https://ips-dc.org/wp-content/uploads/2019/01/IPS_RWD-Report_FINAL-1.15.19.pdf.

Conard, Edward. The Upside of Inequality. New York: Penguin, 2016.

Crenshaw, Kimberle. "Demarginalizing the Intersection of Race and Sex: A Black Feminist Critique of Discrimination Doctrine, Feminist Theory, and Antiracist Practice." University of Chicago Legal Forum 1989, no. 1 (1989): 139–167.

Crenshaw, Kimberle. "Mapping the Margins: Intersectionality, Identity Politics, and Violence against Women of Color." Stanford Law Review 43, no. 6 (July 1991): 1241–1299.

Cumings, Bruce. The Korean War: A History. New York: Modern Library Edition, 2010.

Dahrendorf, Ralf. Life Chances. Chicago: University of Chicago Press, 1979.

Dalembert, Louis-Philippe. "Haïti, la dette originelle." Liberation, March 25, 2010. http://www.liberation.fr/planete/2010/03/25/haitila-dette-originelle_617159.

Dalmas, Antoine. Histoire de la Révolution de Saint Domingue. Paris: Chez Mame Frères, 1814.

Danner, Mark. "The Fall of the Prophet." New York Review of Books 40, no. 20 (December 1993). http://www.markdanner.com/articles/the-fall-of-the-prophet.

Dansereau, Carroll. "Whose Moral Stain? Obama's Immigration Atrocities Led to Trump's." Self-published paper. September 28, 2018. https://www.dropbox.com/s/4603lpfx6y97ohm/WhoseMoralStainReport9.28.18.pdf?dl=0.

Darity Jr., William, Ashwini Deshpande, and Thomas Weisskopf. "Who Is Eligible? Should Affirmative Action Be Group- or Class-Based?" American Journal of Economics and Sociology 70, no. 1 (January 2011): 238–268.

Daut, Marlene L. Tropics of Haiti. Liverpool: Liverpool University Press, 2015.

Daut, Marlene L. "Un-Silencing the Past: Boisrond-Tonnerre, Vastey, and the Re-Writing of the Haitian Revolution." South Atlantic Review 74, no. 1 (Winter 2009): 35–64.

Davis, David Brion. "Free at Last: The Enduring Legacy of the South's Civil War Victory." New York Times, August 26, 2001. http://www.nytimes.com/2001/08/26/weekinreview/free-at-last-the-enduring-legacy-of-the-south-s-civil-war-victory.html.

Davis, David Brion. *Inhuman Bondage: The Rise and Fall of Slavery in the New World.* New York: Oxford University Press, 2006.

Davis, Julie Hirschfeld, Sheryl Gay Stolberg, and Thomas Kaplan. "Trump Alarms Lawmakers with Disparaging Words for Haiti and Africa." *New York Times*, January 11, 2018. https://www.nytimes.com/2018/01/11/us/politics/trump-shithole-countries.html.

Davis, K. G. *Royal African Company.* London: Longmans, Green, and Co., 1957.

Dayan, Joan. *Haiti, History, and the Gods.* Berkeley: University of California Press, 1995.

Debien, Gabriel. *Les Esclaves aux Antilles Françaises, XVIIe et XVIIIe Siècles.* Basse-Terre: Société d'Histoire de la Guadeloupe, 1974.

Debien, Gabriel. "Marronage in the French Caribbean." In *Maroon Societies: Rebel Slave Communities in the Americas*, 3rd ed., edited by Richard Price, pp. 107–134. Baltimore: Johns Hopkins University Press, 1996.

Deibert, Michael. *Notes from the Last Testament: The Struggle for Haiti.* New York: Seven Stories Press, 2005.

Depestre, René. "The Winding Course of Negritude." In *Souffles-Anfas: A Critical Anthology from the Moroccan Journal of Culture and Politics*, edited by Olivia C. Harrison and Teresa Villa-Ignacio, translated by Laura Reeck, 120–125. Stanford, CA: Stanford University Press, 2016. http://pastandfuturepresents.blogspot.com/2015/12/the-winding-course-of-negritude-rene.html.

De Souza, Pascale, and H. Adlai Murdoch. "Caribbean Textuality and the Metaphors of Métissage." *Journal of Caribbean Literatures* 4, no. 2 (Fall 2006): vii–xvi.

Dessalines, Jean-Jacques. "Haitian Declaration of Independence." 1804. https://today.duke.edu/showcase/haitideclaration/declarationstext.html.

Diederich, Bernard, and Al Burt. *Papa Doc.* New York: McGraw-Hill, 1969.

Dillon, Elizabeth Maddock, and Michael J. Drexler. "Introduction: Haiti and the Early United States, Entwined." In *The Haitian Revolution and the Early United States*, edited by Elizabeth Maddock Dillon and Michael J. Drexler, 1–16. Philadelphia: University of Pennsylvania Press, 2016.

Donnan, Shawn, and Andres Schipani. "Obama Urges Trump to Regard US as an 'Indispensable Nation.'" *Financial Times*, November 20, 2016. https://www.ft.com/content/643f6c9c-af84-11e6-a37c-f4a01f1b0fa1.

Douzinas, Costas. *Human Rights and Empire.* New York: Routledge-Cavendish, 2007.

Dowder, John W. *The Violent American Century.* Chicago: Haymarket Books, 2017.

Doyle, Kate. "Hollow Diplomacy in Haiti." *World Policy Journal* 1, no. 1 (Spring 1994): 50–58. Dubois, Laurent. *Avengers of the New World: The Story of the Haitian Revolution.* Cambridge, MA: Harvard University Press, 2004.

Dubois, Laurent. "Avenging America: The Politics of Violence in the Haitian Revolution." In *The World of the Haitian Revolution*, edited by David Geggus and Norman Fiering, 111–124. Bloomington: Indiana University Press, 2009.

Dubois, Laurent. "Thinking Haitian Independence in Haitian Vodou." In *The Haitian Declaration of Independence: Creation, Context, and Legacy*, edited by Julia Gaffield, 201–218. Charlottesville: University of Virginia Press, 2016.

Du Bois, W.E.B. *Black Reconstruction in America.* New York: Harcourt, Brace, and Co., 1935.

Duchet, Michèle. *Anthropologie Et Histoire Au Siècle Des Lumières.* Paris: Albin Michel, 1995.

Dumesle, Hérard. *Voyage dans le Nord d'Haiti.* Cayes: Imprimerie du Gouvernement, 1824.

Dupuy, Alex. *Haiti: From Revolutionary Slaves to Powerless Citizens.* New York: Routledge, 2014.

Dupuy, Alex. *Haiti in the World Economy: Class, Race, and Underdevelopment since 1700.* Boulder, CO: Westview Press, 1989.

Dupuy, Alex. *Rethinking the Haitian Revolution.* London: Rowman and Littlefield, 2019.

Duvalier, François. *Oeuvres Essentielles I: Eléments d'une Doctrine.* Port-au-Prince: Presses Nationales d'Haiti, 1966.

Editors. "How a Broken Migration Policy Has Divided Haiti and the Dominican Republic." *World Politics Review,* March 23, 2018. https://www.worldpoliticsreview.com/trend-lines/24431/how-a-broken-migration-policy-has-divided-haiti-and-the-dominican-republic.

Egerton, Douglas R. "Race and Slavery in the Era of Jefferson." In *The Cambridge Companion to Thomas Jefferson,* edited by Frank Shuffelton. Cambridge: Cambridge University Press, 2009.

Engdahl, F. William. *Manifest Destiny: Democracy as Cognitive Dissonance.* Wiesbaden, Germany: mine.books, 2018.

Esherick, Joseph W., and Jeffrey N. Wasserstrom. "Acting Out Democracy: Political Theater in Modern China." *Journal of Asian Studies* 49, no. 4 (November 1990): 835–865.

Farmer, Paul. *The Uses of Haiti.* Monroe, Maine: Common Courage Press, 1994.

Fatton, Robert Jr. "Development and the Outer Periphery: The Logic of Exclusion." In *The Palgrave Handbook of Critical International Political Economy,* edited by Alan Cafruny, Leila Simona Talani, and Gonzalo Pozo Martin, 119–137. London: Palgrave Macmillan, 2016.

Fatton, Robert Jr. *Haiti: Trapped in the Outer Periphery.* Boulder, CO: Lynne Rienner Publishers, 2014.

Fatton, Robert Jr. *Haiti's Predatory Republic.* Boulder, CO: Lynne Rienner Publishers, 2002.

Fatton, Robert Jr. "Killing Haitian Democracy." *Jacobin,* July 22, 2015. https://www.jacobinmag.com/2015/07/monroe-doctrine-1915-occupation-duvalier.

Fatton, Robert Jr. *The Roots of Haitian Despotism.* Boulder, CO: Lynne Rienner Publishers, 2007.

Feinstein, Lee, and Anne-Marie Slaughter. "A Duty to Prevent." *Foreign Affairs* 83, no. 1 (January/February 2004). https://www.foreignaffairs.com/articles/2004-01-01/duty-prevent.

Ferguson, Niall. "An Empire in Denial: The Limits of US Imperialism." *Harvard International Review* 25, no. 3 (September 2003): 64–69.

Ferguson, Niall. *Empire: The Rise and Demise of the British World Order and the Lessons for Global Power.* New York: Basic Books, 2004.

Ferrer, Ada. *Freedom's Mirror: Cuba and Haiti in the Age of Revolution.* New York: Cambridge University Press, 2014.Fick, Carolyn. "The French Revolution in Saint Domingue: A Triumph or a Failure?" In *A Turbulent Time: The French Revolution and the Greater Caribbean,* edited by David Barry Gaspar and David Patrick Geggus, 51–77. Bloomington: Indiana University Press, 1997.

Fick, Carolyn. *The Making of Haiti: The Saint-Domingue Revolution from Below*. Knoxville: University of Tennessee Press, 1990.

Fick, Carolyn. "Revolutionary St. Domingue and the Emerging Atlantic: Paradigms of Sovereignty." In *The Haitian Revolution and the Early United States*, edited by Elizabeth Maddock Dillon and Michael J. Drexler, 23–41. Philadelphia: University of Pennsylvania Press, 2016.

Fick, Carolyn. "The Saint Domingue Slave Revolution and the Unfolding of Independence, 1791–1804." In *The World of the Haitian Revolution*, edited by David Geggus and Norman Fiering, 177–196. Bloomington: Indiana University Press, 2009.

Fields, Karen E., and Barbara J. Fields. *Racecraft: The Soul of Inequality in American Life*. London: Verso, 2012.

Firmin, Anténor. *De L'Egalité des Races Humaines*. Montréal: Mémoire D'Encrier, 2005.

Firmin, Anténor. *The Equality of the Human Races*. Translated by Asselin Charles. Champaign: University of Illinois Press, 2002.

Fischer, Sibylle. *Modernity Disavowed*. Durham, NC: Duke University Press, 2004.

Foner, Eric. *Reconstruction: America's Unfinished Revolution 1863–1877*. New York: Harper Perennial, 2014.

Foner, Eric. *The Second Founding*. New York: W. W. Norton & Co., 2019.

Fouchard, Jean. *Les Marrons de la Liberté*. Port-au-Prince: Editions Henri Deschamps, 1988.

Fourcand, Jean M. *Catéchisme de la révolution: En l'honneur du docteur François Duvalier, président constitutionel à vie de la république d'Haïti et de madame Simone O. Duvalier, première Marie-Jeanne d'Haïti*. Port-au-Prince: Edition Imprimerie de l'Etat, 1964.

Fox, Michelle. "Morgan Stanley: Belief in 'American Exceptionalism' among Global Investors Has Never Been Higher." CNBC, October 8, 2018. https://www.cnbc.com /2018/10/08/morgan-stanley-global-investors-are-betting-on-us-exceptionalism .html.Fredrickson, George. *The Black Image in the White Mind*. Middletown, CT: Wesleyan University Press, 1987.

Fredrickson, George. *White Supremacy*. Oxford: Oxford University Press, 1981.

Freed, Kenneth. "US Gives Cédras a Lucrative Deal to Get Out of Haiti." *Los Angeles Times*, October 14, 1994. http://articles.latimes.com/1994-10-14/news/mn-50281_1_white -house.

Freedom for Immigrants. "A Short History of Immigration Detention." 2018. https:// www.freedomforimmigrants.org/detention-timeline/.

French, Howard W. "Port-au-Prince Journal: Is Voodoo the Weapon to Repel the Invaders?" *New York Times*, June 24, 1994. https://www.nytimes.com/1994/06/24/world/port -au-prince-journal-is-voodoo-the-weapon-to-repel-the-invaders.html.

Frey, William H. "The US Will Become 'Minority White' in 2045, Census Projects. Youthful Minorities Are the Engine of Future Growth." *The Avenue* (blog), Brookings Institution, March 14, 2018. https://www.brookings.edu/blog/the-avenue/2018/03/14/the-us-will -become-minority-white-in-2045-census-projects.

Gaffield, Julia. *Haitian Connections in the Atlantic World: Recognition after Revolution*. Chapel Hill: University of North Carolina Press, 2015.

Gaffield, Julia. Preface to *The Haitian Declaration of Independence: Creation, Context, and Legacy*, edited by Julia Gaffield, vii–x. Charlottesville: University of Virginia Press, 2016.

Gaillard, Roger. *Les Blancs Débarquent (1914–1915): Les Cent-Jours de Rosalvo Bobo*. Port-au-Prince: Presses Nationales, 1973.

Garamone, Jim. "President Signs Fiscal 2019 Defense Authorization Act at Fort Drum Ceremony." U.S. Department of Defense, August 13, 2018. https://dod.defense.gov /News/Article/Article/1601016/president-signs-fiscal-2019-defense-authorization-act -at-fort-drum-ceremony/.

Garcia-Pena, Lorgia. *The Borders of Dominicanidad*. Durham, NC: Duke University Press, 2016.

Garraway, Doris L. "'Légitime Défense': Universalism and Nationalism in the Discourse of the Haitian Revolution." In *Tree of Liberty: Cultural Legacies of the Haitian Revolution in the Atlantic World*, edited by Doris L. Garraway, 63–88. Charlottesville: University of Virginia Press, 2008.

GARR-Haiti. "Le GARR se prononce sur la déclaration de la 2ème rencontre binationale entre Haïti et la République Dominicaine Spécial." ReliefWeb, February 5, 2014. http://reliefweb.int/report/dominican-republic/le-garr-se-prononce-sur-la-d -claration-de-la-2-me-rencontre-binationale.

GARR-Haiti. "Position de la Plateforme GARR autour du dossier de la dénationalisation des Dominicains/Dominicaines d'ascendance haïtienne." ReliefWeb, January 31, 2014. http://reliefweb.int/report/dominican-republic/position-de-la-plateforme-garr -autour-du-dossier-de-la-d-nationalisation.

Gates Jr., Henry Louis. "Black America and the Class Divide." *New York Times*, February 1, 2016. https://www.nytimes.com/2016/02/07/education/edlife/black-america-and-the -class-divide.html.

Geggus, David Patrick. "The Bois Caiman Ceremony." *Journal of Caribbean History* 25, no 1 (Spring 1991): 41–57.

Geggus, David Patrick. "The Caribbean in the Age of Revolution." In *The Age of Revolutions in Global Context, c. 1760–1840*, edited by David Armitage and Sanjay Subrahmanyam, 83–100. New York: Palgrave Macmillan, 2010.

Geggus, David Patrick. *The Haitian Revolution: A Documentary History*. Indianapolis: Hackett Publishing Company, 2014.

Geggus, David Patrick. "The Haitian Revolution: New Approaches and Old." *Proceedings of the Meeting of the French Colonial Historical Society* 19 (1994): 141–155.

Geggus, David Patrick. *Haitian Revolutionary Studies*. Bloomington: Indiana University Press, 2002.

Geggus, David Patrick. "The Louisiana Purchase and the Haitian Revolution." In *The Haitian Revolution and the Early United States*, edited by Elizabeth Maddock Dillon and Michael J. Drexler, 117–129. Philadelphia: University of Pennsylvania Press, 2016.

Geggus, David Patrick. "Saint Domingue on the Eve of the Haitian Revolution." In *The World of the Haitian Revolution*, edited by David Geggus and Norman Fiering, 3–20. Bloomington: Indiana University Press, 2009.

Genovese, Eugene. *From Rebellion to Revolution*. Baton Rouge: Louisiana State University Press, 1979.

Gest, Justin. *The New Minority: White Working Class Politics in an Age of Immigration and Inequality*. New York: Oxford University Press, 2016.

Gibson, James William. "American Paramilitary Culture and the Reconstitution of the Vietnam War." In *Vietnam Images: War and Representation*, edited by Jeffrey Walsh and James Aulich, 10–42. London: Macmillan Press, 1989.

Gilens, Martin, and Benjamin I. Page. "Testing Theories of American Politics: Elites, Interest Groups, and Average Citizens." *Perspective on Politics* 12, no. 3 (September 2014): 564–581.

Girard, Philippe R. *Clinton in Haiti: The 1994 US Invasion of Haiti.* New York: Palgrave Macmillan, 2004.

Girard, Philippe R. "Did Dessalines Plan to Export the Haitian Revolution?" In *The Haitian Declaration of Independence: Creation, Context, and Legacy*, edited by Julia Gaffield, 136–157. Charlottesville: University of Virginia Press, 2016.

Girard, Philippe R. "Jean-Jacques Dessalines and the Atlantic System: A Reappraisal." *William and Mary Quarterly* 69, no. 3 (July 2012): 549–582.

Girard, Philippe R. "Jean-Jacques Dessalines et l'arrestation de Toussaint Louverture." *Journal of Haitian Studies* 17, no. 1 (Spring 2011): 123–138.

Girard, Philippe R. *Toussaint Louverture.* New York: Basic Books, 2016.

Glissant, Edouard. *Caribbean Discourse.* Charlottesville: University of Virginia Press, 1989.

Glissant, Edouard. *Poetics of Relation.* Ann Arbor: University of Michigan Press, 1997.

Global Research. "America Has Been at War 93% of the Time—222 out of 239 Years—since 1776." *Washington's Blog*, Centre for Research on Globalization, February 20, 2015. Updated January 20, 2019. https://www.globalresearch.ca/america-has-been-at -war-93-of-the-time-222-out-of-239-years-since-1776/5565946.

Goldberg, Richard. "Europe's Sanctions-Blocking Threats Are Empty." *Foreign Policy*, February 20, 2018. https://foreignpolicy.com/2018/02/20/europes-iran-deal-threats -are-empty-trump-iran-eu.

Gordon-Reed, Annette. *Thomas Jefferson and Sally Hemings: An American Controversy.* Charlottesville: University of Virginia Press, 1997.

Gorney, Cynthia. "The Reagan Chart Watch: Astrologer Joan Quigley, Eye on the Cosmos." *Washington Post*, May 11, 1988. https://www.scribd.com/doc/303989261/The -Reagan-Chart-Watcher#fullscreen&from_embed.

Grad, Shelby, and David Colker. "Nancy Reagan Turned to Astrology in White House to Protect Her Husband." *Los Angeles Times*, March 6, 2016. http://www.latimes.com /local/lanow/la-me-ln-nancy-reagan-astrology-20160306-story.html.

Gramsci, Antonio. *Selections from the Prison Notebooks.* Edited and translated by Quintin Hoare and Geoffrey Nowell Smith. London: Lawrence and Wishart, 1971.

Grandin, Greg. *The Empire of Necessity: Slavery, Freedom, and Deception in the New World.* New York: Metropolitan Books/Henry Holt and Co., 2014.

Grayson, William J. *The Hireling and the Slave, Chicora, and Other Poems.* Charleston: McCarter & Co. Publishers, 1856.

Greenwald, Glenn. "Robert Mueller Did Not Merely Reject the Trump/Russia Conspiracy Theories. He Obliterated Them." *The Intercept*, April 18, 2019. https://theintercept .com/2019/04/18/robert-mueller-did-not-merely-reject-the-trumprussia-conspiracy -theories-he-obliterated-them/.

Grégoire, Abbé. *De la Liberté de Consciences et de Culte a Haïti.* Paris: Baudoin Frères, 1821.

Guarino, Ben. "Shaking Hands Is 'Barbaric': Donald Trump, the Germaphobe in Chief." *Washington Post*, January 12, 2017. https://www.washingtonpost.com/news/morning -mix/wp/2017/01/12/shaking-hands-is-barbaric-donald-trump-the-germaphobe-in -chief/?utm_term=.04a2bcfc5e44.

Gusterson, Hugh. "Empire of Bases." *Bulletin of the Atomic Social Scientists*, March 10, 2009. http://www.thebulletin.org/web-edition/columnists/hugh-gusterson/empire-of-bases.

Guyatt, Nicholas. *Bind Us Apart: How Enlightened Americans Invented Racial Segregation*. New York: Basic Books, 2016.

Guyatt, Nicholas. "How Proslavery Was the Constitution?" *New York Review of Books*, June 6, 2019. https://www.nybooks.com/articles/2019/06/06/how-proslavery-was-the-constitution/.

Guyatt, Nicholas. *Providence and the Invention of the United States, 1607–1876*. Cambridge: Cambridge University Press, 2007.

Haiti Constitution of 1801 (superseded 1804). https://www.marxists.org/history/haiti/1801/constitution.htm.

Haiti Constitution of 1805 (superseded 1806). http://faculty.webster.edu/corbetre/haiti/history/earlyhaiti/1805-const.htm.

Hall, Andrew B., Connor Huff, and Shiro Kuriwaki. "Wealth, Slave Ownership, and Fighting for the Confederacy: An Empirical Study of the American Civil War." *American Political Science Review* 113, no. 3 (August 2019): 658–673.

Hall, Peter. *Governing the Economy: The Politics of State Intervention in Britain and France*. New York: Oxford University Press, 1986.

Hallward, Peter. *Damming the Flood: Haiti, Aristide, and the Politics of Containment*. London: Verso, 2007.

Hamilton, Alexander. "Hamilton on the Louisiana Purchase: A Newly Identified Editorial from the *New-York Evening Post*." *William and Mary Quarterly* 12, no. 2 (April 1955): 268–281.

Hammond, Jeremy R. "The 'Forgotten' US Shootdown of Iranian Airliner Flight 655." *Foreign Policy Journal*, July 3, 2017. https://www.foreignpolicyjournal.com/2017/07/03/the-forgotten-us-shootdown-of-iranian-airliner-flight-655%C2%AD.

Hannah-Jones, Nikole. "The Idea of America." *New York Times Magazine*, August 14, 2019. https://www.nytimes.com/interactive/2019/08/14/magazine/black-history-american-democracy.html.

Harris, Leslie M. "I Helped Fact-Check the 1619 Project. The *Times* Ignored Me." *Politico*, March 6, 2020. https://www.politico.com/news/magazine/2020/03/06/1619-project-new-york-times-mistake-122248.

Harrison, Lawrence E. *The Central Liberal Truth*. Oxford: Oxford University Press, 2006.

Harrison, Lawrence E. "Voodoo Politics." *Atlantic Monthly* 271, no. 6 (June 1993): 101–107.

Harrison, Lawrence E., and Samuel Huntington, eds. *Culture Matters: How Values Shape Human Progress*. New York: Basic Books, 2000.

Hartz, Louis. *The Liberal Tradition in America*. New York: Harcourt, Brace, and World, 1955.

Healy, David. *Gunboat Diplomacy in the Wilson Era: The U.S. Navy in Haiti, 1915–1916*. Madison: University of Wisconsin Press, 1976.

Heer, Jeet. "Donald Trump Killed the 'Indispensable Nation.' Good!" *New Republic*, May 15, 2017. https://newrepublic.com/article/142571/donald-trump-killed-indispensable-nation-good.

Hegel, Georg Wilhelm Friedrich. *Hegel's Philosophy of Right*. Translated by T. M. Knox. New York: Oxford University Press, 1967.

Hegel, Georg Wilhelm Friedrich. *The Philosophy of History*. Edited by Eduard Gans. Translated by John Sibree. London: George Bell and Sons, 1902. https://www.marxists .org/reference/archive/hegel/works/hi/introduction-lectures.htm.

Hegel, Georg Wilhelm Friedrich. *The Philosophy of Subjective Spirit*. Vol. 2, *Anthropology*. Edited by Michael John Petry. Netherlands: D. Reidel Publishing Co., 1978.

Herman, Carl. "Earth: 248 Armed Conflicts after WW2; US Started 201 (81%), Killing 30 million So Far. Arrests Are When Now?" *Washington Blogs*, May 17, 2014. http:// washingtonsblog.com/2014/05/earth-248-armed-conflicts-ww2-us-started-201-81 -killing-30-million-far-arrests-now.html.

Herskovits, Melville J. *The Myth of the Negro Past*. Boston: Beacon Press, 1990.

Hirschman, Albert O. *Exit, Voice, and Loyalty*. Cambridge, MA: Harvard University Press, 1970.

Hobsbawm, Eric. "Introduction: Inventing Traditions." In *The Invention of Tradition*, edited by Eric Hobsbawm and Terence Ranger, 2–6. Cambridge: Cambridge University Press, 1983.

Hobsbawm, Eric. *On Empire*. New York: Pantheon Books, 2008.

Hobson, John M. *The Eurocentric Conception of World Politics*. Cambridge: Cambridge University Press, 2012.

Hoffman, Léon-Francois. "Débat." In *La République Haitienne: Etat des Lieux et Perspectives*, edited by Gérard Barthélémy and Christian Girault, 445–448. Paris: Karthala, 1993.

Hoffman, Léon-Francois. "Un mythe national: La cérémonie du Bois-Caïman." In *La République Haitienne: Etat des Lieux et Perspectives*, edited by Gérard Barthélémy and Christian Girault, 434–445. Paris: Karthala, 1993.

Holsti, K. J. "Exceptionalism in American Foreign Policy: Is It Exceptional?" *European Journal of International Relations* 17, no. 3 (September 2011): 381–404.

Hormann, Raphael. "Thinking the 'Unthinkable'? Representations of the Haitian Revolution in British Discourse, 1791 to 1805." In *Human Bondage in the Cultural Contact Zone: Transdisciplinary Perspectives on Slavery and Its Discourses*, edited by Raphael Hormann and Gesa Mackenthun, 137–170. New York: Waxmann 2010.

Horne, Gerald. *Confronting Black Jacobins*. New York: Monthly Review Press, 2015.

Horsman, Reginald. *Race and Manifest Destiny*. Cambridge, MA: Harvard University Press, 1981.

Hughey, Matthew W. "White Backlash in the 'Post-Racial' United States." *Ethnic and Racial Studies* 37, no. 5 (March 2014): 721–730. https://www.tandfonline.com/doi/pdf /10.1080/01419870.2014.886710?needAccess=true.

Hunt, Alfred N. *Haiti's Influence on Antebellum America*. Baton Rouge: Louisiana State University Press, 1988.

Huntington, Samuel. *The Clash of Civilizations and the Remaking of World Order*. New York: Simon and Schuster, 1996.

Hurbon, Laënnec. *Comprendre Haïti: Essai sur l'État, la nation, la culture*. Paris: Les Éditions Karthala, 1987. http://chf-ressourceshaiti.com/data/chfressources/media /ouvrage/Comprendre-Haiti-Essai-sur-lEtat-la-nation-la-culture-Hurbon-Laennec .pdf.

Ignatieff, Michael. *Empire Lite*. Toronto: Penguin Canada, 2004.

Ignatieff, Michael. "Introduction: American Exceptionalism and Human Rights." In *American Exceptionalism and Human Rights*, edited by Michael Ignatieff, 1–26. Princeton, NJ: Princeton University Press, 2005.

International Commission on Intervention and State Sovereignty. *The Responsibility to Protect*. Ottawa, ON: International Development Research Centre, 2001.

Jallot, Nicolas, and Laurent Lesage. *Haiti: Dix Ans d'Histoire Secrète*. Paris: Editions du Felin, 1995.

James, C.L.R. *The Black Jacobins: Toussaint L'Ouverture and the San Domingo Revolution*. London: Allison and Busby, 1980.

Jefferson, Thomas. "The Declaration of Independence." July 4, 1776. https://www.constitutionfacts.com/us-declaration-of-independence/read-the-declaration/.

Jefferson, Thomas. *Notes on the State of Virginia*. Edited by Frank Shuffelton. New York: Penguin Books, 1999.

Jefferson, Thomas. Thomas Jefferson to John Adams. October 28, 1823. Founders Online. National Archives. https://founders.archives.gov/documents/Jefferson/03-06-02-0446.

Jefferson, Thomas. Thomas Jefferson to Aaron Burr. February 11, 1799. St. Domingue (Haiti). *The Thomas Jefferson Encyclopedia*. Thomas Jefferson Foundation. https://www.monticello.org/site/research-and-collections/st-domingue-haiti#footnote27_xj2co5c.

Jefferson, Thomas. Thomas Jefferson to Chastellux. June 7, 1785. Avalon Project. Yale Law Library. http://avalon.law.yale.edu/18th_century/let27.asp.

Jefferson, Thomas. Thomas Jefferson to Edward Coles. August 25, 1814. The Letters of Thomas Jefferson, 1743–1826. American History: From Revolution to Reconstruction and Beyond. http://www.let.rug.nl/usa/presidents/thomas-jefferson/letters-of-thomas-jefferson/jefl232.php.

Jefferson, Thomas. Thomas Jefferson to William Henry Harrison, Governor of the Indiana Territory. February 21, 1803. Digital History. http://www.digitalhistory.uh.edu/active_learning/explorations/indian_removal/jefferson_t o_harrison.cfm.

Jefferson, Thomas. Thomas Jefferson to Indian Nations. January 10, 1809. Founders Online. National Archives. https://founders.archives.gov/documents/Jefferson/99-01-02-9516.

Jefferson, Thomas. Thomas Jefferson to James Monroe. November 24, 1801. Quotes by and about Thomas Jefferson. Thomas Jefferson Foundation. http://tjrs.monticello.org/letter/1743.

Jefferson, Thomas. Thomas Jefferson to Roger C. Weightman. June 24, 1826. In *Jefferson's Empire: The Language of American Nationhood*, edited by Peter Onuf, 2. Charlottesville: University Press of Virginia, 2000.

Joachim, Tanael. "What Makes a Country Great? Meet Haiti's People." *New York Times*, January 12, 2018. https://www.nytimes.com/2018/01/12/opinion/what-makes-a-country-great-meet-haitis-people.html.

Joffe, Josef. *Uberpower: The Imperial Temptation of America*. New York: W. W. Norton & Co., 2006.

Johnson, Chalmers. *The Sorrows of Empire: Militarism, Secrecy, and the End of the Republic*. New York: Metropolitan Books, 2004.

Johnson, Paul Christopher. "Secretism and the Apotheosis of Duvalier." *Journal of the American Academy of Religion* 74, no. 2 (June 2006): 420–445.

Jones, Martha S. *Birthright Citizens*. New York: Cambridge University Press, 2018.

Jordan, Miriam. "Trump Administration Ends Temporary Protection for Haitians." *New York Times*, November 20, 2017. https://www.nytimes.com/2017/11/20/us/haitians-temporary-status.html.

Jordan, Winthrop D. *White over Black: American Attitudes toward the Negro, 1550–1812*. Chapel Hill: University of North Carolina Press, 1968.

Joseph, Délide. *L'État Haitien et ses Intellectuels.* Port-au-Prince: Imprimerie Le Natal, 2017.

Kagan, Robert. *Dangerous Nation: America's Foreign Policy from Its Earliest Days to the Dawn of the Twentieth Century.* New York: Vintage Books, 2007.

Keller, Christian B. "Philanthropy Betrayed: Thomas Jefferson, the Louisiana Purchase, and the Origins of Federal Indian Removal Policy." *Proceedings of the American Philosophical Society* 144, no. 1 (March 2000): 39–66.

Kelley, Robin G. "What Does Black Lives Matter Want?" *Boston Review*, August 17, 2016. http://bostonreview.net/books-ideas/robin-d-g-kelley-movement-black-lives-vision.

Kendi, Ibram X. *Stamped from the Beginning: The Definitive History of Racist Ideas in America.* New York: Bold Type Books, 2016.

Keohane, Robert. "Political Authority after Intervention: Gradations in Sovereignty." In *Humanitarian Intervention: Ethical, Legal, and Political Dilemmas*, edited by J. Holzgrefe and R. Keohane, 275–298. Cambridge: Cambridge University Press, 2003.

King, Jamilah. "How Black Lives Matter Has Changed US Politics," *New Internationalist*, February 2018. https://newint.org/features/2018/03/01/black-lives-matter-changed-politics.

Kolko, Gabriel. *The Roots of American Foreign Policy.* Boston: Beacon Press, 1969.

Kramer, Paul Alexander. *The Blood of Government: Race, Empire, the United States, and the Philippines.* Chapel Hill: University of North Carolina Press, 2006.

Kramer, Paul Alexander. "Power and Connection: Imperial Histories of the United States in the World." *American Historical Review* 116, no. 5 (December 2011): 1348–1391.

Kramer, Paul Alexander. "The Water Cure: Debating Torture and Counterinsurgency—a Century Ago." *New Yorker*, February 17, 2008. https://www.newyorker.com/magazine/2008/02/25/the-water-cure/amp.

Krasner, Stephen D. "Sharing Sovereignty: New Institutions for Collapsed and Failing States." *International Security* 29, no. 2 (Fall 2004): 85–120.

Krugman, Paul. "Fall of the American Empire." *New York Times*, June 18, 2018. https://www.nytimes.com/2018/06/18/opinion/immigration-trump-children-american-empire.html.

Kupchan, Charles. *The End of the American Era: US Foreign Policy and the Geopolitics of the Twenty-First Century.* New York: Vintage Books, 2003.

Kupchan, Charles. "Grand Strategy: The Four Pillars of the Future." *Democracy: A Journal of Ideas*, no. 23 (Winter 2012). https://democracyjournal.org/magazine/23/grand-strategy-the-four-pillars-of-the-future/.

Kuzmarov, Jeremy, and John Marciano. *The Russians Are Coming, Again: The First Cold War as Tragedy, the Second as Farce.* New York: Monthly Review Press, 2018.

Labelle, Micheline. *Idéologie de couleur et classes sociales en Haïti.* Montreal: Presses de l'Université de Montréal, 1978.

LaFeber, Walter. *The Cambridge History of American Foreign Relations.* Cambridge: Cambridge University Press, 1993.

LaFeber, Walter. *Inevitable Revolutions.* New York: W. W. Norton & Co., 1984.

La Redaction. "Edo Zenny crache au visage d'un juge." *Radio Television Caraibes*, September 9, 2012. http://www.radiotelevisioncaraibes.com/nouvelles/haiti/edo_zenny_crache_au_visage_d_un_juge.html.

La Redaction. "Edo Zenny: Je ne suis pas raciste, ma femme, mes amis d'enfance ont leur peau foncée." *Radio Television Caraibes*, September 15, 2012. http://www.radio

televisioncaraibes.com/nouvelles/haiti/je_ne_suis_pas_raciste_ma_fem   me_mes
_amis_d_enfance_ont_leur_peau.html.

Lazare, Daniel. "Concord Management and the End of Russiagate?" *Consortium News,*
July 12, 2019. https://consortiumnews.com/2019/07/12/concord-management-and-the
-end-of-russiagate/.

Lens, Sidney. *The Forging of the American Empire.* London: Pluto Press, 2003.

Levin, Dov H. "Partisan Electoral Interventions by the Great Powers: Introducing the
PEIG Dataset." *Conflict Management and Peace Science* 36, no. 1 (January 2019):
88–106. https://journals.sagepub.com/doi/pdf/10.1177/0738894216661190.

Lichtenstein, Alex. "From the Editor's Desk: 1619 and All That." *American Historical
Review* 125, no. 1 (February 2020): xv–xxi.

Lipset, Seymour Martin. *American Exceptionalism.* New York: W. W. Norton & Co., 1996.

Logan, Rayford W. *The Diplomatic Relations of the United States with Haiti, 1776–1891.*
Chapel Hill: University of North Carolina Press, 1941.

Lopez, Ezequiel Abiu, and Danica Coto. "Dominican Ruling Strips Many of Citizenship." Associated Press, September 26, 2013. https://apnews.com/29602b2aef814e4cbe
493e0fe117a713.

Losurdo, Domenico. *Liberalism: A Counter-History.* London: Verso, 2014.

Macpherson, C. B. *The Political Theory of Possessive Individualism.* Oxford: Oxford
University Press, 1962.

Magdoff, Harry. *The Age of Imperialism.* New York: Monthly Review Press, 1969.

Malek, R. Michael. "Dominican Republic's General Rafael Trujillo and the Haitian
Massacre of 1937: A Case of Subversion in Inter-Caribbean Relations." *SECOLAS
Annals* 11 (March 1980): 137–155.

Malone, David. *Decision-Making in the UN Security Council: The Case of Haiti.* Oxford:
Oxford University Press, 1998.

Manigat, Sabine. "Les Fondements Sociaux de l'état Louverturien." In *La Révolution
Française et Haïti: Filiations, Ruptures, Nouvelles Dimensions,* vol. 1, edited by Michel
Hector, 130–142. Port-au-Prince: Société Haïtienne d'histoire et de géographie et Édi-
tions Henri Deschamps, 1995.

Marienstras, Elise. *Les Mythes Fondateurs de la Nation Americaine: Essai sur le Discours
Ideologique aux Etats-Unis a L'epoque de L'independence (1763–1800).* Paris: François
Maspéro, 1976.

Marx, Anthony W. *Faith in Nation: Exclusionary Origins of Nationalism.* Oxford:
Oxford University Press, 2003.

Marx, Karl. "The Eighteenth Brumaire of Louis Bonaparte." In *Karl Marx: Selected
Writings,* edited by David McLellan, 300–325. Oxford: Oxford University Press, 1977.

Marx, Karl. "Karl Marx to Arnold Ruge, September 1843." In *Letters from the Deutsch-
Französische Jahrbücher.* https://www.marxists.org/archive/marx/works/1843/letters
/43_09.htm.

Massey, Douglas, and Nancy Denton. *American Apartheid: Segregation and the Making
of the Underclass.* Cambridge, MA: Harvard University Press, 1993.

Maté, Aaron. "Don't Let Russophobia Warp the Facts on Russiagate," *The Nation,* December 14, 2018. https://www.thenation.com/article/russiagate-russophobia-mueller-trump/.

Maté, Aaron. "New Studies Show Pundits Are Wrong about Russian Social-Media
Involvement in US Politics." *The Nation,* December 28, 2018. https://www.thenation
.com/article/russiagate-elections-interference/.

Matthewson, Tim. "Jefferson and Haiti." *Journal of Southern History* 61, no. 2 (May 1995): 209–248.

Matthewson, Tim. *A Proslavery Foreign Policy: Haitian-American Relations during the Early Republic.* Westport, CT: Praeger Publishers, 2003.

Mbembe, Achille. *Critique of Black Reason.* Translated by Laurent Dubois. Durham, NC: Duke University Press, 2017.

McCarthy Brown, Karen. *Mama Lola: A Vodou Priestess in Brooklyn.* Berkeley: University of California Press, 1991.

McCoy, Alfred W. *In the Shadows of the American Century.* Chicago: Haymarket Books, 2017.

McDougall, Walter A. *The Tragedy of U.S. Foreign Policy: How America's Civil Religion Betrayed the National Interest.* New Haven, CT: Yale University Press, 2016.

McKinley, William. "Executive Order, December 21, 1898." American Presidency Project. https://www.presidency.ucsb.edu/node/205913.

Menier, Marie-Antoinette, Gabriel Debien, and Jean Fouchard. "Toussaint Louverture avant 1789. Légendes et Réalités." In *Toussaint Louverture et l'Indépendance d'Haïti: Témoignages pour un bicentenaire,* edited by Jacques de Cauna, 61–77. Paris: Karthala, 2004. Previously published in *Conjonction: Revue de l'Institut Français d'Haïti,* no. 134 (1977).

Merritt, Keri Leigh. *Masterless Men: Poor Whites and Slavery in the Antebellum South.* New York: Cambridge University Press, 2017.

Metz, Steven. "Why 2019 May Be the Year America's Global Strategy Finally Unravels." *World Politics Review,* January 4, 2019. https://www.worldpoliticsreview.com/articles/27100/why-2019-may-be-the-year-america-s-global-strategy-finally-unravels.

Michaels, Walter Benn. *The Trouble with Diversity: How We Learned to Love Identity and Ignore Inequality.* New York: Holt Paperbacks, 2006.

Milanovic, Branko. *Global Inequality: A New Approach for the Age of Globalization.* Cambridge, MA: Harvard University Press, 2016.

Milanovic, Branko. *The Haves and the Have-Nots: A Brief and Idiosyncratic History of Global Inequality.* New York: Basic Books, 2011.

Miliband, Ralph. *Marxism and Politics.* Oxford: Oxford University Press, 1977.

Miliband, Ralph. *The State in Capitalist Society.* New York: Basic Books, 1969.

Millspaugh, Arthur C. *Haiti under American Control 1915–1930.* Boston: World Peace Foundation, 1931.

Mintz, Sidney. *Caribbean Transformations.* Chicago: Aldine Publishing, 1974.

Mintz, Sidney, and Richard Price. *The Birth of African-American Culture.* Boston: Beacon Press, 1992.

Moïse, Claude. *Constitutions et luttes de pouvoir en Haiti: Tome 1—La faillite des classes Dirigeantes (1804–1915).* Montreal: CIDIHCA, 1988.

Moïse, Claude. *Constitutions et luttes de pouvoir en Haïti: Tome 2—De l'occupation étrangère à la dictature Macoute (1915–1987).* Montreal: CIDIHCA, 1990.

Moïse, Claude, ed. *Dictionnaire Historique de la Révolution Haïtienne 1789–1804.* Montreal: Editions du Cidihca, 2003.

Moïse, Claude. *Le projet national de Toussaint Louverture: La Constitution de 1801.* Port-au-Prince: Editions Mémoire, 2001.

Moodie, Dunbar. *The Rise of Afrikanerdom: Power, Apartheid, and the Afrikaner Civil Religion.* Berkeley: University of California Press, 1975.

Moore, Jina, and Catherine Porter. "'Don't Feed the Troll': Much of the World Reacts in Anger at Trump's Insult Image." *New York Times*, January 12, 2018. https://www.nytimes .com/2018/01/12/world/africa/africa-trump-shithole.html.

Moraga, Cherríe. "Art in America con Acento." In *In Other Words: Literature by Latinas of the United States*, edited by Roberta Fernandez, 300–307. Houston: Arte Publico, 1994.

Morgan, David. "Clinton Says U.S. Could "Totally Obliterate" Iran." Reuters, April 22, 2008. https://www.reuters.com/article/us-usa-politics-iran/clinton-says-u-s-could -totally-obliterate-iran-idUSN2224332720080422.

Morley, Morris, and Chris McGillion. "'Disobedient' Generals and the Politics of Redemocratization: The Clinton Administration and Haiti." *Political Science Quarterly* 112, no. 3 (Autumn 1997): 363–384.

Morrison, Toni. "On the First Black President." *New Yorker*, September 28, 1998. https:// www.newyorker.com/magazine/1998/10/05/comment-6543.

Movement for Black Lives. "A Vision for Black Lives: Policy Demands for Black Power, Freedom and Justice." August 2016. https://neweconomy.net/sites/default/files/resources /20160726-m4bl-Vision-Booklet-V3.pdf.

Mueller III, Robert S. *Report on the Investigation into Russian Interference in the 2016 Presidential Election*. Vol. 1. Washington, DC: Department of Justice, 2019.

Mulira, Sanyu Ruth. "Edouard Glissant and the African Roots of Creolization." *Ufahamu: A Journal of African Studies* 38, no. 2 (Winter 2015): 114–128.

Murray, Charles. *Coming Apart: The State of White America, 1960–2010*. New York: Random House, 2012.

Nairn, Alan. "He's Our S.O.B." *The Nation* 259, no. 14 (October 1994): 481–482.

Nairn, Alan. "Our Man in FRAPH." *The Nation* 259, no. 13 (October 1994): 458–461.

Nesbitt, Nick. "The Idea of 1804." *Yale French Studies*, no. 107 (January 2005): 6–38.

Newkirk II, Vann R. "Five Decades of White Backlash." *The Atlantic,* January 15, 2018. https://www.theatlantic.com/politics/archive/2018/01/trump-massive-resistance -history-mlk/550544/.

Nicholls, David. "Biology and Politics in Haiti." *Race and Class* 13, no. 2 (October 1971): 203–214.

Nicholls, David. *From Dessalines to Duvalier: Race, Colour, and National Independence*. New Brunswick, NJ: Rutgers University Press, 1996.

Niemuth, Niles, Tom Mackaman, and David North. "*The New York Times'* 1619 Project: A Racialist Falsification of American and World History." World Socialist Web Site, September 6, 2019. https://www.wsws.org/en/articles/2019/09/06/1619-s06.html.

Norton, Michael. "Coup Leader Says Uprising Necessary to Stop 'Apprentice Dictator.'" Associated Press, October 2, 1991. https://www.apnews.com/eeddff991e9a0c410491ed 2d183cea6e.

Obama, Barack. "Inaugural Address by President Barack Obama." Speech, Washington, D.C., January 21, 2013. Office of the Press Secretary. The White House. https:// obamawhitehouse.archives.gov/the-press-office/2013/01/21/inaugural-address -president-barack-obama.

Obama, Barack. "President Barack Obama's Inaugural Address." Speech, Washington, D.C., January 21, 2009, White House. https://obamawhitehouse.archives.gov/blog /2009/01/21/president-barack-obamas-inaugural-address.

Obregón, Liliana. "Empire, Racial Capitalism, and International Law: The Case of Manumitted Haiti and the Recognition Debt." *Leiden Journal of International Law* 31, no. 3 (September 2018): 597–615.

Office of Immigration Statistics. *Yearbook of Immigration Statistics: 2016*. Washington, DC: U.S. Department of Homeland Security, 2017. https://www.dhs.gov/sites/default /files/publications/2016%20Yearbook%20of%20Immig ration%20Statistics.pdf.

Oliver, Melvin, and Thomas Shapiro. *Black Wealth/White Wealth: A New Perspective on Racial Inequality*. New York: Routledge, 1995.

Ollman, Bertell. Introduction to *The United States Constitution: 200 Years of Anti-Federalist, Abolitionist, Feminist, Muckraking, Progressive, and Especially Socialist Criticism*, edited by Bertell Ollman and Jonathan Birnbaum, 5–6. New York: New York University Press, 1990.

Onuf, Peter S. *Jefferson's Empire: The Language of American Nationhood*. Charlottesville: University Press of Virginia, 2000.

Onuf, Peter S. "'We Shall All Be Americans': Thomas Jefferson and the Indians." *Indiana Magazine of History* 95, no. 2 (June 1999): 103–141.

O'Reilly, Kenneth. *Nixon's Piano: Presidents and Racial Politics from Washington to Clinton*. New York: Free Press, 1995.

Orozco, Manuel. *Remittances to Latin America and the Caribbean in 2017*. Washington, DC: Inter-American Dialogue, 2018. https://www.thedialogue.org/wp-content/uploads /2018/01/Remittances-2017-1.pdf.

Ott, Thomas. *The Haitian Revolution*. Knoxville: University of Tennessee Press, 1973.

Page, Benjamin I., Larry M. Bartels, and Jason Seawright. "Democracy and the Policy Preferences of Wealthy Americans." *Perspectives on Politics* 11, no. 1 (March 2013): 51–73.

Pamphile, Leon D. *Haitians and African Americans: A Heritage of Tragedy and Hope*. Gainesville: University Press of Florida, 2001.

Paquette, Robert L. "Revolutionary Saint Domingue in the Making of Territorial Louisiana." In *A Turbulent Time: The French Revolution and the Greater Caribbean*, edited by David Barry Gaspar and David Patrick Geggus, 204–225. Bloomington: Indiana University Press, 1997.

Paul, Emmanuel C. *Panorama du Folklore Haitien: Presence Africaine en Haiti*. Port-au-Prince: 1962.

Perusse, Roland I. *Haitian Democracy Restored—1991–1995*. New York: University Press of America, 1995.

Peter G. Peterson Foundation, "U.S. Defense Spending Compared to Other Countries." May 7, 2018. https://www.pgpf.org/chart-archive/0053_defense-comparison.

Petrella, Christopher. "On Stone Mountain: White Supremacy and the Birth of the Modern Democratic Party." *Boston Review*, March 30, 2016. https://bostonreview.net/us /christopher-petrella-stone-mountain-white-supremacy-modern-democratic-party.

Pettersson, Therese, and Peter Wallensteen. "Armed Conflicts, 1946–2014." *Journal of Peace Research* 52, no. 4 (July 2015): 536–550.

Pew Research Center. *The American Middle Class Is Losing Ground: No Longer the Majority and Falling Behind Financially*. Washington, DC: Pew Research Center, 2015.

Phillips, Anthony. "Haiti, France, and the Independence Debt of 1825." Canada-Haiti Information Project, 2008. canada-haiti.ca/sites/default/files/Haiti,%20France%20 and%20the%20Independence%20Debt%2 00f%201825_0.pdf.

Phillips, Kevin. *American Theocracy*. New York: Viking, 2006.

Pierre-Louis, Michèle D. "Pourquoi Tuer Jean Dominique?" *Chemins Critiques* 5, no. 1 (January 2001): 105–111.

Piketty, Thomas. *Capital in the Twenty-First Century*. Cambridge, Mass.: Harvard University Press, 2014.

Pluchon, Pierre. *Toussaint Louverture: Un Révolutionnaire Noir d'Ancien Régime*. Paris: Fayard, 1989.

Pompeo, Michael R. "Why Diplomacy Matters." Speech, Texas A&M University, College Station, Texas, April 15, 2019. U.S. Department of State. https://www.state.gov /secretary/remarks/2019/04/291144.htm.

Popkin, Jeremy D. *A Concise History of the Haitian Revolution*. West Sussex: Wiley-Blackwell, 2012.

Popkin, Jeremy D. *You Are All Free: The Haitian Revolution and the Abolition of Slavery*. Cambridge: Cambridge University Press, 2010.

Poulantzas, Nicos. *Political Power and Social Classes*. London: NLB, 1973.

Press Secretary. "Statement on Haiti." The White House: President George W. Bush. February 28, 2004. https://georgewbush-whitehouse.archives.gov/news/releases/2004 /02/20040228-2.html.

Price, Alan. "The Economic Basis of the Slave Trade." Revealing Histories: Remembering Slavery. Bolton Museum Archive and Service, Manchester Art Gallery, People's History Museum, The Whitworth Art Gallery, Touchstones Rochdale, The Manchester Museum, Museum of Science and Industry, Gallery Oldham. Last modified 2007. http://revealinghistories.org.uk/africa-the-arrival-of-europeans-and-the-transatlantic -slave-trade/articles/the-economic-basis-of-the-slave-trade.html.

Price, Hannibal. *De la Réhabilitation de la Race Noire par la République d'Haiti*. Port-au-Prince: Imprimerie Verollot, 1900.

Price, Richard. *Maroon Societies: Rebel Slave Communities in the Americas*, 3rd ed., edited by Richard Price, 1–32. Baltimore: Johns Hopkins University Press, 1996.

Price-Mars, Jean. *Ainsi Parla l'Oncle*. Port-au-Prince: Imprimerie de Compiègne, 1928.

Purdy, Jedediah. "Normcore." *Dissent*, Summer 2018. https://www.dissentmagazine.org /article/normcore-trump-resistance-books-crisis-of-democracy.

Quarles, Benjamin. *The Negro in the American Revolution*. Chapel Hill: University of North Carolina Press, 1996.

Rainsford, Marcus. *An Historical Account of the Black Empire of Hayti. Comprehending a View of the Principal Transactions in the Revolution of Saint Domingo. With Its Antient and Modern State*. London: James Cundee, 1805.

Ray, Rachel. "Witchcraft Moves to the Mainstream in America as Christianity Declines— and Has Trump in Its Sights." *The Telegraph*, December 21, 2018. https://www.telegraph .co.uk/news/2018/12/21/witchcraft-moves-mainstream-america-christianity-declines.

RealClearPolitics. "Congressional Job Approval." March 30, 2019. https://www.realclear politics.com/epolls/other/congressional_job_approval-903.html.

Reed Jr., Adolph L. "Marx, Race, and Neoliberalism." *New Labor Forum* 22, no. 1 (Winter 2013): 48–57.

Reed Jr., Adolph L. "Obama No." *The Progressive*, April 28, 2008. https://progressive.org /magazine/obama/.

Reed Jr., Adolph L. "The Trouble with Uplift." *The Baffler*, no. 41 (September 2018). https:// thebaffler.com/salvos/the-trouble-with-uplift-reed.

Reed Jr., Adolph L. "What Materialist Black Political History Actually Looks Like." *Nonsite*, January 8, 2019. https://nonsite.org/editorial/what-materialist-black-political -history-actually-looks-like.

Reed, Adolph L., and Merlin Chowkwanyun. "Race, Class, Crisis: The Discourse of Racial Disparity and Its Analytical Discontents." *Socialist Register* 48 (2012): 149–175.

Reed, Toure F. *Toward Freedom*. New York: Verso, 2020.

Regan, Jane. "A.I.D.ing U.S. Interests in Haiti." *Covert Action*, no. 51 (Winter 1994–1995): 7–58.

Reny, Tyler T., Loren Collingwood, and Ali A. Valenzuela. "Vote Switching in the 2016 Election: How Racial and Immigration Attitudes, Not Economics, Explain Shifts in White Voting." *Public Opinion Quarterly* 83, no. 1 (Spring 2019): 91–113. https://www .dropbox.com/s/qphz9lxy6pxni1k/final_submission_reny_etal_poq_public.p df?dl=0.

RFK Center. "RFK Center Welcomes Landmark Ruling on Dominican Nationality in Inter-American Court." October 24, 2014, http://rfkcenter.org/rfk-center-welcomes -landmark-ruling-in-inter-american-court.

Richardson, Davis. "Glenn Greenwald on Sucker Journalists—and Why There's No Silver Bullet Coming for Trump." *The Observer*, December 20, 2018. https://observer.com/2018 /12/glenn-greenwald-on-sucker-journalists-and-why-theres-no-silver-bullet-coming -for-trump/.

Richman, Karen E. *Migration and Vodou*. Gainesville: University Press of Florida, 2005.

Roberts, Steven V. "White House Confirms Reagans Follow Astrology, up to a Point." *New York Times*, May 4, 1988. https://www.nytimes.com/1988/05/04/us/white-house -confirms-reagans-follow-astrology-up-to-a-point.html.

Robinson, Nathan J. "Bill Clinton's Stone Mountain Moment." *Jacobin*, September 16, 2016. https://www.jacobinmag.com/2016/09/stone-mountain-kkk-white-supremacy -simmons/.

Robinson, Randall. *An Unbroken Agony: Haiti, from Revolution to the Kidnapping of a President*. New York: Basic Civitas Books, 2007.

Roediger, David. *Class, Race, and Marxism*. London: Verso, 2017.

Roediger, David. *The Wages of Whiteness: Race and the Making of the American Working Class*. London: Verso, 2007.

Roorda, Eric Paul. "Genocide Next Door: The Good Neighbor Policy, the Trujillo Regime, and the Haitian Massacre of 1937." *Diplomatic History* 20, no. 3 (Summer 1996): 301–319.

Roosevelt, Theodore. "Expansion and Peace." *The Independent*, December 21, 1899. https:// www.bartleby.com/58/2.html.

Roosevelt, Theodore. "Memorial Day Address at Arlington National Cemetery." Speech, Arlington, Va., May 30, 1902. Quoted in Roosevelt Memorial Association, *The Works of Theodore Roosevelt*. New York: Charles Scribner's Sons, 1926.

Rosenthal, Caitlin. *Accounting for Slavery: Masters and Management*. Cambridge, MA: Harvard University Press, 2018.

Rosenthal, Caitlin. "Slavery's Scientific Management: Masters and Managers." In *Slavery's Capitalism: A New History of American Economic Development*, edited by Sven Beckert and Seth Rockman, 62–86. Philadelphia: University of Pennsylvania Press, 2016.

Rotberg, Robert, and Christopher Clague. *Haiti: The Politics of Squalor*. Boston: Houghton Mifflin, 1971.

Roumain, Jacques. *Oeuvres complètes: Édition critique*. Edited by Léon-François Hoffmann. Paris: Allca XX, 2003.

Sagás, Ernesto. *Race and Politics in the Dominican Republic.* Gainesville: University of Florida Press, 2000.

Saint-Anthoine, J.-Hippolyte-Daniel de. *Notice sur Toussaint Louverture.* Paris: A. Lacour, 1842.

Saito, Natsu Taylor. *Meeting the Enemy.* New York: New York University Press, 2010.

Sala-Molins, Louis. *Dark Side of the Light: Slavery and the French Enlightenment.* Minneapolis: University of Minnesota Press, 2006.

Schatzberg, Michael G. *Political Legitimacy in Middle Africa: Father, Family, Food.* Bloomington: Indiana University Press, 2001.

Schermerhorn, Calvin. *Unrequited Toil: A History of United States Slavery.* New York: Cambridge University Press, 2018.

Scherr, Arthur. "'Cannibals' Revisited: A Closer Look at His Notorious Phrase." *Journal of Southern History* 77, no. 2 (May 2011): 251–282.

Scherr, Arthur. *Thomas Jefferson's Haitian Policy: Myths and Realities.* Lanham, MD: Lexington Books, 2011.

Schmidt, Hans. *The United States Occupation of Haiti, 1915–1934.* New Brunswick, NJ: Rutgers University Press, 1995.

Schoelcher, Victor. *Vie de Toussaint Louverture.* Paris: Karthala, 1982.

Scott, James C. *Domination and the Arts of Resistance.* New Haven, CT: Yale University Press, 1990.

Scott, James C. *Weapons of the Weak.* New Haven, CT: Yale University Press, 1985.

Scott, Julius S. *The Common Wind: Afro-American Currents in the Age of the Haitian Revolution.* New York: Verso, 2018.

Seligman, Lara. "In Reversal, Trump Signals Further Boost in Defense Spending." *Foreign Policy,* December 27, 2018. https://foreignpolicy.com/2018/12/27/in-reversal-trump -signals-further-boost-in-defense-spending-pentagon-iraq.

Sengupta, Somini. "Georgia Park Is to Hail 'Southern Spirit.'" *New York Times,* October 8, 2000. https://www.nytimes.com/2000/10/08/us/georgia-park-is-to-hail-southern-spirit .html.

Sepinwall, Alyssa Goldstein. *The Abbé Grégoire and the French Revolution: The Making of Modern Universalism.* Berkeley: University of California Press, 2005.

Sepinwall, Alyssa Goldstein. "The Specter of Saint Domingue: American and French Reactions to the Haitian Revolution." In *The World of the Haitian Revolution,* edited by David Geggus and Norman Fiering, 317–338. Bloomington: Indiana University Press, 2009.

Sepinwall, Alyssa Goldstein. "Still Unthinkable? The Haitian Revolution and the Reception of Michel-Rolph Trouillot's 'Silencing the Past.'" *Journal of Haitian Studies* 19, no. 2 (Fall 2013): 75–103.

Shane, Scott. "Russia Isn't the Only One Meddling in Elections. We Do It, Too." *New York Times,* February 17, 2018. https://www.nytimes.com/2018/02/17/sunday-review/russia -isnt-the-only-one-meddling-in-elections-we-do-it-too.html.

Shaw, Angel Velasco, and Luis H. Francia. *Vestiges of War: The Philippine-American War and the Aftermath of an Imperial Dream, 1899–1999.* New York: New York University Press, 2002.

Sherwood, Harriet. "The Chosen One? The New Film That Claims Trump's Election Was an Act of God." *The Guardian,* October 9, 2018. https://www.theguardian.com/us-news /2018/oct/03/the-trump-prophecy-film-god-election-mark-taylor.

Sherwood, Harriet. "Christian Leader Jerry Falwell Urges Trump Support: 'He's a Moral Person.'" *The Guardian*, October 9, 2018. https://www.theguardian.com/us-news/2018/oct/09/christian-leader-jerry-falwell-urges-trump-support-hes-a-moral-person?CMP=Share_iOSApp_Other.

Showstack Sassoon, Anne. "Passive Revolution and the Politics of Reform." In *Approaches to Gramsci*, edited by Anne Showstack Sassoon, 127–148. London: Writers and Readers, 1982.

Silverstein, Jake. "An Update to the 1619 Project." *New York Times Magazine*, March 11, 2020. https://www.nytimes.com/2020/03/11/magazine/an-update-to-the-1619-project.html.

Silverstein, Jake. "Why We Published the 1619 Project." *New York Times Magazine*, December 20, 2019. https://www.nytimes.com/interactive/2019/12/20/magazine/1619-intro.html.

Sirvent, Roberto, and Danny Haiphong. *American Exceptionalism and American Innocence: A People's History of Fake News from the Revolutionary War to the War on Terror.* New York: Skyhorse Publishing, 2019.

Slater, Alice. "The US Has Military Bases in 80 Countries. All of Them Must Close." *The Nation*, January 24, 2018. https://www.thenation.com/article/the-us-has-military-bases-in-172-countries-all-of-them-must-close/.

Smith, Matthew J. *Liberty, Fraternity, Exile: Haiti and Jamaica after Emancipation.* Chapel Hill: University of North Carolina Press, 2014.

Smith, Rogers M. "Beyond Tocqueville, Myrdal, and Hartz: The Multiple Traditions in America." *American Political Science Review* 87, no. 3 (September 1993): 549–566.

Sokolow, Jayme A. *The Great Encounter: Native Peoples and European Settlers in the Americas, 1492–1800.* London: M. E. Sharpe, 2003.

Spector, Ronald H. "Vietnam War 1954–1975." In *Encyclopaedia Britannica.* Updated June 21, 2019. https://www.britannica.com/event/Vietnam-War.

Spector, Ronald H. *W. Cameron Forbes and the Hoover Commissions to Haiti.* New York: University Press of America, 1985.

Sprague-Silgado, Jeb. "Global Capitalism in the Caribbean." *NACLA Report on the Americas* 50, no. 2 (June 2018): 139–147. https://doi.org/10.1080/10714839.2018.1479465.

Sraders, Anne. "What Is Middle Class, Really? Income and Range in 2019." *The Street*, January 18, 2019. https://www.thestreet.com/personal-finance/what-is-middle-class-14833259.

St. Clair, Jeffrey. "They Came, They Saw, They Tweeted." *Counterpunch*, February 23, 2018. https://www.counterpunch.org/2018/02/23/99972/.

Stephanson, Anders. *Manifest Destiny.* New York: Hill and Wang, 1995.

Stockdale, Percival. *A Letter from Percival Stockdale to Granville Sharp Esq. Suggested to the Authour, by the Present Insurrection of the Negroes, in the Island of St. Domingo.* Durham: L. Pennington, 1791.

Suebsaeng, Asawin. "Stay Classy: Trump Used to Test His Dates for AIDS." *Daily Beast*, July 25, 2015. https://www.thedailybeast.com/stay-classy-trump-used-to-test-his-dates-for-aids?ref=scroll.

Summers, Larry. "Washington May Bluster but Cannot Stifle the Chinese Economy." *Financial Times*, December 3, 2018. https://www.ft.com/content/d47b2e40-f6ec-11e8-a154-2b65ddf314e9.

Sylvain, Frank. *Le Serment du Bois-Caïman et la Premiere Pentecôte.* Port-au-Prince: Éditions Henri Deschamps, 1979.

Taleb-Khyar, Mohamed B. "Interview with Jean Fouchard." *Callaloo* 15, no. 2 (Spring 1992): 321–326.

Tarrow, Sidney. *Power in Movement*. Cambridge: Cambridge University Press, 1994.

Taylor, Alan. *American Revolutions*. New York: W. W. Norton & Co., 2016.

TFI. "Emile Jonassaint Veut Combattre Les américains Avec La Magie Noire." December 17, 2010. YouTube video. https://www.youtube.com/watch?v=cxnw-kH4_gk.

Thelwall, John. *The Daughter of Adoption: A Tale of Modern Times in Four Volumes*. London: R. Philipps, 1801.

Thelwall, John. *The Politics of English Jacobinism: Writings of John Thelwall*. Edited by Gregory Claeys. University Park: Pennsylvania State University Press, 1995.

Tibebu, Teshale. *Hegel and the Third World: The Making of Eurocentrism in World History*. Syracuse, NY: Syracuse University Press, 2011.

Tocqueville, Alexis de. *Democracy in America*. From the Henry Reeve Translation, revised and corrected, 1899. http://xroads.virginia.edu/~Hyper/DETOC/toc_indx.html.

Tocqueville, Alexis de. *Journey to America*. Rev. ed. Translated by George Lawrence. Edited by J. P. Mayer. New York: Anchor, 1971.

Tomich, Dale. "Thinking the 'Unthinkable': Victor Schoelcher and Haiti." *Review (Fernand Braudel Center)* 31, no. 3 (2008): 401–431.

Tomich, Dale, and Michael Zeuske. "Introduction, the Second Slavery: Mass Slavery, World-Economy, and Comparative Microhistories." *Review (Fernand Braudel Center)* 31, no. 2, part 1 (2008): 91–100.

Torreon, Barbara Salazar. *Instances of Use of United States Armed Forces Abroad, 1798–2017*. R42738. Washington, DC: Congressional Research Service, 2017. https://fas.org/sgp/crs/natsec/R42738.pdf.

Treanor, Jill. "Half of World's Wealth Now in Hands of 1% of Population." *The Guardian*, October 13, 2015. https://www.theguardian.com/money/2015/oct/13/half-world-wealth-in-hands-population-inequality-report.

Trouillot, Hénock. *Introduction à une Histoire du Vaudou*. Port-au-Prince: Fardin, 1970.

Trouillot, Michel-Rolph. *Haiti: State against Nation*. New York: Monthly Review Press, 1990.

Trouillot, Michel-Rolph. "Haiti's Nightmare and the Lessons of History." In *Haiti: Dangerous Crossroads*, edited by NACLA. Boston: South End Press, 1995.

Trouillot, Michel-Rolph. "The Odd and the Ordinary: Haiti, the Caribbean, and the World." *Cimarrón: New Perspectives on the Caribbean* 2, no. 3 (1990): 3–12.

Trouillot, Michel-Rolph. *Silencing the Past*. Boston: Beacon Press, 1995.

Trouillot, Michel-Rolph. *Ti Difé Boulé Sou Istoua Ayiti*. Brooklyn: Koleksion Lakansiel, 1977.

Tures, John A. "United States Military Operations in the New World Order." *American Diplomacy*, April 2003. http://www.unc.edu/depts/diplomat/archives_roll/2003_01-03/tures_military/tures_military.html.

Turits, Richard Lee. *The Foundations of Despotism: Peasants, the Trujillo Regime, and Modernity in Dominican History*. Stanford, CA: Stanford University Press, 2003.

Turits, Richard Lee. "A World Destroyed, a Nation Imposed: The 1937 Haitian Massacre in the Dominican Republic." *Hispanic American Historical Review* 82, no. 3 (August 2002): 589–635.

Turnier, Alain. *La Société des Baïnnettes*. Port-au-Prince: Imprimerie Le Natal, 1985.

Ullman, Harlan K., James P. Wade, L. A. Edney, Fred M. Franks, Charles A. Horner, Jonathan T. Howe, and Keith Brendley. *Shock and Awe: Achieving Rapid Dominance.* Washington, DC: National Defense University Press, 1996.

UNAIDS. "Haiti." United Nations. 2019. http://www.unaids.org/en/regionscountries/countries/haiti.

Urie, Rob. "Why 'Russian Meddling' Is a Trojan Horse." *Counterpunch,* February 9, 2018. https://www.counterpunch.org/2018/02/09/why-russian-meddling-is-a-trojan-horse/.

U.S. Congress. *Annals of Congress,* 5th Congress, 3rd session, 2752. https://memory.loc.gov/cgi-bin/ampage?collId=llac&fileName=009/llac009.db&recNum=169.

U.S. Congress. *Congressional Record.* 56th Congress, 1st session, 1900. Vol. 33, pt. 1.

Van Alstyne, Richard W. "Woodrow Wilson and the Idea of the Nation State." *International Affairs* 37, no. 3 (July 1961): 293–308.

Van den Berghe, Pierre. *Race and Racism.* New York: John Wiley & Sons, 1967.

Vine, David. *Base Nation: How U.S. Military Bases Abroad Harm America and the World.* New York: Metropolitan Books, 2015.

Vitalis, Robert. *White World Order, Black Power Politics.* Ithaca, NY: Cornell University Press, 2015.

Waldstreicher, David. *Slavery's Constitution: From Revolution to Ratification.* New York: Hill and Wang, 2009.

Wallerstein, Immanuel. *European Universalism: The Rhetoric of Power.* New York: New Press, 2006.

Washington, George. George Washington to James Duane. September 7, 1783. Founders Online. National Archives. https://founders.archives.gov/documents/Washington/99-01-02-11798.

Wawa and Rasin Kanga. "Sou Lanme." *Haitian Roots,* vol. 1. Audio recording. General Records and Productions, 1996.

Weiner, Tim. "C.I.A. Formed Haitian Unit Later Tied to Narcotics Trade." *New York Times,* November 14, 1993. https://www.nytimes.com/1993/11/14/world/cia-formed-haitian-unit-later-tied-to-narcotics-trade.html.

Weiner, Tim. "Key Haitian Military Leaders Were on The CIA's Payroll," *New York Times,* November 1, 1993, A1–A8. https://timesmachine.nytimes.com/timesmachine/1993/11/01/issue.html.

Westad, Odd Arne. *The Global Cold War.* Cambridge: Cambridge University Press, 2007.

White, Ashli. *Encountering Revolution: Haiti and the Making of the Early Republic.* Baltimore: Johns Hopkins University Press, 2010.

White House. "Fact Sheet: Sanctions Related to Iran." July 31, 2012. https://obamawhitehouse.archives.gov/the-press-office/2012/07/31/fact-sheet-sanctions-related-iran.

White House. *The National Security Strategy of the United States of America.* Washington DC: White House, 2002. https://2009-2017.state.gov/documents/organization/63562.pdf.

Whitney, Mike. "Where's the Beef? The Senate Intel Committee and Russia." *Counterpunch,* October 12, 2017. https://www.counterpunch.org/2017/10/12/wheres-the-beef-the-senate-intel-committee-and-russia/.

Wiencek, Henry. *Master of the Mountain: Thomas Jefferson and His Slaves.* New York: Farrar, Straus, and Giroux, 2012.

Wiist, William H., Kathy Barker, Neil Arya, Jon Rohde, Martin Donohoe, Shelley White, Pauline Lubens, Geraldine Gorman, and Amy Hagopian. "The Role of Public Health in the Prevention of War: Rationale and Competencies." *American Journal of Public Health* 104, no. 6 (June 2014): 34–47. https://www.ncbi.nlm.nih.gov/pmc /articles/PMC4062030/pdf/AJPH.2013.301778.pdf.

Wilentz, Sean. *No Property in Man: Slavery and Antislavery at the Nation's Founding.* Cambridge, MA: Harvard University Press, 2018.

Williams, William Appleman. *Empire as a Way of Life.* New York: Oxford University Press, 1980.

Williams, William Appleman. *The Tragedy of American Diplomacy.* New York: World Publishing Co., 1959.

Williamson, Kevin D. "The Father-Führer." *National Review,* March 28, 2016. https:// www.nationalreview.com/magazine/2016/03/28/father-f-hrer/.

Wilson, William Julius. *The Declining Significance of Race: Blacks and Changing American Institutions.* 3rd ed. Chicago: University of Chicago Press, 2012.

Wilson, William Julius. "The Declining Significance of Race: Revisited and Revised." *Daedalus* 140, no. 2 (Spring 2011): 55–69.

Wilson, Woodrow. "Address to the Salesmanship Congress in Detroit, Michigan." Speech, Detroit, July 10, 1916. American Presidency Project. https://www.presidency .ucsb.edu/documents/address-the-salesmanship-congress-detroit-michigan.

Woodward, C. Vann. *The Strange Career of Jim Crow.* New York: Oxford University Press, 2002.

Zauzmer, Julie. "Meet the Astrologer Who Brought the Cosmos into the Reagan White House." *Washington Post,* March 11, 2016. https://www.washingtonpost.com/news /acts-of-faith/wp/2016/03/11/meet-the-astrologer-who-brought-the-cosmos-into-the -reagan-white-house/?noredirect=on&utm_term=.05ab65eb5c5c.

Index

Adams, Henry, 40
Adams, John, 12, 21, 67, 140n36, 146n82
affranchis, xiv, 37, 38
Afghanistan war, 24
African Americans: cultural identity of, 107; idea of deportation of, 17–18; inequalities among, 109–110, 111; legal status of, 184n67; quest for citizenship, 19; struggle for equal opportunity rights, 102; struggle for freedom, 18–19, 111; in upper classes, representation of, 115
Albright, Madeleine, 73
"America First" slogan, 88, 99
American Civil War, 9, 10, 18
American exceptionalism: appeal to the past, 120; authoritarian ideology of, 126; claim of equality and, 21; contradictions of, 135n4; crisis of, 120–121; democracy and, 7, 119; diversity and, 117, 119; evangelical version of, 95–96; flexibility of, 98–99, 123, 131; global impact of, 6, 66–67, 120, 126; vs. Haitian exceptionalism, x, 99, 121, 130; imperialism and, xii, 47–48; indigenous peoples and, 21; manifestations of, xii–xiii; market capitalism and, 98; militarism and, 68–69; presumed national innocence of, 146n85, 190n12; racial factor of, 24, 72, 110, 113; religious foundation of, xi, 2, 24, 44, 45–46, 67, 96–97; rhetoric of defense, 5; supremacist principles of, 46; universalist claims of, 64, 66; vitality of, 123–124
American "exemptionalism," 76, 99, 100

American Middle Class Is Losing Ground, The (Pew Research Center's report), 91
American nationalism, 2, 135n4
American occupation of Haiti: dissolution of the National Assembly, 50; economic development during, 56, 63, 77; elections during, 55–56; as element of exceptionalism, 3; Haitian elites and, 53; legacy of, 53, 55; marine invasion, 48–49; policing during, 49, 160n39; racial attitudes and, 50–52; resistance to, 54, 161n5, 161n15
American Revolution, 19, 90–91
Anderson, Perry, 2, 135n4
Appiah, Anthony, 110
Aristide, Jean-Bertrand: American military assistance to, 85; critics of, 83; downfall of, 85, 86, 106; economic policy of, 86; exile of, 85, 106; Haitian diaspora and, 106; nationalism of, 84–85; opposition to US intervention, 105–106; personality of, 174n37; political agenda of, 84; return to power, 84, 85, 87, 105, 106
Arthus, Wien Weibert, 82, 170n73
Asante-Muhammed, Dedrick, 109
Atwood, J. Brian, 86
Auden, W. H., 21
"A Vision for Black Lives: Policy Demands for Black Power, Freedom and Justice," 111

Bailly-Blanchard, Arthur, 50
Baptist, Edward E., 3, 139n25
Bartels, Larry M., 118
Beckert, Sven, 11
Beckett, Greg, 130

Napoleon I, Emperor of France, 13, 29, 34, 153n57
Native Americans, 21–22, 23, 71
neo-colonialism, 164n46
Nesbitt, Nick, 152n54
Newbegin, Robert, 170n3
New Minority: White Working Class Politics, The (Gest), 116
Nicholls, David, 161n4, 173n19
Niemuth, Niles, 144n78
Nieves, Emanuel, 109
9/11 attack, 68, 69
Noirisme, 81, 82, 172n18
North, David, 144n78
Nunn, Sam, 113

Obama, Barack: on American hegemony, x–xi, 168n48, 168n50; ascendancy to the presidency, 115; deportations of illegal immigrants, 93; diverse cabinet of, 116–117; political views of, 189n36; sanctions against Iran, 76; supporters of, 92, 116; tax policy, 118
Obregón, Liliana, 164n44
Ollman, Bertell, 135n6
Onuf, Peter S., 146n88
O'Reilly, Kenneth, 187n17
organic intellectuals, 8, 68–69, 97, 100, 131, 133n6, 135n5, 135n6
Orozco, Manuel, 176n2
O'Sullivan, John, 66, 67
outer periphery: notion of, 175n46

Page, Benjamin I., 118, 119
Papillon, Jean Francois, 27
passive revolution, 122, 190n1
Pax Americana, 23
Péralte, Charlemagne, 84, 161n3
Pétion, Alexandre, 34, 164n44
Philippine-American War, 71–72, 167nn37–38
Phillips, Anthony, 62
Phillips, Kevin, 96
Phillips, Wendell, 145n80
Phillips, William, 48
Pichon, Louis-Andre, 12, 13
plantation economy, 139–140n33, 139n25
Pompeo, Michael R., 123–124
poor whites, 8–9, 10, 138n15
Popkin, Jeremy D., 148n12
Préval, René, 83, 90
Price, Richard, 33, 104
Purdy, Jedediah, 92
Putin, Vladimir, 97, 120, 180n39

Quigley, Joan, 95

race: in American political discourse, 110, 112–113; identity politics and, 107; Jefferson's view of, 110
race-conscious policies, 115
racism: fragmentation of class solidarities and, 112; Hegel's position on, 142n48; legal culture and, 184n67; roots of, 10; spread of, 44; theory of, 158n11
Rainsford, Marcus, 25, 26
Rapid Dominance doctrine, 70
Ray, Rachel, 179n38
Reagan, Nancy, 95
Reagan, Ronald, 95
reconfiguration strategies, 122–123
Reed, Adolph L., Jr., 112, 189n36
Reny, Tyler T., 116
Responsibility to Protect (R2P) doctrine, 75, 105, 185n79
reverse discrimination, 115
revolutionary violence, 25–26
rhetoric of defense, 5
Robertson, Pat, 74
Rockman, Seth, 11
Romney, Mitt, 98
Roosevelt, Franklin, 55
Roosevelt, Theodore, xii, 47, 48, 71–72
Rosenthal, Caitlin, 11, 139n33
Rotberg, Robert, 74
Roumain, Jacques, 94
Royal African Company, 15, 143n50
Russia-gate scandal, 100

Saint-Anthoine, Hippolyte-Daniel de, 27
Saint-Domingue. *See* Haiti
Saito, Natsu Taylor, 21, 23
Sala-Molins, Louis, 151n43
Sam, Vilbrun Guillaume, 49, 159nn24–25, 161n3
Schatzberg, Michael, 95
Schermerhorn, Calvin, 10
Scherr, Arthur, 165n52
Schmidt, Hans, 50, 160n39
Scott, Dred, 145n80
Scott, James, 101
Scott, Julius S., 127
Seawright, Jason, 118
second slavery, 128, 129, 191n20
Senghor, Leopold S., 82
Sepulveda, Juan Gines de, 46
Service d'Intelligence Nationale (SIN), 86
Shafter, William, 167n37
Sharma, Ruchir, 98

Simonis, Judge, 83–84
Sirvent, Roberto, 146n85, 190n12
1619 Project, 18, 19, 144n70, 144n74, 144n78
Slaughter, Anne-Marie, 185n79
slavery: abolition of, 10, 14, 15; Adams on,
146n82; American Constitution and, 17;
American Revolution and, 144n74;
American *vs.* Haitian, 41; class interests
and, 20; democracy and, 8; economic
benefits of, 9, 11, 12, 18, 154n70; efforts to
preserve, 18, 20; founding fathers' view
of, 20; in French Republic, abolition of,
33–34; in Guadeloupe and Cayenne,
reintroduction of, 149n27; Hegel's
position on, 142n48; industrial
capitalism and, 139n25; justification of,
9, 41, 137n7; labor power, 8–9, 191n21;
legacy of, 3, 4, 130; liberalism and, 15–16;
poor whites and, 8, 9; as property
regime, 11; racism and, 11; *See also*
second slavery
slaves: agency of, 20; migration of, 127;
path to emancipation of, 151n43;
punishments of, 150–151n37; three-fifths
clause on, 20
slave trade: abolition of, 130, 145n80,
151n43
Smith, Jacob, 167n37
Smith, Matthew, 129
Smith, Rogers M., 136n11
Somalia syndrome, 106
Sonthonax, Léger-Félicité, 33, 152n54
sovereignty: American approach to,
76–77; gradation of, 77
Spain's conquest of Americas, 46–47
Spanish Santo Domingo: abolition of
slavery, 165n50
Sraders, Anne, 117
St. Clair, Jeffrey, 180n39
Stephanson, Anders, 5, 46
Stockdale, Percival, 25
Stone Mountain, 113
Summers, Larry, 120

Tarrow, Sidney, 101, 102
Taylor, Alan, 41
Taylor, Mark, 96
Taylor, Telford, 74
Terry, Sabrina, 109
Thelwall, John, 25, 26
Thiam, Tidjane, 183n49
Tocqueville, Alexis de, 7–8, 16–17, 137n7,
146n82
Tomich, Dale, 128, 191n20, 191n21

Tonton Macoute (folklore character),
171–172n16
tontons macoute (special operation
units), 81
Toussaint Louverture, François-
Dominique: arrest and deportation to
France, 34, 36, 153n57; background of,
26–27; constitutional provisions on
power of, 57; Constitution of 1801, 27, 56;
death of, 34; Dessalines' relations with,
36; economic and social politics of,
35–36, 59, 162n23; forced labor regime of,
154n70, 162n23, 162n24; foreign policy
of, 27; ideology of, 27; influence of, 40;
letter to Napoleon Bonaparte, 29; plans
for importing slaves, 27, 154n70; in
public memory, 42–43; violence of, 35;
wealth of, 148n12
Trouillot, Michel-Rolph, 1, 25, 32
Trujillo, Rafael, 94
Trump, Donald: American exceptionalism of, xii; anti-immigration rhetoric of,
88, 89, 91; appeal to the past, 120;
"collusion" with Russia, 181n39; defense
budget of, 97; election to presidency, 96,
116, 180–181n39; foreign policy of, 97;
Haitian phobia of, 90, 91; on hand
shaking, 176n5; isolationism of, 97;
notion of true citizen, x; personality of,
176n5; right-wing populism of, 116;
supporters of, 92, 116, 117; tax policy of,
118; tweets on congresswomen of color,
ix–x; xenophobic rhetoric of, x
Trump Prophecy, The (movie), 96
Turnier, Alain, 63

Ullman, Harlan K., 70
United States: abolition of slavery, 130,
138n22, 145n80; black culture, 108;
citizenship eligibility, 136n11; civilizing
mission of, 71, 72; class inequalities, 109,
118–119; comparison to Haiti, 3–4;
congresswomen of color, ix–x; creolization of, 105, 106; cultural exchanges, 104;
cultural stereotypes of others, 51, 73–74;
Declaration of Independence, 18, 20;
defense budget, 97; democratic nature
of, 4, 7–8, 119; demographic changes,
104–105; deportation of illegal immigrants, 93; economic and social
disparities, 9, 98, 182–183n48; egalitarian society of, 138n22; electoral
interventions, 100; embargo against
France, 140n36; expansionism of, 21, 47,

About the Author

ROBERT FATTON JR. is the Julia A. Cooper Professor in the Department of Politics at the University of Virginia. He is the author of several books on sub-Saharan Africa and Haiti. He received the Award for Excellence from the Haitian Studies Association in 2012.